AFRICAN PORTRAITS

By the Same Author
  WATCH FOR THE DAWN
  TURNING WHEELS
  THE HILL OF DOVES

STUART CLOETE

AFRICAN PORTRAITS

A Biography of
PAUL KRUGER
CECIL RHODES
AND
LOBENGULA
Last King of the Matabele

Collins
14 ST. JAMES'S PLACE LONDON
1946

COPYRIGHT
PRINTED IN GREAT BRITAIN
COLLINS CLEAR-TYPE PRESS : LONDON AND GLASGOW
1946

To the South Africans of to-day . . .
The story of some yesterdays

ACKNOWLEDGMENTS

For suggestions, criticisms, and permissions in the preparation of this book, I am indebted to a great number of authors, publishers, and agents. My main authorities have been Sarah Gertrude Millin for Cecil Rhodes; Manfred Nathan for Kruger; and Hugh Marshall Hole for Lobengula. To these three profound students of South African history I owe the framework of the book and to them, indirectly, the idea of writing it—of plaiting, as it were, a triple cord of three great lives. I owe much to other individuals—writers of adventures, histories, and memoirs, such as Sir Percy Fitzpatrick, Melina Rorke, Christiaan de Wet, Negley Farson, Hedley A. Chilvers. I owe something to my own great-great-grandfather, Henry Cloete, who wrote *The History of the Great Boer Trek*. I owe something to my friend Marjorie Juta's life of Kruger. To another friend, H. J. Whigham, I owe a debt for the description of the journey he made with Rhodes to Rhodesia. Thanks are due to Noel F. Busch and *Life* for extracts from Busch's report on South Africa. To my friend, Major Peter W. Rainier, a fellow South African and author of *Pipe Line to Battle*, I am indebted for his criticism and help while I was writing the book.

I should also like to take this opportunity to thank Sarah Gertrude Millin for the help and encouragement she gave me when I first began to write in 1933.

A full list of books consulted is included in the sources.

CONTENTS

		PAGE
Prologue: Three Men Lived		13

PART ONE

IRON

CHAP.		
I	The Pace of the Ox	25
II	The Young Captain	48
III	The Commandant-General	62
IV	The Pathway of Blood	85
V	The Consumptive Lad	97
VI	The Star of Africa	109
VII	My North	128
VIII	The Giants Meet	153
IX	The Gathering of the Eagles	170

PART TWO

GOLD

I	The Ridge of White Waters	181
II	Rhodes	194
III	Doctor Jim	207
IV	Lobengula	223
V	The Death of a King	238
VI	The Third Term	257
VII	The Colossus	272
VIII	The Raid	288
IX	The Fallen Idol	309

CHAP.		PAGE
X	Interlude	326
XI	M'limo	339
XII	A Fourth Term	350

PART THREE

BLOOD

I	The Storm	365
II	Long Cecil	377
III	Mr. Rhodes of Rhodesia	385
IV	The Scholars	398
V	Commando	413
VI	The End of a War and a President	424

Epilogue: The Birth of a Nation — 437

APPENDICES

I	Sources	457
II	Historical Survey of South Africa	460
III	Notes on Native Names	468

INDEX — 471

DIAGRAMS

Boer Trekkers Forming Laager	*page* 37
Boer Method of Mounted Fighting	*page* 40
Zulu Horns Formation	*page* 81

MAP

Basic Map of South Africa	*Endpapers*

PROLOGUE

THREE MEN LIVED

Cecil Rhodes's advice was always: "Go North, young man." His eyes were on the North: on the Limpopo, on the Zambesi, on the Congo and the Nile. There was room in the North. There were riches and wonders. As yet only partially explored, teeming with game, most of it was unclaimed by any European power. The North was open: free to any man or nation ready to play a temporary risk against a permanent acquisition. Some men would die. But men died anyway. Some would go broke. But that also was nothing new. Once the flood started moving, wave after wave of it, some water would remain, and out of this residual human matter an Empire that ran from the Cape of Good Hope to Cairo would be built.

Rhodes was a man of big ideas. The petty never interested him. There was nothing petty about Africa. And, as the most adventurous in America flowed West, so did the most adventurous in Africa flow North. It called to them. It always had.

The Boers on their Great Trek in 1836, and for many years before and after this, had left the Colony to make new homes in the wilderness. Now it was time for the English to leapfrog the Boers and go farther. A new page was to be written on the book of Africa.

No incident, no moment, can be isolated in history. History is a continuous process in which effect, the result of previous cause, becomes the new cause of new effect. No episode can be entirely irrelevant to any other, subsequent episode. So that any given moment in history, as in the life of a man, is the sum, in its widest application, of all previous moments. But certain periods, or dates, can be taken as focal points, as tentative beginnings, as approximations, as something to work up to or back from—as the crescendo where for an instant all the trumpets blare.

Such a moment is the year 1870. In Europe, France under Napoleon the Third had been defeated by the Germans. The

American Civil War had not been over long. The Suez Canal was almost completed, and the European Powers were stretching out their hands towards the tropical areas which could supply raw materials for their insatiable factories. The international financier was coming into being with his manipulations of interest. The public was beginning to understand the stock company. Rudyard Kipling was five years old, and in four years Lord Randolph Churchill was to marry his American wife. Hitler's illegitimate father was working as a customs official in Germany and Karl Marx was fifty-two years of age. Freud was fourteen. Charcot was practising in Paris. King Edward the Seventh was a young man about town. Oscar Wilde was a boy. Rossetti, Lord Alfred Tennyson, Thomas Hardy, and Robert Browning were still alive. George Bernard Shaw was at school. God was in His heaven and all was assumed to be for the best in Queen Victoria's world of five per cent security.

In 1870, diamonds and gold had been discovered in Africa. And with their discovery the old Africa of the hunters and farmers died. Not swiftly but painfully, slowly, over a generation through the manifold sickness that come from a double surfeit. Strange elements were introduced from over the sea. Men and women such as the Boers had never seen before—gold-hunters and prostitutes—travelled over the land, desecrating it, exploiting it, developing it, making the wide veld scrofulous with the sores of their excavations. In the mining camps women auctioned themselves off nightly to the highest bidder, the Sabbath was broken, wire fences were strung, and railroads began to creep over a land that had known nothing swifter than a galloping horse and no sound louder than a lion's roar.

With the finding of gold and diamonds, peace went, and the seeds of war were sown.

Paul Kruger knew this and did what he could to stave off the ruin of his people. Lobengula, King of the Matabele, knew it and tried to keep the prospectors away. Rhodes knew it and played the avarice of the City of London and the courage of his young adventurers against the resistance of the Boers and the Matabele. Here were exploiters ready to be directed by his genius and the exploited doomed to fall beneath it. For Rhodes, if ahead of his time in his concept of money as power, was aware of the time factor which pressed upon him, both physically as an individual, and politically; he knew with Disraeli that the race for Africa was on, that it was to the swift, the rich, and the industralised; and was determined, if he could make it so as a shaper of events, that it should be won by the Empire he served.

The South Africa that these strangers—Uitlanders, as they came to be called—found, was a vast, bare, sunlit land sparsely populated by the farmers who had conquered it. The Boers were of Dutch, French Huguenot, German, and British descent, men who despite their varied origin had one quality in common; their love of freedom and space. "They were the descendants of emigrants . . . and an emigrant is obviously, for better or worse, an exceptional man in his nation. If he were not, he would be at home with others of his kind."

The other inhabitants of Africa were the Kaffirs of various tribes and the vanishing remnant of the Hottentots and Bushmen to whom the country had originally belonged. In addition, there was a special man-made race—the Cape Coloured, a bastard mixture of Malay, Hottentot, Bantu, and European. They were the outcome of women held in slavery and the passion of their owners. The Boers were hunters and farmers, their life one of expansions into native territories and retractions from them. But the retractions were temporary and the expansions permanent. Their ideal was not merely a rude culture, but a way of life into which the new, the strange, and the godless must not intrude.

But in 1870, Cecil John Rhodes, who was both new and strange, arrived—unnoticed—in Africa. To those who met him, he was simply another boy with weak lungs who had been sent out "for the climate!" And Jan Christiaan Smuts, who was born in the Cape Province in the same year, was just another baby. In 1870 Paul Kruger—a man of forty-five—was farming in the district of Rustenburg and had only a local reputation as a fighter and leader. And in the North, Lobengula had just succeeded his father Moselikatze as chief of the Matabele nation. In 1870 the whole world was simmering like a pot about to boil. Aristocracy was being undermined by industry, industry was being attacked by labour, religion was weakening under the spread of the theories developed by Charles Darwin in his *Origin of Species*. Kings were beginning to totter on their thrones.

Africa, until this time an all but forgotten continent, was becoming important, and in South Africa were three men who had never seen each other, but each of whom, though he did not know it, was going to influence profoundly the future, not merely of Africa but of the world itself.

They were Cecil Rhodes, the tubercular boy; Paul Kruger, the Boer farmer; and Lobengula, chief of the Matabele. Each represented a different culture, race, ethic, and ideal. No one of them could be reconciled with either of the others. They were enclosed in a sparsely settled quadrilateral of land whose width was approximately eight hundred miles and whose length measured twelve hundred. Actually the area of real conflict was infinitely smaller, lying between Kimberley on the south and Bulawayo on the north, flanked by Portuguese East Africa on one side and the Kalihari Desert on the other. But men do not exist in a political vacuum. They are what they are, because of what others before them have been; because of their personal characters, heredity, and environment.

Lobengula was the son of Moselikatze, who had fled with his army from T'Chaka, the Zulu chief. Lobengula was a king, a warrior, and the last great savage tyrant. Savagery was all he knew. It was his tradition.

Paul Kruger was one of the Voortrekkers: he had gone as a child with his family from the Colesberg District into the Transvaal: at the age of ten, already a hunter and farmer; at fourteen, a soldier fighting in his first native war; at sixteen, a husband; at twenty-one, a widower. He was twice married. He was the father of sixteen children and destined to be four times president of the Transvaal Republic.

Cecil John Rhodes had come to South Africa for his health. He was the first and greatest of the African millionaires. He never married. He was Premier of the Cape Colony, and added by conquest and by purchase Mashonaland, Gazaland, Manicaland, Barotseland, and Matabeleland to the British Empire. These territories, named after him, make up the two Rhodesias. He believed in a world united by the power of money and the amenities of education. He founded international scholarships at Oxford, giving an undue proportion, more than half, to the United States because they were allotted by states, and he was under the impression that there were still only thirteen in the American Union.

Nowhere else could the drama of the conflicts which were to take place in Africa have been duplicated, for nowhere else was the scene free enough of external and extraneous political matter to make even the troubles which were going on clearly visible. Elsewhere struggles were obscured by the variety of interests concerned, by oblique influences, by hidden stresses and strains. Nowhere else did three cultures—the ancient barbaric, the religious pioneer, and the modern industrial coexist.

It is this fact which makes the modern history of South Africa stand out: its relative simplicity, its clarity, and the fact that not merely three nations, but three worlds warred. These worlds were perfect in their own fashion, having been arrived at by the endless trial and error of the historic process. Each could have gone on, perhaps indefinitely, had not the others, by force of circumstance, impinged upon it.

Three or four hundred years ago the Bantus, of whom the Zulus were but a tribe, had pressed down into Africa from the north, forced down by some unknown circumstance of war, or famine induced by their own fecundity, and had destroyed the little yellow hunters of the plains—the Bushmen and the Hottentots. Later, the Dutch, seeking a half-way house to India, colonised the Cape of Good Hope and pressed north from there. Then the English came and pressed upon the Boers. Pressure upon pressure was exerted on a continent which, though large, was not infinitely elastic. The policy of Bismarck's isolation was deflected by the German people's desire for a colonial empire. Belgium and France joined in the race for new land, empty because it held no white men. The fingers that the Portuguese and British had thrust into the coast-line became hands, vast arms that worked themselves ever inwards towards the entrails of Africa, seeking minerals, land for cattle, vegetable oils, cotton, rubber, cocoa. Rhodes forced expansion on the reluctant Gladstone. Empires on which the sun seldom or never set were established and consolidated. The slave trade had been broken, but the "black ivory" remained: a hundred and fifty million black men. They could be made to work in their own land, coerced by taxation that they did not understand with a *quid pro quo* of benefits that they did not want. The explorer, the missionary, the prospector, the trader, the hunter, and the soldier all played their parts. Religion, cheap liquor, trade guns, syphilis, and arbitrary government by distant chancelleries came to nations of farmers and hunters, both black and white. The great hole at Kimberley was dug. Johannesburg, a miniature New York, raised its towers on the windswept high veld of the Witwatersrand. Slowly, irrevocably, the giant was enchained as he slept.

All this can be said to have begun in 1870, seventy-odd years ago. Among the repercussions of this era were the Zulu War of '79, the Boer War of '80, the Matabele War, the Boer War of 1900, the Herero Rebellion of 1903, the Boer Rebellion of 1914 and the campaigns of German East and West Africa, the Italian Abyssinian War, the Libyan campaign. The Africa of 1870 was already pregnant with them. They were the outcome of events that are forgotten, like the executions at Slagtersnek in 1816, the slaughter of the Matabele cattle in the Rinderpest of 1896, the stock thefts of the Kaffirs, the slave raids of the Boers. But Rhodes, Kruger, and Lobengula are links in the chain that joins the near past to the distant, and to the future.

Back and forth the shuttle of time wove the pattern of their lives, bringing them ever closer till from being separate they were one, merged into a common thread by war. They were merged but not utterly destroyed. Something of Kruger's Boer culture still exists. The Matabele still are there, and a town, Bulawayo, stands on Lobengula's "place of killing." The empire-builder has gone. Rhodes, who was the greatest of them, has left little but the territories which bear his name. He left no children. For he had none of the body; of the spirit he had his scholars. And an ideal which, in the light of present events, can be interpreted as fascistic and imperial. He lies grandly buried in the Matopos with Moselikatze, whose son he conquered.

There are highlights in the lives of these men: great moments. Rhodes, advancing alone to the last stronghold of the Matabele and making peace with them at the end of the rebellion. Rhodes, a young man, a student at Oxford, who, realising the importance of money, was already a financier and a power in the City of London. Kruger, while still a boy, swimming a swollen river to fetch his bride. Kruger, the old cornered lion, blinking his little bloodshot eyes as he declared war on England in the Raad. Kruger, a broken man leaving his ravaged land. And Lobengula finally betrayed.

For many years these men lived as contemporaries in a sub-continent. Here they laboured, fought, contrived, lied, and prayed. Each convinced of the justice of his cause. Each armed—Lobengula with the spears of his impis; Kruger with the Word of God in his left hand and his old roer in his right; Rhodes with the mightiest weapon of all—the golden sovereigns of England. All lived and loved and fought in Africa, which is still dark, but was darker then. Darker with the sun-dried blood of dead and dying men, with the smoke of burning kraals, with the shouts of Arab slave-raiders and the guns of Tippo Tib.

For a thousand years or more Africa was the country from whence things came—slaves, ivory, wild animals, gums, hides, precious stones, and gold: the one to which no one went but the boldest traders—Phœnicians, Arabs. Only much later did the Portuguese, French, English, and Dutch dare to touch its fringe. Every one was afraid of Africa—Bismarck as much as Gladstone. The slavers on the West Coast and the Boers were the only white men who lived there. And the slavers did not live long. Drink and the soft black skins of their concubines soon finished them. Many came and but few returned. The big Bibles that accompanied the trekking Boers saved them no less than their guns.

Strange things and strange tales had come out of Africa. But slowly more and more was discovered. Adventurers came in search less of adventure than of the riches which would enable them to cease adventuring. Traders, mostly Jews, came wandering with their pack donkeys. Africa was exposed—not naked, still shrouded in the veil of mystery; but the veil was diaphanous, her beauties were becoming visible and all Europe went out to rape her.

South Africa was discovered at about the same time as America and for the same reason—the search for the Indies. Columbus sailed west to circumnavigate the world and find a sea route to the Spice Islands that would remove this trade from the overland route to Venice. And the Portuguese, knowing West Africa, proceeded to follow the coast until they rounded the Cape of Good Hope which they called the Cape of Storms.

The Cape itself was only colonised as a half-way house to

India. And from this original settlement, half-fort, half-farm, the Dutch spread north, since they could go no other way, and met in conflict the Bantus who, also because they could go no other way, were coming south. For years the conflict between spear and gun went on. First on the outskirts of Cape Town itself, then on the banks of the Great Fish River, and on, ever on, to the Crocodile and the Limpopo. Then the white men themselves, Boers and English, became embroiled. Having subdued the Kaffirs, they were forced by their separate and irreconcilable cultures into war. These wars—the last Kaffir wars and the Anglo-Boer wars—are at once both the frame and picture, the very substance and texture of the lives of Kruger, Cecil Rhodes, and Lobengula.

Kruger dreamed, and Rhodes, and Lobengula. This is the story of their dreams, of the fruition of those dreams and of their ends. Of Rhodes the ex-Premier fighting to get air into lungs that could not receive it. Of Kruger the ex-President dying an exile in Switzerland. Of Lobengula the ex-King dead, of smallpox, upon a wagon bed in the mountains of Rhodesia.

For a part of their lives these men lived unconscious of the others, unaware of their existence, of the fact that they had been or ever would be born.

Each was set in his ways; each set like a star in its orbit, each moving along his appointed course; each infinitely important in his own sphere ; each utterly diverse from the other. Two white men and a black. Three dreamers of contrary dreams. Kruger dreaming of a world already dead, a patriarchal world governed by the Word of God. Rhodes dreaming of empire, of a *Pax Britannica*, in which he included all English-speaking peoples. Kruger despising money except in terms of land and flocks and herds. Rhodes despising it, but accumulating a tremendous fortune because he saw wealth as source of power. Lobengula dreaming of isolation, avoiding conflict with the white men, and hoping by this method to save the riches of his land from their grasp.

This is the tale of these three stars, travelling independently, in the political firmament of Africa. The story of their beginnings, of the time when their orbits intersected, cutting each other, destroying each other; of the lesser stars, of the passions and impulses which influenced them by the pull of hereditary, conditioned gravity. And finally of their destruction—of the death of the giants.

The tale, which is one of high adventure, must unfold chronologically. It must deal first with each man alone: with the boy Kruger moving North on the Great Trek with his family in 1835; with Lobengula succeeding his father; with Cecil John Rhodes, the consumptive lad, arriving at Kimberley. It must slowly weave the pattern of their friendships, of their conflicts, of wars; of marriages, of deaths and births; of loves and hates; of impacts and counter-impacts; of hopes and fears; of causes and of effects whose repercussions still vibrate.

The Rhodes scholars of to-day owe what they are to Rhodes. The effect in history of such scholarships may be greater than that of the vast country to which he gave his name. The politics of South Africa are still based on the racial prejudice of Kruger and his like, who saw the natives as children of Ham and less than men. And the country is still suffering from the ill-judged acts of the British who attempted to govern a race of free farmers from Whitehall.

The history of men and nations is not a matter of isolated incidents, of inexplicable acts. History is life; it reaches back into the past, touches to-day, and leaps forward to the unpredictable To-morrow. It is written in the names and acts of the great men of each period. They are the heroes. Their names are heavy on the page. They issue proclamations, declare war, sign treaties. But they are nothing. They are the instruments of their time, representative of it, born of it and into it. They ride the stream: they do not make it.

This is the story of a tremendous drama—the end of an era, the beginning of a period. But Africa has known many periods and greater dramas: that of the lost race who built Zimbabwe; of the Bushmen hunted for sport like buck; of the slave forts and barracoons of the Ivory Coast; of the Barbary pirates; of the caravans that penetrated into the Congo before Rome was an empire.

This is the story of map changes, of lands that were uncharted being painted in colour on the atlases of European school-children, of vanished kingdoms, of nations enslaved, of republics broken. But who can assert that these are permanent when so much change has gone before? The Phœnicians mined African gold too; the Arabs traded and were absorbed; the Portuguese, for centuries, wasted their time and substance in Africa. The Germans have gone from Africa, at least politically, but in Kruger's time they had not yet come.

Part One

Iron

The iron entered into his soul.—*Psalms 105: 18.*

CHAPTER ONE

THE PACE OF THE OX

ON THE tenth of October, 1825, at the farm Vaalbank in the Colesberg district of Cape Colony, a boy was born of Kaspar Jan Hendrik Kruger and his wife, Elsie Francina Steyn. He was named Stephanus Johannes Paulus, and was the third child of his parents, who were simple farmers that feared the Lord and disliked the English. Little is known of Paul's early life. It seems likely that he led the life of a Backveld Boer child of to-day—playing with his brothers and the children of the house servants; hunting, riding, and shooting, roaming over the veld; making, as a small child, spans of clay oxen with mimosa thorns for horns and inspanning them to a toy wagon built by his father or an uncle. No doubt, later on, he helped to herd sheep and cattle and to count them into the kraals at night. No doubt he had falls and barked his knees; no doubt he laughed and cried and sat attentive as his father read whole chapters of the Bible to the assembled family.

The earliest known ancestor of Paul Kruger was Frans Kruger, or Cruger, who lived at or near Berlin in Prussia and married Elizabeth Hartwigs. Their son Jacob was born in 1686. When he was seventeen, Jacob went to the Cape of Good Hope in the service of the Dutch East India Company and there married Johanna Kemp. Their fourth son, Hendrik Kruger, was born on April 8, 1725. He married Francina Cloete and they had eighteen children—all the Krugers had large families. The descendants of Hendrik and Francina numbered one hundred and thirty-six persons at the close of the eighteenth century. Gerrit Kruger was Hendrik's second son. He married Suzanna Lasya Buys in 1769. Their second son, Stephanus Johannes Kruger, married Sophia Margaretha Steenkamp. Their second son, Kaspar Jan Hendrik Kruger, was Paul Kruger's father.

Paul's mother died when he was seven, leaving six motherless children. All his life he spoke most lovingly of her and the care and attention she had lavished on him. Between him and two of his sisters there was particularly deep bonds of affection. His father married again soon after his wife's death and Paul always spoke of his stepmother with the greatest liking and respect.

Quick remarriage was essential on the border, where it was impossible to bring up a young family without the aid of a woman. Some idea of the wildness of the times is shown by the fact that at the age of seven, the year of his mother's death, Paul Kruger not only was trained in the use of firearms, but had killed his first head of big game. At fourteen he killed his first lion and had killed men in the Kaffir wars.

In his own *Memoirs* Paul Kruger says, "I can remember very little of my childhood except that an old woman once prophesied that I was destined for a superior position in life."

His first real memory begins with The Trek, when at the age of nine he left home with his grandfather, father, his uncles Gert and Theunis, their families, a flock of nearly thirty thousand Afrikaaner sheep and a few hundred horses and cattle. They went in big tented wagons, painted yellow or blue with red wheels, that were driven by the men of the party.

There must have been days, even weeks, of preparation, before finally the oxen, sixteen to a team, were inspanned, the long whips cracked in the cold air of the morning, and the great wheels turned. These people, men, women, and children, with their flocks and herds, were leaving their homes for good to seek new ones in the wilds of the North. Dried meat—biltong—had been prepared, and Boer rusks, that would keep for weeks. Powder had been bought in barrels, lead bullets had been moulded and the trek gear got ready. All the furniture of their homes, everything inessential, was sold, and the money from the sale used to buy stock which could move on its own four legs.

When they started, the veld was covered with beasts, great flocks of fat-tailed sheep; troops of mares, each with its shrilling stallion, galloped with flying tails; while the cattle, immense horned, moved majestically behind the bulls. There was no road. The trekkers had only the sun and the stars to guide them. There was no safety, only that of their muzzle-loading guns and their belief in the Lord. There was no doctor. The women who were with child would give birth kneeling on ox skins behind their wagons. There were few servants, for these, having been slaves, were left behind in freedom. In all the world, their world, there was nothing but the vastness of Africa in front of them and behind, the law that they defied. The spirit of the trekkers is illustrated by the words of one of their leaders, Piet Retief. He said: " We are now leaving the fruitful land of our birth in which we have suffered grievous losses and continual vexations, and are about to enter a strange and desperate territory. But we go with a firm reliance on an all-seeing, just, and merciful God, Whom we shall always fear, and humbly endeavour to obey."

The Krugers were not the only ones to move: from all over the Colony thousands were going, but they were among the first. And all went for the same reason—a hatred of the English, which had begun with the executions at Slagtersnek in 1816, and that now, with the abolition of slavery, took its final form in an overwhelming desire to trek. To trek means to go: to go towards something or away from something: to go away from the English and towards new pastures. It was a part of the restless Boer nature to trek anyway as soon as any place became overpopulated, or the game was killed off, or the seasons were bad. Most farmers in good circumstances had several farms and trekked from one to another in the course of the year. This is still to some extent true in the Transvaal, where many leave the cold High Veld in the fall, move with their herds to the Low Veld, and return in the spring to wait for the ploughing rains when the ground is soft enough to take the shear.

The Boer's idea of a farm is a block of land of not less than four thousand morgen, preferably eight thousand; that is, sixteen thousand acres. His method of staking it out was to "ride it off" under the direction of the field cornet. Drawing lots for the turns they were to take, each man—and a Boer was a man, a burgher, at sixteen—rode for a specified time enclosing a rectangle of land. Each rode fast and tried to include the best water and land and to avoid the worst. His conception that an area is becoming overpopulated begins on the day that he can see another man's smoke from his house.

Nor, though they disliked the English, can it be said that the Boers liked the Dutch East India Company, who used to govern the Cape, any better; and these very Backveld Boers who moved from the northern parts of the Colony were the descendants of those who had, in previous generations, moved there, against the orders of the Dutch, from the vicinity of the Cape of Good Hope, and for the same reason—a dislike of government and restraint. They saw no need for paying taxes, no need of a police force or of schools. These things they preferred to manage for themselves. What right had any one to make them pay taxes for land that they had wrested from the wilderness? What necessity was there for schools when parents could teach their children to read and write? And why administer the law or formulate codes when the law was clearly and simply stated in the Holy Bible?

So, almost since the founding of the Colony in 1652 there had been movements away from it. Runaway sailors, deserting soldiers, debtors, fugitives from justice, hunters, traders, and adventurers had always joined the farmers and gone beyond them. Some had gone empty-handed, others had gone with livestock and slaves; but where one went others followed. Land was free. It was there for the taking and always, to compensate for the discomforts and dangers of this new life, were the greater comforts of freedom. All these movements, over nearly two hundred years, had passed almost unnoticed. They were in a sense little more than expansions, and the administration kept catching up with them. But this, the trek the Krugers were making, was the beginning of what came to be called "The Great Trek."

The Krugers crossed the Orange River in 1835. In 1836 the main body followed and for ten years hundreds of families moved north—a thousand miles and more across great mountain ranges, across rivers, suffering and dying as they went. And as they went they took up land. Some stopping quickly; others, harder to satisfy, going on.

The names they gave to the farms they took up tell something of the people and the perils they encountered: Leeudrift, lion's ford; Leeukraal, lion's kraal; Rhenosterfontein, rhinoceros spring; Kameelpoort, giraffe pass; Kilpdrift, stony ford; Stinkfontein, foul water; Groenfontein, green spring; Wonderboom, wonder tree; Mooiplaats, beautiful place. The emphasis is almost always on water—a spring, or fountain; a river or a ford; on good water or stinking water, and on the beasts found there.

On lions, or buck, or giraffes which the Boers called kameels because in appearance they appeared to resemble the camel of the Bible, which was their only book.

The cause of this movement was dual. First it was in the nature of the Boer to trek. And being peaceful, farmers rather than fighters, when pressure was exerted upon them in one direction, they moved away from it, according to the law of least resistance, in another.

The second cause was the impossibility of existing under a government which was not merely alien to them, but to their minds unjust. When the slaves were freed by the English, they had no other servants or means of farming without slaves. In addition, the compensation offered to them was not only inadequate, but was payable in England and could only be collected by an agent. The expenses in many cases amounted to more than the capital value of the slaves involved. And even the management of such servants as they had was questioned by the judges of the Black Circuit, who insisted that every punishment inflicted should be noted in a book by farmers who were in many cases unable to write more than their own names.

Added to this was another grievance. Cattle thefts by marauding Kaffirs were constant, and the government declared the beasts to be war booty which must be sold for war costs before they could be distributed among their former owners, who had joined in, and often done most of the fighting which led to their recovery. This discontent was increased by the fact that it was a Boer custom on the birth of a child to give the infant presents of livestock. These came from parents, relations, and close friends of the family—a couple of horses, a cow or two, some sheep or goats—and formed the nucleus of the herd a boy would own when he became a man, or a part of the dowry a girl would take to her husband. The children took particular care of their own animals and became much attached to them. And it was the sale of these animals which infuriated the Boers, particularly the younger ones. They were not merely animals, livestock to be considered as negotiable. They were pets that had names; that had become an actual part of the lives of the families to which they belonged. For the Boers lived very near to the earth and the things of the earth, near to animals both wild and domestic. So the final straw that, a couple of generations later, was to break the back of Britain's South African Colony may have been a pet cow or a favourite ox that was seized by the government and sold to a stranger.

All this was in young Kruger's mind when he left his home. Perhaps not in his mind as conscious thought, as a political creed, but as knowledge absorbed with his mother's milk, with his father's conversations, in the long hours he had spent sitting on his little stool listening to the talk of his elders. For the Boers are great talkers, as they are also men of great and prolonged silences, able equally to cease from talking for hours or to talk without ceasing for other hours when they have things in their hearts which must be stated. The talk of the older men was always of politics, of cattle and crops and hunting, for of these was made the pattern of their lives; and not separately, for each blended into the other. Hunting on the other side of the Great Fish River meant hunting in Kaffaria and possible conflict with the natives, which was a political issue between the Boers and the government. Farming meant the discussion of slaves and talk of stolen cattle.

And over this, woven through all conversation was the thread of hatred for the British. The tales of real and imagined injustice, the dislike of a government whose officials neither understood their language nor their ways.

Unquestionably young Paul Kruger had heard the tale of Slagtersnek many times—from the beginning, where old Frederick Bezuidenhout was killed by the troopers as he resisted their efforts to take him to court for the non-payment of his taxes, to its final outcome, the abortive rebellion of his brother Johannes and the double hanging of the leaders. This was something the Boers never forgot and almost all in the vicinity had been forced to witness it. The rebels were strung up. The ropes broke. And then, despite all the protestations of the onlookers, the doomed men were hanged again. It is a Boer characteristic never to forget a friend or forgive an enemy. Men still speak of Slagtersnek in Africa.

Too young to discuss at the age of nine, Paul was old enough to hear and to absorb what he heard. Seeing only in terms of black and white, of good and bad, Paul turned against the English;

and later, in that time when he was, as the old wise woman put it, "in a superior position in life," as the President and leader of his people, his one idea was to have nothing to do with them, to avoid them and their ways, and, as happened tragically, when no other course was available and there was nowhere further to flee, to fight rather than give way.

But now he was a little boy. All he knew was a hatred of the people who had driven him from his home, had defrauded his parents of their just dues, and had stolen his favourite cattle. Simple thoughts, those of a child who can only love or hate; who knows nothing of toleration, or the interplay of forces, or of cause and effect; to whom the word compromise is without meaning. This was the background of his mind and the basis of his character that was being slowly formed. But in the front of it was the adventure of travel, or hunting, of being hardly more than weaned, and already, by force of circumstance, a man. A thick-set little man on a Boer pony—an entire, for no Boer rode anything but a stallion. A small man mounted and armed; one who worked with the other older men riding herd, counting, looking for good water and grazing in a land all but unknown to white men.

Some had gone before—the boldest, the renegades and rebels. Coenraad Buys had gone early in the century and had married a black queen, the mother of Gaika, by whom he bred a race who exist to-day—the Buys-Folk of the Transvaal. John Dun had married into the Zulu people. Others there were, brigands and murderers, living isolated lives with coloured women. And some great hunters like Louis Trigart. It was their tales of this land flowing with milk and honey that led the Boers on to seek what previously had been only a hope and a dream—a new free land.

Kruger's family proceeded slowly. Some days ten miles, some days five. Some days not moving at all. Never at any time did they move more than fifteen miles in twenty-four hours. The distance covered depended on the condition of the livestock. Cows with young calves, ewes with small lambs, and the ability of both to travel were the measuring rod of progress; and if the Boers had little else they had time in plenty. Their movement was a drift rather than a march.

Each day scouting parties had to go forward to seek the best road for the lumbering wagons, to find water and camping places, to scout for hostile Kaffirs, to shoot meat. Each night the wagons had to be laagered—drawn up in a square, the disselboom of one lashed under the bed of the next. The spaces between the wheels the Boers blocked with small thorn trees and left a single opening, as a gate where, in event of attack, a wagon could be rolled in. The working oxen were fastened in a ring outside the laager, tied by reins—rawhide thongs—to the wagon rails to add a wall of living beef to the protection of the camp.

An ox requires eight hours for sleep and to chew its cud as it lies. Another eight hours is needed for it to graze. So that eight hours in the yoke is as much as an ox can stand and still hold condition. Actually the time they spent yoked was probably much less, five or six hours at the most, allowing for a couple of hours outspan in the middle of the day. And the herds of horses, sheep, and loose breeding cattle, though they could snatch mouthfuls of grass as they moved, had to have time to open out from the herd and seek their fill.

This was young Paul's main duty—herding, driving his beasts on in a compact drove, the strongest leading, the weakest bringing up the rear, and then, when nice glade opened, checking them and allowing them to spread out as they willed.

At these times he probably knee-haltered his horse, allowing it to feed near him, and sat on an antheap watching the beasts with his gun in his hand.

Day after day, night after night, this went on, the country changing yet remaining ever Africa—*Ons Land.* Blue mountains in the distance, lying as softly against the horizon as a woman's scarf, were gradually approached and found to be hard, bitter hills where sometimes the wagons had to be knocked to pieces, carried over by pack oxen, and reassembled on the other side. And then, when across them, new ranges became visible. Rivers were crossed by fastening the wagons to empty barrels and floating them over. Other rivers were forded when a drift could be found, and at still other times the trekkers had to wait for floods from the rains in the mountains to run down before a move of any kind could be made.

And always there was danger from Kaffirs and wild beasts;

thefts by tiny Bushmen, raids by whole troops of lions. Slowly the blue paint was rubbed from the wagon bodies and the wheels. All that was left of the gay red paint was to be found on hubs. Most wheels had been repaired at the portable forges the Boers carried with them, new spokes and felloes had been fitted, the iron tyres shortened, and many axles, that were made of hardwood, had been replaced. Brake blocks had to be fashioned continually; so had disselbooms—the long poles to which the wheel oxen were inspanned. The white new tents of the wagons were torn and red with ingrained dust, and people themselves thin and hard with exposure. The men and boys burnt almost black.

But still they went on, the herds gaining in strength from the new births and losing much of their gain by disease and the depredations of savages and beasts. On, like ships, these eighteen and twenty-foot wagons rolled across the veld, the great rear wheels, six foot high, crashing through ant-heaps and riding over rocks. Sometimes they had to double-span—thirty-two oxen being hitched to a single wagon—to get it through a river drift, or through sand or mud. Then the whips cracked, bending the long sixteen-foot bamboo whip sticks like willow twigs in the hands of the drivers.

Driving oxen is an art, and the Boer loves his span next only to his wife and children and his horse. His wagon is his second home. With it, and the beasts he has trained to draw it, all Africa is his. Each beast knows his name. "*Engelsman! Swartkop! Ireland! Bosveld! Witboii! Rooiland! Witpenze!*" the drivers shout, and the oxen, lying low in the yokes, get their knees under them and pull. Oxen are different from horses and mules and better in many ways. On a hillside, should the wagon stop, they stand in the yoke and will not let their load run back with them. They are fine animals, these Afrikaaner oxen, tall and strong, as fast as horses, with wide sharp horns. They resemble the longhorn of Texas and are probably of the same Iberian ancestry. The Dutch found them in the possession of the natives when they settled at the Cape and it seems likely that from the older Portuguese colonies of the Coast they had spread all over the land. As the Indian corn, that the Boers call mealies, spread from the slave ships that brought it from America.

A.P.

The wagons were heavily laden, some entirely with goods lashed with rawhide thongs. Others were tented living wagons, the rear half-filled by a big kartel or bed that ran from rail to rail within it. Under the kartel were stowed the smaller, more precious objects—a few china cups, perhaps, an odd piece of silver, little bags of money. In each there would be a kist—a chest of fine hardwood with beautifully ornamented brass locks and hinges in which the Boers kept their best clothes. On the Trek the men wore a broad-brimmed hat made of mealie stalks, a shirt, a short jacket, and trousers of fine tanned buckskin. They wore no underclothes or socks and made their own veldschoen— field shoes of rawhide. Each man carried a heavy sheath knife in his belt, bullets, and a powder horn. Over his wrist hung a sjambok, a quirt made of a strip of rhinocerous skin. In his hand he held a gun. Slung beneath each wagon was a long latticed crate for the poultry which got so used to travel that when they saw the oxen being inspanned they would run and jump into it by themselves. A young calf might be in the wagon, its mother, a milch cow, following it closely, lowing all the while. Young puppies born on the road would be kept in the wagon till they were old enough to run; a tabby cat, a pet baboon chained from a belt round its waist, might sit on the tent or run loose beside the wagon. Some Boers even trained baboons to lead the oxen. There might be a cage of bright-coloured wild finches or Cape canaries hanging from the battens of the tent; and on each wagon there were big, black, three-legged iron cook-pots hooked outside, rocking between the wheels, a water barrel, and a small brass-bound barrel of Cape brandy.

Food, the Trekkers—Voortrekkers, those who went in front, as they have come to be called—had in plenty: game and wholemeal bread made from wheat flour. Vegetables and fruit they had none save the few herbs and berries that grew wild or what they could purchase from the natives as they went past their gardens. This was a sore loss to them, for the Boer loves his garden and his orchard. In each wagon there were little bags of seed at which the woman looked tenderly. One day the wheels would stop rolling in a fair land by a fine fresh fountain of water, and then they would settle and plant once more—mealie seed, Kaffir corn, peas and beans, pumpkins, orange pips, the rough stones of peaches, the smooth of apricots, flower seeds, and the bulbs—onions and shallots. For the women were as other women, wanting homes and security, wanting a settled place in which to rear their young, to live and worship God.

If the life of the wagons was pleasing to the young men and boys, it was less so to the women. Their bones ached with the jolting of their springless homes. They were tired of cooking outside, they suffered from cold. The High Veld they had reached was five thousand feet above the level of the sea, and sometimes they cried with the cold as they washed their clothes in the icy water of the rivers. The young girls too were tired of it. The moi meisies—the pretty girls—who all through the trek wore their wide black sun-bonnets and some, the vainest, even masks of tanned goatskin to preserve the whiteness of their complexions, were tiredest of all. They wanted to see strangers. The strange man called to them, the man who would take them away in their ripening womanhood. They were tired of their own families, of the men and boys they had known their lives long, and they saw few others, since it was by families that they trekked.

In 1836 the main group of trekkers led by Hendrik Potgieter joined with earlier trekkers and they all went on together. So far there had been little trouble: the land between the Vet and the Vaal Rivers which they had crossed had been bartered from the native chiefs who ruled it. But now, when they were scattered in small parties, as they had to be in order to graze the vast number of beasts they had with them, they were attacked by the Matabele chief Moselikatze who at that time was the master of the whole country from the Lebombo Mountains to the Drakensberg. Every tribe had submitted to him. He called these subject peoples dogs and treated them as dogs. When vultures passed over his town sailing in great circles over the kraals, he would give orders that some old men and women should be killed to feed the birds that he named his "children."

When Moselikatze heard that men with white faces had come from the South, he sent out two thousand warriors to massacre them, which they did, coming upon them suddenly, leaping at them out of the high grass, hissing through their teeth and rattling their spears against the long shields which gave the tribe its name—the Matabele.

A fortnight later, they returned again to kill more white men and seize more cattle, this time attacking the Boers at Vegkop, in what is now the Free State. But here Potgieter and Sarel Celliers, with thirty-three men, had built a laager and repelled them—the women and children fighting with the men, moulding bullets in the height of the battle, loading guns and handing them to their husbands, fathers, brothers, and sons, even firing them themselves. Kruger, then twelve years old, was with this party. It was his first taste of actual war. As the Matabele approached the laager, Potgieter and some of his men galloped out to attack them. They fired from the saddle in the Boer manner and swung their horses away to load again, all the time retreating towards the wagons, while they inflicted as many casualties as they could. One last charge, the Boers lying low on their horses and firing under their necks; and then the commando came back and the laager gate—the loose wagon that completed the defensive ring—was rolled into place.

For six hours the Matabele attacked, charging with regiment after regiment, shouting their battle cries, their plumes tossing in the air. Thousands of spears ripped through the wagon hoods; hundreds of Matabele fell, but they could not break the laager, and finally they retired, taking forty-six hundred head of cattle and fifty thousand sheep with them as booty. They took also two small white girls. The Boers under Potgieter pursued them as far as the Marico River and beat them in battle at Zeerust, where they recovered a part of the stolen cattle, but not the children.

A number of emigrants then turned east, the Krugers among them, and crossed the Drakensberg into Natal, where there was further bloodshed, Piet Retief and his party of sixty-nine being murdered as they sat unarmed in the kraal of Dingaan, the Zulu king.

After this trouble the Kruger family turned back and settled at Liebenbourg Vlei. Later they went on to the Magaliesberg Mountains of the Transvaal. These were the formative years of Paul Kruger's life. In them he received three months of regular schooling from Tielman Roos, a schoolmaster who had joined the trekkers and taught the children in a grass hut which was built wherever a prolonged halt was made. The rest of his

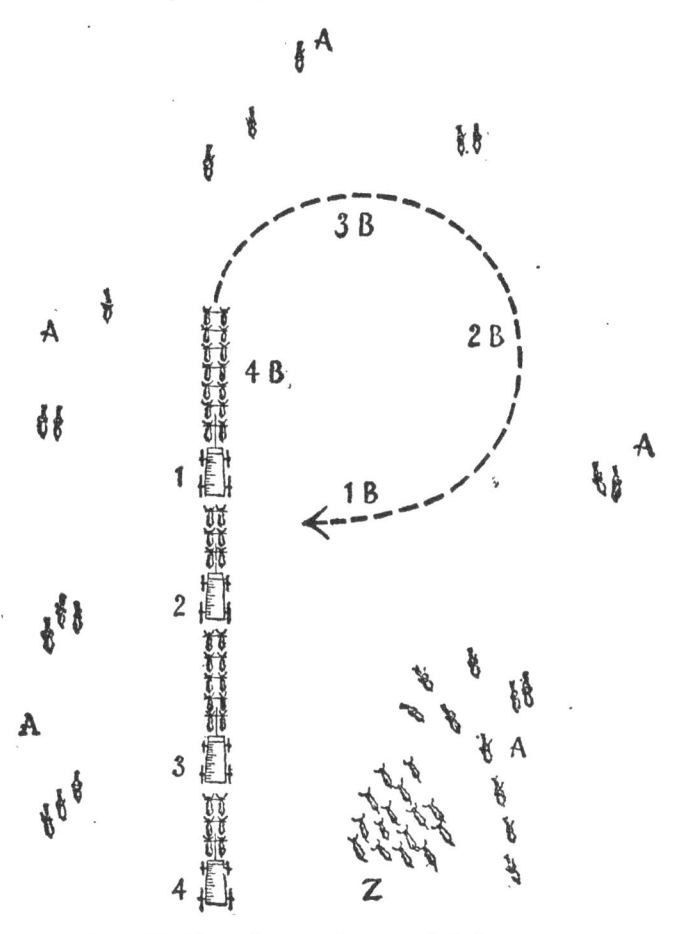

Boer Trekkers forming laager with four wagons

1, 2, 3, 4, wagons in line
1B, 2B, etc., final position of wagons
A, mounted guards
Z, driven cattle

education was given him by his father, who taught him to read and write and gave him his knowledge of the Scriptures. Each day throughout the trek at the table after dinner and supper, the children had to read from the Bible and to repeat or write texts which had been committed to memory.

At fourteen Paul shot his first lion, on the banks of the Rhenoster River in what is now the Northern Free State. This was a big personal event in his life and, added to the battle he had been in, proved his contention that he was a man. The lion had attacked some cattle, and seven Boers, of whom Paul Kruger was one, rode out to hunt it. They went in three parties of two each. Writing of himself Paul says, "I was the seventh but did not count." Among the others were his father, his uncle, and elder brother. Before they came up to the lion, it turned and faced them. The Boers then dismounted and tied their horses' heads together as was their custom when hunting lions, and turned them away from the crouching beast, for should they actually see a lion horses are likely to bolt. Paul was left with the horses, and the lion, ignoring the other hunters, sprang straight towards him, its leap calculated to bring it on to the horses' backs. As it rose, Paul fired, killing it outright and bringing it down so that it almost fell upon him.

One of the party bent down to look at the dead lion's teeth, which were very large, and Paul, thinking no harm, jumped on to the lion's belly. As he did this, the air shook with a tremendous roar and the tooth-measurer fell flat on his face in terror. The others all shook with laughter, for, as all men know, if you tread on a lion's body within a short time of its death, it will roar as though it were still alive. "The breath still in him, being forced from the stomach through the throat, produces the roar." Hugo, the man who had been scared, now wanted to give Paul a good thrashing, but the others restrained him.

It was in this year 1839 that Kruger went out on commando against Moselikatze, which ended in a fight at Strydpoort; but, as Kruger naïvely observes, "It turned out that we were fighting the wrong people." They were Red Kaffirs who had been compelled to join the Matabele. As soon as Potgieter heard of this, he stopped the fight.

Writing in his *Memoirs* Paul Kruger says: "It is of course impossible that I should be able to tell to-day how many wild beasts I have shot. It is too much to remember the exact number of lions, buffaloes, rhinoceroses, giraffes, and other big game ... as far as I know I must have shot at least thirty to forty elephants and five hippopotami. I know I have killed five lions myself."

Kruger's second lion was killed on the Hex River behind the Magaliesberg. A few years later he shot two more lions in the same vicinity. The fifth lion he shot on the Olifants River in the Lydenburg District. In this hunt Kruger's dog seized the lion by the hind leg as it was about to spring upon him, enabling him to kill it with a single shot.

In writing of another lion hunt, Kruger spends a whole page describing the behaviour of a certain dog. "When the dogs found the herd of lions they surrounded it, barking furiously. One of the hounds would go no farther from us than twenty paces. There he stood barking, but nothing would induce him to join the hounds. He was too frightened to do that and too faithful to leave us. One of the lions made for us, and then the poor terrified hound was the only one that did not leave us. He trembled and howled with fear, to say nothing of other more visible signs of distress, and every second he looked round anxiously at his master, hoping, I dare say, that he would fly and that the dog might follow at his heels. But the master stayed and so the dog stayed. The lion was within ten paces of the dog when we shot him. And even now the timid dog was the only one of all the noisy pack that attacked him as he fell under our fire. He nearly died of fear, but remained at his post for love of his master."

This instance of canine fidelity is certainly not without precedent, but is of interest in giving another clue to the character of President Kruger. He was a young man, scarcely more than a boy, when he took part in this hunt. He was an old man who had been very great when he wrote of it, giving the incident a full page out of the 373 in his *Memoirs*. It is a witness to the greatness and simplicity of his mind—that of a man who became great perhaps because he was simple and understood the ways of beasts and men. Nor is this the only reference to dogs in his life. He used them again in a simile before the great meeting at Paardekraal in 1879. Then, when war with the British was imminent,

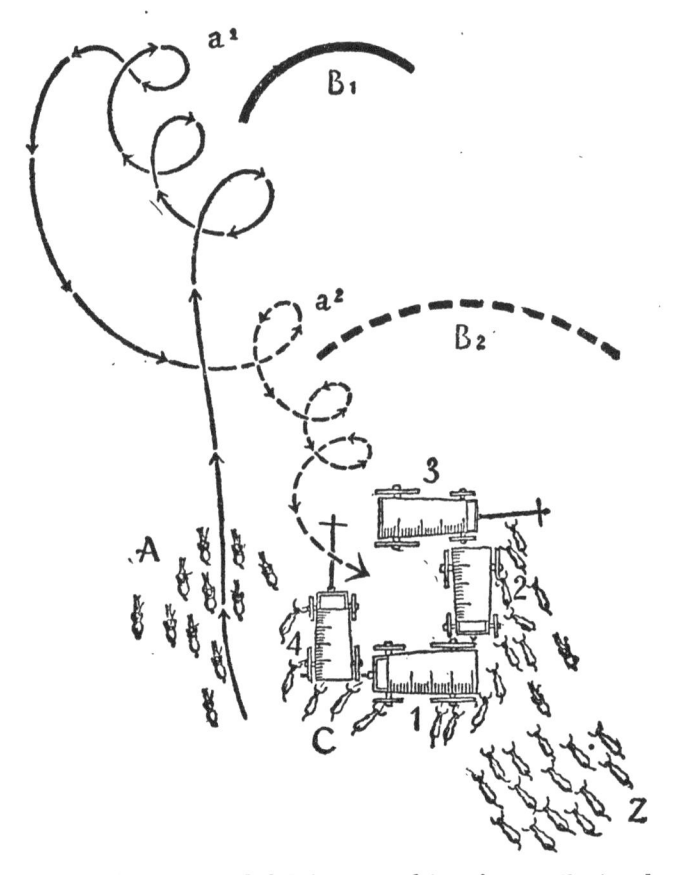

Boer method of mounted fighting . . . firing from galloping horse and then swinging away out of spear range to reload.

A, mounted force attacking
a1, first position
a2, second position before being driven into laager
B1, B2, the Kaffirs
C, draught oxen tied to the wagons
Z, driven cattle

1, 2, 3, 4, wagons in final position of laager. No. 4 is gate that will be rolled up when mounted men are driven in.

he was asked if he would lead the Boers, and said, "When I have a hunting dog, and I say, 'Sah,' he attacks. I am not yet certain if the people are ready—if I say, 'Sah,' that they will fight."

In writing of another hunt, for elephants this time, he speaks with regret of his horse Tempus which was bitten by the tsetse fly and died. These were but incidents in the life of every Boer in the North. All had adventures, disasters, many were killed by wild beasts, burnt up in veld fires, died in accidents and of illness; many fell before the assegais of the natives. They were attacked by the Matabele in the North under Moselikatze and Dingaan's Zulus in the East. These two enemies, though of one race, were dividing among themselves, Moselikatze having fled from Dingaan's predecessor T'Chaka with an army of men. Calling themselves the Matabele, they slaughtered all the natives for hundreds of miles, *eating them up*, seizing their women for wives, their young boys to be trained as warriors, and their cattle for loot, they founded a new nation on the lines of the old. A savage, fighting community that knew no mercy and loved blood for its own sake.

Farming among the Boers was a matter of staying alive, of perpetual vigilance against animals and men, of hunting as much for food as for sport, and much wild game had to be exterminated before any crops could be planted. There were other reasons too for hunting: where the game was plentiful so were the lions and leopards—which they called tigers—that raided the cattle kraals and chicken pens, and occasionally even killed herders in the open. Having nothing but their courage, skill, and the simple tools they had brought with them, the Boers made their homes in the wilderness.

The choice of house sites was limited. They had to be near water—a spring or a river. Usually they tried to make an orchard and a garden to grow vegetables and tobacco, watering it with a furrow taken out of the stream sometimes a mile or more from their homes.

The houses they built of poles placed in holes in the ground and tamped in. The wood had to be hard and immune to white ants. The spaces between the poles and the poles themselves were covered with dagga—clay wetted and tramped till it reached the consistency of cement. It was then thrown against the framework in great dabs and plastered on by hand. The roofs of the houses were thatched with the long harsh grass that grew everywhere. They had no ceilings, and the roof timbers were made, when possible, of white poplars, which grew very straight, were light, and ant-resistant, and which every Boer planted as soon as he could obtain the rooted slips and suckers. The floors were also of dagga mixed with ox blood and hair. Into them, to take up the friction, were inset peach pips. The floors were then polished with beeswax till they glistened. The furniture, except for the little they had brought with them, they made themselves of the woods they found in the North, such as tambouti and boukenhout.

For blankets they had karosses of tanned hides sewn together, and both the seats of the chairs and the bed bottoms were made of riempies—thin rawhide strips latticed across the frames. Having no nails, everything was pegged. This kind of furniture had the advantage of being easily knocked to pieces if they moved on.

What they had not got or could not devise, they had to do without. Powder and lead, essential to them, was brought up by incoming emigrants or by the Jewish smouses on pack donkeys. But it was the custom to cut every bullet out of a beast when it was killed, and fathers would send their sons out hunting for meat with one bullet and one charge of powder. If they wasted it, they were beaten. The result of this upbringing became apparent in the Boer War when the marksmanship of these farmers astonished the world. With good modern rifles a Boer could kill a buck that was invisible to untrained eyes at six hundred yards.

This, then, was the life of a Boer in those days—not much over a hundred years ago. A man who, with his family, had travelled a thousand miles or more, who, having survived the dangers and hardships of that travel, must now face the further danger and hardship of occupying new and hostile land, of making a home out of a wilderness, of building and planning, of planting his garden and orchard, fashioning it like a green jewel, watered by his sweat, in the heart of some valley. Families tended to settle near each other for mutual aid and protection, fathers, sons, uncles, and cousins, occupying adjoining farms, riding them off and starting the small communities which later became towns and villages, or, if disaster overtook them as it did only too often, leaving nothing to show that they had ever been there.

What Paul Kruger, still a boy and subject to his patriarchal father, did was no different from what any other Boer boys did. He, like them all, led a hard, frugal life of hunting, farming, working, and worshipping the Lord. Sometimes there were reunions with other families or with newcomers passing by; sometimes many families met together for Communion—Nagmaal. Sometimes there were dances and feasts at births or marriages, sometimes sadder meetings to mourn a death. There was music made with harmonicas and fiddles, with concertinas and flutes, occasional horse-races and competitions at shooting with a fat pig as a prize.

One adventure did happen to Paul at this time. He and his brother-in-law, Theunissen, who were hunting companions, made a strange compact. It was agreed between them that should one of them behave recklessly, or through cowardice allow game to escape, he should receive a thrashing with a sjambok from the other. On this occasion Kruger had just killed a rhinoceros and had rejoined Theunissen who was hunting a second one—a cow.

As he came near him, Theunissen shouted, "Don't dismount in front of the beast, she's awfully wild and can run like anything." Kruger paid no attention, knowing his brother-in-law to be overcautious, and dismounting ran obliquely past the rhinoceros. She saw him and chased him. Allowing her to come within three or four yards, Kruger fired, but his percussion cap missed, and there was no time for a second shot. There was nothing to do but run, which he did, but his foot struck a root and he fell. The beast was on to him, her horn just missing his back. She had pinned him with her nose and was intending to trample him when he turned under her and discharged his second barrel full under her shoulder blade right into her heart. Of this incident he says, "I owe my life to not letting go of my gun when I fell." His brother-in-law ran up, thinking him killed, but when he saw him get up, belaboured him soundly because he had acted so recklessly. "Soft words and attempts to justify my conduct availed me nothing," Kruger writes, "nor did pointing out that I was already so bruised that I might well be let off my hiding." He was eventually forced to run away and hide in some thorn bushes to escape his brother-in-law.

While still on the trek, Paul Kruger was confirmed by Mr. Lindley, an American missionary who had had a mission station among the Matabele in the Marico District until the Boers in the vicinity were attacked by Moselikatze's men, when, seeing that his work had become impossible, he joined the trekkers. He was a great athlete, a fine horseman and a dead shot, and had a profound influence on Paul and succeeded in grafting something of the New England Puritan creed on to the Calvanistic faith of the "Dopper" people to which all the Kruger party belonged.

At sixteen, Paul Kruger was entitled to choose two farms, like any other independent member of the community; one as a grazing place and the other for sowing crops. He chose Waterkloof and Boukenhoutfontein; later he acquired the farm Saulspoort as a winter grazing farm and many properties in the Rustenburg, the best known of which was Watervaal. He now not merely thought he was a man, but knew it, and was recognised as such, a burgher with full rights. And his thoughts turned to a girl he had met in the country south of the Vaal—a Miss Maria du Plessis. And he set off to fetch her.

When he reached the Vaal, he found the river up and impassable. But Paul was not to be stopped by rivers up or down, and despite the warning of the ferryman, who refused to risk his boat, he drove his horses into the swirling waters and, dressed as he was, swam them across under conditions which courted almost certain death. The ferryman accused him of reckless behaviour, but it is doubtful if the young lover minded much. He had got across, and reached his bride.

In 1845, when he was twenty, Paul accompanied his father as deputy field cornet to Delagoa Bay, to come to an understanding regarding the common frontier between the new land the Boers had occupied and the Portuguese colony. The Lembombo Mountains were agreed upon as the frontier. Moving with their families, including Paul's young wife, the expedition explored the country as far north as the present Lydenburg District, founding the village of Ohrigstadt, but they found no abiding place. Fever, illness, cattle sickness, and over evils drove them to return to the Magaliesberg, where Paul continued to live, and acquire further farms by barter.

Here in 1846, Kruger writes, "I had the misfortune to lose my wife and the baby to whom she had given birth." Thus simply, in one line, he describes his first great personal tragedy. He goes on in the next line: "God gave me another life companion, Miss Gezina Suzanna Frederika Wilhelmina du Plessis." She was a cousin of Maria's, and it was she who requested the sculptor of her husband's statue in Pretoria to make his top hat hollow so that when it rained the little birds could drink from it.

Kruger only waited a year before re-marrying. But there is little doubt that he had known his second wife for a long time, since Boer families are all intimately connected in their personal lives. It was moreover practically impossible for a man to farm unmarried. In all pioneer countries men and women are mutually dependent on each other and form a human unit. This marriage lasted fifty-four years. They had sixteen children, nine sons and seven daughters.

There are certain stories that deal with Paul Kruger's spiritual experiences that are worth consideration, since they occur so often that they are likely to be founded on events which actually took place, though it is probable that time and continued telling have not detracted from the original versions. Oom Paul has become a legend; he was an outstanding figure, and one whom all men watched.

The first tale is that of his temptation. As little more than a boy in years, but already a man if exploits make men, he came upon a young Matabele girl bathing naked in a rocky pool. They were alone. The girl beckoned to him, telling him, in her soft Zulu tongue, that the water was warm. The girl was beautiful. The sun shone on her silky skin. Kruger, young and hot-blooded, moved towards her. And then he heard a voice that said, "Thou shalt not sin." He stopped and then fell on his knees to thank God for his deliverance from evil.

The second experience, which is well documented, tells of Kruger's gift of second sight, or, as we might call it to-day, extra-sensory perception. Always an ardent hunter, Paul was in great demand, and his relations and friends would not go on an expedition without him, for he had had, since childhood, a gift of being able to see the whole surrounding country without first having to hunt over it. Standing beside the wagon at the outspan, he could conjure up a picture in which he saw where the game was. In a state of trance he would describe the exact location of all the animals in the vicinity. To the south, he would say, by a kopje that was almost out of sight, were three elands. To the north a herd of kameels—giraffes—were drinking with outstretched legs, one bull that was very dark in colour; with him were two cows and a calf. To the west in a deep sluit a lion lay waiting to spring upon some zebras that were drifting towards him.

Krüger's descriptions were always correct, and either the beasts he described or their spoor were found when the hunters reached the spot he had described.

For many years he was proud of this power of his, and then one day there grew on him a sense that it was unchristian—that he did it out of vanity. Again, as was his custom when in a quandary, he knelt to pray, this time by a great ant-heap, and asked that this gift be taken from him. It was. He never had another vision of game.

His third experience was the greatest and the most tragic. It was concerned with the death of his little wife, Maria, whom he had swum the Vaal to court. She was very young and appears to have been very silent and gentle. When she bore him a child, he was overjoyed and walked about the house carrying the infant whenever he was in. But Maria and the child did not thrive. Both got weaker daily. Coming into the house from the lands one day, he heard Maria singing. She had never sung before. Going into the bedroom, he found her singing to the child which lay dead in her arms. As he watched her, amazed, she fell back and died.

Heartbroken, Kruger wondered about the meaning of life for months, reading the Bible and thinking. What was the truth? What was life? What was death? Was there a plan? Was the idea of God an illusion? And then one night he went into the mountains behind his house. He disappeared among the crags and hills and none knew where he was. His friends searched the hills in vain. On one occasion a party said they heard someone singing, but only later did it occur to them that it might be the missing man. They went back and found Kruger. He had been the singer. He was almost dead of thirst and starvation, so much so that they had to take water away from him in case he destroy himself by overdrinking. He was not strong enough to ride home, he had to be held in the saddle, but his problem was solved. "The Lord has opened my eyes and shown me everything," he said when he was able to speak.

These three experiences have one thing in common: in them all Paul Kruger sought both consolation and advice from his God. In them all he sought God out on the open veld of Africa, praying to him beside a tree or an ant-hill or in the silence of the mountains. The spiritual factor cannot be denied in Paul Kruger's life and was the complement of his intense virility. The opposite side of this great hunter and fighter was the farmer and the mystic.

Here, then, is Paul Kruger, twenty-two years of age, a re-married widower, a pioneer, a soldier, a deputy field cornet, a farmer, and the owner of great tracts of land and many head of sheep, horses, and cattle. A man whose experience had made him serious and whose upbringing, based upon the Bible, had confirmed this seriousness. Already he had seen life and death—much of it; had faced and overcome many dangers and was, in the rising strength of his youth, equipped to meet all that life would bring forth—the destiny of one who was to have "a superior position" in a way of life that was slow and heavy. Heavy as the lead bullets of the old muzzle-loading flintlocks that went four to the pound.

Slow as the pace of the ox.

CHAPTER TWO

THE YOUNG CAPTAIN

Paul Kruger was appointed deputy field cornet in 1842 at the age of seventeen. Ten years later, in 1852, he was made a full field cornet and accompanied the old Commandant-General Pretorius to the Sand River, where the Sand River Convention, by which the English agreed to leave the Boers in possession of their new lands, was signed.

In the same year Kruger went on an expedition against the Bechuana chief, Secheli, who was protecting another Kaffir chief called Moselele, who had committed a number of murders. When his return was demanded, Secheli sent back a message, saying, "Who wants Moselele can come and fetch him out of my stomach."

The commando under Scholtz, with Kruger as second in command, reached Secheli's town on a Saturday and Secheli sent another message to the Boers, saying that "as to-morrow was Sunday he would do nothing to them, but that on Monday he would duly settle his account." He also asked for some coffee and sugar.

On Monday the battle began. Kruger killed a number of Kaffirs with his four-pounder that he had loaded with coarse shot. During the battle he was nearly killed twice, once when hit in the forehead and knocked unconscious by a ricochetting bullet, and later when a large bullet fired by a Kaffir struck him on the chest and tore his jacket in two.

After it was all over Secheli said that he had had it in his power to drive the Boers back, but that Kruger, once he had laid his hands on his brandy bottle, became invincible. This Kruger complained of as being a lie, since he "never in all his life tasted a drop of brandy."

When the hostilities were over, Commandant Scholtz sent Theunis Pretorius up to the house of Doctor Livingstone, the English missionary, who then lived near the Kaffir town, and there found a complete workshop for repairing guns and a quantity of war material that Livingstone was storing for Secheli. Since this was illegal, the sale of arms or ammunition to the Kaffirs having been forbidden by the terms of the Sand River Convention, they were confiscated, as a result of which Livingstone spent the rest of his life slandering the Boers as enemies of the missionaries and persecutors of the blacks. Part of the Boer resentment against the English was due to the fact that they encouraged the missionaries and demanded equal justice for Hottentots and Kaffirs and white men. As the Boers ruled by the Bible, they considered this attitude infamous and unchristian, since the Bible had cursed the descendants of Ham. "Cursed be Canaan. A servant of servants shall he be . . ." Nothing could be clearer than the Word of God, and this talk of equality was merely to cause trouble between black and white when there was already trouble enough without such outside interference.

As to whether Livingstone did or did not supply arms to the Kaffirs, there is no answer. The Boers say that he did, and he denied it vehemently to the end of his life. Kruger was a truthful man and so it must be presumed was Livingstone.

In 1853, Kruger was again in action under Commandant-General Pretorius against the Kaffir chiefs Mapela and Makapaan in the Waterberg District near Makapaanspoort. This was to avenge the death of Herman Potgieter, who had been killed by Mapela.

Potgieter was the son of the late commandant-general and was a great hunter. Mapela had sent a messenger to tell him of a big herd of elephants in his territory and Potgieter set out to hunt them with his son, Andries, a few burghers, and his coloured groom. He had been for some time on friendly terms with Mapela, who was grazing many cattle for him on shares, Mapela taking the milk of the cows in return for his trouble in herding them. This arrangement had been made at Mapela's request, and on Potgieter's arrival the Kaffirs were very friendly and described the place where the elephants were to be found. The Boers, suspecting nothing, had outspanned their wagons in the village and were engaged in conversation when suddenly the Kaffirs fell on the party. Young Andries and the other Boers were killed, and Herman was dragged to the top of a hill, where, shouting with enjoyment, the Kaffirs flayed him alive in the presence of his groom. He did not die until the entrails had been pulled out of his body.

While Mapela was doing this, Makapaan attacked a number of women and children who were travelling from the Zoutpansberg to Pretoria. It appeared later that these two chiefs had arranged to murder all the whites in their respective districts.

To avenge these deaths, General Piet Potgieter, the nephew of the murdered hunter, set out with a hundred men from the Zoutpansberg and General Pretorius left Pretoria with two hundred on the same errand. Paul Kruger was the second in command of this expedition. As soon as the two commandos met, the Kaffirs were attacked, defeated, and driven back into the mountains. They hid in great caves, where they had stored food and water against such an eventuality. The Boers could not get them out and had no choice but to camp and wait for starvation. to kill them as soon as their stores were exhausted.

Here Paul Kruger decided to break the deadlock by a stratagem. One night he crept into one of the caves where the Kaffirs lay hidden, sat down among them, and began to talk to them in their own language, telling them that it was better to surrender than to die of hunger. Suddenly a Kaffir shouted "Magoa!"— white man—and all fled deeper into the cave. Kruger ran with them and they looked for the white man in every direction except where he was—in their midst. When they had quieted down, he again addressed them, and succeeded in leading a hundred and seventy women and children out of the cave, who never realised, till they were taken prisoner, that it was a white man who had been talking to them. The Commandant-General was very angry and punished Kruger for his recklessness by forbidding him to go near the caves again.

There is in this incident a curious parallel with the action of Cecil Rhodes who in 1897 went alone to the Matopos where the Matabele had taken refuge and treated with them.

There was a further personal incident in this war. In one of the skirmishes, for the Kaffirs, though they were in the caves, kept coming out and making forays, General Potgieter was wounded. At the time he was hit, he was standing very near a ledge, and Kruger, seeing him fall, determined to rescue him. Under the covering fire of the burghers and protected by the smoke of their black powder, he leaped down and succeeded in bringing the body safely back. Potgieter was a big heavy man, and Kruger had to exert all his strength to carry the dead man back to his people.

A heavy Dutchman would weigh at least two hundred pounds, and it is evident that Paul Kruger was a man of exceptional strength. An earlier hunting story confirms this. Once, when he was hunting a buffalo cow, she charged him and his flintlock missed fire. The rains had been heavy, and as he jumped out of the animal's way he landed in a deep swamp. Before he could get up, the buffalo was standing over him. As she butted at him, the cow rammed one of her horns into the mud, where it stuck. Kruger got hold of the other horn and succeeded, using both hands, in forcing her nose under water. The task was harder because the horn was slippery with mud. He then let go with one hand, felt for the hunting knife on his hip, but was unable to hold her; and she freed herself from his grasp, and half-drowned and blinded with mud, she ran away.

A few years before this, in 1845, Kruger had had another narrow escape in the neighbourhood of Sekukuni's town, where he was travelling with his two brothers, Theunis, and their wives. They had outspanned their wagons and Kruger left them to shoot some game for the pot. He was mounted and carried his four-pounder. After about an hour's ride, he came upon a rhinoceros and wounded it. It ran into the bush. He dismounted, but moved only a few paces from his horse in case he had to get away. He fired a second shot, but his gun exploded just where he held the barrel with his left hand and thumb. The lock and ramrod lay in front of him on the ground and the barrel was blown over his head. The rhinoceros charged him, and he had only just time to mount and gallop away, pursued by the rhinoceros, which gave up when it came to a little stream. Kruger then rode quietly towards the wagons.

Next day his people, following the spoor of his horse, found the rhinoceros still alive, and following the trail of blood found his gun and the remnants of his thumb. His hand was in a terrible state, the flesh was hanging in strips, and he bled, in his own words, "like a slaughtered calf." To save his horse being splashed with blood, he had tied a pocket handkerchief round the wound while riding.

When he reached the camp, he found his wife and sister-in-law sitting by the fire, and approached them laughing so as not to frighten them. His sister-in-law, looking at his bloody hand and not knowing him wounded, said, "Look what fat game brother Paul has been shooting."

Kruger then told his wife to get turpentine from the wagon and asked his sister-in-law to take off his bandolier. It was only then that she noticed how white he was—nearly all the blood being drained from his body. He kept renewing the turpentine bandages "to burn up the veins," as the Boers say, and thus stop the bleeding. His youngest brother, who was still a child, Kruger sent galloping off to the nearest farm to borrow as much turpentine as he could get. The farm, which was only eight miles away, belonged to the hunter, Herman Potgieter, who was murdered later, and he came back with his brother and the boy.

"This hand will never heal," he said; "it is an awful wound." He had to dismount quickly because he almost fainted at the sight.

But Herman's brother, who had come with him, said, perhaps to comfort the wounded man, "Nonsense, I have seen worse wounds than that get well with plenty of turpentine."

They helped inspan the oxen and drove over to the farm, where they wanted to send for a doctor to amputate his hand. Kruger rejected this idea, though. Two joints of the thumb had gone, but it looked as if a piece of bone still had to come away. Drawing his sheath knife, Kruger prepared to cut this out himself, but the others took the knife away from him. Later, however, he got it back and performed the operation when no one was looking. The worst bleeding was over, but the operation was very painful. "I had no means by me to deaden the pain," he writes, "so I tried to persuade myself that the operation was on the hand which belonged to someone else."

The wound was slow in healing. The women poured finely powdered sugar on it and from time to time Kruger pared away the dead flesh with his knife. Nevertheless, and despite all care, gangrene set in, and though every known Boer remedy was used, black marks rose on his arm as far as the shoulder. Then the final remedy was used. A goat was killed, and Kruger put his hand into its entrails while they were still hot. This succeeded, and by the time the second goat was used, his hand was easier and the danger already much reduced. The wound took six months to heal, but he was out hunting again before it was quite cured.

Kruger attributes the healing power of the goat entrails to the fact that the goats grazed near the Spekboom River, where all sorts of medicinal herbs grow in abundance.

Again he was saved by the Lord, by the coincidence of his accident taking place in a part where the goats grazed on this particular form of herbage.

Big, thick-set Kruger must have been a young man of exceptional vitality and strength. There are endless stories about him, half-truth and half-legend, but the legends are founded on the half-truth; for to have his exploits spoken about at all among the Voortrekkers, a man would have to be much more than ordinary.

His swiftness of foot was proverbial, and one story of it he told himself—of how, when elephant hunting, he was chased by an elephant and in his race to safety tripped up over a sleeping lion. A lion when waked suddenly almost always panics. "I say almost always," he said, "because there is no always with lions, who differ in character as much as men." This one did panic and ran ahead in a straight line with Kruger running beside him and the elephant trumpeting behind them.

"We were running together," Kruger said. "Sometimes the lion was in front and sometimes I was."

The story was never finished, for it was interrupted by Doctor Leyds, who informed him—he was President then—that the Raad was waiting for him.

When he was eighteen, Kruger ran half a mile against a mounted man and won. This story is confirmed by Poultney Bigelow. Another time Kruger ran against two natives, said to be the pick of their tribe, and won. He is even said to have escaped from a lion by running on one occasion. He was also a great jumper, once in a match jumping twenty-three feet; and when driving oxen and wishing to get to the other side of the span, he often used his long whip stick as a vaulting pole and leaped over their backs. As a horseman he was unexcelled even among a people that lived on horseback. He rarely mounted by the stirrup, but vaulted into the saddle. When buying a horse he galloped it over broken ground to see if it would fall. If it fell, he always landed on his feet, and rejected the animal as unsafe. He rode bareback as well as he did with a saddle, and as easily with his head towards the horse's tail as towards its head, and could still keep it under control. Indeed, when hunting buffalo, he always rode with his head to the horse's tail because the buffalo is almost sure to pursue its hunter and in this position he was able to get in a sure shot. He was in addition a fine swimmer as he proved when he swam the flooded Vaal.

Kruger's life would appear to be a sequence of events and accidents whose outcome always favoured him. Luck some might call it, but to Stephanus Johannes Paulus Kruger there was no such thing as luck. What saved him was Divine Providence, and always—whatever occurred—the hand of the Lord God was stretched out above him. His strength, agility, and courage were certainly factors in his preservation. But to whom did he owe these if not to God?

But to return to the Kaffir War—when it was found impossible to get at Makapaan's people, the Boers, using all their wagons, collected stones and walled up the entrances of the caverns. For this work fifty spans of oxen and some three hundred friendly Kaffirs were employed. In all fifteen hundred drags of trees and stones were thrown down the caves. Many hundreds of Kaffirs died, and so great was the stench of the rotting bodies that the Boers had to move their encampment. A few Kaffirs escaped through small underground passages in the mountains. Those that were caught were court-martialled and shot, for during the explorations and reconnaissances of the Kaffir position, the garments which had belonged to the murdered women were found as well as portions of human bodies which the Kaffirs had roasted on the spit. Commandant-General Marthinus Pretorius says: "I saw it with my own eyes . . . the bodies were mostly those of women. One body, that of a tall man, was frightfully mutilated. All his fingers from the tops of the palms of his hands were cut open; his head was cut off and the trunk was thrown into the water. In one of the kraals melted human fat was found, the hands having been roasted on spits. In addition, we found indications of unbridled ferocity which decency prevents me from describing."

Some Kaffir children were captured and these were ingeboekt —that is to say, apprenticed to various Boer families, where they would be kept under supervision till they came of age.

This question of apprentices was one which later on caused trouble with the English, who found that certain Boers were making slave raids against Kaffirs and Bushmen in order to steal the children, whom they described as orphans, which indeed they were, since the hunters had killed their parents. In addition, since no native knows how old he is, some spent the whole of their lives in servitude waiting to come of age—when they would legally be set free.

The commando having settled with Makapaan now turned its attention to his ally, Mapela, who had entrenched himself on a very high kop which had sheer walls of cliff on every side. Kruger, calling for volunteers to storm it, led the attack with a hundred men. They approached the hill by night and taking off their veldschoen—the soft home-made shoes of tanned leather—they climbed the deep gorge which was the only way to the summit.

Paul Kruger led the first patrol and was half-way up when he was discovered. A Kaffir sentry had allowed him to come right up to him before he fired, and the first thing that Kruger heard was the click of the hammer as it fell on the lock. Fortunately, the gun misfired and Kruger shot the sentry dead at his feet. Surprise was now out of the question: the Kaffirs, aroused, were firing from all round. Kruger's gun-bearer with his second gun fell, and Kruger turned and ran back to the main party.

"Forward!" he shouted. "On with your shoes and have at them without mercy!"

The pass was seized and the top reached by dawn. The Boers mowed down the Kaffirs who were assembling to attack, and put them to rout. The enemy flung themselves over the precipice, where the trees that clung to the cliff and the forest below were festooned with dead and dying men. The Kaffirs were defeated, but Mapela himself escaped.

The commando now broke up, the men returning to their wives and farms. But Kruger had hardly got home before, in

December, '53, he was called out again to act as adjutant to General Pretorius, who was about to attack the chief Montsioa who lived in the High Veld near Marico. He had been raiding cattle and had murdered a farmer; and now that he found himself attacked, had taken refuge in British Bechuanaland.

In this expedition God was again on the side of the Boers, for they reached Setagoli where Montsioa was hiding in the midst of an enormous swarm of locusts which, darkening the sky, hid the dust of the approaching commando from the natives till it was almost in the town, and thus forty burghers were able to rout five hundred Kaffirs, killing many and putting the rest to flight. The stolen cattle were recaptured and again the commando broke up, the men returning to their farms and peacetime occupations.

Kruger, however, did not have much rest. Hardly had he returned when Commandant-General Pretorius fell sick and sent for him. Unfortunately, Kruger was away from home at the time, hunting in Rustenburg Bushveld, and by the time he returned, Pretorius was dead.

"This was most deplorable," Kruger writes, "for who knows what he might have wished to discuss with me in his last moments. On the return journey from Montsioa's town, he had talked to me much on religious matters and he might have had more to say to me on this subject."

A few days after his death, a letter came addressed to Pretorius from the British Commissioners, Owen and Hogg, in which he was requested to take over the Free State from the British government on behalf of the emigrants—that is, the Boers who had taken up land there. This being impossible since he was dead, some burghers, headed by Venter and Boshoff, took over the country, much to the anger of young Pretorius, who considered that the presidency should have come to him as his father's heir. He had been appointed Commandant-General of the South African Republic, and was later elected President when he put forward his claims to the Free State as well and raising some troops camped on the banks of the Vaal, where Kruger, who disapproved very much of his conduct, found him. But when Kruger learnt that the President of the Free State had made an agreement with Commandant-General Schoeman, of the Northern

Transvaal, where the new law was not yet acknowledged, to come to the Free State's assistance, Kruger advised an immediate attack on Boshoff. Neither army was seriously inclined to war, and the messenger Boshoff sent with proposals of peace found Kruger, whom he had been sent to see, on the back of a buck-jumping horse surrounded by his admiring followers. He was told Kruger was competing in a buck-jumping competition. Fortunately, no blood had yet been shed and an agreement was reached. Only one difficulty remained. Two burghers who had sided with Pretorius in the Free State were charged with high treason and condemned to be hanged.

Kruger accused Boshoff of breaking their compact by this sentence.

"We break the compact?" Boshoff said. "What do you mean?"

"Well, you are going to hang two of your people."

"Yes, and we have the right to do so: it says so in the agreement."

"Nothing of the sort," Kruger answered. "You have the right to punish, certainly; but punish means to chastise, to admonish, to warn, and to correct by means of chastisement." And when Boshoff would not agree to this definition, Kruger went off and returned with a Bible and showed that the Holy Writ distinguished between punishing and death. We may chastise a man with the prospect of death, but we may not kill him in order to punish him. The Free-Staters then gave in and the matter was settled.

Many years later, Paul Kruger as President of the South African Republic again gave the same judgment when he condemned the leaders of the Jameson Raid to death. In his mind, no doubt, he was chastising them with the prospect of death and knew very well that he would never permit his sentence to be carried out. But it is questionable if the prisoners were aware of Kruger's opinion or of the consistency of his mind.

Not long after the trouble with Boshoff, Kruger decided to offer his services to the Free State Government to help them settle their differences with Moshesh, chief of the Basuto nation, who had been raiding and killing in their country.

With a small party he went to see Moshesh, sending word that he had not come to fight, but wished to talk about peace. Moshesh sent word that he would come and talk with Mr. Kruger, but Kruger, who was not disposed to wait, climbed the mountains and went straight to Moshesh's town. Moshesh came to meet him, accompanied by Magato, a Kaffir captain from the Rustenburg who knew Kruger. He introduced him, saying to the chief, "This is Paul Kruger."

Moshesh gave him his hand, and said: "Is that Paul Kruger? How is it possible? I have heard tell of him for so many years and now I am so old. How, then, can he still be so young?"

He then took Kruger to his house where they came to terms. During the conversation Moshesh asked him if he was the man who fetched Mapela down from the mountain. His trial had just taken place.

"Yes," Kruger said, "I am he."

"Are you aware that two of my daughters were married to Mapela?" he asked, and then, after a moment's silence, added, "You need not think it was your courage that brought Mapela down from the mountain; it was the dispensation of God that punished Mapela for committing so foul a murder."

This was the kind of conversation Paul Kruger liked, and he asked Moshesh why if he was so devout he came to have more than one wife himself.

Moshesh answered that he had two hundred, but that this was not half so many as Solomon had.

"But surely you know that since Christ's time and according to the New Testament a man may have only one wife," Kruger said.

Moshesh reflected a moment, and then said, "Well, what shall I say to you? . . . It is just nature."

A treaty was then drafted, Kruger acting on behalf of the Free State; and the first Boer-Basuto War ended with Kruger receiving a very fine saddle horse as a present.

All through his life it was religious arguments which interested Kruger the most. He refused, much later on during the Boer War, to meet again a traveller who interested him greatly because he had said that he had been "interrupted by the war from completing his journey round the world."

"Across the world, you mean," Kruger said.

And when the man persisted in his opinion that the world was round, the President would have no further talk with him. He was, according to the Holy Writ, a liar. Kruger refused to believe in coral insects or that islands were continually being made by them, for this, too, was against his beliefs. The world was made in six days—made and finished, completed—and anything to the contrary was heresy.

Yet he did not disdain to use a certain amount of cunning in order to prove his point that the Lord watched over the Boers and that they were the chosen people. There is a story told of how on one occasion when there was no game for the pot, Kruger prayed very loud for divine aid in front of his fellows and made them join the prayers. Next morning, very early, he stole into the bush near the camp and flushed a pau, the giant South African bustard, which flew over the camp and was shot down. The efficacy of Paul Kruger's prayers caused much comment and might have caused more had it been known that he had noted the bird going to rest the previous night before he opened his prayer meeting.

Kruger did almost the same thing on another occasion. This is how it is described by Manfred Nathan in his life of Kruger:

"A party of burghers were out hunting. After waiting a few days, Kruger told his companions he had decided to make it a matter of prayer. For this purpose he proposed to retire into the bush where he was not to be sought after, or disturbed, however long he might be absent. He saddled up and retired to wrestle in prayer. A day or so later the game became more plentiful and the pious farmers set this down to the efficacy of prayer. They did not know that young Kruger had ridden to a Kaffir kraal and explained to them that unless they beat up the game and drove it in a certain direction, keeping themselves well out of sight, he would bring a Boer commando down on them."

Kruger believed in God and in prayer, and it was not going to be his fault if every one with whom he came into contact did not do the same even if it was necessary to trick them a little for their own good. Kruger's God was the terrible, just God of Israel, but his life on the veld and his observations of nature evidently enabled Kruger to endow the Lord with an ironic sense of humour. This combination of the light and the deadly serious was a characteristic of Kruger's. For instance, when Poultney Bigelow, many years later, asked him which he preferred, African or British lions, Kruger answered, "There is no choice. Both are bad."

While still in Moshesh's town a message came to Kruger from the President, asking him if he would return at once and set out as assistant general with a commando against Gasibone, a Kaffir chief on the Harts River, who had stolen some cattle, killed some men, and carried off an old woman and a girl of eighteen.

Kruger jumped on his horse and returned to his farm in the Magaliesberg, in the district of Rustenburg, spending fifty hours on horseback in three days—riding, as most Boers rode when in a hurry, with two horses, one led and one under him, and changing his saddle from one to the other every few hours. Usually Boer horses receive no food but what they can pick up while grazing knee-haltered at night. Each time they are offsaddled, the Boers let them roll, which they say rests them by relieving the stiffness that comes from carrying a heavy man at a canter or triple for long periods. This triple corresponds more or less to the American pace, the horse moving both near and then both off feet together, instead of alternately. Some horses are born triplers and others are trained to it by tying their legs together as colts so that, as the foal leads with his near foreleg, his near hind must follow it. But most horses can be broken by means of a heavy bit and the use of spurs, the horse being at the same time pushed forward and held back, which forces him into this ambling pace which is very comfortable. These horses rarely stand more than fifteen-two and have a great deal of Arab blood. The Basutos are famous for their horses, which can climb mountains and cover great stretches of rocky ground without shoes on their feet. It was not unusual for a Boer to ride seventy miles a day on a single horse. And Kruger's ride would not have been considered exceptional in those days. The main interest of his performance lies in the fact that he spent only one day at home and then rode another three hundred-odd miles to Klerksdorp, where he joined the commando which he was to lead against Gasibone.

On this expedition the Boers were very ill provided with food, having no cattle for slaughter on the road. The usual procedure was to take a herd of oxen, which could travel as fast as the horses, and slaughter what was needed when camp was made.

In addition, ammunition was so short that they could spare none to shoot game. The difficulty of food was got over by rounding up the buck which abounded and driving them into bends of the Vaal River, where they were killed by beating them with sticks.

It is impossible to imagine the vast herds of game which then covered the veld, sometimes blanketing it with a moving carpet of wildebeest, zebras, blesbok, hartbeest, and springbok.

Gasibone and Mahura, another chief who had come to his assistance, were defeated and driven from the caves in which, according to the Kaffir custom, they had taken refuge. The stolen cattle were recaptured and the commando broke up.

Of this period Kruger writes in his *Memoirs*: "For me it had been a busy year."

CHAPTER THREE

THE COMMANDANT-GENERAL

THE NEXT few years were probably the happiest in Paul Kruger's life. He farmed his farm, he fathered more children, he hunted, he performed his duties as a burgher and local administrator. He was a figure among his people—a coming man. He was mature in all his ways, and set in his ways; in his belief in God, in his love of his country and his folk. Above all, he was a man without doubts, one whose life had made him self-confident and assured, not only of the Providence that watched over him, but of his capacity to assist Providence by taking care of himself, his family, and those whom God had put into his care—his family, his burghers, his cattle, horses and sheep, his black servants.

When his father died, Paul Kruger had taken his place as commandant in the Rustenburg. He was now a power in the land, a young captain, a leader of his people, a Voortrekker among other Voortrekkers, a hunter and farmer among other hunters and farmers, a Kaffir fighter among other veterans of the native wars, but greater than them all. A man who, though still relatively young, spoke as he trod, weightily and with certainty; a man whose views were representative of his people and whose politics came straight from between the great leather-bound Bibles of their homes.

Everything was simple and direct to Kruger. Everything the outcome, not of the greater history of nations, but of the parochial history of his folk. He demanded freedom from the English whom he hated with the violence of his childhood memories. He insisted on the black people being subjugated and kept in their places. The missionaries he loathed because they spoke of white and black equality.

Black and white his politics, black and white his views. He saw all things as good or evil, could compromise on little and then only to improve his position while he planned a further blow. Fearless, ruthlessly virtuous, upright, already dogmatic, his feet were firmly set on the rungs of the ladder that would lead him to the presidency.

Rhodes, though Kruger did not know it, had been born in England to plague him. A child now, but one whose character was cast in somewhat Kruger's own mould, though the opposite from it. The one the cast, the other the matrix. The one the positive, the other the negative. Both were men to be loved by those that served them, though at this time only a nursemaid served the infant Cecil. Both were men to whom the ends justified the means, though the one—Kruger—was a man of great integrity and the other—Rhodes—a man of no integrity at all: each represented not only a way of thought but a way of life.

This country where Kruger farmed—the Rustenburg District of the Transvaal—was a wild and beautiful land, well watered, with fine pasturage, and alive with game. Hidden among the stark mountains were lovely valleys. Great cliffs, whitened with the dung of vultures that had nested there for a thousand years, turned pink in the glow of the rising sun and purple in the lilac light of evening. There were plains out of which rose little sugar-loaf hills; isolated from each other they were neat cones of rock that were landmarks for miles. The soil was a rich red clay interspersed with areas of black turf, that grew wonderful, sweet, grazing grass, and which in the drought of winter contracted so much that every yard there was a small crevasse in which a horse could break its leg. In the summer this turf became glutinous under the torrential rains and clung to the wagon wheels, packing them so that travel was all but impossible.

The Boers, like the Krugers who lived on the frontier, were white fingers thrust into the darkness of Wild Africa. Like fingers exploring, they moved here and there, pulling in when they were stung by the assegais of the natives and then clenching into a fist to strike back; contracting when things were bad and expanding again when conditions of safety were re-established. But always groping, always seeking the good and the rich, the fat land, and avoiding the bad. And always behind the hand was the arm of white penetration that led back a thousand miles and more to the Cape, and behind that again, over the sea to the body of white power which forced the hand and arm.

Kruger's hope was to live detached from the body of the world—as if the hand which was the frontier Boer could be amputated from the body that was Europe and the brain that was the stock market of the world. The Bourse of Paris, the London Stock Exchange, and Wall Street were all out, unconsciously, to destroy what Kruger loved—the life of his fathers who had lived isolated in a Biblical vacuum. To avoid the pressure from the South, Kruger had to exert pressure on the North. To live detached from the white, he had to become attached, by war and by the mastery of the conquered as servants, to the black.

At twenty-six, Kruger had begun to show stature as a man of affairs. His physical condition is shown by his exploits in the field, but his appearance has not been dealt with. He was big, standing six feet in his socks, as were his protagonists Rhodes and Lobengula. And like them he was heavily built so that he did not appear to be as tall as he really was. As a young man he remained clean shaven. Later he grew a beard under the chin with whiskers extending up to his ears, his upper lip remaining bare. It has been said that he never had a moustache, but there are two photographs, taken in 1881 and 1882, which show him with a full moustache. After the war of independence his beard began to grow grey and his hair became thinner. In 1883, when he shaved his upper lip, he had more grey hairs than black. As a boy he parted his hair on the left side. Twenty years later he parted it on the right. This would appear to be of some psychological significance, especially as twenty years later on his second visit to Europe, he again parted it on the left. When he was older, no parting at all was visible and he brushed his grey hair straight back, though a long lock fell over his forehead to the right.

Kruger's eyes were a dark brown, almost black. In old age they had heavy bags beneath them and the left eyelid drooped. His eyes at that time were always inflamed and he held them partially closed. His eyebrows were heavy and his mouth large. He held his lips tightly compressed. His nose was prominent with wide nostrils and his ears were big. His expression in maturity was one of settled melancholy, though it could brighten up when he laughed or joked. In comparison with his great body his head was small. His most striking characteristic was his voice. It was startlingly deep, a double bass. When he was irritated, he used it with terrifying effect. It was described as being "not so much a roar like that of a lion as a bellow like that of a buffalo." This bull-like quality of his has often been noted. He even noted it of himself, and said, "In my young days I was a bull."

His Bible was always with him. To him it was not a book, not even a holy book. It was his life-guide and his companion, forever influencing and guiding him. At home a large-print version lay ready to his hand on the table by which he sat, but when angry he would bang his fist upon it without the slightest intention of treating the Bible with irreverence.

Kruger helped to build the first church at Rustenburg, and was so delighted at having laid the ridge-pole beam that he at once climbed to its highest point and alarmed and scandalised the community by standing there upon his head.

He was an ardent Psalm-singer. The "Doppers" allowed no other form of singing, considering even hymns to be worldly, and it is said that the farmers in the vicinity used to come to him to learn the key note for starting the Psalms for the following Sunday service. He used to charge them a double handful of dried peaches for this instruction. Sometimes to amuse himself he gave each applicant a different note and the pupils had to return to him for further instruction. "I nearly bankrupted them of their dried peaches," Kruger said when telling the anecdote.

Dried fruits and konfyts were the only sweets available in those days, and Kruger tells another story about them. He says: "One New Year's Day I sent a Kaffir to my mother's farm" (this would be his step-mother's) "to fetch some raisins. My mother sent me about five or six pounds and said so in a note which the Kaffir conscientiously delivered. But the letter was a proof that the Kaffir had robbed me. I asked what he meant trying to cheat me and why he had eaten nearly all the raisins. ' The letter tells me,' I said, ' that there were a great many more than you have brought me.' ' Baas,' he replied, ' the letter lies, for how could it have seen me eat the raisins? Why, I put it behind a rock and under a stone before I sat down on the other side of the rock to eat the raisins.' "

Kruger was very "down upon" immodesty in woman's clothes.

After an official banquet in London, when someone asked, "Mr. President, did the ladies wear beautiful dresses last night?" he answered, "I don't know. I never looked under the table." Another time in Holland when he was there with General Smit there were many ladies in low-cut dresses. One of them, sitting near the President and unable to get him to speak to her, turned to the General and said, "It seems the President does not like bare necks and arms. What about you, General?"

"No, the President does not like it," Smit said, "but as far as I am concerned the more naked the better."

The lady jumped up, went to her room, changed, and came back with her neck and arms covered and had "a long and agreeable conversation with the President."

On entering a concert hall in Durban with the governor of Natal on another occasion, Kruger looked round, and said, "We are too early. The people have not finished dressing."

Kruger was not sanctimonious, but he would tolerate no trifling with things that he considered sacred. A burgher trying to argue with him once asked if "he believed in the miracles and everything that is in the Bible."

"That I do and always shall believe," Kruger answered.

"Then why, if the ravens brought food to Elijah, why cannot God send me some food with the crows?"

"Because Elijah was a prophet who had a mission, whereas you are only a gluttonous fool, and if God were to send crows to you it would, in all probability, be because he desired the crows not to feed you, but to feed on you."

Kruger had seen many human bodies that had been eaten by vultures, jackals, hyenas, and crows.

His similes and parables had all a Biblical flavour as had his judgments. One of the most famous of these was the way he settled a dispute between two brothers who could not agree about the division of their farm after the death of their father. The eldest said he considered it his right to divide the farm. Kruger agreed with him. "As the eldest and most experienced," he said, "it is your right to divide the property into two portions, but then, having divided it, you must give your brother the first choice."

It has been said that Kruger knew no English, but there

is every reason to believe that he knew it, though he only spoke it on two occasions, the most important being in 1881—while discussing the armistice terms with the British at the end of the War of Independence. A messenger left the tent to carry a message from Sir Evelyn Wood to the commander of the British forces in the field.

"What is that message?" Kruger asked Major Frazer.

"The man is off to notify the army of the prolongation of the armistice."

Kruger then shouted angrily in his bull's bellow, "Stop that man!"

Paul Kruger was never, in the accepted sense of the word, an educated man. He read slowly, following the words with his forefinger. He wrote slowly, laboriously; his hands being more fitted to grasp the barrel of a rifle, the reins of a horse, or the handles of a plough than a pen. But if wisdom is taken as the criterion of education, then Paul Kruger was educated, having passed his years from earliest childhood in the university of life itself. Having seen what went on about him, Kruger had pondered on it and formed a pattern whose archaic quality was more than compensated for by a praticality which was probably greater than that of his academically educated opponents. In learning, as in all other things, the law of diminishing returns sometimes operates with disconcerting results.

Kruger believed that man could survive more than humanity. He knew that a man could exist after his mind had gone, that he could live after his soul had been destroyed. He knew that a man's willingness to fight for freedom was founded on man's fear of spiritual destruction. "Give me liberty, or give me death!" the cry of the American revolutionaries, found its echo a hundred years later in the Boers' passionate refusal to be absorbed by the British. Life without freedom to the Boer is death. And this freedom of his is a very special one, differing somewhat from that of other people's. It concerns an emotion, the spirit, as much as it does the political organisation of his country. It has to do with his right to be alone with his land: to be alone with Africa as though it were a woman. In all Boers there is something deep within them that they never disclose. Anything that applied to the Boers as a people applied to Paul Kruger, who was, as is every great national leader, completely representative of his people.

In the fifties and early sixties, there were only a few men who were not Boers in the Transvaal: a few adventurers and hunters, a few British officers on leave seeking sport, a few traders. But as yet there was no Uitlander problem: these outlanders, foreigners, were to come later. At present there was little to call to them. Europe had not begun to seek colonial empires in Africa; and only the Cape itself was important as a half-way house to India. Here the British East Indiamen had replaced the tall ships of the Dutch East India Company; but except for the flag it flew the function of the port remained the same, its outward appearance was relatively unchanged.

Exports were few—some horses to mount the Indian cavalry, many were sold in the Indian Mutiny of '57; some Cape wines, among them Constantia, had received world-wide recognition; some rare skins, such as those of the leopard and lion, horns for curios, and ostrich feathers were about all that went overseas from South Africa; and the northern Boers had little need to fear the encroachment of the English in a country as wild and inhospitable as theirs. No money was to be made here. Farming was not a business but a way of life, which was only varied by hunting, war, religious and political argument.

The Boers had many customs of their own. The oppsitting or courtship was one which persists in many parts of the Backveld to this day. The young man who wishes to court a maid puts on his best clothes, mounts his best horse, and rides to her father's house. The girl, fully aware that she has attracted his attention —they probably met at a Nagmaal—is prepared for him. When the evening comes, the young couple are left alone and the girl goes to fetch a candle. If it is long, the young man is encouraged, for the custom is that he may sit with her only as long as the candle is burning. If it is short, he knows he is not welcome. Usually it is neither long nor short, and it is only by following up his first visit that he can see how her feelings change towards him—a wonderful social device for a people to whom words came hardly, one saving of embarrassment for both the wooer and the wooed.

This peaceful, or at any rate relatively peaceful, life went on for Kruger till the outbreak of new political trouble which finally became a civil war.

The trouble began with the election of Pretorius, who was President of the South African Republic, to the presidency of the Free State as well on the death of President Boshoff. While he was in the Free State taking up office there, the Volksraad of the South African Republic passed a resolution that their State President could hold no other office; and Pretorius, refusing to give up the presidency of the Free State, resigned from that of the South African Republic. This left the post vacant and Grobler assumed the office of Acting President. Schoeman, the Commandant-General, opposed him on the grounds that he was better fitted for the post. This was a typical Boer reaction. A life of isolation led each man to think himself, if not perfect, at least as qualified to lead as the next man, and perhaps a little better qualified.

Kruger proposed a general meeting where the matter could be settled, but found, when he came to it with his burghers, that Schoeman's people had come armed. Kruger says that even if he had known of their intention he would not have permitted his men to carry rifles, as feeling ran too high and a quarrel might easily have led to civil war. Schoeman tried to seize Kruger, but many were opposed to this, even among Schoeman's party. However, a little while later they brought up a gun loaded with shrapnel and pointed it at Kruger's laager, threatening to shoot unless a certain man by the name of Jeppe was handed over to them. They needed him, as he was the only printer in the republic. His press was at Potchefstroom and Schoeman wanted to have handbills printed stating his case in order to influence the burghers. Kruger refused to give him up, but Jeppe, fearing they would open fire and kill many helpless men and women, gave himself up. There was a parallel incident in the first Boer War of 1880. Printers and presses were important factors in South African politics and wars.

Kruger now inspanned with a parting message to Schoeman's men, telling them that once he had crossed the Magaliesberg they must look on him as their enemy. A little later a properly convened Volksraad declared Schoeman guilty of breaking the law and deposed him from office. Van Rensburg was nominated president and Theunis Snijman as Commandant-General.

During these troubles many members of the Hervormde Reformed Church had accused Kruger with meddling, saying that since he did not belong to this church he was without rights, since according to the constitution only its members were allowed to exercise influence in public affairs. Whoever was not a member of the Hervormde Church was not a fully qualified burgher, they said.

Kruger belonged to the Christelijk-Gereformeerde Church, founded in 1859 by Doctor Postma at Rustenburg. This church was called the "Dopper" or canting church, the word "dop" deriving from a dop, a damper, or extinguisher used for putting out candles, the idea being that the Doppers were against all new ideas and put them out "as a dop put out a candle." Even such ideas as buttons for trousers were extinguished.

The principles of the Dopper Church were based on a strict adhesion to the decrees of the Synod of Dordrecht of 1618, and the services differed from those of other churches in that no hymns except Psalms were sung by the worshippers. A special session of the Volksraad was convened to confer burgher rights on the Doppers, but Schoeman, though deprived of office, raised his followers again and surrounded Pretoria to oppose the measure.

One of Schoeman's men, ignoring the challenge of a picket, had his horse shot under him and was wounded in the arm. This was the first shot fired in the Civil War.

Schoeman now spread a report that Kruger was out on commando with his men to compel the recognition of his church as that of the state. These rumours drew many men to him who felt their religious liberty to be challenged. Commandos were raised and strengthened by both parties, but again, in an effort to avoid hostilities, a meeting was agreed upon and the leaders met half-way between the two camps.

No decision was reached, though Kruger, when accused, said, "I have never thought of making my church the state church. Nay, even if you offered to make it so I should decidedly refuse, for our principles declare that Christ and no other must be head of the Church."

On the following day a battle ensued in which several men were killed and wounded. Schoeman was defeated and retreated to the Free State, where he had a farm, and there rallied more men around him. There was more fighting and another meeting, again held half-way between the opposing camps. A solution was arrived at and the war seemed at an end.

Kruger was then elected Commandant-General of the South African Republic, and in this capacity, a little later, went with a small party to the Free State to determine the boundary line between the two states, where he was surrounded by Schoeman's party, who, though they did not dare take him prisoner, did take his men.

Here Kruger employed one of his stratagems. A Boer when in difficulties always makes a plan—plan maak—and he allowed his enemies to think that he was so enchanted with their country that he intended to settle in it. He even bought a farm there "because there were so many disputes in the Transvaal," and being thorough he sent a message to his family in the Rustenburg telling them to prepare to trek down to join him. However, when he learned the prisoners had been set free and were safe, he returned immediately and joined the government commando on the Crocodile River. He had stayed in the Free State only because he was unwilling to abandon his men. This faithfulness to those who served him he had in common with Rhodes.

There was another engagement, this time during a parley. The Boers, though they fought each other, disliked doing it and always tried to avoid action. It was their fixed principle that whites should not kill whites. There were too few of them in the country and every man capable of bearing arms was needed to fight the native wars which, though they died down, never ceased completely or for long.

In this instance both parties tried to obtain a strategic hill and reached it from opposite sides, coming into collision at the top. Kruger, with a burgher named Enslin, was in front. As he got off his horse and prepared to fire, someone called to Enslin,

"Don't shoot. Let us talk. Why need we kill each other?"

Enslin lowered his gun, but as he did so received a bullet and fell dead in Kruger's arms. A battle followed and the enemy was defeated and fled towards Pretoria.

In this mounted warfare the Boers excelled. Against natives they charged mounted, firing from the saddle; but against white men they dismounted and, using every available piece of cover, fired with greatest accuracy at their enemies. The horses meanwhile were left in dead ground, in a fold of a hill, or behind trees, and stood as they were trained to do without horse holders. A trained Boer pony will stand quite still for hours, even when under fire, if the reins are dropped over his head.

The war, which pleased no one, now reached a conclusion, and the Volksraad discharged from their official positions all who had been directly concerned in the trouble. In view of the unrest which had come with civil war, the Volksraad agreed that a new presidential election should be held. Kruger, to establish his position and to give the people another opportunity of choosing a new commander, resigned his post as Commandant-General, but was re-elected, obtaining more than two-thirds of the votes. Already he had the confidence of his people.

In 1865 the great Basuto War broke out, and once again Kruger was in the field. The Basutos had penetrated far into the Free State and had murdered some Transvaalers. From the settlement of the chief Malap, which was near Moshesh's town, Kruger sent a message to the head chief asking that the murderers be delivered up to him. Moshesh said he could do so in a few days, as he could not lay hands on them at once.

The following day the Basutos, with three thousand Kaffirs and four thousand Zulus, attacked the Boers, surprising them in the darkness. The difficulty of defence was increased by light rain and mist. Kruger had three hundred men with him and it took him till dawn to drive the Basutos from the camp. Kruger's secretary, Nijhoff, who had been drunk and was tied to the wheel of a wagon for punishment the evening before, slept right through the fight and awoke in the morning very astonished to see the carnage and annoyed at having missed the battle.

"Have you people been fighting during the night?" he asked.

Kruger pursued the enemy into the mountains near Malap's town and sent a message to Fick, who was commanding the Free State commando of nine hundred burghers, to join him there. At this place a council was held and it was decided that the burghers of the South African Republic should receive farms in the territory about to be cleared of natives and hold them under the laws of the Free State. An attack was made, the enemy driven off, and large numbers of cattle captured, among them some of Kruger's own beasts.

The joint commando now marched on Moshesh's town and came upon a force of twenty thousand Kaffirs, many of whom were mounted. When they first sighted the natives, the Boers noticed some loose cattle among them, but they seemed so few that it was assumed that they were beasts the Kaffirs had brought with them for food. But when the battle was over, and the cattle captured, the few amounted to eight thousand head, which showed how many natives there had really been. The Kaffirs retreated to their town, where after more fighting they were defeated and a further eight thousand oxen, thirty thousand sheep, and a few hundred horses were taken.

Kruger had hardly got home from this expedition when he was called to Potchefstroom to attend the 1866 session of the Volksraad. On the way he had another accident, this time breaking his leg. At Schoonkloof farm in the Rustenburg, just beyond the Elephant Pass, he had to cross a dry sluit or ditch. The road leading up to it was so boggy that it was impossible to get a cart or a horse through it. Rather than turn back, Kruger turned his Cape Cart round and using his whip on the mules he pushed them at full gallop, hoping to make them jump the sluit and drag the cart after them. They jumped the ditch, but the cart upset, breaking Kruger's leg at the knee. With his leg broken and helped only by the little Kaffir horse boy he had with him, Kruger had to get the cart up, lift it on to the wheels—for it had come off the axle—catch and inspan his terrified mules and drive home again. The leg caused him great suffering and took nine months to mend. His left leg always remained a little shorter than the other.

Before his recovery was complete, he had to lead another commando against rebellious Kaffirs in the Zoutpansberg, where the village of Schoemansdaal had suffered especially from their attacks. Here he twice attacked the Kaffirs, but having used up all his ammunition he was forced to withdraw from the village. He offered to remain until help came, but only one field cornet with his men was willing to stand by him. Kruger then held a meeting and the villagers decided to abandon their homes, load their wagons with their most prized possessions, and driving their livestock return with the commando. Kruger settled them temporarily at Marabastad, which place for the time being then became the biggest settlement in the Zoutpansberg.

On the return journey he fought an action against a Kaffir captain called Machem, who had been stealing cattle in the Makapaanspoort district.

The next year Kruger again set out for the Waterberg and Zoutpansberg to see how matters stood there. He came upon a meeting of chiefs and, without showing any distrust, rode straight into the town where they had assembled. The Kaffirs were surprised to see him, expecting him to summon them rather than to come unarmed into their midst. They greeted him with the words:

"When it is peace, it is peace: and when it is war, it is war."

So again—it was now 1868—there was peace on the frontier. A brittle, uneasy peace, but a respite, and as such welcome to the Boers who in the last few years had spent so much time on service and so little with their wives or on their farms.

Actual peace of long duration was impossible because the Boer cattle were a continual temptation to the Kaffirs. Even the most peaceful were unable to resist minor stock thefts, while among the warlike tribes the young men clamoured continually for action. Raiding and fighting was their way of life.

The term "Kaffir"—used to cover all natives in South Africa—came down from the East Coast from the Portuguese, and is an Arab word meaning "unbeliever." Of all the tribes who came into conflict with the white men, both Boers and British, the Zulus and the Matabele—an offshoot of the Zulus—were the most savage and dangerous. Originally the Zulus were a small community. Their increase was due to their warlike habits. For nearly a century they had devastated the country, seizing cattle and women from their neighbours, killing, raping, burning; and breeding up, by means of the captured women and children, a race of warriors whose like had not been seen before in Africa.

Their history begins with the exploits of T'Chaka, who was born in 1787. He was the son of Usenzangacona, who was the son of Jama, who was the son of Umakeba, the son of Upunga. Usenzangacona was only a petty chief living near the coast between the Umvolosui and Umlatusi Rivers. Little is known of him except that he had thirty wives and two hundred children. One of his wives, the Lady Umnandi, accused of unfaithfulness by her husband, fled from him to another tribe. These are the bones of the story, but there is flesh and blood to be placed upon them—a development of the royal scandal and the hatred of a child; for Umnandi was heavy with child in the Royal Harem —inexplicably so, since the king had not been near her, and her affliction was conveniently described as a dropsy, which was called "Chaka" in her tongue. When she gave birth to a son, it was obvious that he must be a phenomenon without a father, and with great tact he was named T'Chaka in commemoration of the swelling which had so mysteriously disappeared from his mother when he was born.

Since Kaffir marriages are inevitably tied up with cattle, so many being paid for each maid; and since Umnandi was a princess and a great number of cattle had been paid for her, the repayment of these cattle on her return home must have caused great annoyance to her family which they took out on her and her child, both being badly treated.

This ill-treatment by the other children of his mother's tribe may have encouraged T'Chaka's warlike propensities, for already as a young man he had received the name Sigidi, which means "a thousand"—so many had he killed. As a boy the children jeered at him, mocking him for saying one day he would be king. But when that day came, he revenged himself, killing his mother's whole family. But first he endeared himself to the Amatetwa king Diniswayo—the wanderer—by his skill in war.

The Amatetwa were the overlords of the Zulus, and Diniswayo, who had been exiled for a time, had met, while away, a certain Doctor Cowan, who in 1806, with twenty uniformed soldiers, was seeking an overland route to Delagoa Bay. From this man Diniswayo learnt the use of the gun and horse—neither had ever been seen before; and got the idea of uniformed, disciplined troops. Under him the Amatetwa became great and with them the subsidiary Zulus whose chief T'Chaka had become by the death of his father. In 1818, Diniswayo was killed in battle and

T'Chaka and the Zulus seized the leadership. T'Chaka was then twenty-five years of age, and his first act was to murder his brother, Umtetwa. He was a chief after the Zulus' hearts, a man of war, and in the course of his reign he led them to victory after victory. Fifty or sixty tribes were absorbed by the Zulus. All boys had to serve in the army. T'Chaka created a guards corps of fifteen thousand men who were always kept ready to move in any direction at an hour's notice. He built fortified kraals—villages which were occupied by different regiments of his army. Taking on where Diniswayo left off, his troops were drilled in a way which was absolutely new in the history of the African native.

As a boy T'Chaka had fallen in with some sailors who had been wrecked at Saint Lucia Bay and they had told him of Napoleon, which further aroused his ambition. In 1835 a Mr. Nathaniel Isaacs visited him and discussed the affairs of Europe with him. He told him how Napoleon had been defeated and tried to explain the extent of the British dominions. When he had done, T'Chaka said: "Yes, I see now. There are only two great chiefs on earth. My brother King George, he is king of all the whites, and I, T'Chaka, who am king of all the blacks."

Mr. Isaacs stayed in the Royal Kraal for some months and tells of some of the things he saw there. On one occasion a hundred and seventy girls and boys were slaughtered for some offence committed by their parents. The cream of the sport to T'Chaka was that he ordered the girls' and boys' brothers to finish the slaying which he had begun with his own hands. The killing lasted two days, after which there was a great feast and a dance.

One of T'Chaka's palaces, which was of course no more than a ring of grass huts rather more imposing than those of his people, was named the "Place of Slaughter," for here he had put to death a whole regiment of married soldiers together with their wives and children, as a punishment for their defeat in battle. His mother's tribe, the Elangeni, he exterminated, man, woman, and child, burning some to death, impaling others on the sharp stakes of the kraal palisades, tying still others smeared with honey in ant-heaps.

T'Chaka's brutality led to his end. An army he had sent against Usoshengane to the north near Delagoa Bay was defeated as much by the fever of that country and exposure to the summer rains as by the attacks of the enemy. T'Chaka in a rage decided to slaughter the two thousand-odd wives of these soldiers; and the massacre, at a rate of three hundred a day, had actually begun when the remnants of the beaten force got back. Among the women already killed were the wives of two of the king's brothers, Dingaan and Umhlangane, who at once began to plot T'Chaka's death, and succeeded in persuading his servant Umbopa, who had access to the royal person, to assassinate him. The blow was struck on September 23, 1828. T'Chaka was then forty-one years of age, had reigned fourteen years, and had founded one of the most warlike, Spartan states the world has ever seen.

T'Chaka had commemorated his mother's death by killing seven thousand of his people. If they did not weep sufficiently for his mother, they should weep for their own dead. Three times in twelve months did he order his people to mourn the Lady Umnandi, his mother. At the third meeting he caused ten thousand cattle to be kraaled together so that their maddened bellows should be joined to those of the people. Cows with young calves were killed and the calves allowed to starve to death so that they too should know what it was to lose a mother. The gall bladder was cut from thousands of other living calves and their contents poured over the king as he sat in state, naked but for the royal kaross of leopard skins and the red plumes of the green lori in his hair. Sometimes he would say, "That man makes me laugh, take him away and finish him." His kraal was scarcely dry with one man's blood before it was wet again with that of ten or a hundred. The vultures and the jackals waxed fat in the reign of T'Chaka.

T'Chaka, though he kept many concubines, never married, and were a child born of one of his women it was suffocated by a clod of earth being placed in its mouth, and its mother killed. Rivals he might have and did, but he would breed none. "People of the Heavens," the Zulus called themselves. But little had they known, when the name was taken, how they would illuminate the African veld with the fires of their destruction.

It was during T'Chaka's reign that Moselikatze, another Zulu captain, who had conducted a successful raid, decided not to give up his loot of cattle and women, and led his people to the Far North, where he established another kingdom on the Zulu lines—the Matabele.

Dingaan was less warlike than T'Chaka, but even more cruel. His first conflict with the white men occurred in 1837, when a party of Boers visited him at the royal kraal at Umgungundhlovu—which means the "Place of the trumpeting elephant," a Zulu euphemism for the voice of their monarch. The Boers, under Piet Retief and Gert Maritz, left their guns, as no one was allowed to carry arms in the enclosure, and sat down to talk. Mr. Owen, the American missionary who lived among the Zulus, went with them. The palace of the king was a circular hut twenty feet in diameter supported by twenty-two pillars, each ornamented with woven beadwork. Round the king's house were those of his wives and concubines: this group made up the Royal Kraal, and round them again were nearly seventeen hundred huts, each capable of holding twenty soldiers.

An entertainment was put on for the visitors—a grand military show, a parade of the royal guards, four thousand veterans with the ringed heads of married men, each carrying a great white oxhide shield. The Boers then saw two thousand young soldiers with black shields march past. A sham battle took place in which a drove of beautiful oxen and heifers, mixed with the ranks of the leaping warriors, simulated the spoils of warfare. All this went on for some days. Oxen were slaughtered. Kaffir beer was drunk. There were dances—war dances by the men and others by Dingaan's own dancing girls. Retief had with him sixty-nine Boers all well mounted and armed. They had thirty Hottentot servants, led horses and baggage. To round off the show Dingaan had put on, they staged one of their own to illustrate their skilled marksmanship, and the way they managed their horses by galloping them, pulling them up in mid-career and "making them dance," as the Boers call it.

At last Retief decided they had been here long enough. Their business, the ratification of their claims to the land they wanted, was accomplished.

"Stay another day," Dingaan said. "I want to give you a final dance to show you something no white man has yet seen."

On the morning of Tuesday, the sixth of February, Retief had breakfast with Mr. Owen and his wife and sister at the Mission House. Mr. Owen did not accompany him when he joined the other Boers at the Royal Kraal, but spent the day studying the New Testament.

As was usual, and following the routine of the other days, the Boers dismounted when they came to the kraal and left their horses and guns in charge of their servants.

They found the king seated in the centre of a large circle of Zulu warriors of the highest rank—captains, indunas, and princes all in war array with plumes on their heads and bands of hair tied below their knees. They had arms in their hands, assegais and knob kerries; they carried their great oxhide shields.

The Boers were served with beer, with beef, and the dance commenced. Round and round the seated party the warriors swept, leaping and shouting, brandishing their weapons; the dance became faster, still faster, and the circle smaller. The Boers could look right into the bloodshot eyes of the dancing soldiers, could see their dilated nostrils, smell the sweat that ran down their greased black hides; and then it came: Dingaan sprang to his feet and shouted, "Bambani batagati! Kill the wizards!"

Instantly the Zulus fell upon the Boers, twenty or thirty to a single man, and dragged them to the hill of killing where all malefactors and prisoners were put to death. In the valley below them were the whitened bones of the thousands who had died here at the whim of the king; above them in the blue African sky were the vultures that the old king had called his children, circling, waiting. The Zulus dashed out the brains of the Boers with their kerries and speared them as they fell. Then taking the bodies up they hurled them into the void below. This place was called the "Dreadful Hill." Below it, when the Boers conquered Dingaan, they found the remains of their people, the bones, fragments of clothes, and their bandoliers. A great heap of bones, some bleached with age, others still clothed, with remnants of putrescent flesh, lay against the cliff face where gnarled cactus gripped the crevices of rock and great aloes, their blooms like blooded spears, pointed upwards towards the sky.

While this was taking place, Dingaan sent a message to Mr. Owen, telling him not to be frightened, as he was only going to kill the Boers.

The Zulu impis now fell upon the Boers and their families, who were camped below the Drakensberg, where they killed three hundred and sixty-six men, women, and children, and two hundred and fifty coloured servants, coming on them by surprise. The place where this occurred is named Weenen, which means weeping.

Dingaan had the heart and liver of the Dutch commander exposed at the gates of his kraal with certain mystic rites and incantations, believing that this would prevent the entry of other strangers. But the Dutch were preparing their revenge, and, reinforced by other Boers from across the Vaal and some Englishmen, formed a commando of four hundred men and attacked Dingaan's town, where they were "eaten up" by the Zulus and defeated. Dingaan, pressing his victory, cleared the land of white men, and only the arrival of some British troops at the end of 1838 saved the port of Natal.

But the Boers were not to be beaten so easily. They formed a new commando and enlisted the aid of Panda, one of Dingaan's brothers, who came over to them with four thousand of the best Zulu fighting men. This mixed force defeated Dingaan. The king was killed and Panda reigned in his place.

This procession of kings is perhaps the best illustration of the Zulu character. Dingaan murdered his brother T'Chaka; Panda, Dingaan's brother, murdered Dingaan; and Clu Clu, brother of Panda, murdered Panda.

These kings between them built up a great and savage force of fighting men organised into regiments under the command of princes, chiefs, and captains: regiments whose name struck terror into the hearts of the kings' enemies. The Nokenke—the Deriders —whose shields were black and who wore a band of otter skin round the forehead with two plumes of Kaffir finch on the head pointing backwards, ear flaps of green monkey skin and bunches of white cow tails hanging from the chest over the neck and back. The Umhlanga—the Reeds—who wore green monkey-skin headbands, white cow tails and a bunch of ostrich plumes surmounted by a few white on the head. The Umlanbongwenya —the Crocodiles; the Umxapu—the Sprinklers; the Udukuza —the Wanderers; the Udhlambedhlu—the Ill-Tempered; and others: the Sticks, the Blue Horizon, the Straight Lines, the Blue

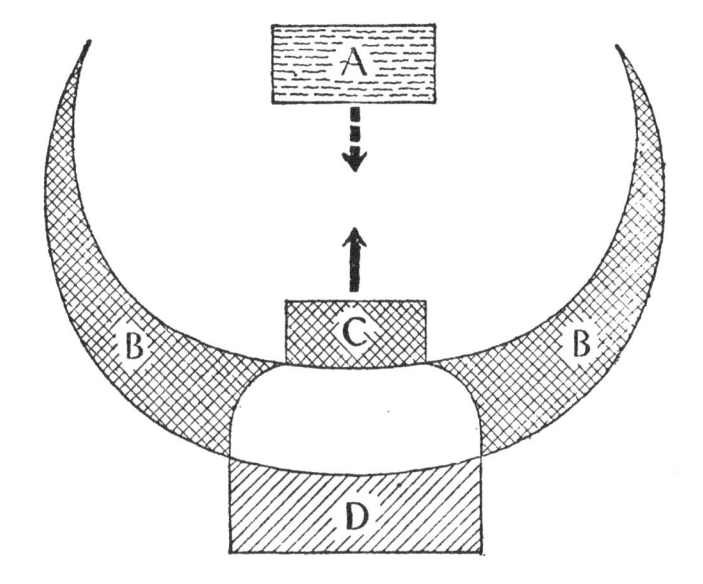

Zulu Horns Formation

The Zulu attack formation was composed of three divisions —two horns, BB, and a main body or chest, C; there was also a reserve, D, who were supposed to be seated with their faces away from the enemy, A, so as not to be excited or influenced by the operations of the main body.

Gum, the Euphorbia, the Benders of Rings, the Snake Regiment, the Evil Seers, the Loiterers, the Sharp-Pointed, the Weight of the Elephant, the Smashers, the Bees, the Gadflies, the Slaughterers, the Invincibles, the Cockroaches, the Warriors, the Hideaways.

Half a million new men were added to the army that originally was said to number one hundred thousand. Three hundred tribes were destroyed and absorbed and the land devastated for five hundred miles to the north. All these vassals were embodied into the tribe calling themselves Zulus, but they were really men of every tribe from Delagoa Bay in the north to the Umzimvubu in the south.

Some regiments were old veterans, up to sixty years; as they aged, younger men were drafted into them. And each corps was savagely proud of its performance and jealous of its insignia. Never in the history of savages was there such discipline, such cruelty, or such panoply. One regiment with red oxhide shields, the next with white, another with white and red, black and white, pure white, or black unmarked with any white. Headdresses were of all kinds, from finch tails and the long plumes of the African widow bird to great headdresses and capes of ostrich feathers and cow-tail kilts. The captains wore kilts of monkey, leopard, and wildcat tails. Dressed like this, running and leaping, shouting, beating their weapons against their shields, and hissing between their teeth, so that above the muffled roar of their beating feet came the sound as if of a wind, the Zulus overwhelmed their enemies.

T'Chaka would permit no man to marry till he was forty, and then only with his permission. Marriage he believed softened men for war. Love affairs and adultery were punished with death. There was indeed only one punishment in those days in Zululand. The warriors went to war naked but for a loin cloth, and some, the so-called naked Zulus, fought even without this. It was T'Chaka who revolutionised Kaffir warfare, substituting the short, wide-bladed stabbing spear for the throwing assegai, which forced the Zulus to fight at close quarters. T'Chaka invented the tactic of the horns, where the main body broke into two racing wings which surrounded their enemy and distracted him from the flanks and rear while the main force closed in. The Zulus always tried to engage the enemy in broken ground with this "pincer-movement" tactic. The formation of the troops was like the head of an ox, the main body being the head and the flanks two horns attached to it. Behind the main body there was sometimes a reserve. When an attack was ordered, the two horns set out to attack the flanks and rear of the enemy, and when there, or when one of them had made its advance and the enemy was fully committed, the main body closed in.

It is difficult to realise the pitch of Zulu discipline, and it is best illustrated by an incident reported by Captain Henry Hallam Parr, who was military secretary to Sir Bartle Frere, who said:

"Not long before the Zulu War broke out, a missionary was explaining to Cetywayo, who had one of his regiments seated round him, the danger he ran of Hell fire. 'Hell fire!' repeated Cetywayo. 'Do you try to frighten me with Hell fire? My army would put it out. See,' he continued, pointing to a grass fire which was burning over a considerable tract, and calling to the officer commanding the regiment, said, 'Before you look on me again eat up that fire.'

"The thousands of which the regiment was composed were in an instant bounding, shouting their war cry, towards the fire, which was eaten up without regard to those who were killed or maimed and permanently damaged."

Next to its perfect discipline the mobility of the Zulu army was its most remarkable feature. A Zulu impi could cover forty and fifty miles a day, its food and sleeping mats being carried by women. Nothing could stop a Zulu impi on the march. Rough country was nothing to them. On coming to a river in flood, an impi formed into close order, the men linked arms, shouted their war cry, and charged the river as if it was a foe. The weakest went down, but the impi got through.

During a lull in the native wars, Doctor Andrew Smith took two chiefs, emissaries from Moselikatze, to see a review of the Seventy-Second Regiment of foot at Capetown. When Doctor Smith, who had gained their confidence, asked them what they would do if they had to fight such well-disciplined and magnificently armed troops as these Highlanders, the chiefs replied, "We should just wait till we got them on difficult ground and then rush in from all sides and stab them, every man, before he could re-load his musket."

This was what actually took place forty-three years later when the Zulus annihilated the Twenty-Fourth Regiment in the Zulu War of 1879.

And now, to add to the troubles of this land of Africa, to the native wars, to the depredations of the wild beasts, to diseases, storm, and disaster, came the thing that Kruger dreaded most, the one thing he was unequipped to deal with—the discovery of gold and diamonds; and with them the influx of aasvoels—the vultures of every land, the seekers of riches, who did not love Africa, but wished to milk her like a cow.

This was the tide that was to destroy Lobengula; to engulf the two little republics of free farmers, and force England into a disgraceful war.

But while these later events were not yet born, scarcely yet conceived, except in terms of the effects of causes still unapparent, in the village of Bishop Stortford, a parson, the Reverend Rhodes, was talking to his wife about the advisability of sending "poor Cecil," who was consumptive, out to his brother in South Africa; and Sekukuni in the mountains across the Vaal was planning to defy the Boers.

CHAPTER FOUR

THE PATHWAY OF BLOOD

AT THE TIME of the Great Trek, Moselikatze—"The Pathway of Blood"—was master of the entire country west of the Lembombo and Dragon Mountains; and when he heard of the men with white faces who had come from the South, he sent an army to massacre them. War between him and the Boers ensued in which Paul Kruger, then a boy, was engaged. Slowly but irrevocably Moselikatze was driven back, but among the captured cattle and loot he took with him were two white children. Of these, as Kruger says in his *Memoirs*, nothing was heard again. But they, or at least one of them—a girl called Sara—was to play a part in moulding history, was to become, though she never knew it, a factor in the conquest of Rhodesia.

After his first actions with the Boers, Moselikatze was certain he had crushed them for good. And why should he not have thought so? His impis had always been successful, no tribe had ever stood up against them. In addition, to give him greater pleasure, there was the loot he had obtained from the Boers— thousands of sheep, thousands of cattle that were twice the size of native cattle; guns and horses, blankets and iron from the tyres of the wagons that could be made into spears and battle-axes.

This frame of mind lasted till Potgieter raised a commando of Boers, Griquas and other half-breeds who had horses and could use firearms, and defeated him in battle, inflicting severe losses upon his men. To add to his troubles, Dingaan, who had succeeded T'Chaka, the Zulu king he had deserted, launched an army against him from the flank; and while reeling under this new blow, the Boers attacked once more, defeated him again, and forced him to take refuge in the mountains and bushveld beyond their reach.

The Boers recovered much cattle, but, failing to find the captured girls, gave them up for lost. And Moselikatze decided that, since the white people were too strong for him, it would be best to retreat still further.

He left small rear guards in the Waterberg to watch and harry the Boers, and led his people over the Limpopo, or Crocodile River, as some call it. This land was unknown to him as it was to the white cartographers of the period, who marked the blank space on their maps, "The Kingdom of Monomopata," and filled in the rest with pictures of elephants, palm trees, camelopards, and lions rampant. This mythical kingdom had been the lure of the Portuguese for centuries. This was the country of Prester John, of gold and silver, of old mines and ruined cities—the land of Ophir—the great unknown. Even the natives had no traditions of this land, no folklore, no stories of it; and into it Moselikatze led the remnant of his warriors.

All that Moselikatze knew of this North Country was the story told by wandering Bushmen, who said that he would come to a great river there. He decided to cross this river and interpose it, as a barrier, between himself and the white men who were creeping north.

The migration started in the summer rains and was frequently help up by flooded streams: the Matabele often had to make great détours through country which was wild and empty. There was game in plenty, but the Matabele were not skilled hunters of anything but men. Moselikatze had two wagons with him, loot from the Boer camps that he had ravaged. The first was loaded with ivory stolen from surrounding tribes or extracted from them as tribute. On the second rode his "great wife" with her son Nkulumana. The other women and children of the nation, his own lesser wives included, marched, or, if they could not, died. Among the straggling crowd of women and children were the two captured white girls and a little Matabele boy, Lobengula, the son of Moselikatze, by an inferior wife. He walked beside his mother, who carried a still younger child—his sister Ningi—on her back. Every day the road became harder. There was less and less to eat; finally nothing but berries and wild fruits. The Matabele had to cut their way through heavy bush, climb mountains that bruised their feet, fight through swarms of mosquitoes that blackened the air; and only the strongest survived. All day the vultures followed the Matabele, waiting to gorge on those who fell. By night they were harried by lions.

Before they reached the Limpopo, one of the little Dutch girls was dead; but the other, Sara, had adopted the customs of the tribe and almost forgotten her early childhood. One day, when more and more were falling from exhaustion, Sara, with some other women found Fulata, the king's Swazi wife, near to death with her children whimpering beside her. The women wished to leave her, saying: "It is the king's wife and these are Lobengula, his son, and his daughter Ningi. But if we tell the king she is dead, he will think we have killed her. Let us, therefore, leave her to the vultures and the children too." They left, but Sara, declining to follow them, picked up the little girl and hoisted her on to her back. Lobengula, the king's son—" He who drives like the wind"—and future king of the Matabele, she led by the hand. She took the children to her adopted mother, Nyumbakazi, who was barren. After that the children were well taken care of, having two mothers where they had lost one—Nyumbakazi and the Boer girl, Sara.

Pressing along the north bank of the Limpopo, Moselikatze struck the Mzingwani. It was in flood and impassable, so here again he deflected his course, marching along the bank and keeping the river on his left. The country grew more and more inhospitable as the mopani scrub gave way to rocks, the rocks to mountains, gorges, and precipices—a wilderness of hills and tumbled boulders from which there seemed to be no exit. In front of them was a great dome-shaped granite head, itself crowned with a circle of other rocks, each many times as large as a native hut.

Moselikatze and his indunas and captains climbed the kopje. Perhaps from here they would see a way out of this infernal labyrinth. But below them was nothing, only more rocks, more scrub and bush, more forest where great tortured cream-of-tartar trees raised their writhing limbs. There was no life here. Not even a vulture or an eagle in the sky.

But as the captains looked, some warriors who had accompanied them dragged up a screaming man whom they had captured. He was a witch-doctor, clothed and ornamented with the inflated bladders, birds' beaks, leopards' claws, and small tortoise-shells of his trade. His waist-belt was a snake skin; from it hung a tattered leather strip of hide. The soldiers said they had caught him in a cave. They said there were others with him, but that they had fled. No one could understand a word he said except one man, a slave, who said the language he spoke resembled his own tongue—Basuto. Acting as interpreter, he found out that the people here were called the Makalanga, and that the hill upon which they stood was named M'lindidzimo and was sacred —the burial place of their chiefs. These hills were, one day, also to be the burial place of Moselikatze, and of Cecil Rhodes. It was the home of an oracle, and Ngwali, the captured witch-doctor, was the chief priest. To him alone, he asserted, did the spirits speak.

As if to prove his words and the sacredness of his person, the storm which had been gathering in the heavens now broke. The black thunderheads reared up like horses over the heads of the king and his princes. The lightning, a blue jagged spear, ripped past them and the crash of thunder echoed from hill to hill. In the silence that followed, a voice spoke from behind the prisoner. But there was no one behind him when Moselikatze and the chiefs turned.

"Make him lead us out," Moselikatze said. The Pathway of Blood was frightened. Ngwali's ventriloquism had worked. "I will give him two oxen if he leads us out," the king said. And he led them.

When they came through the range, a strange sight met their eyes: a new world of park-like rolling land swarming with game, rich with grass and water. The Matabele had found what they sought. The stragglers now caught up with the army which was disposed in the fighting order of the Zulus—a head and two horns, a centre and flanks, as it advanced ready for battle. The men began to sing and rattled their weapons. They marched till they came to a hill where several streams had their source. Here Moselikatze ordered a town built; and the occupation of what became Matabeleland was begun.

But peace was not in the Zulu blood. Leaving the people to build a town, Moselikatze led two crack regiments, the Kanda Guides and M'nyama—those with the black shields—to the north in search of plunder. He needed more cattle, more women to replace the dead, more slaves, more boys to be trained as warriors. An induna named Umnombata was left in charge of the town, which began to take form the moment the king gave orders that it was to be built. They named it M'hlahlanhlele—"Clear the Road"—after their old military kraal in Zululand, which they had occupied in T'Chaka time, before they had deserted him.

Moselikatze had five thousand fighting men with him. The chief he was attacking, Sebitoane, was aware of his coming. Little news came to the town-builders from their king. The North had swallowed him and his five thousand. Then rumours began to float down, tales of disaster. None were confirmed, nor were any refuted; but Umnombata's power waned. Factions, each wanting leadership, arose; and finally, to settle the discord it was decided to consult the oracle in the Matopos again. This time it spoke in unmistakable Zulu. It said: "The king calls you. All must join him. Death will come to those who hold back." The gods wanted the Matabele to go from their land, which was not surprising, since they were Makalanga gods.

But when the Matabele got back to the town again, more news had been received. This time from some Bushmen, who said Moselikatze was dead. They had seen the battle. The Matabele had been caught on an island in a river, where, abandoned by the canoemen they had impressed to carry them over, they had starved to death.

Great trouble now ensued in the town. All remnants of order disappeared. Royal ladies ran away with their lovers, rival claimants fought for the throne. The "great wife" of Moselikatze wanted her son Nkulumana made chief at once, but he was deemed too young. In a fury of disappointment, she vented her hate on Lobengula who was playing on the mud platform outside the royal kraal. Sara hearing his screams rescued him. The queen then called her guards to have Sara caught and killed; but, too quick for her, the Dutch girl seized Lobengula in her arms and fled with him.

In the middle of this disorder, a herder at an outlying kraal ran in to say that he saw fires burning in the night. Not a veld fire, but hundreds of little fires such as soldiers make. And then suddenly, almost as he finished speaking, through the darkness came the sound of a song: "There is work to do at Matshobanes . . . work for assegais . . ." It was the battle song of the M'nyama: the black shields were coming home. They were the picked force of

Moselikatze's veterans hard from war, and when they marched in there was no resistance to them. Not a hand was raised.

In the morning all those who had acted as though the king were dead were prisoners, and the scene set for the first of the great executions which were to take place here for fifty years. One end of the hill on which the new town had been set ended in a precipice. Here in the presence of the army and the people the king sat drinking beer and eating meat while, one at a time, the eighteen leaders of the revolt were hurled over in their bonds. They were thrown tied like parcels, and like parcels they came apart when they struck the rocks below. The royal Zulu salute, "Bayete," given only to kings, echoed over the plains. The spears that had drunk blood were raised—thousand-pointed—to flash in the brilliant sun. That night when the killing was over the people listened to the jackals screaming as they fed.

"The king has given them a fine supper," was the word whispered among the people. "The good old days are back."

Far away, knowing nothing of this, Sara, walking and running with the child Lobengula, the son of the king, approached the wilderness of the Matopos, and was seen by Ngwali, the wizard, who with his acolytes kept a constant watch from the rocks of their sacred stronghold lest the Matabele, respecting neither God nor man, come upon them unawares. Ngwali decided to get Sara and the boy into his power, for both could be useful to him, pawns in the game of power politics—Sara as a bait and a subject for bargaining should the white men, of whom he had heard, come up from the South; and Lobengula, as the son of Moselikatze, was a power in Matabeleland—not in his person, the boy being little more than a child, but in his blood line, that of kings.

The children were watched until, exhausted, they lay down to rest. Then Ngwali's women took them food and milk and brought them in.

"Little ducks," the wizard said, "you have jumped out of a trap. If you go back, you will be killed; but if you stay, you will be protected by the great spirits and be safe."

They stayed, Lobengula growing up and learning much from the witch-doctor, much of the credulity of men from those who came to consult the oracle, and much of the powers of wizardry. And with him always was Sara, who though she lived as a savage had retained something of her past in that she was more gentle than any Matabele. These two influences working together—the latent softness of the white woman in Sara and the arts of intrigue and spiritual power of the doctors—were set against that of the spear, which would have been his only heritage had Lobengula remained among his people.

This went on till 1847, when a story was brought to the witch-doctor's kraal that there were strange bucks on the veld such as men had never seen before. "Bucks bearing their young upon their backs." Sara with Lobengula crept out to see them. He was now a young hunter, skilled in the use of weapons. As soon as she set eyes upon the strange animals, Sara knew them.

"They are Boers," she said, "my kin." And immediately she hid from them. Why she flew no one will ever know. Fear of being found naked and suddenly remembering that nakedness was wrong? Shame at living with savages? This was the reason that the women wrecked in the *Grosvenor* were said to have given when they refused to be rescued from the Kaffirs who had taken them as wives—that, and the fear that they would be separated from the yellow bastards to whom they had given birth. Or perhaps Sara feared something else—the loss of security. Not that her life was secure, except that it was accustomed, but the road back may have seemed too hard. Or perhaps she hated the idea of restraint, having been free so long, since freedom and savagery come so easily to a child. At any rate, she fled and something happened to her in the mountain crags, for she disappeared. Perhaps having saved Lobengula her work was done.

Meanwhile, Lobengula crept up to the Boer camp in the night and watched them; and then, for some inexplicable reason, instead of going to Ngwali he sought out Umnombata, the king's regent of old time, who had been spared at the great killing, but was an outcast, and gave him the news.

Umnombata decided that the time had now come to bring the king's son to the king, who had believed him dead. There was danger in this, for the king might kill them both. But it seemed worth the risk.

"Who is this you bring with you?" Moselikatze said when they appeared. "He is not one of my soldiers, I do not recognise him."

The Induna answered the question with another.

"Does the old bull know all the calves he has sired? May there not be some that he has forgotten? It is Lobengula, son of Fulata, whose father was Malindela, the Swazi chief. He brings news that the white men have come."

Lobengula then guided the Matabele to the Boer camp to fight his first battle.

The leader of the Boers was Hendrik Potgieter, who at last, after many years, had been able to raise a commando to pay off his debt against the Matabele. That he had been successful in this was due to a report sent by Ngwali, the doctor, that the Matabele held a white girl and were ill-treating her. The indignant Boers joined Hendrik at once, and on the way persuaded a number of Bechuanas to join them in the war, promising them loot for payment. Ngwali was using Sara to destroy the Matabele, and his plan would have been successful if Lobengula had come to him instead of going to Umnombata after he had spied on the Boers.

Potgieter got the news of Sara through native hunters sent by Ngwali, who had passed on the word to him at Potchefstroom. Ngwali hated the Matabele, who had stolen his people's land and desecrated the burial place of their kings by their presence. Ngwali led the Boers through the passes of the Matopos, as years before he had led the Matabele. He confirmed the story of the white girl, but pretended that Moselikatze held her in his town. While the Boers prepared to attack the Matabele, Sara, whom they had come to save, was running and hiding in the very hills through which they marked, and young Lobengula, his spears still unblooded, was guiding the Matabele towards the Boer column.

In the early morning before the dawn, the Boers broke camp and marched. This is the hour that is called "the hour of the cattle horns," for then a man bending down can see the horns of his cattle black against the paling eastern sky. It was the Boer plan to surprise the Matabele, falling upon them just before daybreak and killing them as they slept. The ground was covered with a light drifting mist, and the Boers moved through it like mounted ghosts. They were on the flanks of the commando. Their native allies, in whom they had no great confidence, were in the centre.

Suddenly through the grey morning mist the Bechuanas saw cattle: first a few heifers, then more—a herd of oxen. This was what they had come for, for loot; and breaking formation they began to round them up. But the Matabele were ready. The cattle were the bait. The horns of the Matabele army opened wider to allow the cattle and their pursuers to pass through them; then they closed the jaws of their trap.

All chance of surprise now gone, Potgieter withdrew, fighting his way out before the main body of the Matabele could engage him. The expedition had failed, and once again, in the struggle between black and white, the black had won.

It was nineteen years before the white tide rose again. Then it rose irresistibly. A white hunter found gold, and the cry, "There is gold in the North," penetrated all Africa and went beyond Africa into the counting-houses and chancelleries of Europe. Businessmen looked for adventurers who would do their bidding; men who would, for the lure of gold, die, to make their masters rich.

The man who discovered the gold was an elephant hunter called Hartley. He had found old workings—no man knows how old—a few miles north of the Umgulin River in Mashonaland, and had led a German prospector, Karl Mauch, to the spot. The Mashona were a subject people of the Matabele, paying them tribute and doing the work of slaves. Some years later they appear in history as an excuse for the occupation of Matabeleland by the British and the war in which the Matabele were broken; but at this time they were nothing—"dogs" in the words of their masters. A people without rights or dignity.

Prospecting was forbidden in all these lands by Moselikatze, who was now an old man and, fortunately for Mauch, a sick one, or he would not have got out of the country alive with his samples of gold-bearing rock.

Moselikatze feared gold above all else, knowing its lure for the white men; and the only white men who were allowed to move in his country were a few hunters, missionaries, and traders, and these only because it suited the king's convenience. So dangerous was it to prospect that Hartley decided to part company with the German and go back alone.

Among the missionaries living in Matabeleland was one named

Morgan Thomas whom the natives respected greatly for his skill in medicine and called "Tomasi." At the very time that Mauch was making his way south to tell of his discoveries, Tomasi was sent for by the king to ease his sickness. He found him in his hut swollen with gout, riddled with other diseases, supported by two of his wives who kept the flies from settling upon him by waving whisks of ox tails. The king, though he had sent men after the escaping German to capture him, knew that war was coming. War for "the yellow stones," as he called gold.

"Make me strong," he said, "with English mouti"—medicine —"so that I can again lead my armies against the invaders."

The missionary gave the king medicine while his wives held him and the royal guards in capes and headdresses of black ostrich plumes stood leaning on their long shields watching through the door.

But Moselikatze—"The Pathway of Blood, the Black Bull whose roar shook the hills"—was finished. His course was run. He who had slain so many died in his hut like a woman, surrounded by women—a death almost unique for a Kaffir king.

According to the Zulu custom, the body was sewn up at once in fresh-flayed hides of two black bulls. Twelve of his widows guarded it in the royal quarters till it was all but decomposed. Then it was placed on the great tented wagon that the king had used in his travels, and dragged into the heart of the mountains, into the Matopos of the oracle, and a cave named Ntubane was chosen, from among the many, as a tomb. The procession which accompanied the king on his last journey consisted of thousands of warriors and the witch-doctors in full and terrible array. The wagon bearing the body was drawn by a full span of sixteen black oxen which was followed by a second wagon that contained all that had been his in life. Then came the mourners by the thousand, and finally the herd of fifty black oxen which were to be the sacrifice.

The dead king was placed, seated on a throne of rocks, inside the cave. His possessions, his gun, his chair, his eating utensils, his spears, his kaross, were placed in an adjoining cave. Even the great wagon was dismantled and hidden. The caves were then walled up. Thousands of women came in long, black, shining lines bearing red pots of Kaffir beer upon their heads, and fifty picked young men flung themselves upon the black sacrificial oxen, each choosing one and killing it with a single thrust of his assegai behind the shoulder. Great fires were lit and the feast began.

For two days the army drank, gorged meat, danced and sang the praises of the dead king among the piled kopjes of the Matopos. Then they left and the place was silent. Nothing was left of them but broken pots, the bones of the oxen they had eaten, and the ashes of their cooking fires. Nothing was left but the rotting body of the dead king sitting upon his stone throne in the bowels of the hills.

Moselikatze the king was dead. Long live the king. A new king must be chosen. And he was, by the wizards of the Matopos, who in this hour of doubt brought forth their candidate—the boy they had raised and trained. Lobengula was their man.

On the death of his father, fearing assassination at the hands of his rivals, Lobengula had returned to the sanctuary in the hills that had been his home as a child, and was hidden there, protected by the doctors. He had no desire to reign, foreseeing nothing but trouble. Trouble with the white men in the near or distant future he knew was certain. For being brought up by the witch-doctors, he had a sense of the future, of time, an idea of cause and effect rare among the Bantu. Trouble at home, too, because at least one regiment—the Zwong Endaba under M'biko—had sworn that no one but Nkulumana, his half-brother by the king's "great wife," should reign. Only one thing would satisfy Lobengula and the Matabele chiefs. This was that the question should be referred to the spirits, and the spirits obligingly decided that he should be king.

Lobengula at this time was in his prime, a man tall and strong—a warrior. The year was 1870.

The stage in South Africa was now fully set. The protagonists had all arrived upon the stage; and action, which is effect, was to follow cause.

The cause was riches, the gold in the North; in Matabeleland, discovered by Hartley; more gold in the Lydenburg; diamonds in the Free State. These were the little breezes which preceded the storm. The little breezes that were followed by a hot stillness, which stillness was itself followed by currents and the dust devils, that raised all the trash of a continent into the lowering sky.

Nor was it alone in Africa that storms brewed or that whirlwind was so lightly sown. Everywhere men clamoured for space, for empire. Young white men, hot as Matabele warriors, wanted an outlet for their killings and expansions. Darwin had destroyed God with his *Origin of Species*. Freud was already more than a boy and soon to begin writing. The machines everywhere needed raw materials, and the ships of all nations sailed the seven seas in search of provender for factories that had sprung up, like mushrooms in the night. A new world was coming into being, an old world dying. The death pangs of one world were to become the birth pangs of another—the new world which is not yet fully born. Rhodes, with his idea of money, of railroads and factories as weapons, had come upon the African scene. Kruger, still in his prime, represented the old world in which a way of life, rather than the possession of things, was considered happiness. And Lobengula, the young warrior who ruled a kingdom that had only recently passed from the age of stone into that of iron, was king of a race whose God was war.

Gold and diamonds were the catalytics flung by their unwitting discoverers into the cauldron of Africa.

CHAPTER FIVE

THE CONSUMPTIVE LAD

IN THE vicarage of the village of Bishop Stortford on the fifth of July, 1853, a boy had been born. It seems unlikely that his birth caused much excitement. Little in the village and certainly none in the vast bushveld of the Transvaal. What could it matter to Paul Kruger riding over his farm, reading the Bible to his family, proceeding every two or three months to Nagmaal, that a boy called Cecil John Rhodes had been born in England?

Kruger was a believer in God and the words of God. Twenty years later Rhodes, the parson's son, said that there was a fifty per cent chance that God existed. He was even ready to assume that He did exist. It is only surprising that, considering the world as a joint-stock company, he did not say that there was a forty-nine per cent chance in the existence of God, which would have given him control. This was his concession to God.

Kruger knew that God existed. His life in the Rustenburg among the beasts and the birds, among the little sugar-loaf hills that rise out of plains, proved the existence of God to him. The Bible proved it. His escapes from death proved it. The conflict which was to arise between Kruger and this newborn child was in principle one of religious beliefs. That fifty per cent disbelief in God was the unbridgeable gulf that separated them.

The Rhodes family was a large one. There were twelve children —two girls and ten boys, two of them died young. There was also another girl by a previous marriage. Of all these children only two ever married. There is a certain interest in considering the fact that Rhodes left no children and that his race has all but died out, whereas the family of Kruger, direct and collateral, number legion. To increase and multiply and to people the world was the ideal of one man; to own the world as British real estate was the aim of the other. In the fable the tortoise merely won the race against the hare, he did not also outlive and outbreed him. The moral, if there is one, would seem to be that, fascinated by the mercurial passage of the comet, we forget the small fixed star: that admiring the complex we forget that its very complexity must in the end prove its own undoing. In engineering terms, Rhodes's—that is, our—civilisation has too many wearing parts and seems bound to become simplified if it is to last, as the Boer civilisation was bound to become more complex, because it was too simple, if it was to continue.

Little appears to be known of Cecil's childhood. It must have resembled that of other English children of his age and class, as Kruger's had resembled that of other Boer children. It is probable that Cecil had porridge and bacon and eggs for breakfast because all children in England have porridge and bacon and eggs; that he went to his father's church and listened to his ten-minute sermons, because all children went to church. He probably learnt to ride and shoot and fish, though he had little affection for these pastimes. Speaking of his brother, Bernard, Rhodes once said: "Ah, yes, Bernard is a charming fellow. He rides, shoots, and fishes. In fact, he is a loafer."

Cecil did not go to Winchester or Eton like his elder brother. Only the elder sons could be educated so expensively. Instead, he went to Bishop Stortford grammar school, where he won a medal for elocution. At sixteen he left and studied under his father with an indefinite idea of becoming a clergyman or a barrister. But his health was bad. Tuberculosis—consumption they called it then—threatened him, and he was sent to join his brother, Herbert, who was in South Africa. Some years later Herbert broached a barrel of gin too near his camp-fire. It caught alight and he was burned to death.

Cecil landed in Africa, after a two months' voyage, and joined Herbert in Natal where he was growing cotton. Then, as now, cotton proved a difficult crop; subject to drought, to boll weevil, to borer, and a hundred other pests; and the brothers trekked to the diamond fields of Griqualand West.

Cecil was now eighteen. He had broken away from his home, from his country. His adult life, in the desolation of Du Toits Pan, had begun. Perhaps it was because it had begun here that he always loved Kimberley, as it came to be called, so much. He always kept a house there: it was opposite the Kimberley Club in the main street. Built of corrugated iron, hotter than an oven in the summer and an ice-box in the cold nights of winter; sweating with condensation, rotting, with ant-eaten timbers, Rhodes loved it. He furnished it with packing cases and an old iron bedstead on which he used a Gladstone bag for a pillow. He lived here when he was a member of Parliament and had just floated a company for two hundred thousand pounds.

Kruger too lived modestly in his tin-roofed official residence. His farmhouses were thatched with grass, as were those of all Boer farmers. Lobengula's palace was a mud hut.

The first picture we have of Rhodes is as a boy of eighteen, watching the Kaffirs dig in the diamond fields, watching them sift gravel in the creaking cradles—a boy watching and thinking. Many men have written of him as they remembered him in those days, leaning against a shanty dressed in old white flannels, dreaming. Of what was he dreaming? What was he thinking of? Of England, perhaps? Of an empire? Of the money necessary to build it? Of diamonds as money? Of money as power?

This while Kruger farmed. While he went into his kraals to see a newly calved cow. While he watched his matched spans of oxen ploughing up the lands, turning up the red soil in long deep furrows, and dreamed of a Biblical justice and pondered on the history of his race, on their treks and fightings.

Of Du Toits Pan, Rhodes wrote to his mother: "Fancy an immense plain with right in centre a great mass of white tents, and iron stores, and to one side of it all, mixed up with the camp, mounds of limelike ant-hills: the country round all flat with just thorn trees here and there."

It was a tactful letter. It said nothing of the squalor, of the scum of all races who had gathered here, of the coloured prostitutes; of the gambling, the lawlessness, the drinking, the occasional shootings. How could he tell his mother that girls here auctioned themselves off for the night? And that the friends of her purchaser accompanied the happy couple to their tent and stood outside shouting advice to the occupants. Not that she would have believed it if he had told her.

On the lighter side there was spider-fighting, which was a favourite sport among the miners, and a woman writing of her husband on the diggings said: "The only pet we disagreed upon was the spider, an immense, ugly, hairy thing with a spotted body and malevolent black eyes that used to glare at me through the glass top of its cage. It was a fighting spider and for a long time was the champion in that part of the country where spider-fights roused as much interest and won or lost as much money as cockfights. William used to drive miles to enter the horrid thing in mortal combat with some rival spider whose owners had issued a formal challenge, and after a successful battle it was hard to decide who was the more pleased with himself, William or his cannibalistic pet."

But the Rhodes brothers were not actually working at Du Toits Pan. They were at another camp called Colesberg Kop on a farm named Vooruitzicht, which means "foresight." Foresight, indeed, both for the Boer who sold it for six thousand pounds and those who bought it for six thousand pounds. The portion that they were working was the "New Rush"—a kopje one hundred and twenty yards wide and two hundred and twenty yards long. This area was divided into six hundred claims. Each claim was by regulation thirty-one feet square. The number of men, black and white, on the kopje was probably ten thousand.

The Rhodes brothers must have done well, since Cecil wrote to his mother, "I average about one hundred pounds a week." He was making money. Real money. He now, with a Greek lexicon in his pocket, watched his Kaffirs work. A new dream had been added to his earlier ones—Oxford. More education. Now that he could afford it, he saw that education was as much a tool as money, and money was a tool of education. But how to get to Oxford? How to pass the examinations?

Herbert, always restless, left the diggings to look for gold at Pilgrim's Rest in the Lydenburg, and Cecil met Rudd, to whom he took a liking. Leaving him to look after his interests, Cecil sailed for England accompanied by another brother, Frank, who had come out on a trip and was going home to take up his commission in the cavalry. Exam or no exam Cecil was going to Oxford. He wanted to go to University College, but was refused. Oriel was less particular.

In explaining his position to the provost, and comparing it to that of boys in England, Rhodes said: "I am not what they are. I am a man."

He was.

At this time he was twenty. Oxford undergraduate. Diamond claim owner. A boy—a man who had made his first dream come true. He had been admitted to Oxford. He must learn more. He must learn and learn. In both mind and body for the next few years he commuted between Oxford and Kimberley. In Sarah Gertrude Millin's words, "He experienced side by side a youth and a manhood."

At Oxford he was concerned with fortune, with his claims at Kimberley. At Kimberley he was concerned with the philosophy of Oxford. In the dust of Kimberley he read his classics, and beneath the poetised spires of Oxford he negotiated for his pumping plants.

He had his first heart attack at Oxford. The last one was to kill him. Did he think of himself then as dying? Was he in such a hurry because he knew that he must hurry? This was the boy who said he was a man: the man who was a boy at Oxford, though unlike the other boys there. He was also the man who had sold ice cream in the mining camp, and with money he made had bought the claims of those who were tired of digging.

The day was to come when he would run in with Kruger, when he would outmanœuvre Lobengula—the terrible day when they would knock a hole in the side of his seaside cottage to give him air that he could not use. They, his friends, the men who loved and served him. The men he had loved. There was no woman there when he died.

But now he was learning. Walking on the ancient lawns of Oxford, listening to the chime of bells—thinking.

If there are men, Rhodes was a man.

No one after he left school ever called Rhodes Cecil. As a boy in South Africa he signed his letters to his mothers, "Yours affectionately, C. Rhodes." Even while he was at Oxford he was known as "The Old Man," and here we come upon a trait of his— that of spreading himself thick on his friends, giving without stint, never letting one of them down, never even in the later days, when he was Prime Minister of the Cape, forgetting a drunken old-timer who once had served him.

To spread thick is the gift of youth. Most men as they get older, as the number of their acquaintances increases, spread themselves thinner and thinner—give, perhaps, but with ever greater reservations. This was not Rhodes's character. Dying a great man, he remained young all his life, even as his body thickened, as his mind grew in power and his purpose was accelerated by his failing body. However, coupled with this almost adolescent gift of friendship amounting to love—that made him forgive Leander Jameson, that drew him from one of the biggest deals in his life, on the Rand, to Pickering's bedside—was a Voltairian cynicism that made him name his horses after the men he had bought. For he bought men openly, confident that his own, being his friends, could not be bought by his enemies. And they weren't.

He bought the Irish members of the English Parliament. He bought Boer farmers and savage kings. Rhodes, it has been said, was a man without integrity; but one who respected integrity in others. It might be more just to think that he was without integrity when dealing with those who were without it themselves, and to take into consideration the tasks he had set himself to perform, knowing that the limits of his time were not those of other men.

There could never be a to-morrow with Rhodes. To-morrow was too uncertain. Everything must be done to-day. He was without confidence in the time factor or in things working out all right in the end. To begin with, there was no reason why they should—there was little historical precedent which justified this belief in the happy end. And in addition, if by some accident it did end well, he probably would not be there to see it work out. His belief was not in time but in himself—provisionally at least; and within his own sphere he was the master of time. He rode Time like a horse at the gallop, driving it with whip and spur through the space of Africa while Death, another name for Time, crouched like a monkey, growing bigger every day, upon his shoulder.

Most great men—Sir Walter Raleigh, Warren Hastings, Napoleon, even Nelson—have not been remarkable for their regard for legal procedure. Most have not even been, in the restricted sense, particularly honest, because all, putting their mission above themselves, used every means to attain those ends which they felt were demanded of them. Nor have any of the great, with a few notable exceptions, been athletes or sportsmen. Their bodies were the vehicles that bore them, not a mechanism by which pleasure was to be obtained.

The wealth that such men amassed was a by-product of the speed of their achievements—jewelled dust swept into the vortex created by their passing. Gold and jewels clung to them, were discovered by them, were given to them with the honours that were thrust upon them. Rhodes, for instance, never knew where he stood financially. He wrote his cheques on scraps of paper and then forgot to whom he had given them, or the amounts he had paid. He was perpetually overdrawn, but no bank ever refused to honour his signature. He kept his script in all sorts of places. He never seems to have owned a safe. If he had, he would probably have lost the key.

He was too busy to count: he hired other men to do that: too busy to clip coupons, too occupied controlling money to think, except in his early days, of making it. He did not have to. Money bred for him. The play of interest against interest, of advantage against disadvantage, of politics against finance, and finance as a political bludgeon, was his work. The richest man in the world, he never carried a penny in his pocket.

Rhodes remains an outstanding paradox, the dynamic invalid, the rich pauper, the commoner who was the friend of kings; the only white man to whom the Matabele ever gave the royal salute of "Bayete."

Rhodes arrived at Kimberley the very month that England declared to the world that Griqualand West was British territory. There had been some argument over this part of the country. The Orange Free State and the Transvaal both claimed it. Both were insolvent—the Transvaal even unable to float a loan for three hundred pounds, while the Free State functioned on paper currency unbacked by anything except the hope and the prayer, since the Boers were a religious people, that all would come right in the end. Neither republic had expressed any interest in Griqualand till the discovery of diamonds. After it, both said they had claims on it.

Rights are curiously variable. If the rights are to diamond fields, this variability is vastly increased and subject to the pressure of might. The Bastaards had no might and in consequence few rights when the three-way squeeze of the Free State, the South African Republic, and England began for their mountain home. They had with the help of missionaries settled in the land that is now called Griqualand West, where they established a government and proceeded to hunt down the few remaining Bushmen who lived there. From here they wandered nomadically along the Orange River—a pariah race, part farmer, part brigand, part hunter. They squatted on land in what later became the Free State and then sold their rights there to the Boers for four thousand pounds, and crossed the Drakensberg, where they made a new settlement in Griqualand East.

When diamonds were discovered, Nicholas Waterboer, the King Bastaard, wanted, or England said he wanted, England to take over his country. The Free State, since she had taxpayers living in this country, claimed it, and the Transvaal, whose credit was so low that she had been unable to float a three-hundred-pound loan, also claimed this territory, while Parker, a British able seaman, who had been elected President by a select society of renegades, hoisted his own flag in the miniature republic he had created in this debatable area. He was, however, soon forced to haul it down, the South African Republic after some protest withdrew her claims, and England, whose might had become right, bought off the Free State with ninety thousand pounds.

The Bastaards—and proud of it—were a mixed race of Hottentot, Bushmen, and Eastern blood leavened with that of some of the less admirable whites. The land which they had taken from the Bushmen was called Griqualand, as they themselves were called Griquas, the term "Bastaard," flattering as it was to them, not looking well on official documents and dispatches.

Behind the African scene, in the wings but controlling the puppets, were two rivals for power: Gladstone and Disraeli: Gladstone disbelieving in the idea of colonial expansion; Disraeli believing in nothing else. Behind them again was the Queen. And behind Victoria other forces—the royal gardener Brown; the memories of Lord Melbourne, the idol of her youth; her tutor Stockmar, and her husband, Albert. Behind the rival prime ministers were their wives—Mrs. Disraeli, who thought her husband looked so handsome in his bath; Mrs. Gladstone, who probably never saw her husband in his bath. Forces every where—the anti-Semites who disliked Disraeli; the Liberals who thought Gladstone the ideal Englishman. . . .

And Gladstone came into power. To the Boers this was a further proof, if such was needed, that not only did God exist, but that He had answered their prayers. They petitioned, after Shepstone had annexed the Transvaal, not to make them accept British citizenship; but Gladstone, though he was friendly towards them, said he felt unable to support them, since he could not abandon the natives, and possibly the gold which lay beneath the Kaffir kraals. There was always this little question about the natives. But it is hard to consider it alone—without relating it to the mineral wealth of Africa.

The Boers, in the name of God, with their Bibles on the tables at home and their rifles in their hands in the field, were said to be conducting slave raids into the interior. Not exactly slave raids, they were not called slaves. They were apprentice orphans. They were orphans because their parents had been shot. This occurred because they were foolish enough to resist and then to make reprisals, murdering isolated Boers and stealing cattle. One thing led to another. One raid to other reprisals. Each reprisal to more raids. There was something the Boers could not see then and cannot to this day—how the black man can, either in the sight of God or man, be equal to the white. This was a good line of attack for the mining interests, who disguised their acquisitiveness under the cloak of a square deal for the natives.

At twenty it is extremely doubtful that Rhodes had ever had anything to do with a woman. Nor in his whole life is there any ·evidence of intimacy with one. His political success may have been an over-compensation or sublimation of some kind— we have recent parallels. The astonishing thing is that his complaint did not force him towards women. This asceticism must have made him incomprehensible to Kruger, to whom a wife, a home, and children were the ends of life itself. In addition, to a Boer a bachelor was unnatural and suspect. Kruger never said this, but there is little doubt that he thought it, for the first question a Boer asks a stranger is, "How many children have you?" Or perhaps the second question . . . The first is, "Where do you come from?" He wants the story of your travels, which may include news of his friends. Lobengula was certainly no ascetic. Cattle and women, followed by beer and meat, are the things most desirable to the Bantu. First cattle, for they are riches, and also beauty, since ten of them buy a woman. And the woman, apart from working in the fields, pays a long-range dividend in daughters, who in turn are worth ten head of cattle.

But how much of this did Cecil Rhodes know when he was at Oxford? He had never been to the Transvaal where Kruger lived. He did not go there till the discovery of gold on the Witwatersrand—a beautiful name for a beautiful country—"the ridge of the white waters" on the clean and wide High Veld of Africa. Six thousand feet above sea level where the Uitlanders that Kruger hated were to build a city, but where once vast herds of game roamed—blesbok, purple in the evening sun, leaping springbok. Where the koraan, white-bellied, rose out of the long grass; and the duiker and oribi darted through the bush.

His dreams of Oxford had driven Rhodes to its quiet cloisters and quadrangles, but while he was there Africa was his companion. He smelt the acrid scent of the wood and cow-dung fires; he heard the singing of the working Kaffirs. In his mind he saw them raising their picks in unison, turn their flashing heads in the sunshine, pause, and strike. Down they came. As they came down, the Kaffirs grunted—every pick down together; every pick up together. He saw the sweat running down their black, shining hides, their thick lips parted in a grin, their eyes and white teeth flashing. Kaffirs, Africa, the slow plod of the ox team, the lowered heads, the long horns, the yokes and trek chains lying on the ground at the outspan, the smell of coffee. The blue hills of Africa were always with Rhodes.

It was the will of his "fifty per cent God" that he should conquer Africa for England. Conquer the world for England. Insure peace in the world by putting it under the suzerainty of England. Such was the breadth of his dream that later he included America with England.

Vastly affected by Darwin's law of the survival of the fittest, confusing it with God's law, confusing himself with God or at least His instrument, Rhodes rushed on devouring books, men, lands; destroying, amalgamating, drawing to him or removing from his path those who would not be drawn. The fever of the great English adventurers was in his blood as the fever of the tubercle was in his lungs. His story is perhaps the story of the last great Englishman—of the last adventurer who sought nothing for himself and obtained everything. Did he love power? Whether he loved it or not, he obtained it.

History he knew as all men know it, from books. But he did not let his knowledge stop him nor the precedents of that knowledge. History was a process, a ferment. He saw himself as the instrument of history. Pacing the clipped lawns of Oxford, his dreams took shape. A man of intense concentration, the conception was actuality, divided from him only by time, the interval which must elapse while he put his conception into effect.

Lobengula and Kruger, who later were to oppose him, also knew history. Kruger that of his nation—the wars that had been fought against the English and the Kaffirs; against wild beasts; against mountains that had to be passed and rivers that must be crossed; of the hardships of Boer women bearing children behind their wagons; of them fighting beside their men; of massacres: the history, too, of the Old Testament, which in some curious fashion the Boers took for their own.

Lobengula knew the history of tyranny, of government by murder and witchcraft. His knowledge ended there.

And now for Rhodes again, since the others were in ignorance of him, even if he knew of them by hearsay and rumour. This they had in common, these three: the love of Africa that was the home of two of them and the adopted country of the third. Bound by the triple cord that held them to Africa, they loved Africa as woman. And Africa destroyed the three of them. A wanton mistress caring nothing for men—great or small, black or white.

It was to be a long time before Rhodes was to cross the Limpopo and to see the land that was to be Rhodesia. The mountains, the rich valleys, the vast bushveld of grey mopani scrub, the fever trees green-barked and scrofulous. Years before he advised the young men he met to go North. In one of his earlier fits of concentration he said, "The North is my thought." But it was not till 1888 that he amalgamated the Kimberley mines and obtained the Rudd-Rhodes Concession from Lobengula. The Rudd who shared this with him was the one who had looked after his claims while he studied.

In '93 Rhodes took Matabeleland. In '96 his friend, Leander Jameson, led the raid into the Transvaal that destroyed him. In 1902, a month before the Boer War ended, he died.

One of Rhodes's mistakes was that he never understood the Boer: his slow anger; his memory, his patience; his capacity for making a plan and holding to it. "The Boer says nothing. He does nothing. It is all going, one thinks, very smoothly—then his chance comes and he acts. The whole time he has been remembering and planning."

This was a temperament that was beyond Rhodes's comprehension: that of a whole race of farmers to whom money meant less than liberty. Rhodes was a swift man—quick in friendship, quick in anger; faithful in both, and cynical. The Boer does not understand cynicism. There is nothing about it in the Bible. Nor does he like speed.

CHAPTER SIX

THE STAR OF AFRICA

IN MARCH, 1867, at the back of a little mud house on Schalk van Niekerk's farm, De Kalk, near Hopetown on the Orange River, a child was playing a game with stones. He had collected them for himself on the veld, in the dry sluit that ran near the house, and his favourite stone was his blink klippie—his shining stone—the first diamond to be found in Africa. A child had now joined the hunter Hartley as a discoverer of that wealth which was to ruin Africa or make her, according to the point of view. Without that child's toy, or the passing by of the man who recognised its value, there would have been no Rhodes leaning against a shack dreaming his dreams, no Jameson Raid, no Boer War; and the Peasants' Republics would have remained undisturbed, anachronisms, where farmers lived out their lives among their flocks and herds, watching the world, with its inventions, pass them by.

Many Boers knew of the mineral riches of their land, but discouraged all prospecting, knowing that a big strike would produce a competitive chaos with which they were, by their temperament, unfitted to deal. The limit of their mining was to dig for the lead that they used for bullets, and to collect and refine, very roughly, some salt from the natural salt pans. They knew about gold and silver, copper, coal, and iron deposits, but made no effort to exploit them. In fact, it was only after prolonged argument that in 1859 the Volksraad agreed to issue mining permits to individuals, permitting them to seek "for metals indispensable for home use."

John O'Reilly, who discovered the first diamond, had the greatest difficulty in persuading any one that it was genuine. Gregory, an expert, considered the diamond to be a geological accident, since there was no diamondiferous ground in Africa. His mistake caused blunders to be known as "Gregories." Just as later, when the Rand gold fields were discovered, other geologists said that there could not be gold in a conglomerate formation. O'Reilly's first move was to take the stone he had found to Lorenzo Boyes, who was Acting Civil Commissioner at Colesberg. Finding that it cut glass, Boyes sent it to Doctor Atherstone at Grahamstown, who pronounced it to be a diamond.

This stone was finally sold for five hundred pounds, and two years later van Niekerk obtained a second stone by barter from a witch-doctor in the same area for five hundred pounds' worth of cattle and horses. It was an eighty-three-carat stone and was bought by Lilienfeld Brothers for eleven thousand two hundred pounds. Later it was named the "Star of Africa" and assessed at twenty-five thousand pounds.

But the Boers had been right in their premise. With the discovery of gold and diamonds, the strangers, the Uitlanders came; and to cope with them, when President Pretorius was forced to resign because of his mismanagement which had permitted the British to annex the diamond fields, the South African Republic elected a man of modern ideas to lead them.

A Greek, as some thought, to meet a Greek. A thief, others thought, to catch a thief. For the thieves had arrived. Not just smart businessmen and concession-seekers, but real criminals, cut-throats, Australian bushrangers, the scum of London: the vultures, and the females of their kind. What could the Boers make of a girl who, arriving on the diamond fields, announced that she would "meet the boys at the saloon to-night" and then put herself up for auction and knock herself down, for the night only, to the highest bidder—the man who got her paid twenty-five pounds and three cases of champagne?

The Boers were used to a hard life, but it was lived according to the laws of Moses and of custom. And here were people, strangers, who seemed never to have heard of God, or if they had, who scorned Him. Men who did not even agree with Rhodes that there was a fifty per cent chance of God. People who feared neither God nor man, who worshipped nothing but gold and diamonds—wealth that they risked their lives to obtain, and then squandered on women and drink.

An old Boer talking to Sir Bartle Frere once asked him if there were minerals in the moon too. Sir Bartle said there were supposed to be. But the Boer contradicted him. "Meneer," he said, "there are no minerals in the moon, for if there were you British would have annexed it long ago."

The progress the Boers had feared, and had run away from for so long, had caught up with them—even railways, of which many farmers had never heard, were being laid down, and there is a story of a Boer travelling with his wagon across the veld who, when he came to some bright iron rails, decided that this would be a convenient place to halt his wagon. As the front wheels hit the line, he outspanned his oxen and made camp only to be awakened by the roar of a long black object which, flaming with sparks and roaring noisily, advanced upon his wagon, smashed it to pieces, and passed on. " *Verdomple Engels!*"—Damned English! —he shouted. But that did not bring his wagon back.

In July, 1872, Thomas François Burgers took office as President of the South African Republic. He had been educated in Europe. He spoke both English and Dutch, had a Scottish wife, and had been a minister at Hanover in the Cape Colony. He had been much in the public eye, having successfully fought a charge of heresy by the Dutch Reformed Church to which he belonged. The trouble arose because, not believing in the personality of the Devil, he was destroying this belief among his congregation. It was considered as necessary by the Boers to believe in the Devil as in God. The one was indeed the supplement of the other, No Devil, no God; and since God was everywhere, it was deemed impious not to expect the Devil in person, trident, forked tail, and all, to be hiding behind every bush or rock big enough to conceal him.

That Burgers won his case proved that something was changing in the Boer heart. That he was later elected President, confirmed this change

Kruger opposed Burgers's election, and after he had taken oath in Pretoria, said: "Your Honour, I have done my best to prevent your election: principally because of your religious views, which appear to me to be mistaken. But now, as you have been elected by the majority, I submit, as a good republican, trusting that you are a more earnest believer than I thought."

But it did not take Kruger long to see that if his country was to be saved from the progress Burgers was trying to force upon it, he must be removed. Railways, foreign loans and experts were all contrary to the will of God and Paul Kruger. In addition, the treasury was empty and a new Kaffir war about to begin.

Out of the remains of Moselikatze's people, those whom he had not led to the North to form the Matabele, the Bapedi had arisen. This tribe grew as the Zulus and the Matabele had grown—by natural increase and by absorption. It grew strong on the earnings of the young warriors who went to work in the diamond fields, and bought guns and ammunition with their wages. Sekukumi, their chief, raided the Lydenburg to such an extent that the farmers there went into laager and demanded government help. All the help they got was that of two civil servants, who were sent by Burgers to tell Sekukuni to return the stolen cattle and stop making war. Sekukuni's answer was to send two chiefs to Pretoria and say he would give up the cattle if the Boers would grant him the entire eastern portion of the Republic. To enforce his demands, he brought up his impis to threaten Lydenburg itself.

There was only one reply open to Burgers. He declared war. These new troubles Kruger attributed to the fact that the Republic was governed by a godless man. It is also possible that Kruger was jealous. What, after all, had the new president done for Africa? He was a clever minister—too clever by half. A minister in Kruger's opinion should not be clever. The Word of God stood without the necessity of interpretation. But Burgers had never been on commando or drawn up a treaty. He was a book man, a consorter with the Philistines; and when Burgers informed him that he was going to accompany the force attacking Sekukuni, Kruger refused to lead it as Commandant-General, saying: "I cannot lead the commando if you come. For with your merry evenings in laager and your Sunday dances, the enemy will shoot me even behind a wall; for God's blessing will not rest on our expedition."

Burgers accordingly took Nicholas Smit and old President Pretorius with him, and Kruger retired to his farm at Boekenhoutfontein in the Rustenburg to await events. It was no idle sulking. What he had said about the godlessness of the expedition soon got about. It was to all intents and purposes fifth-column propaganda. It probably seemed better to Kruger that the war should fail than that Burgers should remain President. The

Kaffirs he knew he could deal with, but Burgers would betray the people to the modern world of Mammon: to the beast of progress which had shown its brazen face upon the horizon of Africa.

The events he awaited were not long in coming. The commando had enlisted the help of the Swazis who hated the Bapedi, and very quickly took this first objective—Matibi's Kop—which was held by a subordinate chief. Burgers wired to the government, "The Gibraltar of the North is mine."

But it was a little early to call the war won. Sekukuni's main force had not yet been engaged and had retired to their main stronghold—a formidable hill that was very strongly fortified. But success was well within the Boers' grasp, for they had cut off Sekukuni's water supply, and had they been content to wait, the citadel would have fallen. Burgers, though he had no artillery, decided to attack and divided his force into two parties. One party, led by Field-Cornet Roose, attacked and was victorious; but the men with Burgers who should have joined him broke and ran. The President threw himself in front of them. He begged them to shoot him rather than to disgrace him like this—but the Boers ran. God had departed from them for the first time in all their wars. There was a universal cry of "Huistoe"—Let us go home—and mounting their ponies the Boers drifted away. Something, however, had to be done about the undefeated Bapedi and Burgers decided to build a line of forts to hold them. A Prussian officer, Captain von Schlieckmann, was put in command of these outposts and left on the frontier with the force of volunteers that he had been permitted to raise in the diamond fields. They were armed with Westley-Richards rifles and were promised salted horses—that is, horses which have recovered from horse sickness and are considered immunised. These horses were never sent to them, since the government was not able to procure them: possibly because they are expensive and there was no money in the treasury with which to buy them. Apparently the only money that could be contributed to the military chest at that time was twenty-five pounds in small silver. The volunteers were to receive five pounds a month as pay and, at the end of the war, a farm of four thousand morgen—eight thousand acres—free. To meet the expenses of this defensive line, Burgers raised a special tax which many burgers refused to pay, as they considered it unlawful, since the Volksraad had not been consulted on the measure.

In all this Kruger, no doubt, saw the hand of the Almighty. Burgers was unorthodox, so the Lord had chastened him. And now the English joined in on the side of God for a further chastening—not with whips, but with scorpions, which was too much even for Paul Kruger.

Lord Carnarvon called a conference to discuss a union between the British Colonies of South Africa and the Boer Republics. He even chose the delegates who were to attend it. The conference was held in London, where Sir Theophilis Shepstone succeeded in persuading Lord Carnarvon that the Zulus under Cetywayo would join with Sekukuni, and defeat the South African Republic, which was "inherently weak," and could not stand alone; with the result that on his return to South Africa, Shepstone, accompanied by twenty-five policemen, took over the government in Pretoria.

This is the story of the annexation in terms of history. But what was it to Kruger? He saw it as the betrayal of his land, his freedom, his heritage. Was it for this the Boers had trekked? was there no limit? Could his people never go far enough? Must the English, whenever they paused, catch up with them?

Burgers's term of office had been due to expire in 1877. Certain British residents in the Transvaal joined with the Kruger party in denouncing Burgers. They made strange bedfellows.

And then came another London conference. Always London. The compensation for the slaves had been payable in London. And what nonsense, the Boers said, thinking they were unable to take care of themselves. They were only helpless when they abandoned their faith in God. Had Shepstone not come, there would have been a new election and Kruger would have been elected. He arrived on the eve of it, but did not show his hand at once. Attending an extraordinary meeting of the Volksraad, Shepstone said: "In your country there is no government. Your President is not supported. As a friend I offer you England's aid."

But would England have been so generous if there had been no gold or diamonds in South Africa? The Volksraad refused British aid. Then Shepstone spoke up. He said he would enforce aid, but to compromise with Kruger's party he had a protest drawn up against the annexation. This he thought would keep the people quiet. And then, protestation or no protestation, on the twelfth of April, 1877, the South African Republic became a part of the British Empire. On May 24, the Queen's birthday, the Vierkleur—the four-colour flag of the Boers—came down and the Union Jack was officially hoisted by Rider Haggard, the novelist, who then was on Shepstone's staff. Haggard had also assisted when the proclamation of the annexation was read out "in a trembling voice" by Melmoth Osborn, Shepstone's secretary. "His hands trembled so that his assistant, Mr. Haggard, had to hold the documents for him" is the description given by an eye-witness.

With the Union Jack flying over the Volksraad, a last resolution was passed. Paul Kruger was made Vice-President; and since Burgers, a broken man, had retired to the Cape, Kruger found himself the leader of his people. In this capacity he went to England to protest against the annexation. Kruger was then fifty-two years old, a strong, solid man with one leg shorter than the other, with one thumb shot off, with his thick-set body scarred with wounds from savage men and beasts, and his soul fierce with the hatred of this new injustice.

The country had indeed been divided before the proposed election. Most of the burghers who lived in the country were for Kruger and against the President, but the foreigners and a small proportion of town Boers thought that the acceptance of British rule would solve their difficulties which they saw in terms of economics rather than in those of freedom. Boers become denatured by life in towns. Even the word "Boer" means farmer.

The Sekukuni War and the new tax discredited François Burgers completely. The Boers were not accustomed to being defeated by Kaffirs, and taxes of any sort were only raised with the greatest difficulty. They wanted a state, but felt it should not cost them anything. The President was paid three hundred pounds a year, and then only when there was three hundred pounds in the treasury.

The feeling that existed is well illustrated by an incident that occurred at this last meeting of the Volksraad when Burgers slapped Kruger on the shoulder, and said: "Mr. Kruger, you can't deny that the burghers who refuse to pay taxes are in a state of rebellion against their government."

"I deny it absolutely," Kruger said, "on the grounds which I have already stated. They don't refuse to pay their taxes, but they do refuse to pay a tax which you have added without authority. But even if the facts were as you say, I would like to ask you a question. Would you consider it a proof of affection to accuse your wife openly, before her bitterest enemy? That is what you have done to the Republic in the presence of her enemy, and this to me is a proof that you do not love, but hate the Republic."

Shepstone had been standing beside them when he spoke and Burgers's accusations played into his hands, a fact that neither Kruger nor his followers ever forgave him.

Of the annexation Kruger wrote, "This cannot be too strongly branded as an entirely iniquitous act on England's part." By the Sand River Convention, at which he had been present as a young man, England had promised "never to encroach upon the districts north of the Vaal. But as soon as it suited her convenience, perfidious Albion broke her peaceful promises, as she has always done, and always will continue to do, whenever it suits her purpose."

This act of annexation aroused a fury of resentment not only in the South African Republic, which by it had ceased to exist, but also in the Free State and among those of Dutch descent in the Cape Colony. Nor was it universally praised in England. Joseph Chamberlain, then a radical member of Parliament, said later on, "To have continued to maintain the annexation would have been an act which could only be described in terms which had been applied by a high authority to a different subject— 'as an act of force, fraud, and folly.' "

Mr. Carter, later a judge, and the author of *A Narrative of the Boer War*, said: "The motive which urged England to annex was I believe the same as when with longing eyes she looked at the diamond fields, and finally robbed the Boers of that slice of territory. It was greed and love of filthy lucre. This time it was the gold which aroused our cupidity. . . . It is consistent with the manner in which, from time immemorial, we have treated the Boers in South Africa, that our intervention or annexation of that country was the outcome of our love of the Boers? If it was, then the love was of sudden growth; at all events, it was synchronal with the information received in England that payable gold existed in their country."

Kruger, writing as an old man in exile, said: "The late war which has reduced the whole country to ruins and which has cost hundreds of men and thousands of women and children their lives, this war, in which England behaved in so uncivilised and base a fashion as to draw upon itself the contempt of all civilised nations, had its origin partly in Shepstone's annexation. I say partly, for the war had two causes. The first and principal cause was the wealth of the gold fields of the Republic; the second, revenge for ' Majuba Hill.' Only if it had not been for Shepstone's annexation there would have been no ' Majuba Hill ' and no revenge for ' Majuba Hlil ' would have been called for."

Once again the chain of historical cause and effect. The executions of Slagtersnek, the emancipation of the slaves, led to the Great Trek; the discovery of gold and diamonds to the annexation by the British of the republic these peasant farmers had carved out of the wilderness; and caused the first Anglo-Boer War of 1880, out of which was born the Jameson Raid and the second Boer War in which a new stage was set for new troubles and new hates.

In 1877, the Vice-President, Paul Kruger—Oom Paul, Uncle, to his people—accompanied by Doctor Jorisson and Edouard Bok, sailed for England to see Lord Carnarvon, the Colonial Secretary, who alone could restore freedom to his people whom Burgers had betrayed. .

In an election campaign against Burgers, Kruger had said: "When Burgers is President, he knows no Sabbath: he rides through every part of the country on Sundays: of church and religion he knows nothing. . . . Read Leviticus 26:17 with attention and see how literally it has been fulfilled.—I will set my face against you, and ye shall be smitten before your enemies: they that hate you shall reign over you, and ye shall flee when none pursueth you." Nineteen years later, Rhodes, on the eve of the Raid, was to wire Jameson, "Read Luke XIV: 31."

It would seem typical of the times and of Africa that the Bible should have been put to such strange uses: as political propaganda in an election campaign and as a sort of military code book.

Speaking of Europe, Kruger said, "The people are like ants." Their swarming numbers did not impress him. They depressed him. There was no veld here, no wide-open land. The conditions under which the Europeans lived appalled him. He thought nothing of the variety of their Victorian comforts and much of their evil ways. For a man who had seen no town bigger than Cape Town, no water wider than the Vaal, one who spoke no language but the Taal of his race, this trip must have been a tremendous experience. But it was no more than that.

He was well received in England. And more than well received abroad, in France, Holland, Belgium, and Germany; but these countries, even if they were sympathetic to his cause, were in no position to challenge England at the height of her power.

Lord Carnarvon, the Secretary of State for Colonies, received him at Highclere—a magnificent mansion modelled, with some vulgarity, on the houses of Parliament—with a frigid English politeness, but informed him that "an act performed in the Queen's name could not be questioned." The King or Queen in this case could do no wrong. "Dieu et mon droit, Honi soit qui mal y pense." An argument which Kruger found himself unable to understand.

Carnarvon refused Kruger's suggestion of a plebiscite, "because it would involve too much trouble and expense." In brief, he refused to consider the matter, saying it was settled. He believed, or said he believed, that Kruger represented only a small dissatisfied minority. He further believed that Kruger, if he failed in his mission, would become a loyal subject of the new government as he had been of the old. Kruger was supposed to have told Shepstone this, but denies that he ever said anything of the kind and his actions appear to prove his denial. Nor was any notice taken of the blessing of the sister republic of the Free State which gave Kruger a proclamation in which their Raad trusted "the mission of the deputation of the people and the government of the South African Republic will be crowned with good success."

Kruger had left Africa in May, 1877. He reached his home in the Rustenburg again in December. In January, after a few days' rest, he went to Pretoria where thousands of burghers were waiting the report he brought. The farmers were restless and angry with the slow anger of their race. They were citizen soldiers, men who had all been out on commando, all were organised under field cornets of their own choosing. Solid, stolid, respectable men and dangerous to trifle with. They did not like the English. They had no reason to, and they detested the flag that now flew over their land. Despite the fact that the Colonial Secretary had refused to consider the idea, a committee was appointed to arrange a plebiscite, which disturbed Shepstone, who forbade it. Kruger refused to give in, since he had said in England that "the majority were against the annexation and he did not wish to be branded a liar." He added, "If you admit I was right and that the report you sent to England on the feeling of the people was untrue, then the vote will be unnecessary."

Shepstone then gave his consent, provided the burghers came unarmed. The committee met at Doornpoort in April, 1878, and when it appeared, 125 petitions with 6591 signatures had been handed in against the annexation, and 31 with 587 signatures in its favour. This clearly showed the feeling of the people, as the total male white population of the Republic, as given in Shepstone's own report to the Colonial Secretary, numbered only 8000.

Armed with this proof, Kruger again returned to England, accompanied by Piet Joubert and Mr. Edouard Bok, to present his new petition, which declared that "the people of the republic were convinced that the British Government was misinformed as to the real feelings of the Boer population and that they could not believe that England would wish to govern another country against its wish."

The second delegation met with even less success than the first, for Sir Michael Hicks-Beach had succeeded Lord Carnarvon and refused even to meet the delegates, saying everything must be done by correspondence. In the meantime, Shepstone had written to the Colonial Office, attacking Kruger and saying if there was dissatisfaction in Africa it was "he who was the cause of it." Yet while he was in England, Kruger wrote to his friends bidding them to "sit still, otherwise the water will be muddied."

One incident alone stood out on the credit side of the ledger.

An Englishman presented Kruger with a gold ring engraved with the words, "Take courage, your cause is just and must triumph in the end." When he died, this ring was still upon Kruger's finger.

On the return journey the party visited the great international exhibition in Paris and Kruger went up in a balloon. High up in the air, he said to the aeronaut, "Since we have gone so far, take me all the way home."

In the meantime, the Colonial Office had sent James Anthony Froude, the notably inaccurate historian, to South Africa to report on the situation there and to see what prospects there were for a South African Federation. Colonel George Pomeroy Colley was also sent out, ostensibly as a tourist, a word which has now become very familiar, but actually as an agent of the British government.

When Kruger got back to Africa in December, in 1878, the Kaffirs—the Zulus of the East and the Bapedi in the North—seized their chance and broke out with a new series of raids, thefts, and murders. A useless expedition was sent against Sekukuni which achieved nothing and Cetywayo was in rebellion against the English, who, though they had refused to acknowledge the Republic's claim to his territory, now after the annexation said it belonged to them.

New to Kaffir wars, the British Commander-in-Chief asked Kruger the best way to wage a war of this kind. Kruger told him to collect his wagons in laagers at night and to keep himself informed as to the movements of the enemy by spies and scouts. Sir Bartle Frere, the Governor of the Cape, then asked Kruger to accompany the column as adviser and leader. Kruger refused. Frere then said he could name his own reward.

"Very well," Kruger said, "I accept. I will take five hundred burghers and hand Zululand over to you if you will give me the reward I want." Had his people not fought Zulus before, thousands of them, at Blood River and elsewhere? Had they not smashed Dingaan and Moselikatze at the height of their power?

"Do you mean to say your people are so much better than our soldiers?" Frere asked.

"No," Kruger said, "but our method of fighting is much better than yours and we know the country."

He was then asked what his price was.

"The independence of my country and my people."

The Zulu War began without Kruger, and ignoring the advice of the Boers the English were cut to pieces at Isandislawana, where twelve hundred British soldiers died beneath the Zulu assegais. In this campaign, the Prince Imperial, son of Napoleon III. and the Empress Eugénie of France, was also killed. This young man was with the English as a kind of visitor, wishing to see the sport of fighting savages. Out on a small patrol, riding a showy but badly trained horse which he was unable to mount quickly, he was speared as he hopped about with one foot in the stirrup.

Learning the hard way, Lord Chelmsford finally succeeded in defeating the Zulus at the battle of Ulundi and broke their power by capturing Cetywayo, who was betrayed into his hands. Meanwhile, in March, 1879, Sir Owen Lanyon, a soldier by profession, who knew nothing of administration and spoke no Dutch, replaced Shepstone as administrator of the Transvaal.

Shepstone at least knew Africa where as native Commissioner he had crowned Cetywayo. The Zulus called him "Somtszu." The Boers nicknamed him "Ou Stoffel Slypsteen"—a slypsteen is a sharpening stone for knives or scissors. Lanyon, the Boers called "Lang Tang" the Portuguese Governor. He was a West Indian, of dark complexion, which made the people think he was of mixed descent. In consequence they had little respect for him. The British practice of sending administrators accustomed to dealing with natives to rule over the Boers was a mistake, since they were not used to being treated in a high-handed manner. They later objected to Milner on the same grounds. He had been Under-Secretary of Finance in Egypt and treated the Boers as he had been accustomed to treat the fellaheen. Lanyon may have been appointed as a strong man to counter the unrest among the Boers, who, in January, had held another mass meeting, about three thousand of them assembling at Wonderfontein. More, Kruger said, would have been there if the rivers had not been in flood and the horse-sickness season at its height.

Sir Bartle Frere had distributed among the burghers an open letter to Kruger and Joubert in which he said, among other things, that "the annexation was irrevocable." Nothing is irrevocable to a Boer but death, and at Wonderfontein a resolution was passed which declared that the people would not remain content with the decision of the British government, and many burghers thought the time had come to fight. One of them stepped forward and said, "Mr. Kruger, we have been talking long enough. You must let us shoot the English."

Gerrit Scheepers at the head of four hundred mounted men came to Kruger's tent carrying a Boer flag, and said, "This flag which you see here is a symbol of our unity and I express the feelings of all my friends and followers here when I assure you we are ready to offer our blood and goods to defend it and plant it once more on our free and independent soil." Smit called out: "Friends and brothers, this is the flag of our fathers, precious to them, doubly so to us. Let us show that we will preserve it and if necessary give our blood for it."

Kruger then spoke, addressing those who might be fainthearted. "Let neither fear nor shame keep them back, so that it may not be said afterwards that a single person was here against his will. Let there be unity among you and let wisdom give you strength, so that after calm deliberation you may come to a resolution which will tend to the welfare of the country ... leave us all who have been compelled to come here. Once more I say, leave us. Does nobody leave? Well, then, nobody has the right to say anything behind our backs. If anybody does so, I call him traitor."

Gerrit Scheepers said: "Choose, brothers, whom you will serve. Will you serve Her Majesty or take up your arms for freedom? You know how I brought the flag here. Well, if Her Majesty regards this as a flag of war, I am ready to die for it or gain the victory. And you, my friends, if you are with me, then wave your hats." Hundreds of hats tossed in the air as the burghers shouted, "Yes! Yes!" Hendrik Schoeman repeated his cry of the last meeting, "Who wants to subject himself to Her Majesty's dominion?" The excited crowd shouted, "We would rather die."

Kruger answered them with a question.

"If I say Sah will you bite? And if you bite, will you hold tight?"

At this meeting it was resolved to invite Sir Bartle Frere to a new meeting to be held at Kleinfontein, another farm, on the eighteenth of March, 1879, where Joubert ended his speech with the words: "The question which the people must now put to itself is: Shall it submit or not?"

Kruger also spoke and tried to calm the burghers, many of whom still spoke openly of "shooting the English." The committee, he promised them "would not fail to inform them as soon as it thought all peaceful measures had been exhausted." Some burghers even spoke of going to help Cetywayo, the Zulu king with whom the English were now at war. This idea Kruger combated with all his might, maintaining that "it was not Christian and that one must never join with savages in a war against a civilised nation," and he warned the burghers of their danger. "Weigh your words well, think of the consequences of a thoughtless step; wait if necessary till to-morrow. I also want my independence back, but I must once more impress you that this is no light matter when you call out Yes, yes, we want to fight."

Meantime, Sir Bartle Frere, who had promised to attend the meeting, had not arrived. He had left Natal for the North and was travelling very slowly, perhaps on the assumption that his delay would discourage the Boers and that they would, if kept waiting long enough, return to their farms, having accomplished nothing. From Heidelberg he sent word that he would be unable to attend the meeting. The burghers, however, said they were determined to see him, and fearing trouble—there were five thousand Boers assembled on the farm—he changed his mind and came, arriving on the twelfth of April. Many Boers had come two hundred miles to be at this meeting and had been camping on the farm since mid-March.

The leaders rode out to meet Frere, but the burghers when he arrived preserved a deadly silence. Despite his smiles and bows, no one saluted or cheered. He drove with his escort past the thousands of mounted Boers, who sat their horses and watched him with stony eyes. All that was decided was that a new meeting must be held a few days later to discuss the points which had come up.

This time Frere was accompanied by the new Governor, Sir Owen Lanyon, some officials, and an armed bodyguard. Again, as might be expected, nothing was achieved except that Frere acknowledged that he had been misinformed and that "the best men in the Transvaal were against the annexation;" that he would inform the home government of this fact, but that he was still opposed to its repeal. Frere, speaking in this spirit, said to Piet Joubert, "Under the British flag you will have everything you desire; but the flag will continue to fly over the land."

Over the land possibly, but over the people never.

These mass meetings, to which men rode on horseback or in wagons with their families often many hundreds of miles, were typical of the Boer method of government. Living isolated they came together to discuss matters of importance, to pray at Nagmaal or to assemble for war.

Sir Garnet Wolseley was now sent to South Africa with special powers. He was made High Commissioner, sharing that office with Sir Bartle Frere, and told to settle matters with the Zulus and Transvaal Boers. This was the man who said, "So long as the sun shines, the Transvaal will be British territory: and the Vaal River shall flow back to its sources before the Transvaal is again independent."

On December 10, the Boers called a new meeting, on another farm, in spite of Sir Garnet's threat that any one who attended a meeting would be tried for high treason. Six thousand men could not be tried for high treason and six thousand men attended. Kruger told the assembled people some of the things he had seen in England. He told them how powerful England was and said he feared that many farmers, once war had broken out, would become discouraged and go home.

But that night, anxious to see if his remarks had had any effect, Kruger walked through the camp, standing back away from the cooking fires, and listened to the talk. This was a typical Boer action. What simpler plan could have been devised to discover the temper of the people? Instead of inflaming them with patriotic oratory, he calmed them and then went out to see if they would stay calmed.

He heard one man say, "I think Kruger is betraying us."

"No," another answered. "I will never believe that of him, for he has done too much for us and he is still working too hard to be accused of such a thing."

"But," answered the first man, "if he doesn't intend to betray us, why won't he let us shoot the Englishmen?"

Kruger was much encouraged by what he heard. The people were up, their temper raised. Now when he said "Sah" they would bite. When he said "Hold," they would hold.

Next day a resolution was passed: the burghers demanded that they remain free and independent; stated that they had never been subjects of Her Majesty and never wished to become so; and concluded by asking for the restitution of their independence and the restoration of the Volksraad. The last-named body, they said, must take the necessary measures to ensure their independence.

Pretorius and Bok were sent to Sir Garnet Wolseley with this resolution, but both were arrested on the charge of high treason while on their way to the British authorities.

The fat was now in the fire. The guns no longer hung on the farmhouse walls; they were in the hands of a whole people who were ready to ride to the rescue of their delegates. Kruger, who was on his way to Potchefstroom to try to obtain the release of the prisoners, heard of a rescue party which had preceded him, and only by galloping as fast as his horse could carry him did he succeed in turning them back at the outskirts of the town.

That evening the prisoners were released on bail, and Pretorius was persuaded by the British to ride through the country, the government supplying him with mounts, to read a proclamation intended to convince the burghers of the error of their ways.

The burghers whom Kruger had turned back were still assembled, mounted and armed, at Nauwpoort, not far from Potchefstroom, when Pretorius arrived to read this document which said that "the burghers should submit peacefully and that only by this means could they ever hope to attain self-government. . . ."

Kruger then spoke. "Burghers," he said, "do you understand what the British Government offers you? I will try to explain. They say this to you: First put your head quietly in the noose so that I can hang you up. Then you may kick about as much as you please! That is what they call self-government."

The burghers agreed with Kruger, and Pretorius wrote to

Sir Garnet "that it was no use his going on, as the burghers were firmly determined to recover their independence."

A new scheme—that of a Federation of South Africa—was now under discussion at the Cape Parliament. Kruger and Joubert set off for the Cape to fight this proposal, which he succeeded in doing by persuading the Cape Dutch that the Transvaalers would never submit and would not allow foreigners to determine their rate for them. "Do not wash your hands in the blood of your brothers," he pleaded.

While at the Cape, Kruger and Joubert were invited to visit Sir Bartle Frere.

"I will come," Kruger said, "if you can tell me which Sir Bartle Frere it is that wishes to see us; for I know four of them. The first come to see us at Kleinfontein and assured us that he had not come with the sword, but as a messenger of peace. But later on I read in an English Blue Book that on the same day a Sir Bartle Frere, the second, therefore, had written to the British government: *If only I had had enough men and guns, I would soon have dispersed the rebels.* I made the acquaintance of the third Sir Bartle Frere through his answer to our petition for the repeal of the annexation: he then said that he had informed the British government that he had met some five thousand of the best Boers at Kleinfontein and that he recommended their petition to the government's earnest consideration. Afterwards I saw in the English Blue Book that, on the same day, a Sir Bartle Frere, obviously a fourth, had informed the British government that he had met only a handful of rebels. Now these four cannot possibly be one and the same man: if, therefore, you can tell me which of the four Sir Bartles wishes to see us, we will think about it."

That was the end of the invitation.

While Kruger and Joubert were at the Cape in 1880, the Tory government in England fell and Gladstone, who had repeatedly spoken against the annexation, became Prime Minister for the second time. But though he was in power, and, in principle, disagreed with the way things had been handled in Africa, he informed Kruger that he was "unable to annul the annexation or advise Her Majesty to abandon her suzerainty of the Transvaal." "Looking at all the circumstances," he wrote, "both in the Transvaal and the rest of South Africa, and to the necessity of preventing further disorders which might lead to disastrous consequences, our judgment is that the Queen cannot be advised to relinquish her sovereignty of the Transvaal." Gladstone was taking the easy way out. The easy way that was in the end to lead to war.

Everything that patient and forbearing men could do had been done. Further meetings and friendly protests were useless. In Kruger's words: "The best course appeared to be to set quietly to work and to prepare for the worst by the purchase of arms and ammunition. The greatest prudence and the strictest secrecy had to be observed in order to avoid suspicion: this was the only possible way of preparing for the decisive struggle."

This was the picture of Africa in 1880. In the North, Lobengula was staving off the concession-seekers; in Kimberley, Cecil Rhodes was about to form the de Beers Company; and the eight thousand free burghers of the Transvaal were preparing to fight the British Empire of Queen Victoria. Their guns were ready. Their ponies saddled. Their women urgent for war.

CHAPTER SEVEN

MY NORTH

THE DIAMOND FIELDS, which meant one thing to Paul Kruger, meant another to Cecil Rhodes. To Rhodes they were his chance. They were the shining pebbles that would pave his road to the North. "My North—the North is my idea." How often did he say it and to how many men! There was a North then, too; open, relatively unexplored, rich, and if not unwilling, at least unable, to protect itself. In those days strong men could become rich—even had to become rich, one success compensating for ten errors.

Trouble with the Boers at that time did not mean much to Rhodes. During his lifetime his attitude towards them underwent three changes. This was the first—lack of interest. His interest was in wealth, in diamonds as a means of wealth with which to build an empire. Who but Rhodes would have thought of basing an empire on the sale of engagement rings? His second idea—of a combination with the Dutch—was defeated by the mistake of his friend, Doctor Jim. His third was that of a jingo Englishman who saw the Boers as enemies. Though he still talked of working with them, he saw the British as dominant and had no sympathy with the Boer ideal. He died in this frame of mind.

It would be hard to imagine a less adequate description of the diamond diggings than the term "field." A diamond field in operation, whether it be in the alluvial field on the Orange River or a deep-level operation in Kimberley, is a scrofulous sore on the face of the land; a mass of trenches, holes, and heaps of gravel resembling nothing so much as a modern battlefield pitted and scarred with craters. Each hole, of necessity, had beside it the pile of waste which had been dug from it by sweating savages. The workers in those days were savages—Zulus, Matabele, Swazi warriors, who worked to get money for guns and to steal diamonds for their chiefs and kings. As the pits deepened, the heaps of débris grew higher. One man's heap slid into another man's hole. There were quarrels and fights, there were men crushed beneath landslides of rubbish. On the alluvial diggings this was not so bad, for there the diamonds were found near the surface, having been washed into beds by the rivers. But at Kimberley the work was on a pipe, the actual crater where the stones had been formed under pressure when the matter, which is the world, was seething, cooling, contracting, and expanding; when great ranges of mountains were faulted and strata slipped for miles; when the gold conglomerate, that which was to become the ore of the Rand, was boiling like a pot—a pudding filled with currants through which the gold filtered, a flavouring that was to send men mad with greed.

These diamond pipes are the necks of extinct volcanoes that have eroded down to the general level of the country. The bluish indurated mud is excavated, often from a depth of several hundred feet, hoisted to the surface and spread out on floors, where it is allowed to rot for two or three years during which time it oxidizes and disintegrates from exposure. It is then broken up by mills and run over inclined tables where the boys pick out the resinous-looking stones as the water carries them past. A simplification of this process resulted from the accident of a careless overseer who spilt some grease on a table and it was found that diamonds stuck to the grease, allowing other pebbles to be washed past irrespective of their specific gravity. As the gold-hunters the world over have sought the mother lode, so the diamond-hunters sought the mother pipes which must of necessity lie upstream, higher in the watershed. It was thus proceeding upwards from the alluvial fields that mines or pipes were discovered.

Froude, the English historian who had come to South Africa to assist Sir Bartle Frere with his advice—much good it did any one —described the diamond fields as a squalid camp. "Bohemians of all nations came there," he says, "American and Australian diggers, German speculators, traders, saloon-keepers, professional gamblers.... They may be the germ of a great future colony, or if the diamonds give out, they may disappear like a swarm of locusts." Here was the one point where Kruger and the English historian saw eye to eye, except that Kruger preferred the term "aasvoel"—the vulture—to the locust.

A.P.   E

This description of the fields seems accurate enough. But Froude's other remarks about Africa should not be taken too literally. So prone was he to factual errors that the term "Froude's disease" came to be applied to other historians who suffered from what has been described as his congenital inaccuracy.

Anthony Trollope, who went to Africa to help Frere, says: "I am often struck by the amount of idleness which people can allow themselves whose occupations have diverged from the common work of the world. . . . I can conceive no occupation more dreary—hardly more demoralising—than this perpetually turning over of dust in quest of a peculiar little stone which may turn up once a week, or may not."

Kimberley was a hideous place. It scarcely ever rained. Sometimes it had a temperature of ninety-seven degrees in the shade and a hundred and sixty degrees in the sun. Since there were no trees, there was no shade. Since there was so little rain, there was no grass. There were no pavements and the roads were thick with dust: so thick that a driver, to guide them by, had to watch his horses' ears—they were all he could see above the clouds of dust they raised—watching the roofs of the buildings that he passed. Trollope said, "I seem to breathe dust rather than air. . . . I was soon sick of looking at diamonds."

The diggers were the wastrels of the world, idlers who could work neither for themselves nor a master. They had no God, but worshipped the Goddess Luck. In all its history only a few great fortunes were made on the diggings and many backs and hearts were broken. Nor were there great prospects of fortune until diamonds were discovered in the blue ground which lay below the yellow. "A man with a thousand pounds was considered well off in those days," Rhodes said. Perhaps the worst fortune, either in those days or to-day, that could befall a newcomer in the fields was to find in the first few days a reasonably valuable stone. If this happened, he would almost certainly spend the rest of his life looking for greater prizes instead of giving up.

Such trees as there were in the vicinity of the fields soon went, burnt up as firewood; and ugliness, physical and moral, spread over the veld as new strikes were made. Old-timers still regret those days; but old-timers always regret the good old days when they were young and the world was open. High, wide, and handsome they lived and died; and swiftly the dead were replaced by others, for suicide by debauchery has always proved interesting and the blanks of such a society are soon filled up.

There are pink, blue, yellow, and green diamonds. Here is the story of a green diamond. A digger near Bloemhof one day saw a queer black stone, shaped like the end of a pick, lying in one of his final washings. He thought it was a piece of bort—that is, a commercial diamond, used for machinery and drills—and put it in his pocket, thinking it would come in handy to test other stones: a diamond or a bort will scratch anything except another diamond. Kept in bottles, diamonds have even eaten their way through the glass. Several times the digger lost his bort. He took no care of it, but one day it occurred to him to have "windows" cut into it, and when this was done, he was surprised to see a green light shine from the stone. He then had it polished. It was a freak stone and the green glow that came from it was described by some one who saw it as being like "the shade of a signal lamp." After much negotiation, it was sold to an Indian Maharajah.

To the Boers all this was a fantasy, a madness. From 1871, when Fleetwood Rawstone found diamond indications on a kopje on de Beers's farm, the country had been caught in an economic web it did not understand and could not escape. Adriaan van Wyk sold his farm at Dutiotspan for twenty-six hundred pounds, diamonds having been found near his house. Du Ploy, a poor farmer, sold his property for two thousand pounds. In his case a diamond had been found in the clay that he had used to plaster his house; just as later on Struben was to find veins of gold in the stone used in the walls of a farmhouse on the Rand. And still later diamonds were found to have been mixed into the concrete of a station platform in Namaqualand. But the Boers were hurt and amazed at these discoveries. They wanted none of it, and in many cases tried to keep the prospectors away with their rifles. They wanted their homes, their farms, however poor they might be, because a farm was a place and money nothing, since they were without wants. It is this aspect of the Boer character which it is hard for people, reared in a competitive civilisation, to understand.

Many years later, long after the Kimberley mines had been

developed, old de Beers said to his wife, "We should have asked six million and not six thousand pounds for our land."

"But what would we have done with all that money?" she said. "There are only two of us and this house is big enough. We have our front room and our bedroom and our kitchen. What more do we want?"

"We could have a new wagon."

"We have enough to buy twenty new wagons."

"And a new Cape cart to go to Nagmaal—to service."

"That, too, we can afford. Ach, my little heart, be easy. What have we to trouble about? We have enough."

But there was not enough for Rhodes. The nations of the world were not like that of the Boers; and what England did not take, the others would. Rhodes's philosophy was summed up in the word England, and was governed to a great extent by a lecture he heard at Oxford, where Ruskin had spoken of "a destiny now possible to us, the highest ever set before a nation; to be accepted or refused. Will you youths of England make your country again a royal throne of kings, a sceptred isle, for all the world a source of light, a centre of peace? . . ."

But Rhodes went beyond this. His England was not England alone, but also America. He wanted a *Union now*—one language, one currency, a federation with the United States. "We could hold a Federal Parliament five years at Washington and five at London," he said. He thought the only feasible method of carrying out such an idea was "a secret society gradually absorbing the wealth of the world." A gigantic cartel, governed by an English-speaking élite which would be perpetually recruited from those who could make the grade, in a world in which only the fittest survived. He envisaged what to-day we should probably call a "Managerial Revolution" combined with a giant secret society of financiers. That he used Loyola's name in connection with this society shows his idea of a "money religion." This theory has some validity, since Rhodes was very much against power—and money and power are interchangeable terms—without responsibility. He was against inherited wealth, and historically he was correct in associating politics with religion, since the two are in principle inseparable. The priest-kings of the dawn of history held the first political power of which we have any record. In

Rhodes's own time the wizards of the Matopos held Lobengula in the hollow of their hands. In our time the political power of the Catholic Church cannot be denied, nor can the political implications of the Jewish persecutions in Europe, nor the rise of the new political faith of Russia, which is in the widest sense a religion.

England, Rhodes believed with Ruskin, "must found colonies as fast and as far as she is able; formed of her most energetic and worthiest men; seizing any piece of fruitful ground. . . ." This Rhodes believed would found a power so great "as to render wars impossible and promote the best interests of humanity." In 1877 in a document to his friend Stead he elaborates this idea. He wrote:

"It often strikes a man to inquire what is the chief good in life. To one the thought comes that it is a happy marriage, to another great wealth. . . . As each seizes the idea, he more or less works for its attainment for the rest of his existence. To myself, thinking over the same question, the wish came to make myself useful to my country. . . . I contend we are the first race in the world and that the more of the world we inhabit the better it is for the human race . . . added to which the absorption of the greater portion of the world under our rule simply means the end of all wars."

It is this paragraph which has been seized upon by Colonel McCormick, as it was in 1916 by George Sylvester Viereck, to prove that the Rhodes scholarships were devised by Rhodes as the Machiavellian keynote to his arch of British imperial infiltration into the United States that would end in the return of the lost colony to the fold.

But if Rhodes wanted to be useful to his country, so did Kruger. So did Lobengula.

A missionary now enters the political arena. While Rhodes was working in Kimberley, Stanley was lecturing in Germany, where he aroused great interest in Africa. First Paul Kruger's visit to Europe, and now that of a missionary explorer. What they said only confirmed the reports of the German geologist Karl Mauch. Mauch had told Germany of the gold in Africa. Kruger and Stanley told Germany of the troubled political waters from which this gold could be fished with comparative safety.

Leopold of Belgium made his grab at the Congo Basin, and a few years later the Germans occupied Angra Pequina on the west coast, in what is known as Namaqualand, claiming the sovereignty over the seven hundred miles of seaboard from Cape Frio in the north to the mouth of the Orange River in the south, completely surrounding the little British port of Walfisch Bay. Rhodes's "Hinterland" was being ridden off by the European powers as the Boers rode off their farms. Whole countries were being pegged like diamond claims. These waves of semi-peaceful occupation lapped against the African Republics and threatened Rhodes's Cape-to-Cairo dream. Lobengula's empire trembled: the short stabbing spears of his warriors were not long enough to give him immunity.

Not all this had happened yet, but it was in the offing. The straws were in the wind, the writing on the wall, and Rhodes began to make still greater haste. He was already, by the time he had taken his degree at Oxford, a rich man. In 1874 he and Rudd had taken in another partner. Then more partners were taken in and he floated the de Beers Mining Company with a capital of two hundred thousand pounds.

Oxford was now behind him, but he bore its mark till he died. He had said he would go there, and he had. He had been warned against idleness at Oxford, but had said if he was left alone he would pull through, and he did. He never participated in the life of the university. He never took rooms at college. He played no games. He went to few lectures. He became a Freemason and, "cheerfully ignoring anguished protests, made a speech revealing the secrets of his craft:" It is an amusing anomaly to think that while Rhodes, the Freemason, was explaining Freemasonry, Ningi, Lobengula's sister, being courted in Matabeleland by the traders, was wearing a Freemason's little blue apron dangling over her immense thighs.

The making of speeches was one of Rhodes's outstanding characteristics. He loved to talk. He talked expansively, exhaustively, repetitively, shamelessly, about everything that interested him. He was a gregarious man who hated to eat even a single meal alone. He was dependent on atmosphere, on his friends. They were the flint for the steel of his mind. He was in a sense an idealist and as such a cynic, since cynicism is the defence mechanism of the idealist. He was a giver. He had to give money, ideas, land—anything. He had so much and wanted so little.

Here, then, was Rhodes, the young, the rich, the sick young man. Big-made, unco-ordinated, energetic—a man to whom dreams were realities. The man who a little later was to tell his farm manager to buy him the Great Drakenstein Valley.

"How much do you want me to buy?"

"Buy it all."

"All! All the Drakenstein Valley? It would cost a million."

"I don't ask your advice; I want you to buy it. Buy it."

Was a man against him—then he would buy that man. Of one enemy he asked, "What does he do?"

"He sells produce."

"Then buy a thousand sacks of mealies from him."

Rhodes was seldom tidily dressed; he did not like women and never married, though they wrote to him offering themselves as wives or mistresses from all over the world. He drank heavily, according to his enemies; and hardly at all, according to his friends. The truth probably lies between these extremes; but the swollen purple of his face in later life was caused at least as much by his aneurism as his reputed alcoholic excesses. Of himself he said, "My wealth, my life, my dreams were formed here, in Kimberley." And men drank in Kimberley to pass the time in that burning, intolerable discomfort.

Rhodes's temper was passionate. He was quick to anger and quick to repent of his anger. But it will never be known how much his temper, or even his drinking, was due to his knowledge that his time was limited . . . that he had so much to do and so little time in which to accomplish it. Incredibly successful in our terms, he was incredibly frustrated in his own. All work, his own and that of those who worked with him, had to be done fast, done well, done if necessary with a cynicism in which the ends justified the means . . . almost any means. High, wide, fast, and handsome could have been his motto—and big, very big. He was an American in his ideas of size.

The amalgamation of the various diamond mining companies and individual claims which eventually became a monopoly was essential if the price of diamonds was to be kept up, since the output was catching up with the demand; and only by organisation could the thefts of the natives and the operations of the IDB —illicit diamond buyers—be controlled. "On their eight-hour shift in the mine the men were not allowed to wear any clothes, and in the evening when they were brought out of the diggings they had to pass in single file into an enclosed iron shed where they were expertly searched by guards who ran their fingers through their woolly hair, pressed their flat nostrils, felt inside their mouths, under their tongues, in their ears, and up their rectums. Then the native had to lift his arms, stretch apart his fingers and jigger (jump) so that any diamonds concealed by muscular contraction would drop on the floor. . . . A week before a workman left the mines, he was taken to a building called "the detention house," where he was confined with only blankets for covering . . . during this detention period the man's hands were encased in leather gloves like boxing gloves. These gloves, which were locked on his wrists, had a recording watch which automatically registered every time the man went to the toilet. If the watch did not register a daily trip, he was given a cathartic. The toilets were so arranged that water flowed constantly through them, across sieves of various sizes from large to very fine mesh, and thousands of diamonds that the natives had swallowed were thus retrieved. . . . In spite of all these precautions, the natives still managed to steal some stones . . . they would slash open their legs and conceal the diamonds in the open wounds. They would hide them in the navel, or under the skin of the most private parts of the body. The company doctors, by probing any wounds or swellings, recovered many fine stones, for only the finest were worth such self-inflicted anguish."

But the primary factor of waste was by landfalls. Too many men were working in one place; the old thirty-one-foot claims had each been divided into eight parts, and some of them, the best, exchanged hands for a thousand pounds and more. Every cubic inch might contain a fortune. This was after the bottom of the yellow ground had been struck and the real wealth had been found to lie, not above it as had at first been thought, but below it in the hard blue clay. Between these claims, that were like deep wells, ox carts and mule wagons had to pass, and the machinery for washing, sifting, and sorting had to be set up. Mules, oxen, carts, native workers, and even the diggers themselves began falling down the shafts. Flood water filled some claims and when the owners pumped it out, it ran into others.

The mines were shored up with timber, the earth was brought up in buckets running on steel hawsers. The whole of Kimberley was a web of wires along which, in never-ceasing lines, the full buckets came up and the empty returned to the bottom, where men, small as ants, sweated in mud and water.

Melina Rorke said in her biography of Rhodes: "As the buckets came up with their loads of blue ground, swarms of Kaffirs fell upon it with pickaxes and breaking it apart piled it on to barrows to be wheeled away to the enclosed field, where it was left exposed to the sun and rain. After it had suffered a natural decomposition, the Kaffirs worked it into smaller pieces before it was sent to the mills to be crushed, pulverized, and finally washed to get at the stones. . . . The fields of blue decomposing earth looked like a great ploughed waste at first glance, but, as we stood staring across the fence under the watchful eyes of the guards, I could see the bright glitter of occasional bits of crystal and the red sparkle of garnets blinking back at the sun. . . ."

For each load of diamondiferous soil, five loads of overlay had to be discarded somehow. The pits were three or four hundred feet deep and below them again were the shafts that led into the blue ground. A fall of a million tons stopped work for months. Men were continually being killed. This was the chaos into which Rhodes was to bring order by his amalgamations. But others had the same idea. It must have been fairly simple to think of it. But to bring it about, as Rhodes did, step by step, for twenty years, was another matter. His main rivals were two Jews, Alfred Biet and Barney Barnato, both of whom in the end became his partners.

The Jews who had come to Africa in search of wealth were good and bad, probably in about the same proportion as the Christians were good or bad. And among the Jews who came was a character—Barney Isaacs. He was a London Jew from Whitechapel. He landed with forty boxes of mediocre cigars as a stock in trade and set up business with his brother Harry. Music-hall fans, the brothers called themselves "Barnato," and had a fine line of selling patter. They wore loud-checked suits, buttonholes, and waxed their moustaches into points; but they had a good name. Their vulgarity was cancelled out by their generosity; their sharp business sense balanced by their honesty. From selling cigars, Barney took to selling other things, among them diamonds; from selling diamonds, he took to digging for them; and as he made money, he sank it into new claims.

Alfred Biet once said, "I am going to control the whole diamond industry before I am much older."

"That's funny," Rhodes answered, "I have made up my mind to do the same. We had better join hands."

This was one of his earlier amalgamations and was typical of Rhodes. Merge, amalgamate, compromise, join, settle by talk and discussion. It resembles an argument he had with the Boers later when trouble was brewing.

"Blood," the Boer said, "there must be blood."

"Let's have breakfast first and then we'll talk about blood," Rhodes answered.

There was breakfast and no blood. The blood-letting was delayed, and if Rhodes had had his way, none might ever have been spilt. He did not believe in blood.

With Biet in with him, Barney Barnato was Rhodes's only rival. But Barney had an Achilles' heel. He wanted to be a member of the Kimberley Club. He had risen from Whitechapel to become one of the richest men in Africa, but this club business was his obsession. He might have a house in Park Lane, have everything else that money could buy, but the Club—it was a terrible little corrugated iron joint—refused him membership. And this card Rhodes played in the final showdown when they were the last two big men left in Kimberley. Here in action again was the Rhodes who had asked, "What does he sell?" of the produce merchant. The Rhodes who had named his horses after the men he had bought. The Rhodes who held his power over men with the subtle whip of stock-exchange tips. The Rhodes who knew and played on men's weaknesses when he could not play on their love for him. Money, power, women, wine—he knew who wanted which and placed it in their way if they went along with him.

He wanted Barney Barnato. Barney wanted to join the Kimberley Club that Rhodes practically owned. Never had there been a simpler socio-economic equation.

"This," Rhodes said to Barnato as the negotiations hung fire, "is no mere money transaction. I propose to make a gentleman of you."

"It seems incredible," Sarah Gertrude Millin writes of this incident, "that a gentleman should have said it or a man accepted it." Barnato did accept it, but becoming a gentleman was too hard for him, or perhaps, when he found himself with other gentlemen, he did not want to be one after all. At any rate, some years later he ended his life by jumping off a liner in mid-Atlantic.

A girl who knew Barney wrote: "Occasionally father would say rather hesitantly to mother that he felt it was time for him to have Barney Barnato to dinner again, and mother, looking faintly alarmed, would agree. I always looked forward to those evenings, for no matter how formal the atmosphere or how stiff and proper the behaviour of the other guests, Barney would soon melt them into laughter. He had an endless fund of reminiscences and anecdotes, each funnier than the last, and an inimitable way of telling them. He was a short, chubby man with pink cheeks and yellow hair and a droll way of rolling his eyes which used to convulse me with laughter. He was absolutely unself-conscious and would tell the most appalling jokes about himself and his brother and their adventures in high and low society. In the artificially respectable atmosphere of Kimberley he disarmed all the gossips by laughingly parading his family skeletons for their amusement instead of trying to shut them in a closet."

Barney on his way out to Africa—he came steerage—passed in mid-ocean the ship that Rhodes was in as he went to England to try to get into Oxford. When asked, Barney said the difference between himself and Rhodes was that he had come to South Africa with thirty pounds capital and forty boxes of cigars to peddle, while Rhodes had come with a Greek lexicon.

But in 1880 these final amalgamations were still a long way off and Rhodes stood for the Cape Parliament as an independent member from Barkly West, and was elected. He was on his way to the premiership of the Cape Colony before he had got his pass degree at Oxford and staggered the respectable members by appearing in Parliament in the tweeds that he wore in college. "I think I can legislate in them as well as in sable clothing," he said.

But north of the Vaal strange things were taking place.

In the district of Potchefstroom a wagon belonging to Field Cornet Piet Bezuidenhout was put up for sale by the authorities at eleven o'clock on the eleventh of November. The British government had levied taxes which many of the Boers, refusing to recognise the government, would not pay; and to overcome this reluctance their property was sold. But Bezuidenhout was the wrong man to tackle. His name, had the government known the history of Africa, should have rung a bell. It was an ancestor of his, Frederik, who had been shot defending himself against the tax collectors in 1816, and another, Johannes, the brother of Frederik, who had led the rebellion which ended in the tragic hangings of Slagtersnek on the Baviaans River. Whatever else they were, the Bezuidenhouts were not good taxpayers, and as a family very unsusceptible to coercion.

Though the wagon was exposed for sale in Potchefstroom, the auction never took place. A commando of Boers under Petrus Andries Cronje, who was later to become famous as a general, galloped up. Cronje seized Moquette, the court messenger, kicked him, saying, "Away with your government officials: we don't want you," and flung the sheriff from the wagon. The commando then drew it back to Bezuidenhout's farm. It seems possible that the object to be sold for taxes being a wagon was a psychological factor, since a wagon is a Boer's second home: a home on wheels in which he goes to hunt and worship, in which he fetches his bride from her father's house. A parallel was the stupidity of selling the children's pet cattle, which had been a contributory cause of the Great Trek. Less than any other people did the Boers live by bread alone.

The officer sent to collect the wagon came to Kruger and said, "You must admit that this is open rebellion." Every one always seemed to come to Kruger to try to get him to acknowledge that this act or that was treasonable or rebellious.

Kruger answered: "I should agree with you if we had acknowledged the annexation, but that is not the case. We do not look on ourselves as British subjects, and the question of the tax is not a private question of Beizuidenhout's, but a question of principle which concerns the whole country."

As a result of this argument, another mass meeting was held at Paardekraal on December 8, 1880, where, despite the fact that meetings had, as usual, been forbidden, it was unanimously resolved that the Boer government should resume office and call the Volksraad. A triumvirate, consisting of Paul Kruger as Vice-President, Piet Joubert as Commandant-General, and ex-President Pretorius, was appointed. The new government was set up at Heidelberg, which was easily occupied by the Boers, and here on December 16, Dingaan's Day, the Vierkleur, the flag of the Republic, was hoisted. Kruger made a speech that ended by his saying: "I desire to remind you that the cause of the country, however serious, is fully in accordance with law. The people have never departed from the way of the law. They protested after the annexation, they have resisted passively, and would probably have chosen other peaceful measures were it not that the British authority in Pretoria made this impossible. The law of nations is on our side, and however weak we may be, God is a just God. Gentlemen, may the Lord bless your labours and protect our Fatherland."

Cronje with four hundred men left for Potchefstroom, and here the first shot of the war was fired by the English who wounded a Boer named Frans Robertse in the arm. The Boers then sent a message to the British Governor of the Transvaal and appealed "to the generosity of the noble British nation" in order to recover the country in a friendly fashion. Naturally enough, the British claim that the first shot in the war was fired by a Boer. There probably is no war in which both sides have not blamed the other for the outbreak of hostilities.

The British answer was to call out local troops to suppress the revolt. Thus the War of Independence began. Because of their small numbers—there were only seven thousand Boers—the war had to be conducted with the greatest circumspection. Their plan was to isolate all the British garrisons and prevent their concentrating, while the main Boer force proceeded to the border of Natal to stop the approach of reinforcements. Another difficulty was the great shortage of ammunition. At the beginning of the war, Boers had only fifteen rounds to a man—much less than a full bandolier. This meant that the only means of obtaining more was to capture it from the British, which in turn meant, in many cases, the use of English rifles, which the Boers did not like, each man being used to his own weapon.

The engagement at Bronkhorstspruit was not the most important of the war, but it had great repercussions. Here the Ninety-Fourth Regiment of Foot, which was proceeding from Lydenburg to Pretoria, was met by a commando under Frans Joubert. He sent Colonel Anstruther a message, asking him to "return to Lydenburg, in which case no fighting need take place."

The gallant colonel replied, "I am on my way to Pretoria and I am going to Pretoria." And he was, with his band playing, his men marching in close order, their red coats criss-crossed with white belts. A few minutes later two hundred and thirty English boys—they were only that—were dead; and although Colonel Anstruther, in his dying moments—he was one of the first hit—gave Joubert his sword before he died as a present and made no reproach, this attack was later called treacherous. In fact, after the Great Boer War, Field Marshal Lord Roberts telegraphed that he "was now at Bronkhorstspruit where the British had been decimated by treachery in 1881." Joubert stated the Boer position very clearly when he said: "Now the English will, no doubt, fight to show their supremacy. But they must first kill all Boers."

The Boers on the first day of the war dispatched forces to all the British garrison towns. They were not strong enough to take them by storm, but were able to prevent the garrisons from breaking out and effecting a concentration. Pretoria was so closely invested that not till a month after the battle of Majuba did any one in the town know that it had been fought.

A Boer commando invaded Natal and occupied Laingsnek on the east side of Amajuba—the Hill of Doves—a position which General Colley decided to occupy when Colonel Deane, chief of British Intelligence, told him that the Boers had withdrawn from their position. What actually happened was that the Boers kept themselves out of sight and even allowed two British officers to go up to the Nek and make some sketches. Colley then advanced and was repulsed. Eighty-three British of all ranks were killed in this engagement and one hundred and eleven wounded. The Boers lost fourteen killed and thirty wounded.

President Brand of the Free State kept his country strictly neutral, but large detachments of Free-Staters joined under Cornelis de Villiers and reinforced the Transvaal Boers.

Colley now engaged the Boers again at Schuinshoogte, on the

banks of the Ingogo River, in a frontal attack. He had two hundred and seventy-three men of the Sixtieth Rifles, thirty-eight mounted troopers, and four field pieces. The Boers shot gunner after gunner as if they were buck. They decimated the small cavalry force and harassed the riflemen from the flanks. In this action there were sixty-six British dead and one hundred and thirty-nine wounded. The Boers had eight men killed and twenty wounded.

The British press now entered the fray with an editorial in the *Times* which said: " We are now fairly committed to a struggle which we cannot choose but carry through. The resistance of the Boers must be overcome and the insurrection put down at whatever cost. . . . There can be no terms till our military disasters have been retrieved and until the British authority has been restored over the Transvaal."

Sir Frederick Roberts, who afterwards became Lord Roberts, was sent out from England to take command and it has been suggested that Colley, hearing of this, embarked on a new offensive without waiting for reinforcements, in order to gain a striking success before Roberts arrived. At any rate, whatever the cause, Colley proceeded to occupy the top of Majuba, by a night march up its precipitous side. No subsequent reconnaissance was made, and the British were apparently unaware that, though the southern side which they had climbed was practically a cliff, the north side of the mountain was only a gentle slope. No guards were thrown out, and because of the hardness of the ground no trenches were dug.

The Boers, suddenly seeing some British soldiers silhouetted against the skyline, were almost panicked by the thought that they might have guns with them which would have blown their camp to pieces. The Boers, as was their habit, had many of their wives and children in the laager.

Piet Joubert shouted: " There are Englishmen up there now on the mountain! You must bring them down."

Smit was put in command of the attackers with Roos, Malan, and Ferriera as subordinate officers. They had two hundred burghers with them.

The Boers then proceeded to attack the mountain, but in their own fashion. Crawling on their stomachs, they moved from tuft of grass to tuft, from bush to bush, from antheap to antheap, from rock to rock—at no time exposing themselves. It took them five hours to creep up the slope, and all the time they were practically invisible from above. All that could be seen of them at the very end, when they were nearly at the top, was the upturned muzzles of their rifles.

The British, even when the Boers were in point-blank range, still had their sights set at five hundred yards. After the battle, many rifles were picked up with their sights set at this range.

At first the British were safe within the basin-like top of the mountain, with the exception of those who exposed themselves. These fell, hit at once. The British reserves were ordered to clear the slope of the enemy. In scarlet and green coats, with bayonets fixed, they disappeared over the ridge, but were driven back in a few minutes by the rapid fire of the Boers who had them silhouetted against the skyline. By now the Boers were within thirty yards of the top and still advancing. The order was given to fix bayonets for a charge, but it never carried out. The regiments became mixed up, hesitated, and broke. The only way they could run was to the cliff they had climbed the previous night. Men threw away all their equipment and leaped to their death forty and fifty feet below. General Colley, who had been the last to turn, was killed by a bullet in the back of his head.

The British losses at Majuba were ninety dead, one hundred and thirty-three wounded, and fifty-seven prisoners. The Boers had one man killed and five wounded. The casualties in the war which ended with this battle tend to prove Kruger's contention —not that the Boers were better fighters than the British, but that they knew the country and had a better method of fighting.

The defeat created a profound sensation in England. It was "a disgrace that must be wiped out." To the rest of the world it proved the valour of the Boers and established Paul Kruger as the leader of his people.

The correspondent of the *Times*, of Natal, wrote an account of the battle of Majuba and described how the Boers took the death of General Colley. He was shown the body, and asked, "Do you know him? Are you sure you know him?"

I replied, "I give you my word of honour it is General Colley."

No word of exultation passed their lips when they learnt this. I said, "You have killed the bravest gentleman on this field," and they answered, "Yes, he fought well." One man said, "He was a very nice gentleman. He dined in my house when he went to Pretoria." Another said, "He did not think we were wrong, but he was a soldier and he must obey orders." Others remarked, "It was no use fighting against men who had right on their side."

Round the dead general lay the dead and wounded, among them Commander Romilly, of the Naval Brigade, and Captain Maude, of the Fifty-Eighth Regiment.

A poem was published about the General's death in England:

> He needs no tears who in the van
> And forefront of the fight
> Met death as should a gentleman
> Upon Majuba's height.
> Critics (he's dead) will carp and hiss,
> Show how he failed, and why,
> But when they prate, bethink you this,
> "Could they like Colley die?"

The British now had a dead hero and a defeat to avenge. That they had forced a war upon a peaceful republic was a fact easily lost in the roar of public indignation. They were ready to make peace, but something new had been born in England—a hatred of the Boers.

The Boer commandos were mounted infantry who combined the qualities of Cossack irregular cavalry with those of the Virginian trappers and hunters who with their long squirrel guns stalked the British in the American forests in the Revolution. They were inspired with the same quiet fanaticism as the Americans, and were, like them, fighting a War of Independence. Their military organisation of commandos was remarkable for its democracy, and its strength lay in the free association of men from the same district under their chosen leaders. The British were as contemptuous of irregulars in Africa in 1880 as they had been in America in 1776. It was asserted that they could not stand up against regular troops. It occurred to no one that they would not have to—that they would conduct a war in the unorthodox manner of hunters shooting big game.

Mr. A. Aylward's description of a Boer camp is quoted by N. Newman in his book *With the Boers in the Transvaal.*

I shall now proceed (Aylward wrote) to describe a first view of the Boer Camp on the Nek. The generals, there were more than one, were away at the front dimly visible in the distance. The laager contained but few servants. They were in the veld with the cattle carefully watched by a mounted guard. About eight flags fluttered from wagons—these marked those belonging to commandants or field cornets; but the men themselves were off to the Nek, there being positively no one but one idler in all this vast area and he half a prisoner. After a while, there being no one to talk to but an overworked secretary who continually begged to be allowed to go to the Nek also, hunger asserted itself and a lump of flesh half-roasted on a gridiron with a biscuit soon satisfied it. There was tea and coffee too, but these did not taste as they do in other places; they had been cooked in iron kettles that were used for either indifferently. There was salt and sauce also, and there dinner began and ended. From that meal there was no further eating for eighteen hours. The bed was a wagon, and morning brought clouds, mist, and a little rain in the midst of which, accompanied by a superior officer, the party all started for the front. The general-in-chief was here found sitting on a low stool under an old wagon sail not forty yards from the centre of his position. There were three other stools in the tent and around him lay a number of able-bodied men with their guns by them. The general had a bandolier on like his men, and the unacquainted could not have, by the dress, distinguished a lance corporal from a commandant.

Silence and smoke reigned supreme. The chief was writing letters and occasionally reading reports. At noon he had breakfast —salt meat and biscuit with one cup of milkless, flavourless coffee. Then he made an inspection of his posts. It would be as well to note here that the meals were preceded and followed by fervent prayers, during which the attendant officers and soldiers were reverently attentive. It may further be noted that every act of the general's and his officers is done in public. There is neither secrecy nor privacy of any sort in camp or laager, and every burgher, however humble, is welcome to every tent or wagon to sit and smoke as he will, however high the rank of the chief he visits. There is true republicanism in the Boer camp.

The general later addressed one company of the burghers and made a most feeling speech in which he told them "what God had so manifestly done for them, and bade them work to the common end, obey their officers, take care of their horses, and prepare to face an enemy outnumbering them and having every appliance of war and every comfort that civilised organisation can procure to aid them." There was no cheering or nonsense and the men dispersed in silence, nearly all smoking. The general slept in his spurs with his bandolier on.

Long before sun-up scouts began to bring in reports. Later we could see of what stuff the Boers were composed. The outlying pickets reported the British were paraded outside their camp; cavalry mounted. It was coffee time. No orders were issued. The report was not yet confirmed, it might only mean General Wood was inspecting his men; but as the coffee was finished, every man went off to his alarm post and in three minutes the hills were defended. There was no cheering, no bragging, no looking for horses, or asking questions. Every man as he stood walked off to his post and the staff proceeded to inspect the front. Never in the face of real danger, for the valleys were misty and the enemy very formidable, have I seen such cheerful undemonstrative indifference to results. Inquiry now brought to light that there were no differences of opinion whatever among the Boer officers. They were as one man, and their intelligence, news, experience, were, as it were, common property. In the camp were many old gentlemen, veterans of both wars with the English and Kaffirs, but never have I heard a word of anger, censure, or recrimination among them. . . .

After the death of Sir George Pomeroy Colley and the battle of Majuba was over, both sides were ready to negotiate an armistice. Kruger met Sir Evelyn Wood, now in command of the English, at O'Neil's farm, half-way between the camps of the two forces. The British terms did not suit the Boers at all. Sir Evelyn wanted the Republic to be under British suzerainty, a British resident to be appointed in Pretoria, and wished to keep a portion of the Republic—the districts of Utrecht and Wakkerstrom.

After much argument, Sir Evelyn said, "Suppose we don't yield, will you go on fighting?"

Kruger answered: "That is not a fair question. If we do not yield, will you go on fighting?"

"Yes," said Sir Evelyn.

Kruger picked up his top hat. "Then we need not discuss matters further."

Sir Evelyn asked him not to be so hasty. General Smit, who had taken the heights of Majuba and was with Kruger, said, "The best thing would be to let the sword decide." The negotiations, however, continued. Sir Evelyn tried to get off with verbal promises and sent an orderly to inform his people that the armistice must be prolonged while they talked. Kruger had this man stopped. This was the question when he shouted, "Stop that man!" in English, and asked Sir Evelyn as an honest man first to sign the document on the table between them, which he refused to do until Kruger, turning to his men, said, "Burghers, saddle up!" Then Sir Evelyn signed and the orderly went off. What Kruger had feared was that if the length of the armistice had been prolonged, the British would have been able to improve their positions and bring up reinforcements.

The English did everything to disparage the Boer victory.

"How many men did you have killed at Laingsnek?" one officer asked Joubert.

"I had one and one wounded."

The officer laughed and said he had seen more men killed with his own eyes.

"Very well," said Joubert. "Do you go and dig one of them up and bring him here, and I promise you I'll eat him skin and all."

Sir Evelyn asked Kruger, "What were the two hundred men for, whom you were sending to Biggarsberg?"

"We heard you were marching there with twelve thousand."

"And you sent two hundred?"

"Yes, we had no more to send. But I have seen that it would have been enough."

Paul Kruger spent most of the war driving over the country

encouraging and exhorting the burghers. While in the Rustenburg, near his own home, he heard that the Kaffirs under Magato were assuming a threatening attitude. Accompanied by seven men, including his son Piet, Kruger went to Magato's town and found several thousand Kaffirs assembled under arms. He said, "Why did you supply the English in their camp with provisions, although I told you to preserve a strictly neutral attitude in this war which is a war between white men?"

Magato replied that he had received a message from the English saying that they had taken Heidelberg, and that "if I did not obey their orders they would punish me."

The warriors now closed in about their chief and raised their spears. But Piet van der Walt, one of Kruger's men, placed himself next to Magato and said he would shoot him if any harm came to Kruger. The Kaffirs then gave in, and Kruger pointed out to them the error of their ways, which presumably was interfering in a "white man's private war." He then asked Magato for a couple of horses, as he had to get back to Heidelberg at once.

The chief said: "I cannot give you the horses, for if I did the English would know of it to-morrow. But repeat your request in the presence of my people. Then I will refuse and then you must say, 'Very well, then I will take them by force if you will not give them to me.' Then I shall say in my heart it is good, but I shall refuse with my mouth."

Kruger left with two good horses.

After the war the blood of all concerned was up. The Boers, flushed with victory, more than ever convinced that God had been on their side in their fight for justice; and the English furious at having been beaten by a handful of sharp-shooting farmers.

Even the final negotiations almost fell through because the English insisted on calling the South African Republic the Transvaal State. The British Resident came to complain to Kruger about this matter, saying, "The name of the country is the Transvaal State and not the South African Republic."

"How do you prove that?" Kruger asked.

"Why," Hudson said, "by the convention which clearly says the Transvaal State."

"Very well," Kruger answered. "If I sell you a farm and in the deed of sale I say, 'I, Paul Kruger, the vendor,' and so on, then in what follows I am no longer Paul Kruger, but the Vendor, but Vendor is not my name. Even so in this case. In the convention, just as in drawing up a deed, the Republic is referred to as the Transvaal State, but that does not make it her real name, but only her specification. Her real name is and remains the South African Republic."

On the eighth of August the Volksraad met. The country was restored in due form and the Vierkleur flew again. "The dear Vierkleur," Kruger called it. Dear to him and his folk. Dear as the Union Jack to Rhodes.

Why do men fight for a flag? Die for it? Why do they risk their lives for a standard—to save their own or to capture that of an enemy? Through history this has happened equally to the eagles of ancient Rome and the eagles of Napoleon. Equally to the English, the Americans, the French, and the Boers.

In the lives of Rhodes, Kruger, and Lobengula flags play a prominent part. Even recently in South Africa in 1926 there was almost trouble about "the flag question," and many English-speaking people in the Union are still dissatisfied with the small size of the Union Jack that was finally superimposed on the flag.

Rhodes, being what he was, was much concerned with flags, since he was concerned with England—England to him being those places, and the more of them the better, where the Union Jack floated, or more often hung listless in tropic airs of that Empire on which the sun never sets. He thought in terms of maps, or colours, of colouring maps red—of flags. Of the Union Jack which combines the red cross of Saint George on a white ground with the white diagonal cross of Saint Andrew on a blue ground and the red diagonal cross of Saint Patrick on a white ground.

Kruger, too, thought of a flag—the sacred Vierkleur of the South African Republic. This flag had a green vertical stripe nearest the staff and three horizontal stripes of red, white, and blue.

Lobengula did not think of flags except to hate them. Flags to him were the mark of white ownership. Only once did he use one—the white one carried by his emissaries when he was defeated.

His flags were the plumes of his impis, were their oxhide shields and the blue smoke haze of the burning kraals of his enemies.

Flags hung out in triumph, flags insulted and dragged in the dust, flags thrown over corpses, tattered standards in great halls, flags blessed for war by princes of the Church, flags embroidered by women for their lovers, flags emblazoned with the battle honours of ancient regiments; flags associated with the joy of victory, with the horror of defeat, with the birth of kings, the death of heroes, with marriages;—flags born of other older symbols, tabernacles of the Lord God, a strange link between religion, the heraldic devices of chivalry, and the arrogance of a church or nation militant. The shirt flag of distress, the signal flags flown from the full-rigged ships of the line at Trafalgar; and always the white flag of surrender and the symbolic striking of the colours. Why must a flag not fly by night? Why must it be housed in a holy place? Why must men stand bare-headed when it passes? The Union Jack, Old Glory, the Tricolour of France, the Vierkleur of South Africa—the ancient, royal golden lilies of France, the lion of Scotland—what is their meaning? Whence do they come? How long must they, as a form of witchcraft, be endured? For they cause an inflammation to the blood of men; they are martial music to their eyes as the bands of brass are to their ears, and the tramp of men and horses—the wild neighing of the war horses or the rattle of the passing tanks in review. The old men who have served under them stand with tears in their eyes as the flags pass. The young men's eyes are inflamed with blood.

Kruger had much trouble with flags, with the desecration of his own and insults from that of his enemies. The second time he went to Johannesburg—he seldom went there, considering it a Sodom and Gomorrah—the mob, annoyed by the collapse of the stock market, attacked his house, pulling down the railings, and trampled upon his flag—the Transvaal flag. Another time when driving in Pretoria with Rhodes a Union Jack was allowed to fall upon him and envelop him.

In 1896, the Johannesburg Reformers, who should have helped Jameson in his Raid, could come to no agreement about the flag. The best suggestion they could think of was to fly the Transvaal flag upside down: this they felt indicated their spirit of reform and did not commit them to England. They did not want the law and order that England might introduce. Disorder and greater profit was what they wanted. They would certainly have accepted greater disorder if greater profits could have accompanied them. Annexation or Independence—of these the flag was the outward and visible sign, the emblem of authority or rebellion.

CHAPTER EIGHT

THE GIANTS MEET

THE foundamental question of South Africa in those days after the War of Independence was, as it is to some extent to-day, how best the English and the Dutch should get along together. The other question which concerned both the English and Dutch was, what has now come to be called the "native problem," but which was then at a simpler stage: merely the matter of native wars, or, if you lived on the frontier, of survival.

Kruger's first speech in the Volksraad was taken up with discussions of ways and means. He said, "Extraordinary circumstances demanded extraordinary measures." Among the extraordinary circumstances was the fact that the Republic was broke and had to plan some ways of meeting her liabilities. There were liabilities to England contracted before the annexation, there were claims for war damages, there was the widows' and orphans' fund which showed a large deficit instead of a credit, and this was the main point of the problem—the Boers had the greatest objection to paying taxes of any sort, and it was almost impossible to collect anything from them. This left the Uitlanders, the strangers, who were even more unwilling to pay.

Then a brilliant idea occurred to someone—that of monopolies. Monopolies for dynamite, for brewing liquor, for selling gunpowder. Concessions, they called them; and the concession habit spread over the land. Umbandine, the Swazi king, gave away, for a consideration naturally, concessions for everything in his little kingdom—even the concession "to grant concessions." It was impossible for the Triumvirate to realise with their limited education the pitfall into which they had fallen by making use of this financial device. All they knew was that by such a measure the burghers were placated, that the men who received the concessions paid for them in cash and taxes which were easy to collect. As Kruger said, "One hundred pounds was nothing if one had it: if one had nothing, a penny was too much." And the Boers were penniless.

It was impossible for the Boer leaders to recognise the relationship between monopolies and personal incentive, or to realise that this facile measure, which relieved their immediate troubles, would stifle the advancement of the country and form, in later years, the principal grievance of the Uitlanders who were exploited by the concessionaires. Nor did they then see that their own people and officials would be subjected to bribery, which, beginning with free trips to the brothels of Johannesburg and gifts of the new American four-wheel spiders which were made by Studebaker, would end in far greater bribes in cash and kind. How could Kruger and his associates have known all this? There was little in the Bible about economics which could help them.

The next thing the government did was to raise a force of artillerymen. The Boers were all soldiers—irregular mounted infantry of the best kind; but the War of Independence had shown the necessity of having gunners, which meant full-time, long-service soldiers. This force was now recruited, and remained, for as long as the Republic lasted, an élite corps and the pride of Kruger's life. The formation of this corps was obviously a war measure. Certainly artillery was not needed against the Kaffirs. So, if there was peace, war was still in the air.

The next object of the government was a railway, the Delagoa Bay, which President Burgers had tried to inaugurate. In his time the idea of a railroad had been considered impious and contrary to the will of God, who presumably, had He wanted railways, would have created them. But now evil had to be compromised with, and the lesser evil accepted to offset the greater.

This, too, was a war measure, for there would have been little difficulty in linking the North with the Cape, at least as far as finding money to finance the scheme was concerned in the City of London. This railway, which was completed in 1895, gave the South African Republic an outlet to the sea, but one which ran through Portuguese territory. It was something, but not enough. Kruger had hoped for more, an actual Transvaal seaboard, and these hopes were not blasted till, at the urgent representation of Loch, Lord Rosebery annexed Tongaland. When the Union Jack was run up at Kosi Bay, Kruger's dream had vanished, and the South African Republic was truly encircled. Manfred Nathan, in his life of Kruger, says: "There was something Machiavellian in all this. The various conventions, most of which gave the Transvaal a conditional right to construct a line to Kosi Bay, had been dangled under Kruger's nose. And Loch, in whom he had put his trust, had outwitted him."

This, however, is looking ahead. By the time the country's finances had been put in some sort of order by this arrangement of concessions, the railway to Delagoa Bay had been authorised and the Staats Artillery enrolled, native trouble broke out again. Not with Sekukuni, who had been brought to terms, but with his assassins.

Sekukuni, who had been imprisoned, had been released and had returned to his mountain home to live at peace with every one; but in 1882 he, his son, and thirteen followers were killed by a sub-chief named Mampoer, who was his half-brother. The Republic, to maintain order in the Lydenburg District, had to call up a commando. Mampoer fled to seek protection of another chief, Njabel, who was called Mapoch by the Boers. Actually he was the son of Mapoch. Piet Joubert went into action with another commando. Mapoch sent a herald with a white ox to inquire the peace terms, which were unconditional surrender; whereupon Mapoch hid in the caves of the mountains with his tribe, from which it took four thousand Boers to dislodge him, and which they succeeded in doing only by the old method of blockade.

In the meantime people began to want a president instead of a triumvirate to rule them, and it was decided that an election should be held in January, 1883. Kruger and Joubert were the candidates.

There was never any question of policy or difference in programme between them. Both men were the best Africa could produce, both soldiers and leaders, men whose ends were the same, and whose means to accomplish those ends were the same. The voting was just a matter of taste. A man was for Kruger or he was a Joubert man, and that was the end of it. The only argument was which candidate he liked best and preferred to follow. Some liked Joubert's hot, uncompromising temper; others liked the motto Kruger was always quoting: "Be faithful but trust no one." They liked, too, his statement: "In matters of state, as otherwise,

I rest on the eternal principles of God's Word." This was a hard platform to refute.

Physically the two men differed. Joubert was better set up with square shoulders and alert face, but his voice was high and reedy compared to Kruger's bellow, and his figure, though handsome, lacked the power of Kruger's with his barrel chest. Joubert's glance, though it was alert and clear, did not have the penetration of Kruger's savage, half-closed eyes. Paul Kruger was a bull of a man—massive, who moved slowly with his head half-lowered as though ready to charge. His limp, his missing thumb, the heavy flesh which had superimposed itself on the heavier muscle, made him, to a people convinced that more trouble was to come, the best bet; and they bet on him two to one.

As to the troubles, a man did not have to be a prophet to see them. Money was the first of them. The Uitlanders had to be curbed. The method of achieving this was an obvious one—five years' residence before a stranger could become a burgher and a payment of twenty-five pounds. Had Kruger welcomed the emigrants as the United States did after the American Civil War, it seems probable that they would have become loyal citizens of their new home. But Kruger was afraid of them—of being swamped by them.

In 1885 there was nothing Dutch except the names of the streets in Johannesburg. There were, in the whole Transvaal, at this time according to Kruger, eighty thousand foreigners who outnumbered the burghers four to one. Johannesburg was English-speaking, its social character English. In 1888, to jump forward a few years, Kruger addressed a meeting in Johannesburg: "People of the Lord, you old people of the country, you foreigners, you newcomers, yea, even you thieves and murderers . . ." This was his true opinion of the foreigners—thieves and murderers— though when the Uitlanders complained, he said he meant that all should humble themselves before the Lord, even thieves and murderers, were they any such at the meeting.

If any insult was conveyed in these words, he writes, "it applied just as much to the old as to the new population, as any sensible person who took the trouble to follow my train of thought would have perceived for himself."

The cap, however, did fit at least some of the Uitlanders, and it is hard to blame Kruger, since at this time the missionary, Moffat—another of them—was, at Rhodes's instigation, in Matabeleland persuading Lobengula to reject any dealings with the Transvaal and make a treaty with England against all other powers.

In fact, the term murderer was probably meant by Kruger, for he was certain that his emissary, Piet Grobler, had been intercepted and killed on Rhodes's orders. But the bull whom so many said Kruger resembled was brave and strong and cunning, but unable, when he preached—and most of his speeches read in part at least as sermons—to refrain from bringing in the damnation and hellfire angle.

Here is Kruger's version of this incident, written in 1888, when he had been re-elected as President for a second term, again running against and defeating his old opponent Joubert: "At this time Matabeleland and Mashonaland to the north of the Transvaal were governed by the Zulu chief Lobengula, the son of Moselikatze, who had been driven out by the earlier settlers. But Moselikatze, the once so hated and cruel enemy of the Boers, had in later years entered into friendly relations with the Republic and this friendship continued with his son. Lobengula was on very good terms with the Boers and often came into contact with the burghers of the Republic who hunted in his territories. In 1887 he sent one of his principal indunas to Pretoria with the request that the South African Republic should appoint a consul to his domains."

Piet Grobler, who knew the country well, was appointed, and before he left to take up his position Kruger drafted a treaty by which Lobengula placed his country under the protection of the Republic. On his arrival at Bulawayo—the famous "Place of Killing"—he read the document to Lobengula, who agreed to it, but asked for a few days to summon his indunas, as it was necessary by Kaffir law to ask their opinion before signing the treaty.

Grobler decided to make use of the delay to go to meet his wife, who was on her way up to join him and who, according to his calculations, should have just crossed the Crocodile River. On the way he met a patrol of Khamas's Kaffirs who were at war with Lobengula. He rode straight up to them to ask what they wanted, but they took flight. He galloped after them and told them to fetch their captain so that he might hear what their object was. Grobler then left his wagon and went on to meet the main body of the Kaffirs, who opened fire on him. While running back, he was hit, and a young Kaffir girl called Lottering ran up and placed herself between the wounded man and Khamas's men so as to cover him with her own body. Grobler's men then opened fire. He had five men with him and they put the enemy to flight. Grobler was put on the wagon and the journey south continued, but he died the day he reached the river and met his wife. "There is no doubt whatever," Kruger goes on, "that this murder was due to the instigation of Cecil Rhodes and his clique. It was Rhodes's object to obtain possession of the African interior and he was afraid lest his plans be frustrated by Grobler's appointment. . . . Cecil Rhodes is the man who bore by far the most important part of the disaster that struck the country. In spite of the high eulogiums passed on him by his friends, he was one of the most unscrupulous characters that have ever existed. The jesuitical maxim that the end justifies the means formed his own political creed. This man was the curse of Africa."

In the early days of Kruger's presidency, Rhodes tried to get him as an ally and on his way from Beira to the Cape called on him at Pretoria. "We must work together," he said. "I know the Republic wants a seaport: you must have Delagoa Bay."

Kruger answered: "How can we work together there? The harbour belongs to the Portuguese and they won't hand it over."

"Then we must simply take it," Rhodes said.

"I can't take away other people's property," Kruger said. "If the Portuguese won't sell the harbour, I wouldn't take it even if you gave it to me, for ill-gotten gains are accursed."

It would seem probable that Rhodes would have encouraged the Boers to take over Portuguese East Africa and then have seized the opportunity, in the international disorder created by this incident, to strike on his own—with a new annexation of some kind, probably under a different name, since the word "annexation" stank now—which would have brought both the Transvaal and Portuguese East Africa into the British orbit. This is pure hypothesis, but would fit in with Rhodes's character, since there could be no good reason for him to want the Boer Republics to extend their influence for their own good alone.

In 1883 there was much discussion in the Volksraad about the meaning and effect of the Convention of Pretoria. The members did not like it. They did not like the idea of English suzerainty. They did not like the idea of being unable to make foreign treaties without the consent of the British government. They did not like the question of the western border line not being settled, and decided to send another deputation, headed by the President, to England. The new Colonial Secretary in London, Lord Derby, agreed to reopen the discussion, and Kruger, accompanied by the Reverend du Toit and General Smit, sailed on the *Roslin Castle*, October 10—the President's birthday.

Kruger passed his time on board "with a bag of Transvaal tobacco by his side, and the pipe very rarely leaving his lips, reading a Bible printed in double columns, Dutch and English, by which novel method he hoped to learn the English language. But the task did not seem very agreeable to him, his studies were interrupted by long pauses, and evidently it was a relief to him when one of the passengers seated himself next to him and entered into conversation. These studies by means of the bilingual Bible bore no fruit. If the number of English words in the vocabulary of Paul Kruger exceeded two—Yes and No—then it must be admitted that he kept the secret with conspicuous success." This does not jibe with his use of the words, "Stop that man," at the peace negotiations. The most likely explanation is that he understood English, but would not speak it.

To give an idea of the finances of the country: When Kruger had drawn a cheque on the Standard Bank for two thousand pounds to cover expenses for the trip, there were only four hundred left with which to carry on the affairs of State.

On their arrival in England, the delegation stated its case: "We had been fully independent when we had been annexed by force: we had freed ourselves from subjection with our weapons in our hands: England had been magnanimous, and had given back to us nearly everything we had possessed before 1877, but had unjustly retained a sort of suzerainty." Kruger pointed out that by the Sand River Convention of 1852, in which he had played a part as a young man, the Republic had a right to her independence which had been unjustly taken from her and which had not been restored to her in 1881 in the way in which they had been verbally promised that it would be.

Lord Derby acknowledged that there was some justice in the Boers' claim and proceeded to entertain them while the negotiations went on. Kruger went to dine at Windsor, and it is said that when after dinner he poured his coffee into his saucer to cool it, the Queen also drank from her saucer.

But if the delegates were received in a friendly fashion by some people, there were others who were working against them. Sir Robert Fowler, the Lord Mayor of London, at a great meeting protested against the Boers' treatment of the natives and demanded that the government have nothing to do with their claim for the rectification of their western border. The Reverend John Mackenzie cropped up again in defence of the natives. Bechuana chiefs were made to appear paragons of virtue, and the question of enslavement of natives by the Boers was brought up once more. How much of this was a genuine feeling of philanthropy for the Kaffirs and how much was merely an anti-Gladstone demonstration will never be known. And, added to these politicians and missionaries, was the clamour of those who hated the Boers and wanted revenge for Majuba. The old cry that had been heard so often before all over the world, and was to be heard so often again: Revenge—revenge for Adowa in Italy, for Sedan in France. Flags waved. There were cries about national honour.

But at last the Convention of London was signed: oddly enough, on the anniversary of Majuba, February 27, 1884. These anniversaries seem to occur continually in history—a day or a place becomes a psychological and emotional factor. But it had not been all smooth going. At one point, when talking to the Colonial Secretary, Kruger lost his temper and picked up his hat.

"Tell him," he said to du Toit, "we have hammered the British out of the Transvaal once and will do it again."

Another time during the negotiations, Kruger wrote: "Sir Hercules Robinson and I had the misfortune to come into collision. I was pointing out and insisting that certain farms, among others Polfontein and Rietfontein, should come within the boundaries of the Republic, especially as they had formerly belonged to us.

While I made this statement, Sir Hercules Robinson, who was present, whispered to Lord Derby, "It's a lie." I jumped up quite prepared to fall upon Sir Hercules. Lord Derby and the other gentlemen interfered, and Lord Derby said, 'Gentlemen, are you going to fight?' I answered that I had been insulted, but Sir Hercules apologised, saying no offence was meant. Despite this," Kruger goes on, "Sir Hercules and I afterwards became very good friends and remained so until his death. He was an honourable man and a gentleman in the best sense of the word."

The old lion Kruger was not a man to be baited, even in a drawing-room. But his argument about farms, that he knew and had probably hunted over, must have seemed strange to a statesman who handled great affairs in serene objective ignorance. This man with whom he argued was Oom Paul, the uncle of his people, the lover of his land, ready to fight for its name, for every dry spruit and every barren kopje.

However, considering the recent war and the high tempers of the time, things went reasonably well. One thing at least was made clear, and this again was merely a point of honour: the name South African Republic was finally and fully restored to the Transvaal State.

What Kruger thought of his success is best put in his own words. This is what he told the meeting at Paarl on his return: "At the annexation, England took away twenty shillings in the pound from the Transvaal: by the Convention of Pretoria it had returned ten shillings: and now by the Convention of London it had paid another five shillings: but in any event it still owed the Republic five shillings."

Joubert expressed the same idea differently when he said, "It is better to have half an egg than an empty shell."

On leaving England, Kruger went as he had the last time, to the Continent, where he succeeded in raising privately a loan for his Delagoa Bay railway project, to which end the Netherlands South African Railway Company was formed.

Speaking in Holland he said: "We are the lost tribes of parents left by you in the Cape Colony who settled among strangers, but who have preserved all that may remind us of our forefathers ... and if people now say, 'You want to go further and are seeking expansion,' I answer, 'People have undressed me, people have taken away all my clothes: my underwear and my trousers have been returned to me; but where is my jacket?'"

In Germany, wearing his top hat and sash of office, Kruger met Kaiser William I., and Bismarck, the man of blood and iron. They understood each other well, since Bismarck, a North German, spoke Platt-Deutsch which resembled the Taal of South Africa even more than the high Dutch of Holland. It was at this meeting that Prince Bismarck stumbled on the steps of the palace, and the Emperor said, "Prince, you are growing old." Bismarck answered, "Your Majesty, that is usually the case, that the horse grows old before his rider."

Belgium, France, Spain, and Portugal were also visited.

But in Africa, both before and after the Convention of London, there was trouble on the western border of the Republic. Like most other troubles it has its roots in the past. For many years neither Moshette and Montsioa, who headed the Baralongs, Mankoroane, chief of the Batlapins, or Massouw, chief of a mixed race of Korannas and Bushmen, could come to terms about their respective boundaries. And though these chiefs took no part in the War of Independence, they favoured opposite sides. Montsioa called himself an Englishman while Moshette was pro-Boer. After the war, one of Montsioa's sub-chiefs, Machabi, went over to Moshette.

Montsioa, with the help of some English settlers, attacked Machabi. Moshette sent a force to protect him and was attacked by Montsioa. There were several inconclusive fights which both sides claimed as victories. Moshette then attacked Montsioa, who was helped by Mankoroane, while Massouw helped Moshette. The chiefs now enlisted more European help and promised the white men land as a reward. The English volunteers were jailbirds like Scotty Smith and renegades like Commander Bethell who had married a Baralong woman. The Boers helped Massouw. The white men on both sides were called Filibusters. The border now became a sort of Tom Tiddler's ground filled with warring Kaffirs and the scum of Europe—discharged and deserting soldiers, Dutch burghers from the Transvaal, the Cape Colony, and Free State whom neither the British nor South African Republics could control.

The Filibusters immediately began to farm the land granted .

them, and since they came under the jurisdiction of neither the English nor the Boers, formed governments of their own. One community, calling itself the Republic of Stellaland with Vryburg its capital, elected a Volksraad and a President and settled down to govern itself in an orderly fashion. Another lot of Boers proclaimed another republic—The Land of Goshen. This was not well governed and was described by Sir Hercules Robinson as the "Robber Republic."

These were, it might be thought, ridiculous parochial affairs—Kaffir wars in which disorderly white men fought for land, loot, and in some cases for native women. But it is unlikely that the new inhabitants of these little states saw themselves as anything but adventuring farmers—pioneers who had staked claims in a land hitherto unclaimed by white men.

There was, however, another side to the picture and other men about to enter it. It was clear to the British, thanks to the influence of the Reverend John Mackenzie, Sir Hercules Robinson, and Cecil Rhodes—now in the Cape Parliament—that if the Boer government was not checked, it would finally stretch westward and embrace Bechuanaland and the Kalahari. The Boers were also raiding into Zululand. They were in fact expanding in all directions; and if they went far enough would reach both the eastern sea-coast and the deserts of the West.

Bechuanaland, Rhodes, who had his eye on the North, called "the neck of the bottle and the Suez Canal of the trade of the country," since only by this route could trade with the Zambesi and the North be maintained free from Boer interference. If Bechuanaland were lost, there would be an end of British development in South Africa. Lord Derby was roused to putting pressure on the Cape Parliament, which despite his efforts remained apathetic, and whose only action was to send Parson Mackenzie to act as Resident Commissioner in Bechuanaland. He was an ardent imperialist, pro-native and anti-Boer, and, wishing to forestall annexation by the Cape, proclaimed a British protectorate over the territory of Montsioa who at that time was fighting the Goshenites with some success. To do this, Mackenzie raised a corps of mounted police and hoisted the Union Jack at Vryburg in Stellaland.

This annoyed everybody—both the annexationists in Cape

Town and Pretoria and the Dutch farmers in Stellaland whose land titles, which had been acknowledged by the South African Republic, were jeopardised.

Rhodes appealed to the Cape Parliament. "We must not have the imperial factor in Bechuanaland," he declared. To have had this would have ruined his plans, since at this time he was playing both ends against the middle in an effort to bring the British and Dutch together. Rhodes the imperialist was very much against imperialism that he did not control. The methods of the Colonial Office were too slow for him: the machinery too ponderous for even his manipulations. The Cape Parliament at his instigation then sent him up to supersede Mackenzie. Rhodes met the Stellalanders at Commando Drift and persuaded them—he was a very persuasive man—to accept a British protectorate by guaranteeing their titles.

Rhodes's first act had been to go and see van Niekerk, the administrator of Stellaland, with whom he had been able to negotiate before, but van Niekerk's lieutenant, big Adriaan de la Rey, would have nothing to do with any negotiations. "Blood must flow!" he shouted.

"Give me breakfast," Rhodes said, "then we can talk about blood." There was no blood after breakfast. Instead Rhodes stayed with de la Rey a week, became godfather to his grandchild and made a settlement whose chief feature was the cancellation of everything done by his predecessor, Mackenzie.

In Goshen he had no success because Kruger had already annexed it. This annexation was denounced as a breach of the London Convention and Kruger had to withdraw his claims.

But other powers were on the move too. Germany had in 1884 proclaimed a protectorate over Namaqualand and Damaraland and was arousing fears lest she might, by joining hands with the Transvaalers and Portuguese in East Africa, cut the Cape off from the interior. The withdrawal of Kruger's claims had small effect on the burghers of the Robber Republic of Goshenland and a force of four thousand men under Sir Charles Warren was sent north with orders to drive the freebooters out of Bechuanaland, to restore the frontiers, and to take measures which would prevent further plundering. Warren asked Mackenzie to accompany him. He had no desire to meet Rhodes, who he thought had been weak in coming to an agreement with Stellalanders. On the other hand, Sir Hercules Robinson, the High Commissioner, who placed much reliance on Rhodes, insisted on their meeting. There was a general desire, mitigated only by the General's hope of distinguishing himself in some military operation, to arrive at an amicable agreement.

A meeting between Warren and President Kruger was, therefore, arranged and took place at Fourteen Streams. This was the first occasion on which Kruger and Rhodes, who was also present, had met. That Mackenzie was there did not help matters, for his hatred of the Boers was only equalled by their dislike of him. Nor did things go very well. Kruger upset Sir Charles Warren, whose men had not yet fired a shot, by suggesting that it "seemed unnecessary to send four thousand men and a great general to drive out fifty." He then addressed the people, telling them to make no disturbance. "Do not blow upon the fire," Kruger said. The President knew very well that the ashes of the old war were not yet cold. He told Warren to "arrest all wrong-doers and bring them before the courts. I will do likewise." There was further friction about the respective retinues. Warren had with him a bodyguard of skirmishers and scouts. Kruger also had an escort —forty of his newly raised artillerymen—as a guard of honour, though he only brought twenty-five with him to the actual meeting. This was his answer to Warren's question as to why he had come "with an armed party." There is no record about what either Rhodes or Kruger thought of each other on this their first meeting, except that Kruger said, "This young man will give me trouble." Oddly enough, Disraeli had said much the same thing about Kruger when he was in England, describing him as an "ugly customer."

Kruger writes: "This conference had no result except an agreement that each side should nominate a commission to mark off the frontier line as fixed by the Convention and that President Brand should arbitrate in case of disagreements. Rhodes pretended to be on my side in the business. On the other hand, he tried to abuse Joubert until I pointed out to him that he was attacking an absent man. The Commissioners now finally fixed the western frontier. I myself had proposed to settle the matter once and for all by ordering the mounted commando, together with the police and a few burghers who had accompanied me, to ride round the frontier. The ground marked by the horses' hoofs would make a capital frontier line. Warren, however, refused his consent to the proposal, giving as excuse his fears lest it might lead to a hand-to-hand fight between his force and the burghers." It is easy to imagine the shocked disgust of the General at such a simple solution to a problem. That was not the way things should be done. It was not neat, nor tidy, or in order, to ride off a boundary of a country as if it were a farm.

Things did not go well at Fourteen Streams, with Warren's personal guard of two hundred dragoons clanking about with their sabres trailing in the sandy veld; with Parson Mackenzie—the very missionary of missionaries—there to remind the Boers of what they had suffered at his hands. As Sarah Gertrude Millin writes of Warren, "He might as well have brought Satan."

The real trouble grew out of the atmosphere being so military. Warren's authority allowed him to make terms, and acting on Mackenzie's advice he declared martial law over all Bechuanaland, charged Rhodes's friend van Niekerk, the administrator of Stellaland, with murder and disowned all Rhodes's promises. Rhodes protested in vain that he "could govern Stellaland with ten policemen." Warren told Rhodes not to have political discussions with people in this country and proceeded to march on Goshen only to find that the territory had been evacuated by the freebooters. Rhodes resigned, but the result of Warren's work raised such a fury against England that he had to be recalled.

Speaking of his resignation of his deputy commissionership of Bechuanaland, Rhodes said: "I remember when a youngster reading in my English history of the supremacy of my country and its annexations that there were only two cardinal axioms: ' That the word of the nation when once pledged must never be broken and that when a man accepted the citizenship of the British Empire there was no distinction of races.' It has been my misfortune in one year to meet with the breach of one and the proposed breach of the other."

This is the picture of Rhodes, the young administrator, anxious about British prestige, ready on the mounting wave of his power to compromise with any one, and, as yet, unaware of the fundamental differences between "Boer and Briton"—it being inconceivable to him that there should be any doubt in the mind of reasonable men of the advantage to be gained by the absorption of their country by the British. In his mind he probably regarded both President Burgers and Kruger as traitors, since they had been born in the Cape Colony under the British flag. Then, as always, Rhodes underestimated the Boers and placed too much confidence in the British renegades who lived in the Transvaal and trimmed their sails to suit winds of their own interests. When Shepstone had annexed the Transvaal, these men had taken the horses out of his carriage and dragged it to the house where he was to stay. They had been rewarded with champagne and cigars. Champagne and cigars and the handclasps of the great were then, as now, political factors. But their effects are not enduring, and it was men of the same type who in Johannesburg only a few years later avoided fighting with Jameson in the outbreak which they themselves had staged, and by so doing destroyed Rhodes and his grandiose plans of African unity.

It seems likely that when Rhodes made overtures to Kruger, he meant friendship, though naturally that friendship would have been to the British benefit. It would also, over a period of time, have been of benefit to the Boers as well; but Kruger could not see it that way. In the light of his past, this is not surprising. To him the British were Mammon, and to compromise with them was to compromise with evil and would end the day of ruling by God's law and the customs of the Boer people. A relatively modern parallel of the Boer attitude is to be found in that of the Arab Prince Abdul Aziz Ibn Saud, whom the British approached in the First World War, hoping to get him to lead a revolt against the Turks. His attitude, according to van Paasen, was "to keep the Arab world untouched by all modern progress and unsullied from contact with the Christian infidels." It has been said that if Kruger had taken Rhodes's hand in 1894 the history of South Africa would have been different, but this is merely another of those *Ifs* in history. Piet Joubert, the Boer general who fought so well for freedom, was for amicable co-operation between the Republic and the Cape Colony and was attacked on this basis in the Raad. A "Rhodesgesind"—a Rhodes partisan—they called him. This he certainly was not. He was a patriot who saw into the future, and his dying words were, "My poor country, what it might have been!" But the diehards—and that for the Boers is an apt expression—could think of nothing but their country and their freedom. Kruger expressed them, not only as their elected President, but as an individual. He epitomised their beliefs and hopes, he thought their thoughts; down to the smallest detail he lived their lives. Of the Boers he was the most steadfast, a man with all the Boer virtues and all the Boer defects.

The American visitor to Africa, Poulteney Bigelow, gives a good description of him. He said: "Kruger is unique. There is no man of modern times with whom he can be compared. We must go back to mythical days to find his parallel. Kruger is the incarnation of local self-government in its purest form. He is President among his burghers by the same title that he is elder in his church. He makes no pretence to rule them by invoking the law, but he does rule them by reasoning with them until they yield to his superiority in argument. He rules among free burghers because he knows them well and they know him well. There is no red tape, nor pigeon-holes. His door is open to every comer; his memory recalls every farm, he listens to every complaint, and he sits in patriarchal court from six o'clock in the morning till bedtime. He is a magnificent anachronism. . . . At this time Kruger's beard was white, and though probably still capable of feats of herculean strength such as he had performed in young manhood, he was no longer as alert and nimble in the physical sense as he had been of yore. He had many little ailments probably due to lack of exercise, though some attribute this to the fact that like many of his fellow countrymen he was a great meat-eater. It was of meat, bread, and milk that his ordinary diet consisted. Luxuries he eschewed or they were unknown to him."

If the history of Africa were a film being projected upon a silver screen; if time, a hundred years or so, could be run off in a few hours; if we, the sons and grandsons of the players, could put ourselves in their position; or they, our ancestors, could take our place in the audience, the approaching climax would be apparent. The build-up of pageantry is over. The first reels, exciting enough, of savages and beasts, of treks and bickerings, are over. The past is over. Now, we should feel, this is modern, this is contemporary—the story of gold, diamonds, power, politics, and intrigue. The tempo has changed. Kruger is getting old. Rhodes is forcing the pace. Lobengula is sore afraid. Kruger has accused Rhodes of the political murder of Grobler, his agent to the Matabele. A war has been fought and won against the British: a defeat that rankles in the English heart. The temporary annexation of the South African Republic is still an unscabbed Boer wound. The Kaffirs are uneasy, sensing, as animals might, the great struggle. The young men whet their spears. The Uitlanders are eager for greater gains and authority, wanting dual nationality, so that reaping advantage from two nations they can evade the responsibilities of either. Rhodes and Kruger, the great Boer and the great Englishman, have met, and have parted in distrust: Rhodes contemptuous of the rustic Kruger; Kruger certain that "Mr. Rhodes is just as loyal to his country as I am to mine: but you can't come to an agreement with a man who never goes to church."

CHAPTER NINE

THE GATHERING OF THE EAGLES

THE GERMAN EAGLE was now stretching its wings; the Gallic cock was dead—at least temporarily—and the British lion, which had growled under Disraeli, purred in Gladstonian domestication. "Deutschland über Alles" was becoming more than a song. It was becoming a belief.

The lectures of Stanley, the visits of Kruger, the stories of gold and diamonds, had excited Europe to such an extent that Bismarck, who had just finished forging the German states into a solid body, was forced to abandon his idea of isolation and look to the formation of an overseas empire. Leopold, King of the Belgians, was about to reach out the itching hand that was to decimate, by murder, the natives of the Congo. German missionaries were asking for protection which the English would not give them on the West Coast, while on the East, Karl Peters was collecting the concessions which he took home to peddle. The general feeling in Europe, the tendency of the times, was a sort of tumescence which was to end with the rape of Africa.

The first German move took place in 1883 when a Bremen merchant, Franz Adolph Luderitz, purchased land from a chief between the Orange and Little Fish Rivers on the coast of South-West Africa and decided to establish a factory there.

His government desired to know if Her Majesty's Government exercised any authority in that locality and would afford him protection in case of need. If not, Germany would extend to the factory the same measure of protection as she gave to her subjects in other remote parts of the world—"but without the least design to establish a footing in Africa." Lord Granville replied that he must consult the Cape Parliament, which showed no disposition to occupy any territory south of Walfisch Bay.

Neither the denials—we knew less of them then—of the German diplomats, nor the appeals for protection by German missionaries, most of whom were also geologists and explorers, created any suspicion in England. For a quarter of a century the German missionaries in Namaqualand had made repeated complaints of ill-treatment by the natives. Very few people took the colonial movement of Germany seriously. Luderitz, now assured of his government's backing, sent a ship to Angra Pequena and concluded, through his agent, a treaty with an old native chief called Frederick. For two thousand marks and some old muskets he obtained sovereign rights to two hundred and fifteen square miles of land and the ten miles of sea frontage which still bears his name. Next day, the first of May, 1883, the German flag was hoisted for the first time in a German colony, and in October a German gunboat took up her station there.

In 1870 *Harper's Magazine* in America published a cartoon of a woman, Europa, carrying a child on her back. The child wore a spiked helmet—a pikelhaube. The caption was "The Man of the Future." Here, at Luderitz Bay thirteen years later, we behold him, an adolescent, on the quarterdeck of his little gunboat.

Karl Mauch's reports of gold deposits were pulled out of their pigeon-holes in Berlin. The co-ordination of all such knowledge was begun, the foundation of Geopolitik laid, and German tourists began to look for world markets and, oddly, when they found nice places, *in remote parts* of the world, to settle in them. England, showing signs of that decadence which culminated at Munich in 1938 and was only ended over the English skies in 1940, sent a warship, H.M.S. *Boadicea*, to uphold the rights of British concessionaires in West Africa, but, on being told that she was in German territorial waters, turned about and sailed back to Table Bay.

In London, Count Hatzfeldt made official inquiry of the government asking: "If the British government claimed sovereignty over Angra Pequena and the adjacent territory, and, if so, on what grounds."

Germany now had her first colony—German South-West Africa. How they were to treat their colonies is worth considering. The Herreros who lived here, one of the finest races in Africa, were decimated by the Germans, but, as Negley Farson writes, "infinitely worse than the usual atrocity story are the numerous accounts of the ways the German settlers tried to swindle the Herreros out of their magnificent herds of cattle."

In 1904, when the Herreros rebelled, the Germans killed fifty thousand of them.

The tribe began with a population of ninety thousand, and when the rebellion ended in 1907 there were fewer than thirty thousand left. To-day there are still fewer; they are a dying race. They are dying out because the women "will bear no more children into slavery." It is claimed that the women have such a knowledge of abortion that many of its secrets are still unknown to their own wise men. Officers who fought with Botha in 1915 were astonished at the gap in the Herrero population. "You hardly ever came on a child younger than eleven. It was as if since 1904 the Herrero women had stopped breeding." In the non-commissioned officers' messes the German garrisons made Herrero women wait on them naked; while the officers at Fort Mamutoni's "used to make a pretty Herrero girl strip and then lie on the table and they would play cards on her stomach."

In the Cameroons, another colony which Germany obtained later, a German officer, Major Dominick, hanged the king of Duala and burnt his followers with gasoline in trenches. In Tanganyika, it took the Germans from 1892 to 1896 to defeat the Wahehe, another great fighting tribe, and their chief Mkawawa committed suicide rather than fall into their hands.

Looking back, we can see into what was then, in 1883, the impenetrable future. The child that Europa had carried on her shoulder was still a boy. The gunboat that patrolled Luderitz Bay was an unimportant part of the infant's navy, something almost as negligible as a child's toy boat floating in its bath, in comparison with the British fleet. But there were other factors: there was trouble in Egypt and the prospect of trouble with Russia, both of which could have been fomented by Germany.

This was the *quid pro quo* in the game of power politics, or, as it might more aptly be described, of blackmail. Angra Pequena, the Germans said, or we will make trouble.

The annexation of Angra Pequena was supposed to, and perhaps it did, come as a complete surprise to Lord Granville. Up to the last minute he had been assured that neither Bismarck nor the Reichstag would support the German Colonial Party. Flourishing a document before the German lawmakers, Bismarck said he had been unfairly treated by the British Government which had sent him no answer to his despatch in which he had said Germany was about to take over this land unless England claimed it. He did not add that, though he had sent it to Count Munster, he had himself forbidden the Ambassador to present it to Granville.

There was, in addition to the possible trouble-making factor by Germany, the feeling in England that she should not be "a dog in the manger" and resist German and other claims to an empire in Africa. There was also the fact that the Kaiser was related to Queen Victoria, which was why, later on, Heligoland passed from British into German hands. Indeed, so strong appears to have been this bond that the Queen gave the Kaiser Kilimanjaro as a birthday present—Africa's tallest mountain to wear like a stickpin in his tie.

Though in 1881, after the Boer War of Independence, and with the fall of Disraeli, the British Government had been anxious to cut responsibilities to the utmost, public opinion slowly changed, influenced in part at least by Rhodes, so that by 1897 the area under British rule had been doubled. The approach of other competitors had a stimulating effect on the nation as had the riches of the diamond and gold fields. Investment followed discovery, as discovery followed the missionary and hunter. Occupation, or, to sweeten the pill, protection, had to follow investment. English investment meant colonisation by England.

More, the Gladstone haters in their desire for revenge denounced the peace he had made with Boers as "Majubanimity." The jingoes, the Kipling readers, became afraid that the Germans, pressing east through Damaraland, would link up with the Boers trekking west and form a Teutonic belt confining the British to the south of the Orange River.

But in all this there were cross-currents. Rhodes's ultimate dream was a *Pax Teutonica* enforced by a federated British Empire, Germany, and the United States. So, though he feared German expansion, he at the same time wanted a kind of agreement with them.

Kruger had not the slightest objection to German encroachment. At least as far as he was concerned, it was better than English encroachment.

But Rhodes did not welcome a German and Boer junction.

On the other hand, he was playing ball with the Dutch element of the Cape Province. Thus, Rhodes's ambitions were exactly opposed to Kruger's. Rhodes was determined to secure for England the vast "hinterland," as he called it, of Africa. Kruger equally determined, was for Boer consolidation of the Free State and the Transvaal linked by rail to a port on the East Coast. Rhodes wanted a Cape-to-Cairo railway. Kruger refused to allow a British line to cross his territory.

The word "imperialism" was coming into use now. It described very aptly Rhodes's policy. Kruger still hoped to see the Vierkleur waving from Table Bay to the Zambesi. He stated it in these words: "Then it shall be from the Zambesi to Simon's Bay, Africa for the Afrikaaners." Germany was in sympathy with his views, or appeared to be. Even before the Boer War of 1880, Ernst von Weber had suggested a German settlement in Matabeleland, where the Boers might join their German kindred in a colony free from British influence. This argument was later used by Rhodes in his negotiations with Lobengula to prove that the British, not the Boers, were his friends.

By Warren's settlement of the Bechuana question, Boer aggression, as it was described, was arrested. Germany was presumed to be warned, and access to the North through *the neck of the bottle* preserved.

But Rhodes's idea did not end here. In addition to keeping the neck of his own bottle open, he wanted to close the neck of another bottle—that of the Boers. For they, too, were beginning to understand this bottle business. Everybody was trying to bottle every one else up. Kruger wanted to enclose the English; the English wanted to enclose the Boers. And now the British had their chance, which came indirectly through their own errors.

Wolseley, in his settlement of Zululand, had created thirteen little kinglets, who he felt would neutralise each other. They did this with such success that the Boers filtered into the country and on the death of Cetywayo proclaimed his son, Dinzulu, king and, in 1884, obtained a large concession of land from him. Under the leadership of Lukas Meyer they formed "The New Republic" with a capital at Vryheid and claimed territory as far as the sea.

At last Boers, though not Transvaalers, owned a strand of their own. They even had a bay, Saint Lucia, that could become a harbour. This move offered Kruger his long-coveted outlet from the Transvaal. And here, working through Luderitz and the South African Republic, Germany prepared to repeat the coup of Angra Pequena—for a private merchant of Bremen, Herr Luderitz got around a great deal. And Colonel Schiel, a German in the service of the Republic, got new concessions from Dinzulu in the neighbourhood of the Bay, while Bismarck drew a red herring of objections to British encroachments in the Niger watershed, to cover up these new movements. Lord Derby, however, seeing that appeasement towards German expansion had not been rewarded with the good-will which he had hoped for, ordered H.M.S. *Goshawk* to Saint Lucia Bay, where she dropped anchor. And by virtue of an old treaty with King Panda, the Union Jack was hoisted there in December, 1884, and the only possible harbour between Durban in Natal and Lourenço Marques in Portuguese East Africa was annexed by the British. The New Republic appealed in vain to Holland, France, and Germany. Germany, being the only one that was a danger to British interests, was given concessions in the Cameroons to keep out of the matter.

Under the lid of uneasy peace—that is, of undeclared wars—Africa was simmering like a pot. The Zulu War was only recently over; the first Boer War was just over; the Sekukuni War was just over. Three little Republics of Freebooters had sprung up. Battleships, British and German, were dropping their hooks and hoisting flags among the mangrove swamps of uninhabited shores on the Atlantic and Indian Oceans. Hunters and concession-seekers were swindling native kings; missionaries of all countries were clamouring for protection from the savages that they had settled among and in most cases failed to convert. Explorers like Sir Harry Johnston and Karl Peters raced each other in discovering new animals, such as the okapi, and in the act opened up new territories and created new interests in lands that no one had thought of for centuries. In the North there was the Egyptian War; Chinese Gordon, Rhodes's friend, had been killed in Khartoum. Leopold of Belgium was preparing for his land grab in the Congo, while the diamond-diggers sweated, and the gold prospectors wandered over the kopjes of the High Veld.

Millionaires, like Rhodes and his associates, were commuting between South Africa and the City of London. Boer generals, like Joubert and Cronje, were national Boer heroes.

Old Paul Kruger—Oom Paul—sat on the stoep of his little house in Pretoria and advised his people about all things, from what to ask for a farm that they wanted to sell to the best method of breaking-in a shooting pony. In the North, Lobengula lay naked on his bed while his wives covered him with English sovereigns that had been earned by his warriors while they worked on the mines, or played with the diamonds they stole for him, and which he kept in two tin kerosene cans. The wild game still roamed in hundreds of thousands, perhaps in its millions, over Africa. The rinderpest had not yet come to destroy it, but already the old Africa had gone, the shadow of Europe was over it. The old land was pregnant again, with the child of wealth in gold and diamonds, in rubber and cocoa, and nut oil; and her pains, which would come near to killing her, already were begun.

The success of Bismarck's policy of twisting the British lion's tail depended to a great extent upon the co-operation of the French government under M. Jules Ferry, and when that ministry was about to fall, he changed his tactics and called for an Anglo-Portuguese-Congo-Zambesi Agreement Conference, in Berlin. By this, the theory of spheres of influence, as opposed to territorial acquisition, was arrived at. At Versailles in 1871, Bismarck had said: "I want no colonies. They are only good for providing offices. For us colonial enterprise would be just like the silks and sables in the Polish noble families who have no shirts."

In 1872 he said to the British Ambassador in Berlin: "Colonies would be a source of weakness because they could only be defended by powerful fleets and Germany's geographical position does not necessitate her developing into a first-class maritime power."

In 1881 he said to a deputy at the Diet: "So long as I am Imperial Chancellor, we shall have no colonial policy. We have a navy that cannot sail, and we must have no vulnerable points in other parts of the world which would serve as booty for France as soon as we went to war with her."

Evidently France was to be milked again one day.

But even Bismarck himself was not strong enough to check

the national desire for colonies. His view was that of a soldier—of Germany becoming a world power by fighting wars on interior lines in Europe.

Yet for two hundred years Germans had been forming societies whose sole purpose was to assist German emigrants. In 1667 William Penn visited Germany and six years later a body of Germans settled in Pennsylvania. Colonists went to Brazil. There was even a society founded in 1842 for the "protection of German emigrants to Texas." These colonists adhered, in all cases, to their own language and customs and were ethnological German islands set in all the countries of the world.

Germans were complaining. "For how long must Germany do nothing but dot Africa with the bones of her explorers?" was the cry.

In 1882 a powerful German colonial organisation was formed by Baron von Maltzan and Prince zu Hohenlohe-Langenburg to encourage German emigration to the United States, Canada, and South America, where they were to form small settlements under the German flag. First secure small trading stations, and then secure government protection for them was the pattern of this peaceful penetration.

Both England and Germany, officially at least, appeared to be unable to see the difference between official policy and private action, but the basis of all colonial expansion has always been the "incident": a missionary killed, a small store burnt, a cry for help, and then the punitive expedition, the establishment of a fort to protect the post—more factories—more forts—more flags —a meeting of diplomats, and the annexation is complete.

Once Bismarck had begun to expand and had seen that it would work, he reversed his policy and went on in a hurry. In less than five years Germany was in possession of Togoland, the Cameroons, and Tanganyika. The end of Luderitz, the man who had begun all this, is obscure, but he is supposed to have been drowned in the Orange River while prospecting for diamonds.

Tides had swept over the continent of Africa before. Great tides of invasion which had overwhelmed and absorbed whole peoples—slow, lapping waves: the lap of the Boers against the Kaffirs; of the English against the Boers' heels; but it had always been a flowing tide of conquest in which the weak crumbled before the invader. The direction had been set, the advance slow—of the Kaffirs against the Bushmen, of the English against the Dutch. Even the flashing spears of T'Chaka's impis had been slow—attacking, eating up, and then resting from their labours of killing.

But now this was changed. There was a wind rising, the waves of the new tides were lashed high into the spume of controversy and war. Tide against tide, wind against wind, drift and current, all contrary, all at odds with each other, and the sky forever darkening with new thunderheads, with further threats of death.

The steel of the pioneers' guns and the iron of their great turning wheels had bred gold, and the gold was now to breed more steel; the Maxim gun and the pom-pom were about to breed blood—that of Matabele warriors dying in their last glorious charge of tossing plumes and spears. The blood of Boer farmers, fathers and and sons who had ridden out to fight together. The blood of simple English boys—the soldiers of country regiments who died without knowing why on the alien veld that the Boers inexplicably loved so much that they would not relinquish it.

Part Two

Gold

Instead of rejoicing you would do better to weep: for this gold will cause our country to be soaked in blood.—*Paul Kruger.*

CHAPTER ONE

THE RIDGE OF WHITE WATERS

IN 1885 the affairs of the South African Republic were again in a poor way. There was no money in the treasury, the country was in the depths of one of its seven-year depressions, the gold-finds of Barberton had petered out; and then suddenly a new strike was made on the High Veld of the Transvaal—on the windswept ridge that the Boers called the Witwatersrand—the ridge of white waters.

The burghers were overjoyed. Now they would have markets for their produce—the cattle, mealies, and truck that they produced and could not sell; for obviously a nation of farmers has no outlet for farm produce. To sell it there must be a non-farming community which consumes but grows nothing for itself. Paul Kruger, however, was doubtful of this new advantage. To him it was a new curse set upon the land. It was Baal, Moloch. It was Mammon. Riches to him lay in the land itself, not beneath it: in the herds of cattle, in stone houses and kraals, in rivers and fountains, in shade trees. Only in these things did happiness and contentment lie. Money, necessary as it seemed to be, frightened him with its potential of luxury, of softness, of corruption.

"Do not talk to me of gold," he said, " the element which brings more dissension and unexpected plagues than benefits in its train. Pray to God, as I am doing, that the curse connected with its coming may not overshadow our dear land, as it has come to us and our children, again. Pray and implore Him, who has stood by us, that He will continue to do so, for I tell you to-day that every ounce of gold taken from the bowels of our soil will yet have to be weighed up with rivers of tears, with the life blood of thousands of our best in the defence of that same soil from the lust of others yearning for it—solely because it has yellow metal in abundance."

Kruger's yellow metal. Lobengula's yellow stones.

Kruger saw into the future. Saw the new influx of foreigners that would swamp his people and destroy their ways; saw the difficulty of ruling a majority of Uitlanders with a minority of Boers; and foresaw in the seduction of his people the almost certainty of a new war.

Once diamonds had come in the nick of time to save Africa—or to destroy her. Now gold had come to save—or to destroy her. In either case, whatever the opinion, they had come. They were there and men would dig for them. Who were these men? The gold men were much like the diamond men; some were diamond men who had trekked up from the fields, but there were others, complete strangers to Africa. Americans from "'Frisco"; men from Ballarat, Cornishmen, Russians from the Ural mines—a new flock of miners, adventurers, gamblers, and prostitutes. There were good hard-working men among them, but the bad predominated, and the insatiable. Men like Deeming, who murdered four men in a single night in Johannesburg and then escaped from the country by killing a fifth and using his papers.

The miners lived in tents, wagons, and thatched huts, and ate "from iron pots in which meat and vegetables were boiled together in a sort of broth. Knives and forks were luxuries."

The Boers were not businessmen. The Rand was a cold, bleak ridge where it was hard to make a living from the land, and the farmers almost gave their land away, selling immense farms for a few pounds, or a few hundred pounds, swapping them for a horse and bridle, a span of oxen, or a piano. Later, when they were wiser, they asked and accepted thousands for land worth millions.

The gold was discovered, as the diamonds had been, by an accident. Robert Lys, an Englishman who had become a South African burgher, found his wagon stuck in some mud and threw stones under the wheels to make a track for them. The stones interested him. He was, like most pioneers, a prospector, and he took samples of this "pudding stone," as he called it, to Pretoria to show Doctor Karl Mauch, the German geologist, whom years before Hartley had taken to the Far North to investigate the ancient workings there. Mauch said the samples contained gold and Lys told him where he had got it. It seems likely that Mauch informed the German Foreign Office of the wealth he had found in the Transvaal and that this contributed to the interest that the Kaiser took in South Africa. A friend of Lys's, Fred Struben, was also convinced that gold would be found in large payable quantities on the High Veld, which was contrary both to the popular and the expert opinion of the time—Charles Gardiner, the famous mining engineer, even refusing to get off his horse to look at the conglomerate formation when it was shown to him. Going into partnership, Struben and Lys set up a five-stamp mill and began to work what they knew to be a minor reef while they searched for the mother lode. "If my friends had not thought me a fool in the early eighties, we might have bought the whole of the gold-bearing farms of the Witwatersrand for a song," Struben said many years later.

He did actually have the chance of buying the main reef, but turned it down, thinking the sample shown him to be "fools' gold"—pyrites. The two men, Honeyball and George Walker, who had brought in the sample, were carpenters, and had struck the main reef when out for a walk on the veld. But Honeyball refused to allow Struben to crush and pan the chunk of rock he had chipped off the outcrop, which made Struben think the whole thing a plant. Again the hit-or-miss of accident, the paradox, the strange concatenation of effect and cause—the bogged-down wagon, Karl Mauch turning up again, and the stroll of a couple of carpenters that ended in the city of Johannesburg springing up to flaunt itself six thousand feet above the level of the sea.

It is a comment on the story of Africa that Walker, who discovered the reef whose content has been assessed at two billion pounds, died in poverty. The farm on which the reef was discovered was Langlaate, the property of the Widow Oosthuizen, who, on the advice of Paul Kruger, finally sold it for six thousand pounds to I. B. Robinson.

The formation in which gold is found on the Rand is called "banket" because it resembles a Dutch almond sweetmeat of that name. The gold is mixed up in conglomerate beds, composed of quartz pebbles bound together by siliceous cement containing iron pyrites, in reefs which dip down to tremendous depths.

The origin of this reef and how it came to be tilted so that the upper end touches the surface, while the lower, curving like the inside of a bowl, is sunk to depths that have not yet been reached, is explained by Mellor and Reinke, whose theory is that at one time a great river ran from the north and turned the Witwatersrand into a lake. The river sometimes became torrential and carried with it large pebbles and gold in suspension which ultimately formed part of the sediment deposited in the lake bed. The gold came from the denudation of gold-bearing rocks that have vanished. At its mouth this river ran through a delta by several effluents, and the richest reefs almost define their beds. At a later date the whole deposit was covered by other beds which form the quartzites of the Witwatersrand series. Then came a period of upheaval when the granites forced their way upward, tilting and faulting the reef, compressing and cooking the conglomerate into its present form.

The Rand was no poor man's gold field. It needed capital, and big capital, to develop it, and that capital came at first from the diamond fields and later from England and America. The shafts were sunk, and are still being sunk, from this highland plateau to below sea level—six thousand feet down—seven thousand. And down there the work is done by hundreds of thousands of "boys" under white gangers. Some of these Kaffirs in the early days were recruited from the hot Low Veld, hundreds of miles away in the North, and suffered greatly from the cold when they reached the Rand. "Hundreds," John Hays Hammond said, "die on their march to Johannesburg." He goes on: "As labourers the Kaffirs are not only tractable, they are a fun-loving lot. It was, however, frequently necessary to resort to flogging to maintain order among the boys on the compounds. Afterwards the natives would come to the managers to thank them as a dog crawls to lick the hand of its master after a deserved whipping. . . . The boys often reported for work in a shockingly intoxicated condition, sometimes so helpless that they fell from the cages and were horribly mangled and killed."

The picture of the Rand begins to compose itself. The township of ramshackle, corrugated-iron frame houses, with a few of brick; some hotels, saloons, and brothels; wired-in compounds filled with savage warriors who for a time abandoned their spears to work in the mines. Boers coming in with their ox wagons laden with produce. Second-rate magnates drinking champagne and smoking first-rate cigars. The keynote was one of anarchy and bewilderment. Bewildered Boers, who had sold their farms for next to nothing, watched a city spring up. Bewildered Kaffirs shot down in cages to work in the bowels of the earth. A bewildered patriarchal and parochial government found itself confronted by an influx of strangers who could not speak their language. Bewildered adventurers found themselves rich overnight—directors of companies simply because they had been clerks in London or Hamburg and could add and subtract with a certain degree of accuracy. Bewildered London barmaids found themselves married and ladies because they happened to be white. One difference, which we tend to forget, between these early days and to-day is that then a man could be both young and rich. He could stake his life and gain a fortune while he was still young enough to enjoy it. It did not require years of work, it did not require capital. Initiative and courage and brains, good health and a little luck, were enough.

These changes in Africa were sudden. They superimposed themselves on the older, almost Biblical, pattern of life which had existed in the Republic. It was like a picture in which the life of one period was overlaid by the life of another, like two photographs taken on one plate—that of a train superimposed upon one of an ox wagon.

In the past the Bantus had flowed over the Bushmen, the Boers over the Kaffirs, the English had lapped at the heels of the retreating Dutch colonists. T'Chaka had substituted the short stabbing assegais for the throwing spear and revolutionised, by conquest and murder, the composition of Africa. The Matabele, realising that firearms must be victorious against even their own short spears, bought firearms, which they never learned to use properly, from the white gun-runners, with the wages they earned on the diamond diggings. These changes had, on the whole, been gradual. But the gold mines appeared almost overnight. No one was ready for them.

Meanwhile, all the old problems were still there. The Kaffirs, though continually driven back, kept returning for more, and Rhodes's imperialism, gaining strength from these new discoveries, impinged still further on Kruger's policy of isolation. The Rand and the town of Johannesburg that was springing up upon it were, as Kruger had foreseen, going to be the cause of trouble. Gold had been discovered in astronomical quantities. Kruger had no use for gold. Strangers came to mine it. Kruger had no use for strangers: "delvers," he called them; delvers of gold. He also called them "uproar-makers." A town was being built. Kruger had no use for towns. There was even no word for town or city in the Taal. "Stadt," "Dorp," "Burg," do not really mean towns. A hundred or two hundred houses grouped round a great outspan, a church and a few general stores, formed the Boer conception of a highly populated locality. And industry? Surely a man could make what he needed for himself: only a few things need be bought.

In Africa the ideas of Darwin and Huxley warred with the Old Testament conception of world origins and entered the lists as much as the modern rifle. Ruskin, Nietzsche, and Kipling were here on the South African veld with Job and the prophets of Israel; with American mining experts like John Hays Hammond, and writers like Rider Haggard, Trollope, and Froude. Ideas are too often forgotten in history. It was the idea "that God was not with the burghers" that made the Boers run when they attacked Sekukuni. It was the idea of empire that forced Rhodes on. It was the idea of patriarchal freedom that had driven the Boers North from the Cape and made them fight their War of Independence, and which, while they refused to have anything to do with a railway from the South, made them push forward still farther into the wilds, seeking an outlet to the sea independent of British control. The Boer's idea of Africa was that of the veld, open, wide, inviolate, and free. His method of insuring his own privacy was to own great areas of space and then to sit smoking on his stoep to contemplate them. This idea was in direct opposition to that of the new townsmen —the exploiters, who demanded the privacy of locked houses, and gave not a damn for the land unless mineral wealth was to be found below it.

Rhodes read history and biography. He found peace and beauty there. Kruger read the Bible for the same reason. Rhodes saw the beauty of his own creation when he looked down into the great hole he had made in Africa. Kruger knew it when he watched his wide-horned cattle herded into the kraals at night. The joy of hunting, of his own great strength, was Kruger's in his youth. Rhodes had no health and he had had no youth. He was the "old man," even as a boy. He was hasty because he had to be. Illness and death were at his elbow. Kruger was slow, confident in his faith in God which the adventures of his life seemed amply to justify.

The meeting of these two men was that of the irresistible force and the immovable object of the old conundrum. Rhodes obviously knew all about Kruger. It is probable that Kruger, too, had heard of Rhodes, of his almost miraculous rise to fortune, of his election to the Cape Parliament, but it is unlikely, until their meeting, that the man Kruger thought that the boy Rhodes—for to him he was no more than that—would ever endanger the South African Republic, or that already in 1880 the train was set with everything, as we look back upon it, arranged with almost inescapable, mathematical precision.

Now the pattern so slowly woven from such diverse threads was taking shape, the form becoming apparent, the shuttle moving swiftly. At last the naked warrior, the bearded Boer with his gun and horse, the London merchant, the British adventurer, hunters, concession-seekers, missionaries, miners and prospectors, were all recognisable in the tapestry of events, and all were moving in towards the golden heart of Africa to attack or protect it. All forced by their circumstances; all out of control; all contrary or supplementary and complementary; all at odds; all combining, breaking away, changing form, massing, disintegrating, marrying into parties, divorcing themselves from their partners of yesterday; all digging furiously or furiously watching the digging; all arming, buying; all amalgamating, evading amalgamation; all fighting, making peaces that were provisional, signing proclamations and conventions, substituting new conventions for the old, litigating, demanding, acceding to ¡demands, seceding, planning, lying, cheating, murdering even, in this land of Africa where all but the Bushmen were alien.

This argument, this lack of agreement between the English and the Boers, was fundamentally religious. An argument of

Gods and about Gods. The God of Israel and the God of Mammon. Kruger's point of view and Rhodes's were only exaggerations of the points of view of their followers. Kruger's remark to Jorrisen on his voyage to England, when Jorrisen was explaining the Darwinian theory to a fellow passenger, "Why, if what you tell him is true, I might as well throw my Bible overboard." Rhodes's fifty per cent chance of God. Kruger's belief that alles sal regt kom—all will come right; Rhodes's haste. The Boer refusal to fight on Sundays even in Kaffir wars. The Uitlanders' Sunday races. Kruger's cry, "Africa from the Zambesi to Simon's Bay for the Afrikaaners." Rhodes's great hand on a map of Africa; "I want it all British red." Kruger's refusal to compromise; Rhodes's desire for it ". . . I find it as easy to do business as to fight with any one." The Dutch hatred of money as a source of evil and the fantasy of the street stock exchanges, where "the streets were filled with hatless yelling brokers buying and selling the script of newly formed companies."

Kruger died worth a few thousand pounds, most of which was in land—the farms he owned. Rhodes died worth between twenty-five and forty-five million pounds. He could have made a hundred million if he had wanted to, as John Hays Hammond explained to the American millionaires, who, when he returned, asked him, much to his annoyance, how much Rhodes was worth. And then the anomaly: Rhodes, who cared for wealth, but saw it in terms of power, not bothering to make all he could; and Kruger, who cared nothing for it, supposed to have taken the gold hands from the clock in Pretoria when he left the country, leaving his Bible behind. That he left his Bible, if he did, is explicable. He also left his old dying wife and the Bible was an heirloom that held the records of his family in its pages. If he took the gold hands—which is doubtful—it would fit in with the rest. Some say he took all the gold he could lay his hands on: it is supposed to be buried in the Low Veld, and men have lost their lives looking for Kruger's millions, as they are called. The war was not over when he fled, and gold to Kruger was power too—the power to continue the fight against Mammon. Gold to defeat gold. But the Boers were unable to carry on, and no European power would come to their aid. Yet still to-day many Boers hope for a Republic again. "If the gold goes"—and it could, by devaluation, by the refusal of native labourers to work for low wages in the mines —" then the English will go and the Boers will remain," farming as they always have. Already grass is growing in the streets of Kimberley. The diamonds of West Africa have destroyed Rhodes's creation, and if the gold went, too, the pace of Africa would be reduced, not perhaps to the pace of the ox, but to that of a T-model Ford.

But now in the late eighties speed was coming to disturb the Boers. Fast transport by railways, faster driving in American Studebaker spiders, faster living by the strangers in their midst. Ladies, the wives of financiers who smoked cigars, wore a monocle, and drove their own four-in-hands, now were here with ideas almost as upsetting to the respectable Boers as the whores who had preceded them. Whores they understood, though they had none of their own. There was a lot about them in the Bible.

In all this gold-mine development Cecil Rhodes was late. He was too busy in Kimberley to give the new reef his full attention, particularly as he had been misinformed about its value. The expert he had sent up to look at it thought it was just a flash in the pan—that it would not last—that the deposits were too low-grade and too hard to work to be profitable. There were memories of other strikes of which a great deal had been thought, but which had given out. In addition, the eyes of England—and capital—were upon Australia, where new gold mines of supposed incredible riches had been discovered. Africa was for diamonds. It was absurd on the face of it to suppose that in a single country, within a few hundred miles, there could be both the richest gold mines and the greatest diamond deposits in the world. It was contrary to the laws of Nature, average, and common sense. They did not realise in London that Africa never had made sense, that it had always been the land of paradox and anomaly. They assumed the darkness of the continent to be related to the colour of its inhabitants, to the fact that it was unexplored, and not to psychic causes, to ancient gods, to the fact that if a continent can have an aura of tragedy, this was the one. For its population, other than the Boers who understand its tempo, or the natives, no country has suffered more from death and destruction, from disease, from fighting, floods, droughts, from sudden death in swollen rivers, from suicides or accidents. None has seen swifter rises to fortunes and swifter falls from it. This is the land of Boers and Negroes, of men who love the land, or for Englishmen who have actually settled there.

As a milch cow Africa is a failure. Her milk turns sour in the stomach of the adventurer. Only this can explain the strange love of those who love her desert veld, her stark mountains, her incredible bareness. Africa is a wife, and no mistress. Even Rhodes mistreated her, and the grandeur of his achievements can scarcely have compensated him for the pain of his death or for the greatness of his disappointments. "So much to do, so little done," were his dying words. Did he, Colossus as he was, flatter himself that he could do things to Africa?

Cecil John Rhodes, Africa's impresario. He sold Africa to the world. He sold her long. He sold her short. He advertised her riches, her beauty. He adorned her with cities, he hired her out to his friends. He sought to put a sub-continent in his vest pocket and died from the fever of his thwarted love, for in the end Africa would have none of him. The Rhodesia that he had taken loved him, but not the South that he had courted so ardently and betrayed so thoroughly.

Paul Kruger rode the slow tide of the country. What haste he made, he made slowly. Cecil Rhodes, on the contrary, in a reversal of King Canute's behaviour, tried to hurry events. Still to-day in Africa Kruger's method is the best. For a while the stranger can hurry the country with his new and foreign energy. For a while he can lift the great stone that lies over her heart and peer into her secret riches; and then one day his foot slips and he is crushed.

While Rhodes was of the opinion that the ore of the Rand must prove too costly to work at a profit, Alfred Biet, a Hamburg Jew who later was to become his friend and associate, was buying up all the best properties; and when Rhodes did finally reach Johannesburg, the cream was gone. He did not feel about gold as he felt about diamonds. "I cannot calculate the power in these claims," he said.

That was Rhodes's gift, to look at a piece of mineralised land and calculate its latent dynamic power as translated into money as a political weapon. But when he actually was in the middle of some important negotiations, he left Johannesburg to rush back to the deathbed of his friend, Neville Pickering, who had been the secretary of de Beers Company. He said he never regretted this decision to leave one of his biggest deals unconcluded to go to the deathbed of the young friend who was the beneficiary under his second will.

Rhodes loved men, but none—not even Doctor Jameson—did he ever love as he had loved Pickering. This capacity for giving and inspiring friendship was an outstanding characteristic of Cecil Rhodes. His friendship with Hofmeyr, which was broken by the Raid, was more than friendship. Stead was another friend. So when he was older was Grey, who he said was "that finest of English products, an English gentleman." General Gordon who was killed at Khartoum was his friend. So was General Booth. Friends, people, influence, love, power, were an intrinsic part of Rhodes's pattern. Power by talk, by magnetism, by purchase, by influence direct and indirect.

Believing in himself and his destiny, he told Jameson, when he asked him how long he thought he would be remembered: "I put it at four thousand years."

Finding it forever necessary like an adolescent to explain himself and his views to an audience—his hopes, his ideals, his beliefs, his philosophies—he disliked being alone. Like an adolescent he believed in people; like an adult he combined this belief with a paradoxical cynicism. But where was the cynicism when some friends told him they had bad news—his lovely house, Groot Schuur, had been burnt to the ground—and he answered, "Thank God. I thought something had happened to Doctor Jim." This was a part of his philosophy, of his fundamental wisdom. A friend was irreplaceable; a house, even a great one, could be rebuilt. Rhodes was a practical man, so practical that he understood impalpables like friendship.

But he was a man without humour. If a funny story was told, he would look blank, wait for the laughter to die down, and go on with his discussion. At this time Rhodes is described as big and blond. He would talk with his grey, heavy-lidded eyes fixed on space as though he was seeing thousands of miles of veld and mountains. His voice would get higher and shriller as his enthusiasm gathered momentum. No one could get a word in edge-wise once he began to outline his plans for Africa or embarked on the subject of gold or diamonds.

There has probably never been a greater maker of wills than Rhodes. He made six of them, and they all indicate his character and that of his friends. Whatever step he took, he made a new will: one when he entered Parliament; one when he consolidated his gold fields and de Beers; another when he took Mashonaland; another when he became Prime Minister; and another when he took Matabeleland.

His later wills are less flamboyant than the early ones. He substituted English-speaking for British, but in them all was the same thought of England. In his first will he wanted the colonisation by British subjects of all lands where the means of livelihood are attainable—the entire continent of Africa, the valley of the Euphrates, the islands of Cyprus and Candia, the whole of South America, the islands of the Pacific not heretofore possessed by Great Britain, the seaboard of China and Japan, the ultimate recovery of the United States of America as an integral part of the British Empire—the foundation of so great a power as hereafter to render wars impossible and promote the best interests of humanity.

Later on he wrote to W. T. Stead, "Union with America and universal peace, I mean after a hundred years, and a secret society organised like Loyola's, supported by the accumulated wealth of those whose aspiration it is to do something. . . ."

Was Rhodes so wrong in his hopes and guesses? Are not the great cartels a power of accumulated wealth, but set to an evil purpose? Is not the alliance of England and the United States and other great nations nearer than it has ever been before? Is not war, if we take Rhodes's date, which would be about the year 2000, perhaps going to become impossible? Is Rhodes himself not a sort of Hitler, but one who was humanitarian in the long view?

Rhodes's principle was that of Nordic superiority. He believed in aristocracy and expressed in another will that his humble belief was that "one of the secrets of England's strength has been the existence of a class termed the county landlords . . .;" but he goes on, "I object to an expectant heir developing into a loafer."

Of him Spengler wrote: "In our Germanic world the spirits of

Alaric and Theodoric will come again. There is a first hint of them in Cecil Rhodes."

Ill health had brought Rhodes to Natal. Diamonds had taken him to Kimberley. Gold was now leading him North to the South African Republic into the orbit of Paul Kruger and Lobengula, leading him to his doom and their own.

CHAPTER TWO

RHODES

KRUGER'S remark when he received Frere's invitation to visit him—"Which Frere is it? I know four Sir Bartle Freres"—could be applied with even greater justice to Cecil John Rhodes. With which Rhodes are we dealing at any given time?—the sickly parson's son, the Oxford man, the financier, the premier, the farmer ... Rhodes was a man who parodied his own virtues, whose whole life was a paradox of Machiavellian simplicity. An expatriate who devoted his life to the aggrandisement of the country he had left, and all but ruined the Africa he loved. Hero to some. Murderer to others. The godless man whom men worshipped almost as a god. The Colossus with lungs of clay. The great cynic, the great idealist. The financier who was always in debt. The imperialist who shares with Simón Bolívar the liberator the honour of having a great country named after him. The man who chose a mountain for a tomb. The only white man who ever received the Zulu royal salute of "Bayete" from the very people he had destroyed; and who, exposing another facet of his character, left uncompleted the greatest deal of his life to go to the deathbed of a friend. The maker of a million settlers' homes who had none, in the real sense, of his own. The uncrowned king of half a continent. The man, to whom hundreds of women offered themselves in concubinage or as wives, who never touched a woman. The student of history who forgot men were not bloodless pawns.

Sarah Gertrude Millin says: "Greatness is a sort of genius—a quality, not an accident or an achievement, a gift and not an inheritance. It inhabits a man like poetry or courage ... and as there are minor poets there may even be lesser great men—village, if not world, great men." "The reason," Emerson says, "this man or that is great is not to be told. It lies in the man."

Both Rhodes and Kruger were great. But Kruger's was a

more parochial greatness than Rhodes's, who used to say he left England less in search of adventure, and because of his health, than to get away from cold mutton. Cold mutton could be translated into hot roast beef on Sunday or any other conventional habit. He was not a man who lived by rote or thought in terms of precedent. His idea was to force on a reluctant Africa a federation resembling the American federation of states. But he went beyond this. He wanted to get America back and said—"Even from an American point of view, just picture what they have lost." At another time he wrote to Stead, "Fancy the charm to young America to share in a scheme to take the government of the world."

This was Rhodes's master plan—the orderly government of the world by a superstate. The limited plan he came near to achieving was the African federation.

The race for Africa was now really on. The preliminary canter was over. The Belgians were in the Congo—led by Stanley, the explorer; the French were in the Congo—led by another explorer, de Branza. Germans were everywhere hunting, prospecting as engineers for gold, as missionaries for souls. The silences of the great rivers were broken by the shots of the hunters and the hymns of the ministers. Soon they were to echo under the crack of the kiboko and the cries of natives being thrashed for failing to produce their quota of rubber. Portugal was claiming more rights. Germany had established her colonies. France was creeping down the Niger. England must make her way up from the Limpopo and join the Cape to Egypt. Is it wonderful, therefore, that the Boers were afraid? That they sought protection, that they wanted an outlet of their own to the sea? That they, who to live, needed farms so large that they could live by the increase of their herds alone, felt themselves hemmed in? Above all they hated and feared England, and England guided by Rhodes was on the march. "I look upon the territory of Bechuanaland as the Suez Canal of the trade of this country," Rhodes said, ". . . the key of its road to the interior. Some honourable members," he went on, "may say this is immorality. The lands they may say belong to the chief, Mankoroane. . . . Now I have not these scruples. I believe the natives are bound gradually to come under the control of Europeans. . . ." Here Rhodes paraphrased Darwin. He knew what he had to do. He felt conquest his duty—not merely to England, but to the world. Sarah Gertrude Millin, Rhodes's biographer, says, "Take up a picture of a group of men significant in their day, and he demands the eye, something different, something for both good and evil, unique."

Rhodes always looked older than he was, thirty when he was twenty; forty when he was thirty. He is described as thick and heavy—square, with big hands, a double chin, a sensual mouth, and a high falsetto voice. Bismarck, the maker of Germany and competitor for Africa, another big man, had a similar voice.

Rhodes, the so-called solitary—this is part of the fiction that has been built up about him—hated even to have a meal by himself. He loved to surround himself by friends and if friends were not available enemies would do. He had to talk, he had to have an audience. And often, when he had done talking, his enemies became his friends. He hated loafers and, like many childless men, had definite ideas about education. A good education he felt was essential. "Then kick all the props away. If they are worth anything the struggle will make them better men; if they are not, the sooner they go under the better for the world." Here we get the theory of the survival of the fittest introduced into family life. Rhodes studied Aristotle; he was profoundly affected by Ruskin. The *Origin of Species* he combined in his mind with Winwood Read's *Martyrdom of Man* and Disraeli's foreign policy. Rhodes was what we should call a realist to-day. He tended to ignore psychic and emotional causes and in consequence was unable to foresee effects due to such phenomena. His estimates were based on the factual, on figures, on the fallibility of men and their susceptibility to temptation, rather than on their faithfulness to a principle or idea or ideal. He investigated God factually and gave God his chance—a fifty per cent chance. He decided that Charles Darwin was the best interpreter of God's work, which in terms of fact appeared to be that "dog eats dog": the bigger dog destroying the lesser. It remained merely for man to follow this lead and God's will was done.

God's finest product, according to Rhodes, was the Englishman. Here was the one race which had true ideals of justice, peace, and liberty without any suggestion of equality. With the English he included the British colonials and the Americans. An English-speaking block that should in his opinion and God's, if God existed, rule the world. Oddly enough, while he was working all this out, Nietzsche was doing the same thing in Germany. It is unlikely that Rhodes ever read any of his works, since none were translated into English until after his death. But the idea of a superman and a super-race was permeating the world. Ideas can be considered as fluid, as travelling the air waves so that different people who have never seen each other get the same idea at the same time. Darwin, in whom Rhodes believed so strongly, was merely first in the field. Wallace's discoveries and conclusions were very similar and tend to prove the contention of the fluidity of ideas. This period could perhaps be considered as the time in which modern fascism began to take actual form. Rhodes, Sarah Gertrude Millin says, was, whether he knew it or not, a Nietzschean. She put it this way: "To begin with, he was not much of a Christian. He was, whether he knew it or not, a Nietzschean, an ancient Teuton. He considered himself a Darwinian. 'At some future period,' says Darwin, 'not very distant as measured by centuries, the civilised races of man will almost certainly exterminate and replace the savage races throughout the world.'"

Rhodes's attitude to the natives varied with the political wind. At one time he said—this was when he wanted the natives on his side—"I do not believe they are different from ourselves." But he also said on other occasions, "The natives are children." On the native question at least Rhodes and the Boers had no quarrel. It was their one and lowest common denominator. Rhodes said, "I am no negrophilist"—a superfluous assertion, since he threw so much emphasis on pigmentation. All that was Nordic blond was good to him—in which conclusion he agreed perfectly with the thoughts of Nietzsche, whom he had never seen.

In a letter Rhodes wrote in 1877, he says: "I contend that we are the finest first race in the world and that the more of the world we inhabit the better it is for the human race."

It is impossible to imagine Kruger thinking on these lines. Kruger is explicable while Rhodes was and remains a phenomenon.

At twenty-four when still an undergraduate he made a will in which he left to Britain the fortune he had not yet made and stipulated that it was to be employed in absorbing the rest of the world into the British Empire. Spengler saw Rhodes as the new enlarged man, "as a captain of industry become statesman, a man who has really ceased to feel his enterprise as his own business and its aim as the simple amassing of fortune." Rhodes was only twenty-seven when he said, "I went down to the Cape Parliament thinking, in my practical way, I will take the North."

He has been described as overbearing and ruthless. And he was. But he was also reasonable and conciliatory, colloquial; and explanatory when it was worth his while. He was for a time —and not a short time either—successful in being all things to all men. Whether he fooled them or fooled himself, or whether he thought circumstance itself would come to his aid, it seems impossible to determine. He did not believe with Kruger that "alles sal regt kom"—that all would come right; but appears to have thought that he could make things come right if he had control.

Rhodes's charm was undeniable. Barnato said, "You can't resist him." Hofmeyr said, "We had a talk and were friends ever afterwards." The Matabele whom he destroyed said, "You have come again and now all things are clear, we are your children." General Gordon said, "Stay and work with me." Then he asked him to come and help "smash the Mahdi." Rhodes's reply was typical. He would not fight the Mahdi, "but deal with him." To "deal" or to "square" were pleasant euphemisms for bribing: a simpler and a cheaper method of settling difficulties than war. Rhodes is even supposed to have said to Parnell, when he said, owing to his divorce, the priests were against him, "Can't you square the Pope?" Nothing daunted Rhodes. After getting Barney Barnato into the Kimberley Club, "to make a gentleman of him" and bring him on to his side of the diamond fence, Barney said, "But your crowd will never leave me in. They will turn me out in a year or two."

"Then we'll make you a life governor," was Rhodes's answer.

This final act of amalgamation took place in Doctor Jameson's cottage. Rhodes and Biet were on one side. On the other were Woolf Joel and Barnato. The stakes were for millions and none of the men concerned was yet thirty-six years old. The argument went on till dawn, Rhodes talking, Rhodes exhorting, cajoling, threatening. Rhodes's high voice stringing out long estimates of costs and profits. Rhodes getting up and sitting down. The room was filled with smoke. The men were drinking as they talked. Someone would lean forward to adjust the light of the lamp, turning the wick up or down. "If you have an idea and it's a good idea, if you will only stick to it, you will come out all right," was Rhodes's argument, and the amalgamation of the diamond fields and consolidation of diamond interests was a good idea. And then, as the sky began to pale, Rhodes threw in his final argument: he promised Barney Barnato a seat in Parliament. That finished it. Barney gave in. Life governor of the Kimberley Club and the right to put the magic letters M.P. after his name.

"He ties me up as he ties up everybody," Barney said. No man could resist Rhodes because he always attacked his Achilles' heel.

After the amalgamation, Rhodes addressed his shareholders, explaining the complications of the negotiations and the profits that would accrue from it in a speech as long as a short novel, without once referring to a note. Rhodes was an able if uninspired speaker. Here is an example: "Now at fourteen shillings a carat, producing nine thousand loads per diem yielding eleven thousand carats, only claiming a carat and a quarter per load, we should obtain seven thousand five hundred pounds per diem, which would cost us eight shillings per load. . . ."

A simple device for buying a man was to buy a horse from him. It was implied to the seller that this horse Mr. Rhodes wanted was an extremely valuable animal and that the price for the alienation of the horse's affection, from one master to another, would naturally be taken into account. The horse was in fact merely a symbol, a cheque stub, as it were, which would cover the bribe. And then, when Rhodes had the horse, with that cynical humour that distinguished some of his acts, he named if after its previous owner.

Ambition. Rhodes's was endless. He even wanted the stars, he said. "These stars that you see overhead at night, these vast worlds which we can never reach. I would annex the planets if I could. I often think of that. It makes me sad to see them so clear and so far away." This takes us back to the story of the old

Boer who said there were no minerals in the moon because if there were the British would have taken possession of it long ago.

But what chance had men like Lobengula, and the others who were against him, with Rhodes? The man who wanted the stars, whose thoughts were so big that men were less than ants. Perhaps he saw them as ants toiling to make the world red for England.

A contemporary, writing of Rhodes as a young man, said: "I have seen him many times in the main street dressed in white flannels leaning moodily with his hands in his pockets against a wall. He hardly ever had a companion, seemingly took no interest in anything but his thoughts, and I do not believe if a flock of the most adorable women passed through the street he would go across the road to see them." That is Rhodes the misogynist, and set in opposition to this is Rhodes the friend, who once gave Alfred Biet, who was in difficulties, six signed blank promissory notes, saying, "Whatever I have got is yours to back you if you need it."

In these hard-boiled times, when lack of feeling is regarded as a sign of sophisticated culture, it is worth examining some scenes from the not very distant past. Here is one of them described by Sir David Harris, who was a very close friend of Rhodes. It was a few days after Neville's death. Rhodes and Willie Pickering, Neville's brother, were alone in the board room. Harris says: "I saw two men sitting at a bare writing-table. Something made me stop and I stood quite still. They had no papers in front of them and did not say a word. Damn funny, it looked. They were both in the same attitude; one hand on the brow shutting the eyes and supporting the head, with the elbow resting on the table, the other hand and arm lay flat on the table. Damn funny, I give you my word. I stood there stock-still, sort of fascinated. Then on the table between them I saw a gold watch and chain in a rough pile which Rhodes and Willie Pickering were alternately pushing from one to the other. First one would give it a shove and the other would only shake his head and push it back again. And I give you my word they were both crying. All I heard was, ' No, you are his brother,' and again, ' No, you are his greatest friend.' "

When Rhodes had left the gold fields before completing the

deals he had negotiated there to get back to Pickering's bedside, he said. "Pickering's dangerously ill. I am going back by to-night's coach."

All seats were booked. Rhodes's answer to this was: "Buy a seat from someone who has already booked. Get a special coach —anything; I am going to-night." Rhodes's tears and affection for his friend. Kruger's tears and love of his land. Nelson's last words of "Kiss me, Hardy . . ."

John Hays Hammond, who was closely associated with Rhodes, describes him as typically Augustan with his heavy forehead, his strong mouth, and square cleft chin. This impression of his origin was strengthened by the curly blond hair, always in confusion. His grey-blue eyes could be as cold as ice, but when he smiled, as he frequently did, they were cold no longer. His hands were blunt and powerful, expressive of himself. He rarely moved them to gesticulate . . . his big-boned frame seemed to tower over most of his companions.

Mrs. Hammond appears to have agreed with her husband and wrote: "He has the superb head of a Roman emperor. He is a man, the most impersonal man I have ever known—strong, broad, and splendid. He is not fine, keen, nor sensitive. The world is his omelette and the men the eggs which compose it. I believe that he would lap human bodies like sandbags to build his fort . . . he can crush, cut, but never pinch. Money is his steed, instinct his spur, and a generous power his aim. . . . Mr. Rhodes is a great man. His brain is great and level as Table Mountain. There are no spiritual pinnacles to his nature. He lives entirely beyond the pale of everyday life. The tender, gentle things are not for his consideration. His life is speeding at too great an impetus for him to be seen in detail, or to feel in detail. The man is the most impersonal personality that I have ever met. Mr. Rhodes can be as bloodless as Fate when people are not of use to him. He simply has no use for a disused member. They are as out of place in his life as a bit of broken machinery would be in a steam engine."

John Hays Hammond writes of him: "The South African natives are said to have thought Rhodes mad. If so, it was the kind of madness that appealed to them and made them trust and follow him. It is certain that he was possessed of an energy so inexhaustible that to the ordinary man he must have seemed almost a demon. Coupled with this energy was a driving desire for power.... On Rhodes's wrist there was a small aneurism which by its throbing indicated to him that he had reached the danger point of over-exertion. His heart had never been equal to his spirit: as he grew older it fell steadily behind."

"The great fault of life is its shortness." was Rhodes's continual complaint; "just as one is beginning to know the game, one has to stop." Kipling expressed his spirit:

> Dreamer devout by vision led
> Beyond our guess or reach,
> The travail of his spirit bred
> Cities in place of speech.
> So huge the all-mastering thought that drove—
> So brief the term allowed—
> Nations, not words, he linked to prove
> His faith before the crowd.

Natives are good judges of character and they called Rhodes Lamula M'kunzi—he who separates fighting bulls. Samabulane, the Matabele induna, said, "We, the Matabele, all know the great Johann." He was speaking of Johann Colenbrander. "We knew him as a promising youth. We remember his daring deeds as a young man. We know he was the voice of the great men sent to our king Lobengula. But as compared to the great white Chief, the Great Johann is only the tick bird that picks the ticks off the rhinoceros."

A man's home is a reflection of his personality. The books, the pictures, the furnishings, the thousand things that a man, in a lifetime, collects round him to be his inanimate companions, are a key to what we call his character. The only safe way to disguise this personal taste is to use an interior decorator—for a man is known no less for the surroundings he chooses than for the friends with whom he associates; no less for inanimate than the animate, since both must be included to form the picture of his chosen environment.

Rhodes's house was remarkable. Groot Schuur—the great barn—is a two-storey house of thirty rooms. It has gables like most old Cape houses. The windows are large, have small panes and are shuttered. The stoep roof is supported by white pillars and faces the mountain. The floor of the stoep and hall is a checkerboard of black-and-white stone tiles. The furniture is beautiful old Colonial Dutch, which, like the houses of the Colony, is Dutch in feeling softened by the voluptuous curves of the Eastern slave craftsmen from Batavia who built it. It was all big and sparsely distributed. Even in his house Rhodes had to have room. Even in his house, as servants, he could not stand "women fussing." His servants were men. He did have two pictures of women in the house. The one was a Raeburn he had fancied as a boy and was later enabled to buy; the other, that hung in his bedroom, was a photograph of an old Kaffir crone—Moselikatze's widow who had helped him to make contact with the Matabele chiefs. Among the pictures in his home were one of Napoleon's coronation—had this any significance?—and another of Bartolomeu Dias discovering the Cape. He had also a model of the sacred bird the Phœnicians were supposed to have left in Rhodesia, and a bust of Napoleon. The sacred bird motif was carried out right through the house. The fifteen bedrooms had two bathrooms and were remarkable for the absence of adequate mirrors. Rhodes's own room had no full-length mirror and no bookshelf. His bed had an uncomfortable mattress on it. On a table he kept a big atlas. Maps and atlases were his passion. Africa was his passion. From his bedroom he could look through the great crescent of windows at the mountain he had decorated with hydrangeas. It is somewhat typical that he should have so much liked scentless flowers, hydrangeas, cannas, and bougainvillæa. They were all hardy, they had big blooms, they massed themselves well, in great flamboyant clumps of bleeding colour.

It was typical, too, that he loved the Cape and the view of the sea where two great oceans meet, where the rollers from the Antarctic ice crash against the golden strand of Africa; where two seas and the tip of a continent amalgamate in a symphony of sun and storm. "Come, let us walk up the mountain and see the two oceans," he would say to his guests. One ocean was not enough for the Colossus.

"Men," Milner said, "are ruled by their foibles and Rhodes's foible was size."

Rhodes was a mountain man, though he came from flat country. When he attacked the North—"My North"—he marched not along the coastline as the Portuguese had done—the flats were good enough for the Portuguese—but along the great central plateaus, along the highlands, along the very backbone of Africa. His idea of bigness was three-dimensional, including plain and mountain; including, best of all, the plain on the mountain, the great High Veld mesa of Africa. It was a mountain-top that he chose as a burial place.

The books in his house were characteristic of him. He had Gibbon's *Decline and Fall*. He admired it so much that he ordered his bookseller, Hatchards of Piccadilly, to collect, type, and bind uniformly all Gibbon's authorities. This order cost him eight thousand pounds. He had two hundred and fifty volumes of history; biography, one hundred and thirty-seven volumes; Africana, one hundred and seventy-five volumes. In addition to these there were a number of books on the Cape Colony and fifty books on Egypt. The Cape was in his pocket as Premier; Egypt he hoped to have. They were, as it were, the two ends, the beginning and the terminus of his Cape-to-Cairo railroad dream. The middle, the thousands of miles that separated them, he was satisfied to leave relatively unexamined. No great power stood between him and the Mediterranean. Rhodes had twenty books about Napoleon, one life of Alexander the Great, and several on the rulers of India. There were other books about travel, about social science, about federation, geography, and constitutional government. He had seventy books of reference, twenty-five novels, twenty-four books on art and science, seventeen works of literature—such as Ruskin and Shakespeare—and nine on architecture. He had Frazer's *Golden Bough*. He had no piano in his house and among the books no rare editions. He did, however, have some Gobelin tapestries.

The rooms of Groot Schuur were panelled or whitewashed. The feeling the house gave was one of space, of calm, and, in human terms, of coldness, of massive weight—big, strong, heavy, high, wide, handsome, large, magnificent. "You should count in hundreds and thousands," he said, "not dozens. That is the only way to produce any effect or make any profit."

Inyanga, his Rhodesian farm, covered a hundred thousand

acres; his dam held back fifty million gallons of water. His fruit trees were planted by the hundred and fifty thousand. Discussing with Sir Herbert Baker a building he wanted designed, he said, "Make it big, simple—barbaric, if you like." "Think simply," "Truth is ever simple," were others of his sayings. One wonders if he thought that he thought simply himself. If he did, it was paradoxically, with such grandiloquent simplicity and truth about his desires, that no one could believe him.

He kept wild beasts at Groot Schuur. He had lions there and great paddocks where buck and zebras roamed. Many of his animals were poisoned in the period of his decline from power. And in this zoo of his, we find his spirit which wanted to possess, in opposition to that of Kruger who kept no beasts but his dogs and horses. Rhodes enclosed his animals while Kruger founded the greatest wild-animal reserve in the world on the Sabi River on the Portuguese border.

In all his acts Rhodes acted on his principle of "Do not be mean." And meanness or smallness was not in him.

"You the same Rhodes, sir?" asked the doctor who had examined him as a boy, on a later visit to England. On saying that he was, the doctor said, "Impossible. According to my books you have been a corpse these ten years."

Never has there been a more dynamic corpse, never a man who, knowing death was near, made greater haste to accomplish his ends. "Happy? Good God, no." But Rhodes knew that life was not made for happiness; that after all we do not live for happiness but for life, whatever it brings. For some obscure reason Cecil John Rhodes's life force was tied to his belief in his country's supremacy, to his conception of the blond, Nordic superman.

In 1891 he fell from a horse—he was a poor horseman—and broke his collar bone. In the same year he had influenza. His fear of death was accelerated. He thought he would only live till he was forty. At forty-eight he died. With "so much to do, so little done," with the regret of a dying man who envies those who survive him because "they will see it all . . . and I shall not."

All? Did Rhodes really think any one would see it all?

Wilfred Blunt wrote, "Rhodes is dead. I did the rogue an injustice when I thought he might be shamming." Meredith said,

"I would scourge him with the crown still on him." In life Rhodes had been crowned and scourged, but the scourgers dared not raise their lash till his crown had fallen.

"Everything in the world is too short," was another of Rhodes's saying. "Life and fame and achievement. Everything is too short. From the cradle to the grave, what is it? Three days at the seaside."

Only one thing was unconquerable to Rhodes—*Time*. Time was against him and time was winning.

CHAPTER THREE

DOCTOR JIM

Doctor Leander Starr Jameson—Doctor Jim as he was called—was born in the same year as Cecil Rhodes, and came out to South Africa for the same reason, ill health; he became Rhodes's greatest friend and closest associate after Pickering's death; almost ruined Rhodes with the Raid; and finally became Premier of Rhodesia, the country that he had helped Rhodes to conquer. Doctor Jim was a small dark man with a high forehead. He carried himself badly with stooped shoulders. His attitudes were careless. He rode his brown cob "Moscow" with slack rein and a loose leg. Dismounted, his tendency was to lounge with his hands in his pockets. Though he was feverishly restless, with a fantastic craving for action and adventure, none of it showed in his bearing except that he was a great, almost a chain smoker of cigarettes.

Melina Rorke, who knew him as a child, says, "I always enjoyed myself in his presence. There was something so warm and friendly about him. Whenever his dark, wide-set eyes rested upon me, I felt myself an integral part of the group. . . . Actually he was thin and insignificant with just a fringe of dark hair below his shining bald dome, but no one ever thought about his looks, so big was his heart, so inspiring his enthusiasm, so great his charm."

John Hays Hammond describes Jameson as "of small stature, slightly built. His brown eyes, alert and brilliant, were set far apart. His personality was forceful with magnetism which led his men to follow him in whatever enterprise he might recommend, however desperate. . . . He was a most engaging companion; there was in him a spirit of daring, and a willingness to risk all on the throw of a dice, that was at times regarded by the less adventurous souls as foolhardy . . . no sooner was one problem out of the way than two new ones presented themselves. The solution of every one required immediate decision and positive action. Jameson loved the excitement of this adventurous existence. He cajoled the Matabele chiefs when he could; when he could not, he fought and conquered them." With Jameson war was a continuation of politics by other means.

It was Doctor Jim who met the commando of Boer Filibusters under Ferriera when they were going to jump the British claim in Mashonaland and not only turned them back but persuaded their leader to join him. Here again is the irony of Africa: Doctor Jim turning back one lot of Boer raiders, and then, not many years later, when he was himself leading a raid into the Boer country, being captured and condemned to death.

On one occasion, hearing that a Zulu boy who had run amock and killed a white man, a woman, and a child was about to be lynched, Jameson jumped on his horse and galloped to the jail where he found fifty men about to break into it. Without dismounting he shouted:

"Gentlemen, I ask you to pause. Remember the country is on the eve of a boom. For God's sake, don't do anything to stop it."

The lynching party became hesitant: above all, being miners and settlers, they wanted a boom. Jameson then invited them over to the Masonic Hotel for a drink and to talk things over. He assured them that justice would be done. They sang "For he's a jolly good fellow"; they sang "God Save the Queen," and then they dispersed. There had been no lynching. Like his leader Rhodes's "Let's have breakfast before we talk about blood," Jameson had put his idea over by negotiation and alcohol.

This incident had a sequel. The baker who owned the lynching rope sent in a bill to the government for fifteen shillings, alleging that in the confusion of the moment the Doctor had made off with it. Perhaps he had.

The general picture of Doctor Jim seems to be that of a small, nervous, highly-strung man, an excellent surgeon, a man who held himself in, who rode himself on the heavy curb of an affected calm that deceived no one as to the urgency of his character. He was a lawmaker and by contrast a lawbreaker. He was once arrested for gun-running to a native tribe, he led his police into the Transvaal on the Raid that immortalised his name, ruined Rhodes, and epitomised the final phase of British expansion—that of conquest by adventurers. That he failed in his coup was due to the fact that the time of the gentleman corsair, the political Raffles, had passed. A fighter, a gambler, a passionate, and able man; a man of great erudition; a delicate man—who succeeded in overcompensating his weakness by the strength of his will and the tenacity of his purpose. His piles tortured him, yet he would stay in the saddle all day. Like Rhodes, he never married. Condemned to death by Kruger after the Raid, he was imprisoned in England; was released on account of ill health after a short term, thus turning his defective physique into an asset; became Prime Minister of the Cape Colony; was knighted; and finally buried in state. His charm was undeniable, his capacity beyond question, his love of Rhodes and of England the mainspring of a life doomed by illness to adventure and by temperament to kill the things he loved best—Rhodes and the prestige of England.

Jameson's life and Rhodes's are inextricably bound together in the twofold cord of their love for each other and for the country of their adoption. They were complement and supplement. They were master and man. But the man was the master, physician, and adviser. He was Rhodes's genius, and in the end his evil genius. Yet even for this Rhodes forgave him.

After the Raid he said, "Jameson has upset my apple-cart." Just as when he got the news of the burning of his home, he said, "My God, I thought something had happened to Doctor Jim." Never was there a word of blame for Jameson from Cecil Rhodes.

Jameson was, " to at least half the people of South Africa, the personification of flagrant breach of faith, oversea acquisitiveness, and cynical violation of the most elementary principles of law . . . the circumstance that this political felon was allowed to boss the show at Cape Town within ten years of the Raid merely increased the intensity of some people's ire. Jameson never succeeded in shaking off either his indiscreet admirers of his irreconcilable persecutors. . . . Owing to his predilection for frequent and lengthy trips to Europe, Jameson was practically a stranger to Africa except the Cape and Rhodesia. . . . Backed by a small majority he accepted the Cape premiership in 1904. He did this without the slightest vestige of enthusiasm. His immediate party friends he describes as ' the most awful crew ' and the honourable members as ' this beastly house.' Nostalgia for golf courses in England never left him."

Jameson's attitude is still not uncommon. Many of the better-off settlers from England know only their own districts and commute between their farms, where they work, and home—England. Africa and its people are unknown to them even after many years of residence. Jameson travelled a long way in Africa—from Kimberley to Bulawayo, from Bulawayo to the disaster at Doornkop where he was captured. From there, to a condemned cell in Pretoria, to England and subsequent freedom, to the premiership of the Cape Colony, and a home, as Premier, at Groot Schuur that Rhodes had left for the use of those who should follow him. But all the time, except during his adventurous days in the North, he seems to have pined for home. In 1907 he wrote to his brother Sam, "I shall beat you at golf when I come back." In 1911 he wrote from London to Sir Thomas Smart, one of his lieutenants, that he wanted "to leave politics." On April 10, 1912, he did leave politics.

On November 26, 1917, Sir Leander Starr Jameson died in London. The First World War was then in its critical stage and America had just come into it against Germany. In 1904, when he became Premier of the Cape, Paul Kruger died. Jameson's life was a link between the days of the Great Trek of the Boers and the First World War.

The life the pioneers led in Mashonaland was hard in the extreme. They were short of everything, of all supplies. There were no women there, no comforts of any kind, and little food except the game they shot. And yet they succeeded in making farms and establishing mines. By and large, these men whom Rhodes had sent up were not farmers. They were young Englishmen in search of adventure who had been inspired by Rhodes and Jameson to go North—"to my North . . . the hinterland that is my thought"—and create there a new extension of the Empire. They lived in native huts built of mud and thatched with grass. They ate when they could and drank all they could lay their hands on. But the prices of everything were very high. Eggs eight shillings and sixpence a dozen, butter six shillings a pound, milk twelve shillings a quart, candles three shillings a pound, paraffin fifteen shillings a gallon, English beer thirty-two shillings a dozen pints.

In 1891, when Lord Randolph Churchill's surplus stores were

sold, a bottle of three-star brandy fetched five pounds, a case of whisky fifty pounds, which led to the speculators rushing up liquor. For some weeks nothing else was imported and the prices fell rapidly—so much so that the local paper, which was printed on a little hand press, informed the public that the "cost of living had fallen to five shillings a bottle."

The settlers were easy marks for the confidence men who followed them. A pair of mules for breeding were sold to one man. Another trickster arrived with a small sum of capital that he had made in the Free State by vaccinating Boers against smallpox with a mixture of condensed milk and water at two and sixpence a throw. In Mashonaland he employed this capital by buying a number of cattle from a Boer. The sum paid in gold and notes appeared wrong to the Boer who considered himself "slim" —a hard trader—and he proceeded to prove his contention that he was ten pounds short by referring to a *Ready Reckoner* he carried. He produced the book to support his claim. The Doctor, as he had been called after his vaccination trick, looked at the book carefully and then flung it down. "Why, man alive," he said, "that's no good. That's last year's *Ready Reckoner*."

Currency was also a difficulty. There was a great shortage of it and its place was taken by cheques. As the nearest bank was at Mafeking and it took the post eight weeks to make the round trip, there was great risk in accepting any cheques issued by people who were not in a settled position. The Chartered Companies' cheques were accepted as standard currency, but as they were often for odd amounts transactions were difficult. Marshall Hole tells of how he went to a dispersal sale to buy a bag of potatoes, which were a great luxury, for the mess. He bought them for seventeen shillings and sixpence and tendered his cheque, the only money he had, on the Company for five pounds three and fourpence. "No change," said the auctioneer, "but we'll soon put that right," and before Hole could say anything knocked down a pair of field boots to him for two pounds ten and a bottle of brandy for one pound. He then offered to toss double or quits for the balance, and offered, when he lost, another bottle of brandy or a doubtful cheque for twenty-five shillings. Hole took the cheque which he says he eventually induced someone to accept for a pound of Boer tobacco. The members of the mess when he took home his purchases reluctantly accepted the brandy, since they needed the potatoes, but refused to have anything to do with the boots. They were no use to Hole, since they did not fit him, and he got rid of them only by giving them to his native servant in lieu of a month's wages.

Another interesting financial incident took place when at a revivalist meeting—the Salvation Army had arrived by this time—a man called Donaldson said he was saved and standing up before the crowd said, "This is not the old Donaldson addressing you but an entirely new Donaldson." He was interrupted by someone shouting, "But what we want to know is will the new Donaldson pay the old Donaldson's debts?"

There would have been no point in obtaining Bechuanaland—"the neck of the bottle," as Rhodes called it—for England unless it was going to be used. Bechuanaland led to the real North. The djhins—hunters and prospectors: they came and went back and came again with others—poured out of the bottle in a trickle at first, and then the bottle became an hour-glass, its belly forever swelling with new acquisitions. But at no time, especially in the beginning, was the job easy. It was not merely a matter of negotiations with Lobengula, of outwitting Kruger who was also negotiating, but of finding the right man to carry on the work and of organising transport and turning an occupation by a lot of young, rather wild young Englishmen into a settled colony with towns, farms, homesteads, hospitals, schools, churches, and hotels.

It was Rhodes's genius which saw all these in his mind as complete long before his Chartered Company was formed or his treaty with Lobengula signed. He saw good farms, fields of green mealies, patches of alfalfa, towns with the streets so wide that a full span of oxen could turn in them. And as he saw it in his mind so was it made, and it was made because he had seen it in his mind: because he had the capacity to make others see with him and believe with him. But in the beginning it was a gamble, a race in which Rhodes entered the best men he had: Jameson, Rudd, and the young men who were known as the "Twelve Apostles." Had Jameson not come to Africa the conquest of Rhodesia might never have taken place, since there was no one with ability comparable to his to whom Rhodes could have entrusted the job. And his coming was an accident—another of those strange tricks that Fate seems to have played on history. A sick man, Jameson applied for the job as surgeon to the new hospital at Kimberley. The position had been offered to Doctor Henry Wolff, an American graduate of Harvard Medical School. His letter of acceptance was never received and when he arrived, he found Jameson already at work.

Rhodes's road to success was paved with delayed despatches. But here at least was one with which he could not be accused of tampering.

Something must be said about the upper-class Englishman of the time—the eighties and gay nineties. It was the grand period of the snob, of the gentleman. In the early nineteen-hundreds the *Illustrated London News* had a double-page drawing of a party entitled "Entertainment for children of the patricians." In 1905 in the same paper there was a picture of Bernard Shaw with the caption "Socialist—yet not a ragamuffin." In his description of the Zulu War, Captain Montague writes of his servant holding out his tunic in which he had found a louse, saying to his master that it was "one of the things the men have." The old school tie, which is relatively democratic, had not come in yet, since all gentlemen wore frock coats, top hats, and the great Ascot ties which were derived from the stock of an earlier period.

This was the period of the great London clubs, of blackballing, of "good form," of English jingoism, of Kipling's Tommy Atkins, of an almost incredible class distinction, of a formal morality which covered a looseness which would not be tolerated to-day. Anything was permissible for the rich, provided it was not discovered or flaunted. Many Englishmen in Africa came from great homes and had been brought up within the restricted frame of Victorian custom. Young sons, expecting to inherit little or nothing, had to make their own way and Africa was as good a place as any in which to do it. They had ridden to hounds since childhood, had been taught to shoot pheasants by their father's head keeper, and though they revolted from this life and went, as it was called, "abroad," or "to the colonies," they retained many of the forms to which they had been conditioned in their childhood.

They are interesting as a class which has vanished, as a lost and intermediate species, as examples of an aristocratic mutation.

For the making of an empire no better stuff could have been found as clay to Rhodes's hand, unless it had been the Elizabethan adventurers, or the men who served the old John Company in India. As Rhodes was an intermediate type, something between a Warren Hastings and a modern financier, so were these young men intermediate, something between the officers who fought under Wellington at Waterloo and the officers who died in the First World War in France, Belgium, and Mesopotamia. They were a military, plutocratic-by-marriage class, a caste of which there are only a few hardly recognisable remnants to-day. They were the instruments, but it was Rhodes, Jameson, and Biet who made Rhodesia. An Englishman, a Scotsman, and a German Jew who by some accident had all been born in the same year. All were invalids. Rhodes with his weak lungs and heart; Jameson with his weak lungs, hemorrhoids, and gallstones; and Biet almost psychopathically nervous: a curious trio of bachelors. They did not like games. They were not interested in team sports. Rhodes rode every day of his life and shot game, but he could never ride or shoot. He played cards and could not play. Jameson liked solo whist and always lost at this his only sport. Biet at one time kept a racing stable in Germany, but never saw one of his horses. If these men had a common denominator, apart from the year of their birth, it was a love of art, of beauty. As a group they were abnormal—intellectuals, celibates, who had sublimated their desires into the worship of a central idea which one of their number, Rhodes, their prophet, had sold them.

The prelude to the concessions, Rhodes's or any one else's, are the concessionaires—the seekers, the men wanting something for nothing, or for as little as they can pay. Even here there is a pattern and the seekers are preceded by others—the missionaries; the traders who come a-bartering beads for ivory, trade guns for quills of gold. Then the sportsmen and hunters. These last get the first real concession, the right to hunt, which is the right to explore and to map and prospect. It is more or less possible for a chief to stop a man from taking samples of rock, but he cannot stop him from looking at anything or marking down what he sees on a rough little map in his log-book. Who would bother to take a country until they knew it was worth taking? But for many years reports had been coming down from the North. The little concessionaires were established there by the grace of God, brandy for the king, a measure of good luck, constitutions which could withstand the ravages of the climate and consciences which could support the orgies of massacre that they were forced to witness as the king's guests.

All this had happened in Moselikatze's time. The missionaries —he even had a favourite missionary, Moffat—had come; the hunters like Hartley, and a few traders. This was the position in Matabeleland in 1870 when Moselikatze died and his son Lobengula took his place. The white men were there in his land, but not yet boldly demanding—many of them even servile, crawling on their bellies like his own subjects towards him.

Here is a description of Lobengula, the mountain of black flesh that had once been a Matabele warrior: a tall fat man naked but for his head ring, the feather of a parakeet in his hair, and a sporran of blue monkey skin about his loins. Before him, posturing, leaping, shouting, comes his m'bongo, his praise-maker. "Behold the king," he shouts, " the black bull, the elephant whose tread shakes the world. When he opens his mouth, the heavens roar. Stabber of heaven . . . eater of men."

See Lobengula, "he who drives like the wind," in the bath chair that was his throne; see him on his wagon beneath the Tree of Justice.

Hear him condemn a man to death who has drunk the king's beer. See him with his wives and his concubines. See him in his kraals, in his house. See him drunken on the champagne the white men have taught him to drink, and the brandy. It had to be good champagne and old brandy. See him yearly grow fatter, see him suffering from gout. Suffering from fear. Fear of his own warriors and what they will bring down upon him. Yes, they can kill if they must, but not too much, and only Mashonas. Above all, they must not touch a white man. In fear that too many white men will come, he sends out patrols to stop them and turn them back. The missionaries must be held in check too. A little Christianity was good, too much would undermine him.

Lobengula was not the last great black king. Khama, the king of the Bechuanas, was greater than he. But Lobengula was the last great king to stand against, and finally to fight, the white man.

This was the period of feelers and of tentacles. Englishman, Boer, and Kaffir were all putting out feelers, fingers, tentative antennæ to try to find a way out of their dilemmas, to seek weak points; or thrusting out tentacles to throttle their opponents and steal their wealth.

In 1887 Lobengula sent his emissaries to Kruger to effect a treaty. Kruger was negotiating with the Swazis, but was more than ready to put Lobengula's territory under the protection of the South African Republic as well. Before this treaty was completed, however, Kruger's emissary was killed by Khama's Bechuanas: an act which Kruger attributed to Rhodes. There is no proof of this, but, as Sarah Gertrude Millin says, "Fate was on Rhodes's side in the matter of inconvenient emissaries. They did have a tendency to vanish from his path.".

Rhodes rose in righteous anger at Kruger's desire to expand to the North, which, if it had been successful, would have checked his own plans for expansion in the North. "When I see that Paul Kruger, with not a sixpence, when his object was to expand his country over the whole northern interior"—*my North, the hinterland that is my thought*—"when I see him sitting in Pretoria with Bechuanaland gone"—Rhodes had taken it from him—"and other lands around him gone from his grasp, I pity the man. I know very well that he has been willing to sacrifice anything to gain that object of his. If you think it out, it has been a most remarkable thing that, not content with recovering his country, he wished to obtain the whole interior for a population of his own."

But Kruger's move had frightened Rhodes. He now had to move fast. An ability to do this was his strong point. Sir Hercules Robinson, the High Commissioner, was his first contact. A message was sent immediately to the deputy commissioner of Bechuanaland, who happened to be Rhodes's old friend Sir Sidney Shippard, and by another of those happy accidents Sir Sidney's assistant was Moffat, the son of that Moffat who had been Moselikatze's favourite missionary. By another coincidence Moffat happened at this very moment to be in Lobengula's town. A message was sent to him to ask how things were going between Lobengula and the Boers, with the added instructions that he was to get in ahead of them, which he did. Lobengula agreed not to cede any part of his kingdom without the sanction of the British High Commissioner.

Even assuming an element of luck, there seems to be too much of it here to make the assumption that it was all luck hold water. A better solution, considering Rhodes's character, would be that there was a combination of planning and luck. Like Napoleon, Rhodes believed in lucky men, considered himself lucky, and employed others whom he believed to be lucky. But also, like Napoleon, he planned as well, and put lucky men in positions where they could make use of their luck. Take the concatenation of circumstance. Rhodes's friend Sir Sidney was deputy commissioner. Moffat, his assistant, was in Matabeleland at the time when Kruger's messenger was assassinated, and ready to negotiate with the chief who had been his father's friend when the moment came. Unquestionably Rhodes did not know exactly what would happen, but he had an idea of the trend and got his men into key positions—pawns to be moved by the Colossus when the moment came to play them.

Meanwhile, other native chiefs were worried. Lobengula had committed himself: how much even Lobengula did not know yet, but the chiefs of other tribes—Lewanika, chief of the Barotse, and Khama, king of the Bechuanas—wanted more information.

Khama wrote to Shippard, fearing that England might favour Lobengula, saying: "I fought Lobengula when he and his father's great warriors came from Natal, and drove him back. He never came again. Yet I fear Lobengula less than I fear brandy. I dread the white man's drink more than all the assegais of the Matabele which kill men's bodies and it is quickly over."

The old fire-water story. The white man, partly inoculated by generations of dissipation to the poison of spirits and his own diseases, like syphilis, tuberculosis, and influenza, did more in all parts of the world to destroy the native cultures than he did with his rifles; and Khama feared, not only that Lobengula's warriors would be armed with rifles and attack him, but that the precedent of white penetration would be forced on to his own people.

In this spirit he wrote to the king of the Barotse, who was also under the protection of England: "I understand that you are now under the protection of the Queen of the English people. But they say there are soldiers living at your place, and some headmen sent by the Queen to take care of you and protect you from the Matabele? Are you happy and quite satisfied? Tell me as friend. Are the ways of the white man burdensome to you?"

What did they know of all this in England? What do they know of England who only England know? What did the old Queen, the widow at·Windsor, know about the black warriors who now claimed her protection or tried to avoid it?—the shining black men and women who knew neither clothing nor restraint. What was this new frieze of naked ebony that Rhodes had painted on the red plush and gold of her great drawing-rooms? England wanted no more expansion or annexation. There were already too many naked men claiming protection. Why, the Zulus, the fathers of the Matabele, had only just been conquered. Colonies cost money to administer. Colonies were a nuisance.

But Rhodes, an Englishman, now acted. His rivals, the Exportation Company, Bechuanaland and the Exploring Company, who had the ear of Lord Knutsford, the new Colonial Secretary, were trying to jump his claim in London. To forestall them he rushed three men up-country to Lobengula—Rudd, his first partner; Rochfort Maguire, an Oxford friend; and Thompson, his compound manager at de Beers who knew the Matabele language—and many of the men who, having worked in the mines, had returned to their kraals. The Exploring Companies also sent a man called Maund to represent them. Lippert represented another group at Lobengula's court. They were the lobbyists. They spent their time conspiring to attain the ends desired by the companies they represented.

The Matabele warriors hated all the white men who hung about the royal kraal, and wanted to make an end of them. Only Lobengula stood between them and their assegais. He was afraid of a white man being harmed because he knew the repercussions caused by such a murder would end in the defeat of his impis. Caught in the cleft stick of fearing to offend his people, and fearing equally to offend the British, he vacillated. His hope was to play one British interest off against another. But at last Rhodes's agents won the race and concluded an agreement with Lobengula by which Rudd and his associates were to pay him a hundred pounds a month, give him a thousand Martini-Henry rifles, a hundred thousand rounds of ammunition, and an armed steamboat on the Zambesi. For this Lobengula granted "complete and exclusive charge over all metals and minerals in my kingdom, together with full power to do all things necessary to win and procure the same."

A missionary, Helm, wrote out the concession and read it to the king. Sir Hercules Robinson endorsed the document, describing Rudd in a letter to London as a "gentleman of character and standing . . . who would check the inroads of adventurers." That is to say, an adventurer with sufficient backing to stop other adventurers such as the Boers or the Germans.

Lord Knutsford, however, was worried about the rifles. "Do you think," he cabled to Sir Hercules, "that there is any danger of complications arising from these rifles?"

Robinson answered that there might be, but that if Lobengula did not get them one way he would get them another—through other countries. Helm, of the London Missionary Society, who had written the agreement, favoured giving the rifles because the substitution of long-range rifles for the stabbing assegais would tend to diminish the loss of life in the Matabele raids and thus prove a distinct gain to humanity.

Like the use of gas in modern times.

The Bishop of Bloemfontein disagreed with Helm "on account of the increased facilities likely to be thus afforded for cruel raids."

Khama was still worried about Lobengula having modern firearms while he had none. This problem was solved by Rudd also giving Khama arms and ammunition, so that, in Sir Sidney Shippard's words, "The relative position of the chiefs would be unchanged." An armament race in Africa had begun—a kind of very simple preview of operations later to be conducted in Europe by Sir Basil Zaharóff and his kind.

But Rhodes, though he had Lobengula's signature, had not yet got his concession or floated his Chartered Company.

Now began a great shuttling to and fro, a great commuting, and fluttering of every kind of wing. Rhodes dashed from London to South Africa and back again. Young men dashed North. Hunters hunted wildly, seeking not game but roads. Financiers preened their splendid plumes and wetted their bills for the kill the brave young men would make. The croupiers of the stock exchanges raised their rakes while investors licked their lips. Rhodes was a hero: Rhodes was a scoundrel: Rhodes was this, Rhodes was that. Clergymen thundered against him; clergymen appealed for him, and to him. Great things were in the air. Men were moving; guns were moving. English guns to the Matábele and Khama—and naturally to other chiefs. German Mausers, *sub rosa*, to Kruger. More guns, also *sub rosa*, to the Uitlanders in Johannesburg who felt that they should be armed—against what they did not know, since they were doing very nicely, but against something. Every one was very much what they were—intensely nationalistic: as much the young Matabele warrior as the young English adventurer, or pioneer, to use the popular euphemism; as much the stolid Boer on his farm as the London broker, who, though he never took a greater risk than that of falling out of a hansom cab, was perhaps the greatest flag-wagger of them all. The waters were troubled for rich fishing and the fishers were ready, their hooks barbed and baited, their financial loins girded for profit. Eagle-eyed young aristocrats fingered their rifles, the barnyard roosters of commerce bought new red-ruled ledgers.

And this all because a black king, drunken on champagne and brandy, had sold away his kingdom.

The last garment of the North, the vain courage of the Matabele warriors, was about to be ripped away. The dance of veils was almost over. No one said it, but every one knew it. There would be an incident, and then—the North would lie open, naked, and violate.

But the charter must be obtained before anything broke. It must be prepared with indecent haste to cover with legality this indecent nakedness which was about to come. For there were those in England who objected to it; to whom such a rape seemed indecent. The liberals, the radicals, the men who had kicked at the annexation of the Transvaal a few years before and who were as ready to be sentimental about Kaffirs as Boers. This document of charter corresponded to the letters of marque given to a privateer, and Rhodes, the captain of the vessel, intended to get it. A new East India Company was to be formed in London, a new John Company. "We've got the men, we've got the guns, we've got the money, too," was the principle, and "Who's to stop us?" was the attitude.

Slowly England had been led along the path by Rhodes. He had shown the people vista after vista, he had shown them the gold and the wide spaces. He had talked about his hinterland— my North; he had told of its wonders, its vast herds of game, its great rocks and mountains, its mopani scrub and towering timber trees. He had excited England at a time when England was ready for excitement. When England was bored with Alfred Tennyson, tired of Swinburne, and titillated by Kipling. Or had the idea of a black Dolores at their mercy a sudden appeal, for this African Dolores was rich? At present only God and Rhodes knew how rich.

While Rhodes sought his charter, Lobengula waited. And old Oom Paul waited, his thumbless hand upon his old four-pounder, his pipe in his mouth, his Bible open upon his knees.

But Lobengula did not only sit and wait. Somehow the significance of this act began to dawn on him and he wrote to Queen Victoria: ". . . They asked me for a place to dig for gold and said they would give me certain things for the right to do so. A document was written and presented. I asked what it contained and was told that in it were my words and the words of these men. I put my name to it. About three months afterwards I heard from other sources that I had given by that document the right to all the minerals in my country."

Is this not the complaint of every man who has been swindled —does each not say and believe "this contains my words and the words of these men?" In them all is there not a hidden clause which is never mentioned till the deed is signed, a paragraph in minute print that changes the aspect of the whole?

Would it be possible that the missionary Helm misrepresented the contents of the deed? It would obviously be easier to make converts in a conquered country. Could the ends have justified the means? The missionary has rarely objected to the gunboat or police protection which backed his authority to convert. The Spaniards used force to convert Mexico in the sixteenth century and the precedent they established has been followed all over the world. Oddly, the savage has needed to be coerced before he would abandon his tribal culture and adopt the Mother Hubbard and the religion that the white man preaches, but so rarely practises himself. Oddly, without books or what we call knowledge, the native knows justice and truth and is at a loss to understand the sophistry to which we have been conditioned.

Rhodes disputed the authenticity of this letter of Lobengula's to the Queen. But surely no other course was open to him. At any rate, Lobengula, persuaded that he might be able to get out of his bargain, since he did not see how he could have made a treaty with the Queen as her emissaries had not been present, decided to send a mission to England to see her. He sent two indunas with Selous the hunter, Maund the representative of the Exploration Companies, and Johann Colenbrander, a Dutchman well known on the frontier. These three white men, now acting against Rhodes, were later to serve under him.

While the Matabele captains were being shown the sights of London, including the fat little old Queen, Rhodes acted. Not only would the charter not wait, but life would not wait. With all his money he could not buy health, not a single extra year in which to accomplish those ends which were his driving force.

He spent his time interviewing, buying out rivals, intimidating the enemies he could not buy, satisfying, explaining, and igniting the fire that was eventually to consume South Africa. There were enemies in London: Mackenzie the missionary, and Bradlaugh and Labouchere, the London Chamber of Commerce, the Aborigines Protection Society, Albert, who afterwards became Earl Grey, and his friend, Joseph Chamberlain. The Irish members of Parliament he had bought for ten thousand pounds, giving it to them "in poor Parnell's cause." But the root of the trouble lay in the fact that, though he had Lobengula's signature, the Exploration Companies had applied to the Colonial Office for a charter in the North before he did. To this there was only one answer, and that answer was to Rhodes's own taste—amalgamation. His manœuvres had been a masterly jockeying for position which left him the inside track. They had the first application, but he, Rhodes, had the king's signature.

CHAPTER FOUR

LOBENGULA

LOBENGULA was king of the Matabele. To know how little or how much he was king, we must go back to the day that he assumed the title. At that time he had two friends only— old Umnombata, who did not long survive his achievements as a kingmaker, and his own sister Ningi. But he had many enemies. He was in the thrall of the wizards of the Matopos—the priests of M'limo, who had brought him up. He was never free from their prying, for they had agents among the Matabele, lesser priests, the so-called witch-doctors, who smelt out any one who did not pay them blackmail and had them killed by claiming that they were the king's enemies. If one of the king's wives was sick, or did a royal ox die, someone was smelt out. The sorcerers worked for the king too—on his hint. If, for instance, a man was too rich and the king desired his wealth or if a man was too powerful and the king feared his power, then that man was found guilty of witchcraft and killed.

But they, the sorcerers, not he, the king, were the masters. The irony of it was that Lobengula, as king, was also the high priest of the nation. Ningi, his sister, hated the sorcerers and was hated by them. She was the friend of many white traders, and of the bottles they brought, and advised Lobengula on many things from the choice of a new wife to the advisability of making an alliance or a war. But eventually the witch-doctors were too much even for her and she was killed at Lobengula's orders. Then indeed he was alone.

Her end was very simply accomplished. Lobengula's chief wife, Lósikeyi, daughter of the king of Gazaland, gave birth to a stillborn son. This could only be due to witchcraft. Someone was responsible and Ningi was accused. As evidence the doctors produced a small brass locket that the king had given to his sister many years before.

"From the child's throat we drew this forth," the doctors said.

"And in Ningi's hut we found this." Another doctor came up with a dead toad, its body pierced with a wooden skewer. Also they added, "We have cast the bones and they say that she is guilty."

"Do not let me look on her face again," the king said. "Let her be served as she has served my son." In a few minutes it was over.

Frank Oates gives a description of Ningi, or Nina, as he called her: "Suddenly the royal sister appeared and presented a most singular, not to say magnificent, appearance. It was something like the appearance of the prima donna at the opera, or the leading spirit in some gorgeous pantomime. She is very stout, and tremendously embonpoint, and her skin is of a coppery hue. She wore no dress, and the only covering above her waist was a number of gilded chains, some encircling her, some pendent. Round her arms were massive brazen bracelets. A blue-and-white freemason's apron appeared in front, and looked strangely anomalous there, though really not unbecoming. From her waist also there hung down a number of brilliantly-coloured woollen neck-wraps, red being the predominant colour. Under the apron was a sort of short black skirt, covering the thighs, made of wrought ox-hide. Her legs and feet were bare, but round her ankles were the circlets of bells, worn by the women to make a noise when they dance. Her headdress was decidedly pretty—a small bouquet of artificial flowers in front, and amongst the hair, standing in all directions, feathers of bee-eaters' tails. A small circular ornament fashioned of red clay was on the back of her head. She put herself in posture for the dance, but did not move very much or energetically whilst keeping time; she suffered too much from adiposity. She held one of the large oval black-and-white ox-hide shields, surmounted by a jackal's tail, such as are carried by warriors."

Oates described Lobengula in 1873 as being of an intense black colour. On the other hand, Sir Sidney Shippard says his skin was "of a fine bronze." Oates says he had a benignant smile. The French missionary Coillard in 1878 corroborates this. While Maund in 1885 describes him as "a gross fat man with a cruel, restless eye."

Generally Lobengula was naked except for his kilt of blue monkey skins. Shippard says, "in spite of his obesity he had a most majestic appearance." The French explorer Lionel Declé thought him "the most imposing monarch he had ever seen except the Tsar Alexander."

When he received Selous, Lobengula wore a greasy shirt and a dirty pair of trousers. When Oates saw him, he wore a broad-brimmed hat, an unclean cotton shirt, unbraced baggy trousers, and large clumsy shoes. Cooper Chadwick, who was in almost daily contact with Lobengula from 1887 to 1890, said: "Lobengula stands over six feet in height, but is so enormously fat that it makes him look smaller, though his proud bearing and stately walk give him all the appearance of a savage king. His features are coarse and exhibit great cunning and cruelty. But when he smiles the expression completely changes and makes his face appear pleasant and good-tempered."

There are no pictures of Lobengula because he refused, on superstitious grounds, to be photographed; and the few sketches that exist bear little resemblance to each other and probably little to Lobengula. The composite descriptions of those who saw him appear to portray a tall warrior with a not unpleasant expression in the earlier stages of his reign, but one who became more gross and cruel as he was undermined by his power of life and death and the champagne and brandy with which the traders kept him supplied. His size at least he had in common with Kruger and Rhodes. His pride was that of the Zulu: like that of those chiefs who surrendered to the British after the war of 1880. This pride is illustrated by an incident which took place when an officer, wishing to possess something of Mahanana's, a Zulu kinglet, asked him to give him the stick he carried.

Mahanana raised his eyes for a second and replied in his low soft voice: "This stick has touched my hand and there may be some royal sweat upon it. I am a king and nothing of a king's can touch a stranger and not be defiled." The officer, foiled about the stick, asked for the tiny snuff-box he carried in his ear. Without a word the Zulu raised his hand and took it out with hardly a motion of his body. Then he held it out and let the tiny bit of horn fall into the Englishman's hand. The latter in return brought out some sticks of tobacco and a couple of boxes of matches, both worth their weight in gold in the Zulus' eyes, and offered them to Mahanana. He quietly held out one hand and, as the presents fell into his palm, just passed them over to his follower sitting next to him as if these things were utterly beneath his notice. "And yet this man," Captain Montague goes on, "was a prisoner and beaten. It is amusing to talk to the Zulus, they are so magnificent in their ignorance and so full of their own superiority."

The same pride in loyalty is shown by an event in Lobengula's kraal. A Holi slave had been caught drinking some royal beer from a jar left on the ground by a girl.

"Bring the dog here," said the king.

The man was led up to him.

"Your lips have tasted the king's beer. Cut off his lips."

"Cut off his nose which has smelt the king's beer."

"Cover his eyes which have seen the king's beer."

The skin of his forehead was peeled down with a knife till it hung like a curtain over his eyes. His eyes covered, his nose and lips cut off, he was led away to be hurled to the crocodiles in the River of White Stones, while the trader who had been present during the proceedings went outside the kraal and was violently sick.

Yet Lobengula was a constitutional monarch and pleasing to his people, except that he was too peaceful for them and restrained them from war with the white men.

The royal palace at Gibbexegu—the noose of the old man—which was later, and aptly, named Bulawayo—the Place of Slaughter—consisted of two brick houses built by an English sailor who had a knowledge of bricklaying and had found himself in Matabeleland, having wandered up there from the coast. Behind the king's houses were the huts of his wives constructed very neatly of poles and cow-dung cement with thatched beehive roofs. Each was enclosed by a palisade of reeds. Near by were the courtyard for meetings, and the goat kraal where the king presided over the mysteries of rain-making and which was specially guarded as a holy place. The whole group of buildings was surrounded by a zareba of tree trunks, while a further area was cleared of bush and marked off for military parades and ceremonial dances. Outside the royal quarters and parade ground were the huts of the common people in separate, fenced-off groups. The atmosphere of the palace was indescribable. The royal yard was littered with the heads and skins of oxen slaughtered for the king's feasts, heavy with the stink of putrescent flesh, black with the flies which clustered on the offal and men alike; superimposed on this stench was the smell of goats and dung from the kraal, of sour milk and beer and sweat. The only shade in the shimmering pool of heat was given by the king's indaba tree, beneath which he sat to administer his terrible Matabele justice. Shining naked warriors of the guard lolled about, leaning on their spears. Shining naked girls, in never-ending strings, brought in beer and meat, carrying it on their heads, balanced in great red Kaffir pots. The king's wives, fat mountains of black flesh, crept on their knees to their master. Children, naked too—calves of the royal bull—played in the dust, while dogs fought for scraps, and chickens no bigger than bantams strutted, crowed, and scratched in the ground stamped hard by the king's killers.

The dogs were so savage that no one was safe from them. They were said to have pulled down and killed one of the king's captains. On one occasion, when a trader complained of them, Lobengula showed him his own trousers which one of them had torn.

Overhead in the burnt-out sky of Africa vultures circled endlessly while they waited for justice to be done. Not far off the crocodiles waited, too, also for the justice that was their food. All that was most savage in a savage land was here concentrated into a single acre of blood-stained soil. This was the centre, the very home of death, the Place of the Slaughter.

To this kraal came Sir Sidney Godolphin Alexander Shippard, K.C.M.G., in a spring wagon drawn by eight mules with an escort of a captain, a sergeant, and sixteen smart troopers. He came nominally to inquire about Grobler's murder. But the dead man was only the excuse: the real purpose was a question of boundaries. Grobler had been the South African Republic's emissary, and according to Kruger his murder had been planned by the British.

Sir Sidney was a little important man with Dundreary whiskers. He was in a bad temper, having been stopped at the border by a Matabele patrol who refused to let him go on till they had informed the king of certain circumstances.

Her Majesty's envoy stopped by a horde of savages with spears! It was intolerable. But Her Majesty's envoy was stopped and held up while the king was informed of his suspicious actions. The matter, as far as the Matabele captain was concerned, was important—one of medicine, of witchcraft.

This is what the spy he had sent to his camp had seen: The white induna—Shippard—he said, "took off all his clothes and sat in a pool of boiling water. He rubbed his body all over with a terrible white frothing medicine and squeezed the boiling water over himself with some strange vegetable. Without doubt he is a powerful wizard."

This is why Lobengula greeted the representative of Queen Victoria as a wizard. Shippard was asked why, if he was friendly, he travelled with soldiers? Why, if he was not a magician, he travelled by night "like wolves and ghosts"? To a people afraid of the dark, it would not occur that it was cooler to travel by night.

Meanwhile, Lobengula was worried. Knowing something of sorcery, he disliked sorcerers and feared them, but at the same time he wished to see this man. To add to his fears came the counsel of the other white men who hung about his kraal—some represented the Boers, others represented German interests, still others had been sent by the Portuguese. The young warriors were almost out of hand. Regiment after regiment came to Bulawayo to ask permission to turn the intruders out and to massacre all the white men in the country.

Lobengula had a gift—not common among native Africans—of being able to look ahead and to see under the surface of events, of having at least some knowledge of the law of cause and effect. To kill the white men would be easy, but . . . To give concessions here and there would be easy, but . . . Always buts and ifs; always the act and the repercussions of the act. Yet he had to do something to get away from his worries and from the men, all of whom wanted something from him—gold, concessions, land grants, trading rights, even sleek Matabele girls.

And the answer to his problems was to come to an agreement with Shippard and to substitute one big worry for a lot of little ones, to consolidate his liabilities of worry as if they were debts that he was taking to a loan company. Sir Sidney Shippard was the agent of that company. The wealth of Matabeleland was the security Lobengula was about to mortgage.

Helm the missionary attended the meeting between Shippard and the king, acting as interpreter. Major Gould Adams and Moffat were there also. Adams was in command of the escort: Moffat was supposed to be in Matabeleland on a social visit to the king. Shippard, though it was midsummer, wore a tightly buttoned frock coat on which was pinned the star of his order. He had on grey kid gloves, patent-leather boots, carried a malacca cane with a silver top, and wore a white sun helmet. Dressed like this and accompanied by the captain of his escort, he picked his way through the offal of the king's yard to the royal wagon from which descended the king, dressed in a monkey-skin kilt with a strip of blue calico about his loins.

Mutual compliments were exchanged and interpreted. The sun beat down upon the group by the wagon. The flies rising from the rotting ox heads settled on the face of the Queen's emissary. The crowd of warriors, councillors, royal wives and concubines pressed nearer.

Lobengula lit his pipe, Shippard lit a cigar. The king ordered the people back and said to Shippard, "What is it you really want from me?" By "you" he meant the English.

"I want nothing," Shippard said, "but to bring you a message of good will and to hear what you have to say about the boundary between you and Khama." It was Khama's men who had killed Grobler.

"Let the boundary wait. I want to talk about the white men at my kraal. For a long time they let me alone, but since I marked the paper for Joni"—this was what he called Moffat—"they worry me. They say they are friends of the Queen, but they are not friends among themselves. How do I know if they lie or not? And who is Ulodzi?"—this was Rhodes. "Is he one I can trust?"

"Yes, you can trust him."

But Lobengula was not happy about the paper that Rudd, Maguire, and Thompson had presented to him, that Helm had translated and read to him. He had been promised rifles, ammunition, a gunboat on the Zambesi, and money—a hundred pounds a month. This was real gold, and surely better than gold in the ground in Mashonaland that he and his people would never dig for. But was it real gold?

"How do I know you have any money?" he asked Rudd.

Rudd was ready for him: he pulled out a bag from his pocket and emptied a pile of sovereigns into a wooden platter on the ground at the king's feet. As a result, Rudd went off with the signed document, but the other white men stayed whispering into the king's ear: Rhodes was an imposter, he had no real power. How did he, Lobengula, know there was even a queen in England? Who had seen her?

Lobengula now decided to send emissaries of his own to London. "You shall be my eyes," he told them, "and shall come back and tell us what you saw."

The indunas went and saw the sights of London and the Queen, but Rhodes was there before them.

After they had gone, the king's worries continued. "Do you know what you have done, king?" the agent of a German speculator asked. "You have sold your whole country. It is not gold Rhodes wants, it is your land. Thousands will come. They will rob you of your cattle and your women."

Trouble grew, and when unrest was at its height in rode Doctor Jim. He had seen the king before and had cured his gout and diseased eyes. Now he set about calming the king's mind as once he had calmed his body. For weeks he stayed in the kraal promising, cajoling, calming, explaining that Rhodes was an honest man and that the king, according to his contract, had not parted with an acre of his land. He promised that Rhodes would never interfere with him as long as the Matabele let him dig for gold in peace.

But Lobengula knew that the white men would come; that having come they would encroach on his old raising grounds; and that one day there would be a clash—the incident that Rhodes too had foreseen and wanted, the explosive whose fuse was the Rudd concession. At one end of the political situation was Rhodes with a match, at the other end Lobengula sat on the powder barrel.

Lobengula knew this, but he could do nothing. He had sent his indunas *to see*. He had written to the Queen. All he could do was to wait, to drink champagne and brandy, to play with the hundred golden sovereigns that were given him each month, to handle the stolen diamonds his men brought him as tribute from

Kimberley, to mourn his sister Ningi—and regret the day he had become a king.

Cecil Rhodes now had his concession and his charter, but he had no road. It was one thing to be allowed to dig for gold in Mashonaland, and another to get there without meeting Lobengula's impis—whom the king was unable to control fully. If once they saw numbers of white men with horses and wagons in their country, they would attack them; and the moment for war had not yet come. An incident, like a boil, must have time to ripen. There must be inflammation and pain. It would not look well if it came too soon. The partisans of the Negroes in London and Rhodes's personal enemies would make it look like an invasion of native territory. It was nothing else, but it must be made to seem something else; and here Frédéric Courtney Selous, the last of the elephant hunters, came in. He had hunted all over this country since boyhood. Lobengula had never liked Selous and had always hoped that an elephant would kill him. However, no elephant had killed him and Selous changed sides—having been to England as Lobengula's emissary, he now worked out for Rhodes a practicable route for what was actually the invasion of Mashonaland.

Jameson, after four months in Lobengula's kraal, had got him to agree to giving a safe passage through his lands to the pioneers by goading him and worrying him till at last, distracted, the king said, "I never refused the road to you or your impi."

But this was not enough. Promise or no promise, without Selous's road there would have been war. But Rhodes's luck persisted: Selous agreed to guide the expedition which Frank Johnson had undertaken to equip in nine months for the sum of eighty-eight thousand pounds.

Selous and Johnson, who had been among the earliest concessionaires and as such Rhodes's opponents, were now on the directorate of the Chartered Company. Quite how this happened is hard to explain except by Barney Barnato's remark, "You can refuse Rhodes nothing . . ." There must, however, have been a *quid pro quo* of some kind.

Doctor Jim accompanied the column when it marched, but almost at once there was trouble, for Selous crossed the Matabele border to look for the two indunas who had been detailed to show the permitted road at a doubtful point. Lobengula sent this message to Jameson at once: "Has the king killed any white men that an impi is collecting on his border? or have the white men lost anything they are looking for?"

Jameson hurried to Bulawayo to see the king.

"The king told me I could make the road. Did the king lie?" Jameson asked.

The king, who was sacrificing a goat, answered, "The King never lies," and turned back to the goat.

There was no further interference and the Union Jack was hoisted on a plateau four thousand feet above sea level. The place where it flew was called Salisbury.

Rhodes had chosen Mashonaland rather than Matabeleland for his pioneers because if it came to an argument he preferred to argue with the unwarlike Mashonas who were tributaries of the Matabele, rather than with the Matabele themselves. For though Lobengula did not know it, the German had been right —he had given away his country.

His emissaries were back now, having seen with their own eyes —the eyes of the king—the great white Queen. They informed Lobengula of her existence. Lobengula with his back to the wall now sent for Helm.

"Read that," he said, and gave his copy of the concession to Helm who had written it out, "and tell me faithfully if I have given away any of the land of the Matabele."

"Yes, king, you have. How can white men dig for gold without land?"

"If gold is found anywhere, can the white men occupy the land and dig for it?"

"Yes, king."

"If the gold is in my garden, can they dig for it?"

"Yes, king."

"If the gold is in my kraal, can they enter and dig?"

"Yes, king."

The king's *eyes*, his indunas, who had been to London, had seen much, but accomplished nothing. The king's letter to the Queen had accomplished nothing: it had arrived too late. Oddly, this letter sent through Sir Sidney Shippard took one hundred days to arrive in London, while Maund's, who wrote at the same time, took forty-seven.

Lobengula now could write as much as he liked, send as many *eyes* as he liked—the Union Jack flew on the Mashona High Veld.

Nor did the Queen's answer that the indunas had brought back comfort the king. She advised him to give no hasty concessions.

" It is not wise," she wrote, " to put too much power in the hands of the men who came first and to exclude other deserving men. A king gives a stranger an ox, not his whole herd of cattle, otherwise what would other strangers have to eat?"

A more important question, Sarah Gertrude Millin says, might have been, " What would the king himself, if he gave away his whole herd, have to eat?"

While Lobengula was regretting that he had ever made his mark on any paper whatsoever, while the pioneers were finding little gold and neither milk nor honey in Mashonaland, Rhodes had become Prime Minister of the Cape Colony.

Mr. Rhodes was on his way up.

Lobengula was on his way down.

Paul Kruger was static, sitting heavily in his office watching events and making his plans—plans so simple that when they were put into effect, the English world was shocked at his duplicity. The Machiavellian old man had been buying guns from Krupp and Creusot and had got ready with a handful of sharp-shooting mounted farmers to challenge the greatest empire the world had ever seen.

Mashonaland was really a No Man's Land, a raiding ground for the Matabele, a kind of reserve in which they went hunting when they wanted sport and loot in the form of girls, cattle, and slave boys for herders. Since this North was unsurveyed, even unexplored, there could be no actual boundaries. There were claims to this river, to these mountains, but these were really only indications of spheres of influence, and elastic—expanding if there was force to expand them, contracting again if the force weakened. It was known where Matabeleland was, or where the South African Republic was, or where the Portuguese colonies were: that is, it was known where the seat of government was; but where, at any given moment, their influence might extend was certainly not known.

The Boers under Ferriera that Jameson turned back were on their way into Mashonaland, yet after Rhodes's annexation the Portuguese claimed Mashonaland. Lobengula claimed land which certainly came into the Portuguese sphere. On one side of Mashonaland were the Portuguese half-castes who ruled in the name of Portugal and on the other the Matabele; both raided for slaves, while the Boers and the English were engaged in trying to take the country by a mixture of concessions and filibustering expeditions. This had gone on for so long that the Mashonas lived in perpetual fear of every one. They were farmers and tradesmen, not soldiers. They alone manufactured iron, melting it and forging it into spear heads. Some even think the Mashonas to be the descendants of the men who built Zimbabwe and mined the ancient gold of Ophir. Living in mountain villages in constant terror the Mashonas soon learnt to work for the white men who had dared to occupy the plains and feared no Matabele.

Having got the land and the concession, Rhodes's next move was to occupy his acquisition—that is, to settle it. Prospectors and miners were not settlers. Though Jameson had extracted from Lobengula his half-hearted promise of safe passage, the pioneers avoided Bulawayo and used Selous's road that ran through the No Man's Land on the Portuguese East African border. Lobengula might promise, but he could not guarantee, that his young warriors would not attack the column. Semi-military in character the pioneers were accompanied by five hundred mounted police equipped by the Chartered Company. With them went Johann Colenbrander, the half-English, half-Dutch frontier-born pioneer who knew the Matabele well and was the friend of Lobengula. It was he who took him the one hundred pounds each month for which he had sold his country.

Each night the column laagered their fifty wagons in a square, setting Maxims at the corners. Establishing Fort Victoria on the way, they reached Mashonaland in September, 1890, at the beginning of the rainy season. All food had to be railed and carted from the Cape, seventeen hundred miles away. Doctor

Jim was appointed administrator for the Chartered Company in 1892.

Among the settlers were Americans from every part of the United States, men from every part of the British Empire—the Australian contingent being the strongest. There were Boers and Englishmen of every kind from lords to ne'er-do-wells. There was even Frederick Burnham, the famous Indian scout, who arrived with his wife and child in an American buckboard which because of its lightness was something new in Africa and caused great surprise. This was further increased when Mrs. Burnham insisted that her husband unpack her sewing machine so that she could make herself a new dress and her seven-year-old son some new shirts. Hers was the first sewing machine—no doubt a Singer—to be set down in the wilderness. A white woman, a buckboard, and a sewing machine were events in those days. Another woman who was there in the early days was Melina Rorke who describes a third and most remarkable woman —Maria Colenbrander, the wife of the pioneer scout and interpreter—whom she saw first tearing by in a perfectly fitting riding habit on a magnificent chestnut horse. She had dark hair and large, dark, flashing eyes: a woman of ungovernable temper who thrashed her servants, who would ride any horse yet foaled, and had no use for other women and little for any man but her husband, who was suitably mated to Maria: a great blond man, he stood six foot two, was absolutely fearless, and rode over every one, black or white, rough-shod.

Something of the stamp of man who made this country comes out in a tale Melina Rorke tell of this Colenbrander: "I saw him approaching. Something about the way he was sitting his horse, about the anxiety of the black boy running beside him, told me something was wrong, and then, as he came abreast, I saw that he was covered in blood, his shirt in tatters, and his right arm dangling useless at his side. At my exclamation of involuntary pity his blue eyes blazed down at me out of the pale mask of his face as though defying me to question him. I said nothing and his lips twisted into a sardonic grimace. Nodding shortly he rode on. Later it appeared that he had shot a lion, wounding it, and then as he tried to shoot again his rifle jammed. The lion charged and he used his rifle as a bludgeon until the stock broke off and then with his bare fists and gun barrel he had fought the infuriated beast until he had succeeded in killing it. The lion had ripped and clawed him until his chest was a mass of torn flesh and streaming blood and his right arm in shreds. He had made his black boys heat the rifle barrel red-hot to sear his wounds and then, refusing to be carried, had mounted his horse and ridden home."

Johann Colenbrander was the pioneer at his most highly developed stage, a white savage, the most terrible of men, the bravest, most resourceful and uncompromising: a man who had beaten natives to death in anger, who had killed a lion with next to nothing but his hands: the mate of a woman as handsome and savage as he was himself. The natives feared and followed him devotedly. Rhodes was Spengler's man of the future; Colenbrander certainly also answered to his description of what men should be—"full of pride, knowing oneself feared, admired and hated for one's fortune and strength, and the urge to vengeance upon all, whether living beings or things that constitute, if only by their mere existence, a threat to this pride. . . ."

Colenbrander died, drowning in a flooded stream in Zululand to please a motion-picture director who wanted some dramatic action. Once again the irony of Africa: her answer to those who served, loved, and defied her. Their bones, since the beginning of time, have whitened the veld. Their name is legion, from the early Arab and Portuguese hunters of wealth, to the modern seekers of diamonds in the waterless wastes of Namaqualand, to the hunters like Selous, who died in the East African campaign in his seventies when once again he was in the saddle and back at his work as a scout.

Gold unfortunately was not found in Mashonaland and the farming was bad. For a land described as flowing with milk and honey, it was singularly arid. The shares of the Chartered Company were falling in the London market. The stockholders were disappointed. They had hoped for so much. They did not understand Africa.

There is the story of one company which had built a storage dam for water. First they waited for the rainy season, and when it came the water began to rise, and with the water the price of the shares. Spreckly, who was in charge of the work, was told to wire to London the amount of water in the dam each day. The wires came: "Three feet of water in the dam."—"Five feet."—"Ten feet."

The cablegrams were published, every one was counting the profits. Then came the next cable:

"Dam bust."

Spreckly was killed by a Boer bullet at the head of a squadron of Rhodesia Horse in the Anglo-Boer War.

In the meantime there was peace in Mashonaland but no prosperity. But the old-timers, who were laughed at as scaremongers, thought even peace too good to last. Doctor Jim said, and rightly, that Lobengula did not want war and as long as the white men did not encroach on Matabeleland proper, he would be able to hold his young men in check. But it occurred to no one that the Matabele might not keep to their own territory, or that they might be tricked into an attack. Unfortunately, if Lobengula wanted peace, Rhodes had to have war.

CHAPTER FIVE

THE DEATH OF A KING

IN 1893 the inevitable incident took place. Before dealing with the incident, it is necessary to see the necessity, from Rhodes's point of view, for an incident. In 1890 he said to those who asked him about the new territory of Mashonaland, "You must remember I have only the right to dig for gold." To the settlers in the same year he said, in effect, "So long as the Matabele do not molest my people, I cannot declare war on them and deprive them of their country; but as soon as they interfere with our rights, I shall certainly end their game; I shall then ask your aid and be very glad when it is all over. I shall grant favours to those who assist me."

To justify himself there had to be pillage and murder. This was the pattern of precedent, and essential to save face in a world which knew the real truth but demanded the cloak of sophistry to clothe its unpleasant nakedness—the political bathing suit designed to satisfy the scruples of those who hesitated at nude aggression. Already a year before the trouble the *Financial Times* in London said the "Chartered Company is doing all in their power to provoke Lobengula."

It is important to note that the shares of the Company at this time were waste paper. No gold had been discovered in Mashonaland, and the settlers were not only finding farming with no markets near them unprofitable, but were also suffering badly from fever. Incidentally, the Cape-to-Cairo telegraph—Rhodes's dream—had to go through Matabeleland over which he had at this time no jurisdiction. First a telegraph, then a railroad. Then, with communications secured and bases to the north and south, in Cairo and Capetown, the reality of a British Africa could follow the dream.

But Rhodes was a lucky man. At this juncture five hundred yards of telegraph wire was stolen by the Mashonas. They

THE DEATH OF A KING 239

wanted wire to make ornaments for the ankles of their women, but someone had to pay for it if the prestige of the white man was to be kept up. The telegraph was, if not the sacred cow, the sacred calf. It must grow: nothing must interfere with it. Five hundred yards—next time it might be five thousand.

A fine was imposed and paid in cattle. It was paid with remarkably little argument by the Mashonas, since the cattle they gave belonged to Lobengula, king of the Matabele. It seems absurd to imagine that Jameson did not know that they belonged to Lobengula, since among all natives the cattle always belong to the king, and this rule would certainly have its fullest application with a subject people. Actually the Mashonas herded the king's cattle and in return got the milk they gave.

Since Lobengula was lord of the Mashonas and was responsible for their actions, he could neither let them steal the Company's wire nor allow them to pay an indemnity for their theft with his cattle. He therefore sent an impi under Manyao, one of his indunas, to punish the thieves, the punishment, of course, being death. Lobengula even told Jameson and the officer in command at Fort Victoria that the people were not to be alarmed. "I send you warning," he said, "that my impis will pass your way, but have orders not to molest any white man."

By some accident this message, like so many others from Lobengula, did not arrive in time. Rhodes was the lucky man, not Lobengula, in matters of this kind, and the first thing the settlers knew was that a force of Matabele warriors was sweeping through the country butchering Mashonas, many of whom, having become their servants, sought their protection. The spears of the young men of Matabele were thirsty, they had been dry too long, and they killed with gusto; they raped with vigour and stole cattle in the grand manner of their Zulu past. Some European cattle were picked up along with the Mashona beasts.

Jameson ordered the beasts returned and told the police at Victoria to drive the Matabele back over the border.

"Which border?" asked Lobengula. "I am not aware," he wrote to Moffat, now assistant British Commissioner, "that a boundary line exists between Doctor Jameson and myself. Who gave him the boundary lines? Let him come forward and show me the man that pointed out to him these boundaries: I know nothing of them, and you, Mr. Moffat, you know very well that the white people have done this thing on purpose. That is not right. My people came only to punish the Mashonas for stealing my cattle and cutting your wires."

Of this incident Kruger, certainly no friend of Rhodes's, wrote, "It is affirmed in Africa that it was Rhodes who informed Lobengula that the Mashonas had stolen his cattle and that it was his duty to punish the raiders. Lobengula at once despatched a band of his people, as was the custom in these cases, to revenge the robbery. Rhodes used this fact to demand Lobengula's punishment on account of the massacre of the Mashonas." Whether this view is true or not, one thing is certain: Rhodes was to have his way and his war.

In the magazine *Truth*, Labouchere wrote:

> Mashonaland was found to have no paying gold. The shares of the Company were unsaleable rubbish. A pretext therefore had to be found for making war on Lobengula and seizing Matabeleland—all the circumstances show that the coup had been carefully prepared long beforehand. When the train was laid, a quarrel was picked with the Matabele who had entered Mashonaland at the Company's request and they were shot down by this same Jameson while doing their best to retire in obedience to his orders. Instantly the whole of the Company's forces, all held in readiness, entered Matabeleland under the pretence that they, the Matabele and not the Company, were the aggressors. Lobengula's savages were mowed down by thousands with Maxims. Those who were taken prisoner were killed to save trouble. The king's envoys sent to make terms were murdered. The king himself fled and died before he could be captured. His territory was parcelled out to the band of freebooters who had been collected by promises of loot. A million new shares were created—and in the subsequent boom were unloaded on the British public at prices ranging up to eight pounds a share.

But as yet there was no war. The time was not yet fully ripe. Lobengula could be counted on to keep the peace till they, Jameson's men, were ready. At all costs he wanted peace. This was the period of inflammation, of psychological war and preparation. Rhodes's defenders say that he did not engineer the war because the Company's funds were exhausted. But if this was against war, it was also for it—a means of replenishing the exchequer, by the conquest of new mines which would be the security for new loans and the issue of new shares. Another reason given is that the Company had disbanded almost all its trained forces. They had been cut from seven hundred to forty, the place of the expensive police being taken by the Mashonaland Horse, who were volunteers. It would, however, seem possible that this was a ruse, since most of the men were still in the country as settlers and were still armed and available for service.

Here are the series of telegrams sent by Jameson at this time: "The Victoria people have naturally got the jumps . . . Volunteers called out, rifles distributed . . . Will wire you when I hear the Matabelle have all cleared . . . At present this is merely a raid against the Mashona and not against whites . . . I hope to get rid of the Matabele without trouble . . . War from the financial point of view would throw the country back till God knows when. . . ."

This last wire scarcely squares with the facts, since once the war had started, the Company's shares jumped to unprecedented heights. It seems possible that these telegrams were sent to be produced later if there was trouble about the war and the annexation of Lobengula's territory. What better evidence of good intent could there have been than this documentary proof of good intentions?

Jameson, now in Victoria—he had come from Salisbury—sent for the Matabele indunas and said, "If you have not gone when the sun is there"—he pointed to the sky—"we shall drive you."

They answered, "We will be driven. Where is the border?"

An hour and forty minutes later an officer and thirty-eight mounted police followed the retreating Matabele.

A shot was fired.

Some say a Matabele fired it: others a white sergeant. The first shot in any war, the act which makes war differ from what the Boers call "a demonstration of force," is always in doubt, each side claiming that the other fired first—which makes their answering shot an act of self-defence instead of aggression.

Thirty-three Matabele were killed and many wounded. No European was hurt. The Matabele offered practically no resistance, which seems odd, for warriors whose spears were wet and whose minds were inflamed with blood. It would suggest that they obeyed the king, who had said, "Molest no white man," which was lucky for Jameson. He had called up the Mashonaland Horse, but only about forty troopers had assembled when he gave the order to attack.

John Hays Hammond, who was in a position to know, says, "What the Matabele thought when the little line deployed before their hundreds can only be conjectured." He continues: "The very bloodiness and swiftness of the contemplated invasion (by the British settlers of Matabeleland) offered the only chance in its favour. The grim determination of the white man, when stripped of the veneer of civilisation, is more relentless, more persistent, and more terrible than the ferocity of the most formidable black warrior who ever trod the African continent. Apart from this consideration, it seemed, from a military point of view, a hopeless venture. What chance would a handful of settlers have against the impis of well-armed Matabele? The fact that this raid was successful and that Jameson's later raid of 1895 was unsuccessful does not detract from an inevitable comparison. Here, as in the later raid, Jameson betrayed a lack of judgment. In this instance, however, fortune smiled on him. None the less, he had tempted fate. The defeat of the advance guard would have meant the massacre of every white man, woman, and child north of the Limpopo River." And that this force of white men was not defeated was simply because, obeying their king, the Matabele did not fight them.

While this was going on and before the actual conflict between black and white began, Johann Colenbrander was at Lobengula's kraal trying to make peace, or, more accurately, conducting negotiations which would delay Matabele mobilisation and confuse the issues while Jameson pressed on his preparations. Lobengula had sent for him, for he still wished to make terms. Colenbrander had advised him before when there had been trouble in the air.

Johann came, and with him, much to Lobengula's annoyance, came his wife Maria, riding a big white stallion. Lobengula told his attendants to leave him and stood alone with the white man and woman in the sacred goat kraal. Of all the white people who came and went in his country, these were the two that he held in the greatest esteem. Both spoke Zulu perfectly, both were fearless, the woman as fearless as the man, and as arrogant. Dressed in a khaki drill habit, a hunting crop in her hand, on her head a broad-brimmed felt hat, Maria stood beside her husband facing the king. Had his respect for her anything to do with the other white woman he had known in his childhood, the Dutch girl Sara who had reared him? Did courage and arrogance call to courage and arrogance? Did the savage in the black understand the savage in the white? At any rate, to Lobengula, here were honest people and fearless, who knew his tongue, the liquid Zulu of his fathers, as well as they did their own.

"Johann," Lobengula said, "I gave Ulodzi and Dakatela leave to dig for gold"—Ulodzi was the native pronunciation of Rhodes, and Dakatela meant Doctor, Doctor Jim—"yet they have brought up an army and the land is full of young men who call it their own. Am I then no longer king? Is Dakatela king? Why do they do these things in my country?"

Colenbrander knew why these things were done. He knew, too, what the king feared, having been, before he went to Rhodes's camp, one of the emissaries Lobengula had sent to London to accompany his indunas.

"Rhodes and Jameson know you are king," he answered. "They only want the gold which you have given them. But how are they to work it if your young men attack and kill those that work for them on the mines?"

Maria now broke in: "I am the king's friend, I speak to him as my brother. The king does not understand the heart of the Englishman. The king has given them leave to dig for gold and now it is too late to stop them. Each day more come. At present they are content with the country of the Mashona, but if the king's soldiers molest Mashona who are working for them, they will fight and then they will come and attack the king in his own town."

"What does a woman know of such things?" Lobengula said. "You have never seen my armies in battle. These white men will only make breakfast for them. Have you forgotten what happened to the white soldiers at Isandhlwana?"

"Yes, king, I am a woman, but where is Cetywayo now? Be wise in time and try to keep the peace with these people lest you be eaten up by them as Cetywayo was."

An induna who had joined the group now spoke: "Pay no heed to this yapping she-jackal, Great One. Tell her to go back to her husband's kraal and attend to his food and drink. We are not children to be scolded by a woman."

Maria turned on him: "You have not stood up to Englishmen in battle. You have spent your life beating out the brains of children and ripping the bellies of old women. Keep your baby-killers in check, O King, or they will drag you to your ruin and your country will belong to others—Sala guhle, Kumalo—Go sweetly, Elephant." Maria turned, and signing her husband to follow, mounted her white horse. She gave him a blow on the quarters with her whip that made him lash out to scatter the Matabele who were round them and galloped off.

That night the Colenbranders were waked by the noise of their working oxen being spanned. The scared driver told them that it was the king's orders. "He has been told that the Baas's wife is a sorceress and will work him harm. You are both to go and go quickly." The last link between the white and black was broken; their only contact now could be that of spear and of rifle; their only bond the blood that ran equally from the black man and the white.

Lobengula at once withdrew his offer to pay an indemnity of cattle and demanded that the Mashona his men had come to punish be handed over to him. He told the Company that they had "come, not to dig for gold, but to rob me of my people and my country." He refused to accept the hundred pounds due to him each month under the Rudd concession because he said "it is the price of blood."

Jameson, now that he was ready, wired to Rhodes, asking if he could march into Matabeleland. Rhodes answered, "Read Luke XIV: 31."

Doctor Jim read Luke XIV: 31: "What king going to make

war against another king sitteth not down first and consulteth whether he be able with ten thousand to meet him that cometh against him with twenty thousand."

Jameson wired to Rhodes: "All right. I have read Luke XIV: 31."

On August 14, the day that Lobengula refused his subsidy, Jameson made an agreement with his settlers. It was known as the Victoria Agreement and promised land, gold, loot, and other advantages to those who would follow him. The word "loot" is used in the document, which was secret and unauthorised; the Colonial Office did not know of it nor did the High Commissioner. What they did know and have on file were the wires which would prove, when the time came for him to use them, that Jameson did not want war.

On August 24, ten days later, Lobengula wrote to Queen Victoria: "Your Majesty, what I want to know from you is if people can be bought at any price. Your Majesty, what I want to know from you is: why do your people kill me? Do you kill me for following my stolen cattle which are in the possession of the Mashona living in Mashonaland? I have called all white men living at or near Bulawayo to hear my words showing clearly that I am not hiding anything from them when writing to Your Majesty."

What Lobengula meant by this reference to white people was that the few traders, missionaries, and hunters who were living in Matabeleland had been told to leave the country before war actually began or come into his own kraal for protection. He kept his word: of those who stayed not one was hurt. Still even now he worked for peace and succeeded in holding his maddened impis in check.

Moselikatze, Lobengula's father, would have attacked at once, but Lobengula differed from his father. He was partly civilised, a man who looked into the future. He knew that this trouble could not be patched up once it was begun. He knew that if he destroyed the white settlers the English would never rest until they had defeated him.

So while Jameson got stronger daily as more men joined him, Lobengula decided to send more emissaries. James Dawson, an Englishman who had a store in Bulawayo, wrote a letter for the king and agreed to accompany Ingubobubo, the king's brother, and the two other indunas who were to deliver it.

On the eighteenth of October the envoys reached the camp of Major Gould Adams at Tati. He had come up with his police to help the Chartered Company's volunteers against the Matabele. with him, too, was a Dutch Colonial in the Company's service who had recruited a force of Boers in the Transvaal against Kruger's orders, and eighteen hundred of Khama's Bechuanas—the hereditary enemies of the Matabele. The Bishop of Mashonaland was also with them. The Church and the Company marched together.

Gould Adams arrested the envoys. In his despatch he called this *the obvious course*. It would seem odd that three elderly natives should so obviously have to be arrested, unless it was also obviously impossible for the course of war to run true if they and their message of peace should reach their destination. They could hardly have been a danger in a camp of three thousand armed men. They were arrested and told that they would not be harmed unless they attempted to escape. They did attempt. One induna was shot, another clubbed to death, and Lobengula's brother returned to the king with the news. Dawson had abandoned them.

"Killed while attempting to escape," has often been a convenient cloak for murder. The charge is unproved, but the fact remains that messengers who were suggesting things contrary to the interests of Rhodes were subject to delays and accidents.

Jameson had to have war. Peace now would have been disastrous. The men were moving, the money—Rhodes had sold fifty thousand of his own Chartered Company shares for what they would fetch—already spent. The settlers had told Gould Adams they would either "do something to bring on a row or leave the country." Rhodes was taking a chance, but he delighted in chances and was confident of his luck. "I felt," he said later, "that if there was a disaster, I was the only person to carry it through." But no doubt he also felt if there was no disaster, he wanted to be free, and be under no financial obligation to any one when it came to making terms.

Lobengula was ready to unloose his black dogs of war. Regiment after regiment was camped on the slopes round

Bulawayo. It was the midsummer, the rains had not yet come, and in this heat the thousands of warriors sat waiting, dressed in their war clothes, carrying their guns and spears. All wore the war plumes of their fathers, and carried the great shields which had given them their name—"Those of the Long Shield." The oiled skins of the warriors twitched like those of racehorses waiting for the start. Their eyes were bloodshot, they licked their lips as they waited. And then the king appeared. A ripple ran over the waiting men, a muttering that rose to a shout: *Nanku! Nanku! There he is!* And then silence.

Lobengula came with his old dignity, mastering his gout and his fat; he came naked, his body streaked with blue paint, a long feather in his hair, an assegai in his hand. Slowly he paced down the incline towards his men. Then he turned to the east where the white men were advancing on his country and with a shout drove his spear into the ground.

This was the signal. Every warrior sprang to his feet, each plunged his spear into an invisible enemy as he hissed *Jiya! Jiya!* between his teeth.

By midday the regiments—the Insukamini, the Isizela, the Hlati, the Amaveni, the Imbezu, the Induba—and the others were gone.

But something had gone wrong. In the excitement none of the soldiers saw it, but when Lobengula drove his spear into the ground, the point had broken. Why had it broken? Had it struck a stone? Had it been badly forged by a Mashona slave who, knowing nothing of sabotage under that name, had nevertheless committed it? The king had been brought up by doctors and believed in omens, in the throwing of the bones and signs. He spent that night with his sorcerers peering into the entrails of a goat, seeking counsel in the heaving bowels.

Before dawn two of his wagons left the kraal loaded with ivory. It was buried on the banks of the Umgusa River. A fire was built over the pit to disguise it and the slaves who had gone with the wagons never returned.

The king's own wagon was also loaded with his bath chair and other personal belongings. It was said that the king was going to the front to take supreme command, but the king stayed in his kraal, not showing himself to any one.

"The total effective force at Jameson's disposal was about a thousand, white and native, all told. (This figure does not appear to include Gould Adams's force.) They entered Matabeleland in two columns which united at Iron Mine Hill. They adopted Boer tactics. The twenty-two wagons, each drawn by sixteen oxen, were driven in a double column protected on all sides by mounted men and artillery. Within three minutes of the alarm being sounded, it was possible to form the wagons into a laager and place a piece of artillery at each corner. It was decided that if defeated, the horsemen should retreat within the square and that the final stand to oppose the onrush of the Matabele should be made with the wagons as a barricade." But the onrush was never made.

The Matabele War was a neat little war, a Blitzkrieg. The settlers and troops did not go through the Matabele like a hot knife through butter. On the contrary, the Matabele with furious and futile courage flung themselves against the hot iron of the British and were melted to nothingness. The thousands of Lobengula's warriors poured themselves with wanton, prodigal courage into the stream of bullets that came from the English Maxims and Lee-Metfords. What had they but courage and blood to spend, what had they but spears which they knew how to use, but could not come close enough to use, and Martini-Henry carbines that they could scarcely shoot? It had indeed been wise to sell them firearms. They thought that by putting up their sights they shot straighter. Had they kept to their short stabbing spears and attacked only by night, the British column would have been overwhelmed. As it was, in the first battle on the Shangani River, the Matabele lost six hundred men and one of their generals committed suicide by hanging himself from a tree rather than fall into the hands of the English when he was disabled by wounds. The volunteers lost one trooper killed, one coloured driver killed, and six men wounded. In the second engagement on the Inhembesi River, two Matabele regiments, the Embezu and Ingubu, were, to use Willoughby's words, "practically annihilated." "I cannot speak too highly," he says, "of the pluck of these two regiments. I believe that no civilised troops could have withstood the terrific fire they did that day for at most half as long." In this battle the Company's force lost four killed and seven wounded.

Lobengula had waited too long. His belief in magic had been responsible for Martini-Henrys—the fire rods of the white man. Having lost none of their courage, the Matabele had lost the tactics of their Zulu fathers. They did not meet the enemy in broken ground or ambush him in the defiles. Instead, the plumed thousands flung themselves into reckless battle and the might of the last great warrior race in Africa was broken.

A comment on this fighting is seen in the fact that when Sarah Gertrude Millin's biography of Rhodes was filmed and shown in London at the height of the Abyssinian War of 1935-36, a sequence showing the slaughter of the Matabele is said to have been cut out, so greatly had the temper of the English people changed and such was their horror at the Italians' methods of war.

When the white men left Lobengula, the half-caste Jacobs got his chance. He was the Bastaard son of a Fingo woman and a Dutch bywoner—sharecropper. As a child Jacobs had been abandoned by his mother and raised in a mission where he learnt to read and write English. He had then drifted to Kimberley, where he was arrested and sentenced for illicit diamond-buying and did time on the Breakwater at the Cape. Later he was used as a stool-pigeon by the police, but proved too untrustworthy to be of value. His next exploit was a criminal assault on a woman, for which he received lashes and had to flee civilisation. In his illicit diamond-buying operations he had come into contact with many of the Matabele who were working on the diamond mines and decided to go up to their country.

Lobengula, deprived of the missionaries and traders who usually acted as secretaries to him, used Jacobs in their stead, and before long he had become the king's adviser. To add to his influence with the king, he courted Losikeyi, the king's "great wife," and became her lover. Losikeyi had an eye on the king's treasure of gold and diamonds; she may even have known where his ivory was buried, being the wife in whom Lobengula reposed his confidence, and felt that Jacobs with his knowledge of the civilised world would make a good accomplice as well as a paramour.

Jacobs was with the king when the news of disaster came—his only adviser a Bastaard criminal.

The king's remaining treasures were loaded on to the wagon that stood waiting, his span of black oxen were inspanned, his chief wife hoisted on to it, and the great wheels rolled. The noses of the oxen pointed north. To flee from the English, the Boers had gone north; to flee from the Boers, the Matabele under Moselikatze had gone north; to flee them again, the Matabele went still farther north, while the English pressed north behind them. The North was not only Rhodes's idea, it was every one's idea. The North to the fugitive of any colour meant freedom, if not safety.

Round the lumbering wagon clustered the king's wives and concubines and the women and children of the soldiers—the whole population of "the Place of Killing." Round the women and children came the remnants of the army, like bulls guarding a herd, prepared to fight a rear-guard action, to sacrifice themselves to save a nucleus from which their people could begin again as they had done before—as their fathers had done in the old days, as their grandfathers, the Zulus under Dingaan and T'Chaka, had done before that. They would find new land, steal new cattle, and women to breed from. Much was lost but not all. They still marched erect, the remnants of each regiment together, But they sang no war songs: neither songs of victory nor of defeat. There had been no victory, and they were not yet defeated.

Their first halt was at a hill that the Matabele call, from its shape, "The woman big with child."

The king looked back in the direction of his town.

He had lost it, but they should not have it. Towards dawn what he was waiting for happened.

As the Company's troops approached Bulawayo on the fourth of November, there was a great explosion, a black cloud rose over the town, spreading its pall of smoke like a mushroom—covering it. The ammunition Lobengula had received for his guns had been blown up. The British troops marched into the ruined town, headed by an old pipe major of the Royal Scots, and raised the Company's flag by the great indaba tree that stood majestically amid the ruins of the royal kraal.

Once again a flag was raised. A piece of bunting that hung listlessly silhouetted against the airless, smoke-blackened sky, while notes of Scottish pipes proclaimed Victory. The war that Rhodes had wanted and had fought was won. Jameson now sent a letter to the fleeing king. "To stop this useless slaughter, you must at once come to see me at Bulawayo, where I will guarantee your life will be safe and that you will be kindly treated. I sign myself your former and I hope your present friend, L. S. Jameson."

Jameson was magnanimous. First, the telegrams proving that he did not wish to make war, and now a letter that asked for peace and protested against "this useless slaughter."

The letter was taken by some mounted men who carried a white flag and were brought to the king by his outposts. John Jacobs was now called in to read and translate the message.

"What does the letter say?" Lobengula asked.

Jacobs did not like the letter at all. If the king went back, he would have to go with him or lose his job as secretary and his hope of loot. His lashes still were sore in his mind. There was another warrant out against him and he had no desire to put himself in a position where it could be executed.

"Dakatela"—the doctor—"says you must come to Bulawayo, Great One, to talk to him of peace." He paused. "Doubtless he plans to trap and kill you."

The king then asked his indunas, "Is this a trap?"

They, the old captains, remembered the precedents. "Remember what happened to the messengers the king sent to the Queen? They were killed, O King. And if Dakatela wants peace, why does he not come himself to see you here?"

The seed of suspicion Jacobs had sown flowered instantly in the fertile soil of these earlier betrayals.

Jacobs spoke again. "Tell them, king, that you will come if Dakatela will build a house for you to live in. For your own is burnt. This will give you time to get away."

The answer was written. "I have the honour to inform you that I have received your letter and have heard all what you has said so I will come. But allow me to ask you where are all my men which I have sent to the Cape. And if I do come will I get a house for me as all my houses is burnt down and also as soon as my men come which I have sent then I will come and you must please be so kind and send me ink and pens and paper . . . I am yours etc King Lobengula."

Lobengula knew very well that the men he was waiting for were dead, killed as they tried to escape from Gould Adams's camp. His message, therefore, expressed his distrust and played for time—time for escape, for further negotiations. Given time, he might be able to consolidate his people and get better terms, he might be able to get guarantees. Lobengula was trying to add *Ifs* and *Buts* to an act in which there were no Ifs and Buts—trying to qualify something that was already consummated. The marriage of Rhodes's men to Matabeleland was already an accomplished fact. They had had their titles before the first Matabele blood was spilt upon their new farms. This was the loot they had fought to obtain.

Jameson waited three days for Lobengula to come in and then pursued him; and at last, after a fortnight, he had almost run him down, had almost tired the old king out. Lobengula was a sick man, a frightened man. Only one thing was left. He now tried to buy himself out of his predicament. He called his indunas.

"Matabele," he said, "the white men will never cease following us while we have gold in our possession. Collect now all my gold and carry it to the white men. Tell them they have beaten my regiments, killed my people, burnt my kraals, captured my cattle, and that I want peace."

Lobengula the Zulu, the king of the Matabele, was beaten to his knees. This was the final gesture, the throwing out of the child in the sledge to the pursuing wolves.

Lobengula's men collected a thousand sovereigns. Ten months of his subsidy, ten little canvas bags stamped in black with the name Standard Bank of South Africa. These were taken out by a terrified mission. Before they could come up to the main body of the British pursuing force, they met two mounted troopers, who took the money from them and sent them home. The gold was never delivered. Afterwards there was an investigation, which helped Lobengula not at all, for he was dead. The two men were condemned to fifteen years of hard labour. But when, after serving two years, they appealed on the grounds that the evidence against them was insufficient and the sentence beyond the magistrate's jurisdiction, they were freed.

In December, deputations of Matabele came to Bulawayo to sue for peace, and the war, which had begun with the Mashona

THE DEATH OF A KING

stealing five hundred yards of copper wire in May, was really over. Rhodes had, indeed, as he had promised, "ended their game."

But to complete his triumph, Rhodes, who had arrived in the captured capital, had to have the person of the king. There could be no real or lasting peace while Lobengula was at large.

To achieve this, a patrol of forty men under Major Allan Wilson was sent out to capture the king. They were well mounted and well found. At intervals six returned with despatches. The remainder did not come back and nothing was heard of them till their bodies were found in February, 1894.

In 1893 the spring rains had been late. The country was dry, desiccated, shivering in a mirage of heat when the patrol had set out; and then suddenly the skies had broken apart and the rains had come. Wilson's horses could no longer help him. The Shangani River came down in torrential flood and he was cut off.

Wilson should have retreated when he noticed that the Matabele were showing themselves in increasing numbers, but he was expecting reinforcements from Colonel Patrick Forbes, and camped. At dawn he was attacked and after some hours realised that the odds were hopeless. With the river down, it would be a fight to a finish unless by some miracle more troops could be brought up by another drift. He told Frederick Russell Burnham, the American scout who was with him, to break through the masses of Matabele who surrounded them and get the news through. Burnham selected Ingram, another American, and Gooding, an Australian, to accompany him. Using every trick they knew, they got past the Matabele, managed to ford the river, and reported, as they swung from their saddles, "We are all that are left."

The Matabele remnants who had gathered round their fleeing king closed in on the Englishmen who were left. First one white man fell beneath their shots, then another; the wounded horses plunged. Wilson gave the order to dismount. This was the end. They were going to die and the way they died impressed even the Matabele who killed them. As the warriors were preparing to make their final charge, the "closing in" they loved, "the overwhelming," with hungry spears, they saw one of the white men stand up and shout out an order. The others stopped firing and also jumped to their feet. They all took off their hats. There was a sound of singing. As they sang, two more were shot. Then, when it was over, when the last notes of "God Save the Queen" had died in the veld, they all shook hands with each other and remained standing with their faces towards the Matabele.

The moment had come. The warriors closed in, their spears rattling against their shields, their plumes tossing in the air, their feathered cloaks flowing out behind them. *Jija! Jija!* came the hiss of death at the short stabbing assegais went home. It was over. All were dead except one man: Wilson had managed to reach an ant-heap and stood firing with a pistol in either hand. He was brought down with a shot from a Martini, but even as he fell he fired a final round. Only now was it done.

"Strip them," ordered the Matabele captain, "but do not cut their bodies, for these are not Mashona dogs, but brave men. Leave their bodies where they lie. The vultures and the jackals will do the rest."

There was another comment, for the men with Wilson were young, almost boys. "These are but boys," the Matabele said, "and if umfaans—children—can fight like this, what will we do when the bearded men come to avenge them?"

It had cost Lobengula eighty men of the blood royal and five hundred warriors to kill Wilson and his thirty-four men.

The sad end of the Wilson patrol was the only fly in Rhodes's rich ointment of success. Everything had gone wonderfully. The Christian prayers of the Bishop of Mashonaland had been answered and the wicked Matabele destroyed. The settlers sucked up Rhodes's flattery. "It is your right," he said to the pioneers, "you have conquered the country," as they proceeded to enter into the kingdom of Rhodesia. A farm of three thousand morgen each—six thousand acres—twenty gold chains each and an equal share of Lobengula's cattle. There were two hundred thousand head to be distributed. And the first private wagon to enter Lobengula's "Place of Killing," like the first that had entered Fort Salisbury, brought a load of whisky, four tons of it, gross—and nothing else.

"Will you go against twenty thousand with ten thousand?" Saint Luke wrote in his Gospel. Well, according to Rhodes, his gallant settlers had done much better than that. For the record Rhodes told them of their own achievements. He said they had done with nine hundred men what it had been estimated it would take ten thousand to do. He neglected to add the troops under Major Gould Adams or the Bechuanas or the Cape Boys or the Dutch Freebooters. In all there were nearer four thousand men employed than seven hundred against the Matabele.

There was also an economic question. The settlers had done the fighting, and the cost, as far as the London shareholders were concerned, was negligible: only a hundred thousand pounds. After the conquest the capital of the Chartered Company was increased from one to two million pounds by an issue of a million new shares. No wonder Rhodes was pleased with his settlers.

The Bechuana auxiliaries had gone home before the campaign was quite finished because smallpox had broken out in Mashona and Matabeleland. And smallpox was to be of more value to the English than the Bechuana, for it was of smallpox that Lobengula died.

Still fleeing with a remnant, that little band which always seems to remain loyal to any cause or king and which always seems to contain an Iscariot, Lobengula found himself in the fly belt on the M'lindi River, less than forty miles from the Zambesi. Here the remnants of his cattle died—even his draught oxen, and the wagon which had brought him so far was still. A believer in signs, the king knew this was the end. It needed no casting of the bones for him to know that his course was run. His spirit was broken, his limbs swollen with gout. His brandy, that had proved such a solace to him, drunk; his cup of bitterness full and overflowing. He called his indunas about him and told them to look to Rhodes, his conqueror, for protection.

"He will be your chief and your friend." To his warriors he said, "You have done your best, my soldiers; you can help me no more. I thank you all. Go now to your kraals. Go sweetly. Go in peace."

Among the few who still were round him were three of his sons, some of his wives, a few faithful indunas, and some of the soldiers of his bodyguard. Old Mjaan and Bozungwane stood by him to the end, and the two captains paid their dead king what due they could. But there was little ceremony. There were no oxen to sacrifice, no warriors to mourn. Two of the surviving beasts, miserably thin, were killed, and the swollen body of the king sewn into their bleeding hides and buried where it lay on the banks of the M'lindi.

The king was dead. There were none to cry, "Long live the king," for those who should have cried were also dead, and the Matabele, the last of the Zulus, broken.

CHAPTER SIX

THE THIRD TERM

ON May 10, 1893, the year of the Matabele War, Paul Kruger was inaugurated for a third term as President of the South African Republic. He had obtained in the election 7854 votes. Joubert ran him close with 7009.

Kruger was sixty-eight years of age, and, despite Joubert's competition, was the master and father of his people. He spoke of "My Country," "My Raad," "My burghers," as Rhodes spoke of "My North," and with more right. Rhodes acknowledged this and said, "When I refer to Paul Kruger as the Transvaal, I think I am speaking quite correctly. . . ."

The rivalry of these two men was now apparent to both. It was not merely a divergence of opinion, but a clash of temperament, of ethics, of religion, and of interest.

As early as 1888, Rhodes had said in a political speech to his followers: "My ideas have always been directed towards the broad question of South African politics, and I believe that, if I succeed in the object of my political ambition—that is, the expansion of the Cape Colony to the Zambesi—I shall provide for you in the future success in the prospecting for and the production of gold far beyond what has occurred to you in the development on the Vaal River . . . I am tired of this mapping out of Africa in Berlin. My belief is that the development of South Africa should fall to that country, or countries, which by their progress shall show they are best entitled to it. . . ."

"Africa for the Afrikaaners from the Zambesi to Simon's Bay" —at the Cape of Good Hope—was Kruger's wish.

The principle was the same with both men. Each wanted to possess South Africa. Since this was impossible, each tried by political manœuvres to attain his own ends and thwart the ends of the other. Each tried to win over those of the other race into his camp. Rhodes tried, by making friends with Hofmeyr and the South African Bond, to bring the Cape Dutchmen on to his side. Kruger tried in his speeches to the Uitlanders to include them as friends while, being afraid of their voting power, he denied them the franchise.

Rhodes's hope was ruined by the Jameson Raid: Kruger's by the Uitlanders who, banded under the Reform Committee, incited the Raid because of their—at least in part—imagined grievances. The most real of these grievances was the attempt by the South African Rebublic to call out British subjects on commando in 1894. Most foreigners—the Germans and Hollanders—went willingly, but the English claimed exemption and the National Union of Reformers issued proclamations declaring that "people who had no privileges were not bound to fight." Inevitably, the clash between "Boer and Briton" was coming. As politics failed, war approached.

The country, at least the areas where mining was taking place, was turbulent. Sir Henry Loch, who had gone North to discuss the affairs of the Swazis, went to meet the President in Pretoria with intructions from London to intervene. The crowd that met him was unruly. The President could hardly reach Sir Henry to greet him. "God Save the Queen" was sung. Many men wore red, white and blue favours. A man carrying an enormous Union Jack mounted the box seat of the President's carriage in which he sat with Loch, and whether by design or accident allowed the flag to fall on and envelop the President. When Loch got out at the Transvaal Hotel, the horses were taken out and the President left sitting in it alone. Some burghers got new horses and drew the carriage to the government buildings where Kruger got out. There is general testimony that "The President remained completely calm, unperturbed, and never lost his temper" during this incident. Yet the President was not a temperate man. He was a passionate man who not so many years since, on being "opposed in the Raad, had waved his arms frantically and literally roared with rage. He tore his green sash of office from his chest, kicked it from the dais of the House on to the floor. Several members tried to appease him and prevent him leaving the House for ever. He shook them off so forcibly that two of them went staggering to the end of the dais and fell."

It was not that the President was not angry about the Pretoria demonstration. It was that he was a Boer and hunter, a man trained by his way of living to bide his time: the man who in the Bechuanaland troubles had told his burghers "not to blow on the fire." He had plans laid. If the explosion was to come, and he was by now certain it must, he wanted to delay it till he was in as advantageous position as possible. Here again, as with Jameson and Lobengula, was the insistence on time and on timing— the effort of both contestants to strike when the other was off balance.

Though as yet Rhodes and Kruger had not come into actual, open collision, they were accepted as not merely the heads of their respective peoples in South Africa, but as completely representative of their aims and ends. Rhodes meant English expansion. Kruger meant Boer expansion, or, if this was impossible, Boer isolation. In May, 1892, Rhodes, addressing his shareholders in London, said—he was talking about the Boer trekkers who had crossed into Mashonaland under Colonel Ferriera—"I am on the best of terms with President Kruger. But I pointed out at the time of the crisis that if President Kruger crossed the Limpopo we should have very severe differences." These trekkers were independent Boers and their advance into Mashonaland, far from having been instigated by the President, had been forbidden by him.

Had Rhodes an immense capacity for self-deception or had he the gift of deceiving others? Kruger must not be a dictator, but Rhodes became a dictator in all the territories he acquired. Kruger must not cross the Limpopo, but Rhodes painted the map red up to the great lakes and hoped to go farther.

"I find in my life," Rhodes once said, "it is far better to tell the town crier what you are going to do and then you have no trouble." The people who were with Rhodes made no trouble because they believed in him and his ideas. And he had no trouble from his opponents because they always thought he was bluffing. If he was going to do something, he would not say so, was their line of thought.

Speaking of his North he said to his settlers that this, the North, "was a happier thing than the deadly monotony of an English country village. Here, at any rate," he said, "you have the proud satisfaction of knowing that you are civilising a new part of the world. Those who fall in that creation fall sooner than they would in ordinary lives, but their lives are better and grander."

This was the truth, but how many young men believed him? The young man in war or adventure sees only death for others. He is always a glorious and honoured survivor, however lost the cause. It was Rhodes's belief that men should live dangerously.

This man Rhodes, and Rhodes's men, were the enemies of the South African Republic: the enemies to the ideas, ideals, hopes, and fears of Kruger's burghers—the exact antithesis of them. The hope of either one was the fear of the other. They were as flint and steel, as inseparable, as conflicting, as certain—as the friction increased in its intensity—to produce fire.

This period could be described as the period of manœuvre, Rhodes had got his North, which meant that Kruger had lost it. Rhodes now made another move to surround the Transvaal and cut it off from the sea. In 1884 he had tried to render it absolutely dependent on the Cape Colony by making overtures to the Portuguese Government to obtain control of the traffic through Delagoa Bay if not the actual possession of the harbour of Lourenço Marques.

Rhodes's side of the picture is shown by a letter he wrote at this time: "I have acquired an admiration for Oom Paul Kruger, for had he not conceived the noble scheme, from his point of view, of seizing the interior, of stretching his republic across to Walfisch Bay, of making the Cape Colony hidebound, and of ultimately seizing Delagoa Bay, and all this without a sixpence in his treasury?"

In 1890, not so long ago, Rhodes had suggested that Kruger seize Portuguese East Africa. Now he was after it himself, which alarmed the German Government which did a considerable trade with the Republic. A not unimportant part of these exports were the guns and ammunition the Germans sold to the Boers, and in agreement with the government of the South African Republic, two German warships were sent to Delagoa Bay. It worked as it had at Angra Pequena, and Rhodes withdrew his claims. According to van Oordt, this prompt intervention by Germany saved the situation for the Republic.

What actually saved the Republic was the fact that Lord Rosebery's Liberal Government paid no attention to the matter and that Rhodes was prepared to let the British lion sleep while he consolidated his other Northern gains. Let the British Government forget Africa for a while, another chance would come. Rhodes felt himself able to make it come if it did not come without assistance.

This was the second time the infant German navy had challenged the might of British sea power.

The Germans were much elated by this diplomatic victory which they had achieved·by armed threat.

This incident was followed by an official dinner given for the Kaiser's birthday by the Germans in Pretoria, to which President Kruger was invited. Here the President made a speech lauding the Kaiser and telling how well he had been received in Berlin when he was in Europe. He went on to say: "If people make clothes for a little child, they must not make them so that they fit a big man. But in proportion as the child grows up, it must have bigger clothes or the old ones will burst asunder. When I asked Her Majesty's Government for bigger clothes, they said, 'Eh! Eh! What is that?' and could not see we were growing. . . . If the time arises when the Republic must wear bigger clothes, you will contribute much to that result . . . and I wish also to give to Germany all the support a little child can give to a big man. . . ."

These two incidents—the speech and the presence of German warships in African waters—were used by an anti-Kruger press to fan the flames of the Uitlander opposition. The Rand capitalists, despairing that their grievances would ever be remedied by the Transvaal Government, now joined the Reform Movement. Among them was the firm of Wernher, Biet and Company, which had the backing of Cecil Rhodes, who was the managing director of the Goldfields Company. Rhodes at this time, in 1895, was Premier of the Cape Colony, a privy councillor of Great Britain, and head of the Chartered Company.

Jameson was now sent on Rhodes's behalf to Johannesburg to learn the true situation. He reported the Uitlanders full of discontent and ripe for revolution. Where Jameson got his idea it is hard to discover unless his wish was the father to his thought. He would certainly have liked to believe it true. The fact was that not five per cent of the English in the city were interested in obtaining the vote. They were in Africa to make money and they were making it. When they had made enough, they would go home to England to live; as for the capitalist leaders, very few of them were ready to risk their own skins in any cause. Jameson's only support came from the more irresponsible members of the population and the few who were not doing well financially, and these he began to arm with guns sent North in packing cases and containers marked as mining machinery. At the same time the Chartered Company's forces, the heroes of the Matabele War, were massed on the Bechuanaland border ready to march in to help the Uitlanders should it be necessary to assist them. That such a raid would be against international law and a contravention of the Foreign Service Enlistment Act appears to have occurred to no one.

Guns were now coming from the south into Johannesburg for the Uitlanders and to Pretoria from the east through Portuguese territory for the Transvaal burghers. Any one with eyes to see or with ears to listen to gossip could see the storm approaching. The news reached England and the Chartered shares moved upwards. Trouble in Africa meant profits. Obviously this time there would be no Majuba. This time it would be a real war which the British would win in a few weeks.

In April, 1895, Major the Honourable Bobby White was sent to the Transvaal as Intelligence Officer. In his diary, which was found later, he wrote: "Visited the artillery camp at Pretoria. Saw some very old pieces of ordnance. One gun of the date of the Second Empire, a Maxim Nordenfeldt, a nine-pound muzzle-loader . . ."

The Boers must have laughed. They had shown the Honourable Major their artillery museum. There were at the time of his visit in the fort at Pretoria twelve field pieces, ten thousand rifles, and twelve million rounds of small-arms ammunition.

In this year, too, the Delagoa Bay Railway was opened. Kruger now had access to the sea by rail, and was in direct contact with Germany and France, which meant with Krupp and Creusot. Each day his regular artillerymen became more proficient and his burghers more watchful. Kruger, too, was waiting. "One day," he said, "the tortoise will stick its neck out." "How," he asked, "do you kill a tortoise but by waiting till its neck is unguarded and out of its shell?" The neck was Jameson's police force at Pitsani. All Africa waited breathless with cocked rifles for a move. In a game of waiting the Boer always had the advantage.

Asked by an English Member of Parliament, if there was war with England, what chance he would have of winning? the President said he "wanted no such war," but went on to develop his thoughts in terms of a hunting parable that was so typical of him. "Suppose," the President said, "you are going down a road with nothing but a pocket knife and you meet a lion, would you be so reckless as to attack it with a pocket knife? Certainly not. But suppose that the lion attacks you, would you be such a coward as not to defend yourself with your pocket knife?"

"I would certainly try," the M.P. answered.

"Well, sir, there you have the answer to your question."

Le style c'est l'homme—the style is the man—and Paul Kruger's style was well expressed, as was Rhodes's, by the way he lived and the things he said. His similes were bucolic, savouring of the veld and his continuous Bible reading. His humour—and he had plenty—was heavy and inclined to be rough. It is hard to find inconsistencies in his words or his behaviour. He was what psychologists would call an uncomplicated character. He was forthright. He was without repressions. A man who struck when he was angry, but who, with a hunter's wisdom and a farmer's patience, was able to wait upon circumstance, certain of divine protection and convinced that in the end the good triumphed over the evil. The husband of two wives, the father of sixteen children, the grandfather of one hundred and twenty, the killer of innumerable big game and many Kaffirs in his wars against them, he remained a simple man and a poor one.

He lived in a small house which he had built on Church Street in Pretoria in the eighties. It had a big sitting-room, a medium-sized dining-room and bedroom, with some other smaller bedrooms, a kitchen, and an office or study, behind which was a still smaller room where he could obtain complete solitude and to which no one was allowed to penetrate. In front of the house was a wide stoep whose steps were later flanked by the two marble lions presented to him by Barney Barnato, the mining magnate. Kruger rose at daybreak as he had done when he was a farmer.

His first action was to go into his inner sanctum and read a chapter of the Bible. He next had a cup of coffee; after that he went out and sat on the stoep where he would receive all comers.

At eight o'clock the family had breakfast, which was preceded by prayer and the reading of another chapter of the Bible and ended with a blessing.

The house was always full of children who were checked when they worried Oupa—old father—grandfather. If they listened too closely, the old man would inquire if they were "counting the old people's teeth." At meals the women and girls of his household had to sit with their heads covered.

Kruger ate his meals fast and suffered from indigestion, as he was a heavy eater of meat and bread. He never ate rice and seldom touched vegetables. He was very fond of bread soaked in milk. He drank no liquor except under orders from his doctor. He hated drunkenness and in his age suffered from asthma and heart disease. He smoked heavily, his favourite pipe being a meerschaum with a curved stem. It was rarely out of his mouth. When he was in the Volksraad and could not smoke, he ate oranges with great rapidity. He drank a great deal of coffee and spat freely, always having a spittoon near his chair, which he seldom hit.

After breakfast the President would put on his long black morning coat, his green sash of office, and his silk hat. In his earlier years he wore klapbroek trousers—the wide flapping pantaloons favoured by the Voortrekkers. But later he changed to trousers of a more fashionable cut. He was never comfortable in these town clothes and looked just what he was—a farmer dressed up for Sunday, but the President's Sundays came every day.

Once in his life he received a threatening letter of assassination. He treated it with contempt. He was "in God's hands and if his time were to come it must come."

At nine o'clock he arrived at his office, where, owing to the over-centralisation, everything had to be attended to by the President in person. At ten o'clock he would go to the Volksraad to listen to the debates. His memory was extraordinary. He remembered men, dates, facts, figures, even letters that he had written or read years ago.

The President's wife, "Tante Sanna," was a housewife. She took care of the President's house, bore his children, and helped to raise the grandchildren. When visited by Lady Green, the wife of the British agent, she was peeling peaches into a large basin that she held on her lap. Most people described her as "a dear old lady." Politically her main duty was to care for her husband and supply the gallons of coffee his stream of visitors drank each day. There was always coffee ready on the kitchen stove.

Kruger's lunch was light. With it he always drank a glass of milk. By two o'clock he was back at the government buildings. At four he returned home and received visitors again. He retained his hat on his head, sat with his pipe in his mouth and his big Bible on the table beside him. He drew slowly on his pipe and "presented an expression of simple sleepy beatitude. But the lion was not slumbering. If some one made a remark he did not like, he would pound the Bible beside him with his fist and shake the room with the vehemence of his anger. Then he subsided and beamed again."

Visitors came to see him from all over the world. Among them was Mark Twain. Another was Stanley, the missionary and explorer, who described the President as "a Boer Machiavelli, astute and bigoted, obstinate as a mule, remarkably opinionated, vain, puffed up with the power conferred on him, vindictive, covetous, and always a Boer, which means a narrow-minded and obtuse provincial of the illiterate type."

The memory of Kruger's remarks about his friend Doctor Livingstone and the gun repair shop he said he was running for the Kaffirs must have remained with Mr. Stanley. British explorers and missionaries were seldom unbiased when expressing opinions about the Boers or their President.

Captain Slocum of Boston was another visitor. He was circumnavigating the globe all by himself on his little boat, the *Spray*.

He said the President told him with conviction that "the earth, with certain minor exceptions, such as high mountains, was flat and always had been so." He appeared to consider that the Transvaal was the chosen land of the globe and the eyeball of the world. Slocum says, rightly or wrongly, the President gave him "the impression that Pretoria was practically the centre of the earth."

The McAdoo Negro minstrels, when they came to Pretoria, invited the President to a concert. McAdoo said his choir sang very well. The President said, "You have never heard me sing. I sing bass."

Kruger had both wit and wisdom. A burgher once came to him and asked for a job with the administration. Kruger said, "You are too stupid to be a clerk and at the moment there is no vacancy for a head official." An English peer, dissatisfied at his treatment by the President, told the interpreter to tell him that he was a member of the House of Lords and had once been a viceroy.

"A viceroy—what is that?" asked Kruger.

"Oh, a sort of king."

Kruger smoked his pipe in silence and then said to the interpreter, "Tell the gentleman I was once a shepherd."

Kruger hated gamblers and had no patience with them when they complained of their losses. One burgher who had been badly bitten in the boom of 1895 came to the President to complain about his losses.

"You remind me," he said, "of a baboon I once had. It was very fond of me, but one day when it was sitting between my feet its tail got burnt in the fire, whereupon it turned and bit me. So it is with you. You go in for reckless speculations and then you blame me for the consequences."

Another time someone asked him why he never went to the races. He replied, "I am an old man. And I know very well that one horse runs faster than another. It makes no difference to me which one it is."

Kruger's third presidency began and ended with difficulties. From the beginning his life had been hard—the Trek as a child, the Kaffir wars of his youth, the War of Independence in his late maturity, and now, in his age, the threat of a still greater war. Privation, danger, unhappiness, betrayal—Paul Kruger had known them all and still retained his faith in God and the ultimate success of his people. With the rough he had also known the smooth—the hot love of his youth, when he had swum his horses across the Vaal to seek his bride; the excitement of the chase; the pleasures of comradeship with the burghers whom he had so often led to war; the joys of family life; and the curious pleasure to be obtained by tilling the soil and the raising of stock.

A simple farmer, a shepherd boy, as he called himself, Kruger had been to Europe, had seen the Queen of England in all her glory, had visited many countries, met many people, and nothing had changed the granite of his disposition. His road and his duty were clear to him. And out of it all, out of all his experiences, had been born his philosophy—that of a bucolic Solomon, of a farmer sitting in the judgment seat of a nation of farmers. An old thick-set David who now, in his age, had to prepare his sling for the Goliath of England.

Kruger was often compared to a lion or a bull. The bull now felt himself being edged into the kraal: driven a little, coaxed a little, incited to attack and refusing, but always nearer to the kraal that he feared; and all of it he blamed on Cecil Rhodes.

Of the Uitlanders who composed the Transvaal National Union, Kruger wrote: "They make it their business to keep the Johannesburg population in a constant state of ferment and to manufacture complaints against the government. Every method of agitation was put into force by these gentry for the furtherance of their intrigues. Apparently they were agitating for the franchise; but their real object was a very different one as will be seen. That Rhodes's influence was here too paramount was proved by later events."

The truth of this assertion is found in some of the correspondence between Sir Lionel Phillips, president of the Reform Committee and partner in the house of Wernher, Biet and Company to his partner Alfred Biet. Sir Lionel—he was Mr. Lionel then—was a great letter writer. On June 10, 1894, he wrote: "I do not know what must be our next move. The government clearly thinks it has done well for the industry and our opposition will of course irritate old Kruger." He was right, it did. "The old man is, however, in no case friendly to the industry, has the most perverted ideas on political economy, suspects we were all working in concert with his deadly opponent C. J. Rhodes, sees imaginary amalgamations looming in the distance and the country bought up by Rhodes. . . ."

Rarely have any man's fears been more justified. Buying up and amalgamating was Rhodes's strong line. Biet, to whom Phillips wrote, was Rhodes's partner. Guns were being smuggled into the Simmer-and-Jack Mine in which Rhodes was the largest shareholder, and Jameson was raising the Rhodesia Horse, a regiment of irregular cavalry, north of the Limpopo. On June 16, Phillips wrote another letter to Biet: "Captain Rhodes (Cecil Rhodes's brother) has urged me to go to Cape Town and consult C. J. Rhodes as to the position and our line of action. I don't of course want to meddle in politics, and as to the franchise I do not think many people care a fig about it."

Few people did care a fig about it, but nevertheless it was the excuse. The British businessmen in Johannesburg were represented to themselves, and to others at home, as an ill-used minority. Hobson on this subject says: "Many of them hated the Boer and believed him corrupt and incompetent. Some of them exhibited a certain fervour on the franchise issue, but none of them had undergone any serious personal trouble with police or other officers of state . . . as for general liberty and even licence of conduct, it existed nowhere if not in Johannesburg. Every luxury of life, every form of private vice, flourished unchecked. Every man and woman did what seemed good in his or her eyes. The Helot," Hobson goes on—this was the romantic pseudonym given to the Uitlanders, who were considered to be in the position of helots, "bore his golden chains with insolent composure . . . the entire wealth of the land, drawn from the bowels of the earth by Kaffir labour, passed easily into his hands with the exception of the toll taken by the government . . . in a land of simple-mannered plain-living farmers he alone had material luxury and the leisure to use it. . . ." Looking back on those days the average old-timer says regretfully, "There'll never be such days again."

Thirty-five thousand Uitlanders presented a petition to the Volksraad, asking that their grievances be redressed. But as Sarah Gertrude Millin says of this petition: "Almost anybody will sign anything. If one has the necessary education it is easy, and somehow adventurous, to sign one's name."

It is interesting to note that the Chartered Company taxed their settlers' gold fifty per cent while Kruger taxed the foreigners in the Transvaal only ten per cent. Logic, however, has little place in argument about wealth.

A Boer had the rights and responsibilities of a full burgher at sixteen, whereas a foreigner had only these same rights, if he could qualify, at forty.

Kruger, to achieve a compromise, had created a Second Raad, inferior to the First Raad, which had the right of veto on anything decided by the lower house. Two years' residence entitled a stranger to vote in the Second Raad, provided he was a Protestant and over thirty years of age. Another two years, and if he had property in the Republic he could be elected a member. It took a further ten years to give him the rights of a sixteen-year-old Boer boy.

By this device Kruger hoped to equalize the difference in numbers between the "Come and Go" foreigners and his Boer burghers.

The point is that few of the Uitlanders wanted to become burghers and give up their own nationality. What they wanted was both to have and eat their political cake. They wanted dual nationality. They wanted to be able to vote themselves into power in the South African Republic where they were temporary residents, and then, having amassed fortunes, to return to their own countries—to England, Germany, France, Switzerland, Sweden or America.

It should be noted that the burghers were outnumbered by four to one. The oppressed minority was actually an extremely rich majority which the leaders of the Reform Movement felt should not only have a voice in the government, but actually rule the country.

To the Boers, who had made this land, who had fought and died over every acre of it, this idea had small appeal, since they had come so far to avoid this very thing—the domination of their race by the English. It was this desire that led to what has been called the "Incident of the Drifts."

Kimberley had been the magnet which attracted the iron rails till the discovery of gold made the Rand the financial centre of Africa. But with shift of economic gravity to the North came the necessity of railroad extension and expansion. The Transvaal Boer, however, did not belong to the railway epoch. Left to himself he would not have had a yard of railway track in the Republic. The question of carrying up heavy machinery and of feeding a large urban population which could not be fed or serviced by ox wagons moving at a speed of ten miles in twenty-four hours did not interest him at all.

The Free State not having an immigrant problem was more co-operative than the Transvaal, and allowed the line to creep up through its territory to the very borders of the South African Republic—only fifty miles from the mines. But here the line was blocked, by Kruger's order, on the banks of the Vaal. So far and no further. He would allow no railway to come into his country until his own line from Delagoa Bay to Pretoria was completed. In 1895 the strip of veld between the terminus of the Cape-Free State line and the consuming centres of the Rand was probably the only place in the world where the ox wagon competed with the locomotive. Here everything was off-loaded from the freight cars and loaded on to the long Boer wagons. But even this was not enough for Kruger. In order to exclude the competition of the Cape railroad—for even with all this unloading and reloading it was cheaper to bring goods by this line than on the Boers' own line from Portuguese East Africa—Kruger closed the two drifts —fords—across the Vaal.

"Jou kerls"—fellows—"have had enough of the Johannesburg trade," the President said. "I have made up my mind that the Delagoa Bay line shall have the lion's share."

The drifts were closed. Goods piled up on the veld. Firms in Johannesburg were in despair, there were riots. Only the Boer burghers were unaffected. They did not believe in railways anyway. But the closing of the drifts nearly precipitated war between England and the Transvaal. The action of the President was contrary to the Convention of London, which stated, in Article 13, "Nor will any prohibition be maintained or imposed on the importation into the South African Republic of any article coming from any part of Her Majesty's dominions. . . ."

Faced by this fact and the tone of the British Government, Kruger backed down, the drifts were reopened; but relations between the Boers and the Uitlanders and the British Government were in no way improved by the incident. War was appreciably nearer. Twenty-five thousand pounds was spent on a fort in

Pretoria and the site of another commanding Johannesburg was chosen. Mr. Van Zweten, a Hollander in the employ of the republican government, was sent to Europe to engage soldiers of fortune and buy arms. An order for heavy guns was placed with Krupp's and a battery of quick-firers was mounted on Hospital Hill directly overlooking the streets of Johannesburg. Every one was uneasy, Boer and Briton alike. No one could settle down. The roar of the great batteries crushing the gold-bearing rock sounded like gunfire on the High Veld. Doctor Jim was reading about Clive and inclined to believe Lionel Phillips when he said, "The Boer prowess is much overrated since they licked our troops. . . ."

The War of Independence had been more or less inconclusive. This was the time to strike "for England, home, and beauty:" to strike as Clive would have struck in India. Dull clods, these bearded, homespun and leather-dressed Boers. Faced by enough regular troops, dashing leaders, and the due allowance for British pluck and luck, they would soon be defeated. The names of Clive, Hastings, Nelson, Wolfe, rang in Jameson's ears. What had they got that he had not got? It was just a matter of having enough audacity. Someone—was it Napoleon?—had said "audacity and always audacity." The Doctor ignored two other sayings— the first about "an army marching on its stomach;" the second about things having to be prepared "to the last button on the last gaiter."

CHAPTER SEVEN

THE COLOSSUS

Rhodes the Colossus now straddled Africa. He had one foot planted in the Cape of Good Hope where he was Prime Minister and the other on the Zambesi territories where he was the Chartered Company. His eyes were on Egypt. Beneath his loins was Kimberley, the great pit that bred his strength. Rhodes's feet were on the ground, on the ground of Africa; his head was in the clouds of Olympus.

Rhodes, a man of brass, an idol, an anathema. Rhodes, the great man at his greatest. Rhodes, the sick man hurrying. My God, how he, the beloved of the gods, must hurry. *So little time, so much to do.*

Rhodes, a god surrounded by his archangels—Doctor Jim, Rudd, Alfred Biet, John Hays Hammond the American engineer. The archangels surrounded by the lesser angels—the young pioneers, the tough old-timers, the scouts and hunters. And hovering over the holy tabernacle from which flowed all good things—and all good tips—was the angel of death shooting his darts into Rhodes's lungs, hurling his bolts into Rhodes's heart—riding him like a horse, checking him with a choking of his breath or a catch at his heart; flushing him; making him pale. Rhodes, the giant with lungs of clay.

Upstairs the gods were laughing at the man who disbelieved in gods. They were getting something ready: one of these jokes so beloved by them. The gods were going to hoist him on his own petard—to have him destroyed by his own best friend, and then to watch him slowly die. The gods had loved Rhodes for long enough. They were fickle gods, and Rhodes had no weapon against them. He had a Bible like Paul Kruger, but he kept it in his bedroom with his atlas. They must have cancelled each other out. For Rhodes had no faith: a fifty per cent chance in the existence of the Almighty is not faith and can give no comfort. Nor was there a woman to comfort him, nor a child; and perhaps a Bible should not be kept with an atlas—the sacred not be mixed with the material. At this time, in the height of his power, Rhodes was only a few yards away from death and he had already chosen his tomb in the wild Matopos, the home of the god M'limo: the piled maze of rocks and mountains where King Moselikatze lay staring with eyeless sockets at the North that Rhodes had taken from Lobengula, his son: the resting place of Wilson's brave patrol. They had been buried there by Rhodes's order. Did he want their bold young spirits to accompany him into the Presence as Moselikatze's slaughtered slaves and herds would accompany Moselikatze? Was God to be impressed . . .?

But now, at this time in 1895, the Premier of Cape Colony and managing director of the Chartered Company, Rhodes was riding hard, using whip and spur in his race against the scythed horseman who rode easily in his saddle certain of victory eight lap years ahead. Did Rhodes look back and see him, and then look forward at the course? How far would he get? Each day the thunder of the white hoofs grew louder behind him.

That this was so is Rhodes's only excuse. "To-morrow was not also a day" with him, as it was to the Boers. Nor had he their belief that "all would come right in the end." Pace was what counted with Rhodes and the pace was killing.

A political juggler, Rhodes was second to none in the number of balls he could keep in the air at one time. The ball of his North, that of his diamond and gold interests, that of his position as Prime Minister, that of the confidence of his shareholders in London, that of the contradictory balls of his encirclement of the Dutch Republics and his friendship for the Dutch of the Cape, And while he played with these balls, tossing them up and catching them, there were the strings he had to pull, the reins of the hundred human horses that he drove—the Irish members of Parliament, his settlers, his constituents. A fantastic cat's-cradle of divergent interest and hopes of which he was the centre, the master only so long as he let nothing go, let nothing slip.

He had continually to meet changing conditions, to adjust himself to them, force other conditions, to change his direction. He loved power; he had it, and he needed it. But even his genius, his skill, and his charms were only just enough for his purpose.

Only he, a giant, could have managed, and then only for so long. And set against his growing power—it was still growing in 1895—was his waning health.

Rhodes formed an alliance with Hofmeyr's Africaaner Bond, persuading him that their ends were his own—a United South Africa. Jan Hendrik Hofmeyr, who originally, before the betrayal of the Boers by Gladstone, had been for a South African Union, turned against the idea and linked his party with that of the Dutch Reformed Church minister du Toit. Du Toit's Farmers' Defence Association's platform was a " United South Africa under its own flag"—but not under England. Its influence had spread from the Cape Colony into the Free State and the Transvaal. It had soon become clear to Rhodes that he must bring Hofmeyr in on his side, and in Rhodes, Hofmeyr found an Englishman with whom he could work. They became close friends and this friendship lasted until the Raid when it broke bitterly, shattered on the rock of imperial aggression. Hofmeyr compared himself to a wronged husband. He had been betrayed, charmed back into complacency, and then betrayed again. This betrayal simile was evidently appealing to the Boers, since Kruger had also used it when referring to Burgers's remark in front of Shepstone at the time of the annexation.

Rhodes, a practical man—he was certainly that as well as being a dreamer—took the Dutch view on the question of natives. And only later, when the Dutch had given him up, did he want "common rights of franchise for every civilised man whatever his colour." But at this time when he was consolidating his position, he was ready to play along with the Bond since their ends were similar to his own—a United South Africa.

Hofmeyr wanted it under one flag, but not under that of England. Rhodes's idea, expressed later, was: "If I forfeit my flag, what have I left? If you take away my flag, you take away everything."

A typical inconsistency is another of Rhodes's flag statements when after trouble with England he threatened to "raise my own rag." If there had been no Raid, Rhodes might have managed some compromise with Hofmeyr. One of his axioms was: "Always be sure to satisfy the other fellow. Any trade that is not satisfactory to him is not satisfactory to me." Perhaps here, too, with Hofmeyr he had a plan up his sleeve that would satisfy them both.

Rhodes agreed with the Boers and most of the Colonial English about the natives, and it seems likely that this would have been the keystone of his African structure. He could have promised support of British capital and no interference with the native question. He saw them, as did the others, as the source of all labour in Africa, and realised the necessity of creating a labour pool from which natives could be drawn when needed by means of taxes that they had to work to earn, and by encouraging at least a partial civilisation which created wants previously unknown and, equally, necessitated money to satisfy them.

This idea of creating a labour pool even included the arming of natives, first as a means of tempting them to work and next as an excuse for breaking them and reducing them to the status of serfs. Rhodes was bringing modern industrialism to Africa. There had to be a hungry unemployed population seeking work at low wages. It should be remembered that savages in their tribal state are accustomed to living without what we should call real or regular work.

After the Basuto War, which had cost the Cape millions and was inconclusive, Rhodes addressed Parliament on the subject of guns, taking a stand against native disarmament. First he pointed out the cost of such a policy, since natives would resist it. Next he took the line that it was none of the white man's business what went on in the native territories, particularly as they were not big enough or strong enough to enforce a policy on them. " Are we a great and independent South Africa?" he asked; and then answered his own question. " No, we are only the population of a third-class English city spread over a great country."

These were appeals to reason. They were cold, objective, almost cynical reasons, but justified, in the sense that if the Colony and England ceased selling arms and tried to take back the guns in the possession of natives, other countries would supply them and nothing would have been gained except further and more bloody wars. But it seems possible that Rhodes had another reason for wanting the trade to go on. Guns were the big inducement that brought the savage from his kraal up-country to the labour compounds of the de Beers Company. It was only the desire for guns, the white man's magic, that could keep the mines working, or hold the natives there, virtually prisoners away from their homes and women, for the three years of their contract.

Among savages a gun has only one purpose: it is not used for hunting game. But businessmen took the short-sighted view, gambling an immediate labour supply against the certainty of war. There have been recent parallels in the supplies of scrap and oil to their potential enemies by British and American interests. There is in South Africa to-day a system of native poll tax which, since firearms are no longer allowed to be carried by the natives, forces them to labour in order to defray it. The reward of the rifle has been replaced by the penalty of prison if the tax is not paid, and the labour pool remains intact.

There is still another possibility—since the man we are considering was a genius—that Rhodes wanted the natives to have arms, not merely for the primary reason of securing his labour supply, but for the secondary reason that, having rifles, trouble between the white population and the natives became more than ever certain as it had in Matabeleland. If he wanted the whole North—and he certainly wanted it—Rhodes had to have wars and be able to use the fact that the natives had modern weapons to justify them. He must be able to say, "They have rifles—they are dangerous." He would, to some extent at least, be able to justify himself and be less open to attack on the grounds of using well-armed troops to shoot down natives armed only with spears.

Anthony Trollope believed that work and wages civilised the Kaffirs. "One is tempted sometimes," he wrote, "to say that nothing is done by religion, that very little is done by philanthropy. But the love of money works very fast."

Rhodes said: "I will lay down my own policy on this native question. Either you have to receive them on an equal footing as citizens or to call them a subject race. I have made up my mind that there must be class legislation, that there must be laws passed. These are my politics on native affairs, and these are the politics of South Africa. If I cannot keep my position as an Englishman on the European vote, I wish to be cleared out, for I am not going to the native vote for support. . . . We must adopt a system of despotism, such as works well in India, in our relations with the barbarians of South Africa."

Here is another point on which Paul Kruger would have agreed with Rhodes in the nineties of the last century. It remains a point with which most South Africans of to-day are in agreement. Despite this, and in contradiction to it, Rhodes did play for the native vote when he had alienated the Boers. Rhodes later described himself as a "rabid jingo." He maintained that the missionaries should be "taught a lesson." And the Dutch certainly were ready to have missionaries taught lessons, but were incapable of getting on with a jingo. To the Boer the missionary is a traitor who betrays the white man, "under the cloak of religion," to the black.

Mackenzie was the missionary all white Africa hated. He went about denouncing every one—Rhodes, Kruger, Hofmeyr, and Bismarck.

Here, on the question of Bismarck, Rhodes was in agreement with him. He did not want Germany in Africa. The criss-cross currents of policies and personalities become more and more apparent—enemies desiring one thing; friends parting because they could not agree on something else; tension in one place causing relaxation in another.

Rhodes insisted that a United South Africa was his first objective. Had he achieved it, however, with Hofmeyr or Kruger, there is little doubt that he would then have swung Africa into the orbit of the Empire. Rhodes wanted Kruger to take the harbour of Lourenço Marques from the Portuguese. There is little doubt that had he done so Rhodes would have absorbed both the Transvaal and Portuguese East Africa by the simple expedient of restoring order by annexation.

It is ironic that his Rhodesias, the lands he created, are the very ones which to-day refuse to enter the Union.

In 1894 "Rhodes's health was failing, he looked exhausted, his hair grey, he was in a very nervous state, his face becoming blotched and swollen."

"Never hurry and hasten anything," Rhodes had said. "We can work slowly and gradually" was another of his statements. He accused Hammond of being impatient. "The trouble with all you Americans is your desire to complete everything immediately."

But now he had to reverse himself. He had to hurry, to crush years of work into months, months of work into weeks, weeks of work into days. And time was not the only thing that was running out. Luck was running out as well. Swaziland had passed into the control of the South African Republic. His scheme for a telegraph from the Cape to Cairo was quashed by Belgium, who, at the instigation of Germany, withdrew her concession of a strip of land through which it had been agreed it should run. Rhodes's policies were those of corridors, or necks to bottles. If he could be granted an inch, he was sure that he could get the ell. First a telegraph. To lay it a road would be built. Then the road would be improved. Then a railroad would somehow be laid on the right-of-way. Then the railroad, which would be a great capital investment, would have to be protected by forts. Rhodes's tentative arrangements for the purchase of Lourenço Marques from Portugal fell through, again through German intervention. In addition, the gold which had not been present in Mashonaland was also absent in Matabeleland.

The only real gold in Africa was on the Rand and the Rand belonged to Kruger. "If only one had Johannesburg," Rhodes said. "If one had Johannesburg, one could unite the whole country to-morrow.... Then you would have a great commonwealth; then you would have a Union of States; then I think, apart from my mother country, there would be no place in the world that would compete with it . . . there is no place to touch this; there is no place to touch it for the beauty of its climate and the variety of its products."

This is the voice of a man speaking of his beloved. It is the voice of a man covetous, of a white man lusting for the charms of a subject Negress, the love song of Solomon, Rhodes, who loved no woman, applied to a great land. These are the words of a financier with his eyes on Kruger's golden vineyard. Meanwhile, the Rhodesia Horse continued to be equipped, and Kruger was importing arms, and the Chartered Company's shares were mounting in value again. The London stock exchange knew Rhodes's dictum: "In South Africa where my work has lain, the laws of right and equity are not so fixed and established."

Where things were not established, they were in flux, and in flux was the possibility of profit—nor was there any secret about it. "If there was conspiracy, it was one of the most curious the world had ever seen, since every one spoke of it." Revolt, rebellion, war, was on every man's tongue. If only one had Johannesburg—if only gold in any quantity had been found in Mashonaland or Matabeleland—if only he had been able to deal with Kruger. The greatest intermediator and compromiser in the world had been unable to deal by negotiation with his most important opponent. Like a rock old Kruger squatted, pipe in mouth, rifle and Bible in hand, in Rhodes's path.

If only Kruger had been susceptible to intimidation or bribery. If only he could do in the Transvaal what he had done when he took over Pondoland. Here Sir Henry Loch, the High Commissioner, had been insulted by Sigau, king of the Eastern Pondoland, which was a British protectorate. Sigau had kept Loch waiting three days before he would see him. Incidentally, Pondoland lay between the Cape Province and Natal—another corridor. And it was generally acknowledged that it was merely a matter of time before it would be annexed—that is to say, before an incident would occur, as inevitably it must, which would justify annexation.

This insult was the cause and Rhodes handled it in a typical manner. No one can question Rhodes's courage or his sense of drama. To annex by force was against his principles. He hated blood. He also hated the trouble caused by war and the waste of money which inevitably accompanies the spilling of blood. So Rhodes went to Pondoland in a coach with eight cream-coloured horses and an escort of eight policemen. If Hollywood had thought this one up, it would have been considered ridiculous. A prime minister driving off in a coach drawn by eight palamino stallions and accompanied by eight policemen to visit a barbaric chief in his mountain fastness.

Among the luggage Rhodes had some machine-guns. This was the rabbit he was going to pull out of his pith helmet.

When he arrived, he made Sigau wait three days as Sigau had made Loch. Then to show Sigau what would happen if there was any trouble, his troopers mounted their machine-guns, aimed them at a patch of mealies—corn—and proceeded to mow it down.

The country was annexed. The two German concessionaires who were operating there were deported and some policemen left in charge. A nation of two hundred thousand people had been annexed without a shot, except those fired at the mealie patch, at a cost of seven thousand pounds. Sigau received a pension of five hundred pounds a year. Lobengula had received twelve hundred, but then the Pondos were not the Matabele. Less belligerent, less was required to appease them.

Such drama as this would have been impossible to Paul Kruger. He did not believe in the spectacular. There are those who say that had Rhodes and Kruger met alone the first time at Fourteen Streams instead of with Warren and the parson Mackenzie, everything might have gone well; but they tend to ignore the basic differences between the two men: to forget their discrepancy in years, in blood, in upbringing, in their separate ambitions and destinies; and above all, to forget that gold lay beneath the Ridge of White Waters and not in the Cape Colony or in Rhodes's newly acquired North.

Rhodes's god was England. He continually lamented the loss of America. He wanted "union with America and universal peace." Perhaps he was not far wrong. Certainly America and England, allies in two world wars, have travelled a long way along Rhodes's path. Again he goes on: "The only feasible thing is a secret society gradually absorbing the wealth of the world. I am not going to say that you could make a United States of Africa to-morrow, but I say that this thing could be done gradually by promoting the means to the end."

Ends and means. Manipulations, movements on the chessboard of Africa: Rhodes on one side, Kruger on the other. The kings and the queens and bishops and knights were white, and the pawns, on both sides, black; and when the game was not going right, Rhodes shook the table a little. The game of high politics is without an ethic, it is the art of promoting means to ends.

If Rhodes's god was England, if his ambition was to paint the map red, through war if necessary, in order to achieve peace, his prophets were an interesting assortment: Spengler, Nietzsche, Ruskin, Darwin. Rhodes was a believer in the superiority of blond people—the Aryan myth of to-day. He believed that the civilised races of man will almost certainly exterminate and replace the savage races throughout the world.

And here again is another of Rhodes's great inconsistencies as to the natives. He said at one time, "I do not believe they are different from ourselves," and at another, "The natives are children."

What his real opinion was it is hard to decide. The English, by and large—because he was a great Englishman—followed him. To keep the Dutch on his side he had to state definitely, "I am not a negrophilist," which ranged the missionaries against him as they were against the Boers and left the Boers still against him.

His first act as Prime Minister was to support the Strop Bill (to "strop" is to flog). This was a bill which would allow magistrates to impose the lash upon recalcitrant Kaffirs. Its aim was to punish natives who had no objection whatever to going to prison, where the food was better than that to which many of them were accustomed, and the work relatively light. Rhodes knew this bill would not pass. It is doubtful if he approved of it and his support was merely a means to an end.

The Glen Grey Act was a kind of native charter designed to solve the native problem. It was really an experimental native reserve. Six hundred acres were surveyed and given in allotments to deserving natives. If they did not work, they lost their rights. They could inherit property, but the law of primogeniture was enforced so that these properties would not be broken up among numerous children. This dividing-up of farms equally, until they become economically unworkable, which was the Dutch law, has been a primary cause in the production of poor whites. It was the younger sons of England who constituted Rhodes's best pioneers. He thought that the younger black sons of his Glen Grey settlement would form the best labourers in Africa, since they were drawn from picked families and were forced out to work.

Rhodes was attracted by a book on Russia by Sir Mackenzie Wallace who had written enthusiastically of separate holdings of this kind. The traditional Kaffir culture was that all land should be held communally. Rhodes believed that individual ownership, even under this modified form, would stimulate ambition as it had done in Russia. Oddly, less than forty years later the Russians had given up small holdings and had adopted Communistic collectives which bear at least some resemblance to the old Kaffir system.

No white men, or at least only a few traders and missionaries and officials, were allowed to live in the reserve and the idle natives were taxed ten shillings a year. Rhodes hated loafers, black or white.

The Glen Grey Plan has been largely applied, but is more of a palliative than a solution. Natives increase and land does not. Cattle increase and land does not, with the result that most reserves are bare of grass which has been eaten by the cattle, goats, and sheep: bare of trees which have been burnt in the cooking fires. It seems probable that there is no single solution to the native problem, but many, none of them perfect, but which together, over a period of time and by degrees, may work. But Rhodes's principle of reserves is likely to be the basis of any plan.

Of the natives Rhodes once said, "I have no native policy. I could not afford to have." He also said at another time, "This is my native policy," and went on to speak of class distinctions. His difficulty was that he had to have a policy to suit each party and each man as it seemed expedient. In Rhodes's time only Christians had rights. Natives had no international importance or rights. If a land was taken over, the natives in it were taken over with the wild game. Rhodes considered himself a valuable instrument for the cheap extension of Empire. He was at once the privateer captain sailing under letters of marque and the financier of the expeditions. "I am sometimes told," he said, "that my ideas are too big. Yes, I answer, they would be if I were living on a small island, say Saint Helena or Cyprus, but we must remember that we are living on the fringe of a continent. . . . We must try to keep the continent together . . . if we were to go up in a balloon, how ridiculous it would appear to you to see all these divided states, divided tariffs, divided peoples. . . ."

In the same line he continues: "When the thought came to get a continent, it was a mad thought. It was the idea of a lunatic. It is not now a question of the lunacy of the project: it is merely a question of the years it will take to complete. . . . In reply to the question, ' But where will you stop?' I will stop where the country has not been claimed."

"It has fallen to few," he says in another speech, "to be the author so to speak of a huge new country. . . . I shall never abandon my object. . . . When I find myself in uncongenial company or when people are playing their games or when I am alone in a railway carriage, I think of my great idea ... it is the pleasantest companion I have."

The natives, Rhodes maintained, "are increasing at an enormous rate. The old diminutions by war and pestilence do not occur ... the natives devote their minds to a remarkable extent to the multiplication of children. They had in the past an interesting employment for their minds in going to war and consulting their councils as to war. By our wise government we have taken away all that employment from them."

The Boers could never follow the hypocrisy which permitted the British to claim that the black man was the white man's equal and brother in the sight of the law and of God and yet permitted them to rob and despoil him. The Boer understood this double standard as little as the British understood the Boer "slimness," which is its equivalent. No slavery, said the British. Then they took a man's land, imposed a head tax on him, and forced him to work. This seemed especially wrong to the Boers, since in this way the master was without responsibility towards his servant, whereas under the old Boer law the owner of a slave not only had to support him in old age, but was personally responsible for his torts. The Boers said: "Do these black men look like our brothers? Do they smell like our brothers? And if they are your brothers, why don't you treat them as such?"

The native question in Africa is not yet solved. There are six million natives in the Union of South Africa and two million white men. Given franchise, the white Uitlanders—which they are, ethnologically speaking—would be swamped, and the situation, which Kruger feared in the Transvaal and which caused the Boer War, would be duplicated, the natives replacing the white outlanders of the Transvaal. Nor are comparisons between the South African Bantu and the American Negro profitable, since the African native is at best only two generations removed from the savage warrior, whereas the American Negro has been associated with the white man and his culture for a minimum of a century and according to some authorities only five per cent are without any white blood at all.

What happens in Africa in the future lies in that future, is hidden, and time, by trial and error, will show the only solutions:

much time, no doubt, and many errors. But in Rhodes's time there was little division of opinion among the residents of Africa, British or Dutch, about the way the natives, who then beyond any doubt were savages, should be treated. Trollope said, "This savage! this is something more, but very little more than a monkey," when describing them. On the native question Rhodes described himself as "a rabid jingo." One wonders if a man can be jingo about one question and not another. The word "jingo" came from a popular song that was approved by the British politicians who wanted to bring England into the Russo-Turkish War of 1877 on the side of the Turks. The chorus was:

> We don't want to fight,
> But by jingo if we do
> We've got the men, we've got the guns,
> We've got the money too.

Mrs. Brown Potter was its great exponent and used to sing it at the Palace Music Hall in Shaftesbury Avenue. Like all popular songs it illustrated a phase of national thought.

Rhodes did not believe in the secret ballot. "I object to the ballot *in toto*," he said, "because I like to know how a person votes." Rhodes believed each man had his price: if he knew how they voted, he could deal with them. This was one of the political uses of money and of knowledge, but it was useless unless he could know how a man voted, for he might say one thing and do another. Knowing the expedient himself, he believed that others also knew it and that he could overcome every one by bribery; by charm, or, when charm failed, by intimidation; but charm rarely failed.

By one means or another, lands were continually being absorbed by Rhodes. First Bechuanaland, then, in 1890, Barotseland—a territory "two hundred thousand square miles in extent" —was bought for two thousand pounds a year from Lewanika. A concession in Manicaland, for one hundred pounds a year, followed, but the Manica chief complained to the Portuguese, who tried to intervene. He said, as all chiefs said after they had signed on the dotted line, that he had not understood what he was giving away. The Portuguese intervention failed and Rhodes's young men marched in. Gazaland was bought for five hundred pounds a year, but when Jameson arrived there the Portuguese arrested him for gun-running. And after some negotiations with England, Gazaland was assigned to the Portuguese. Having lost something, Rhodes was not prepared to lose all. He needed the Portuguese harbour of Beira for his pioneers in the North, just as Kruger needed Lourenço Marques for his burghers in the Transvaal. Both men sought outlets into the Indian Ocean. The next question was how Rhodes was going to achieve his end. His method was simple. He sent a young man there with merchandise and waited to see what would happen to him. Of course he might be shot. "No, my dear fellow," Rhodes said, "they'll only hit him in the leg." Actually the Portuguese shot at him with blanks. Willoughby, who later shared many enterprises with Rhodes and Jameson, was the human trial balloon. Rhodes through England protested and the Portuguese gave way. It seems possible that the Portuguese in their excitement might have used ball cartridge, missed the young man's leg, and hit him in the head. If they had, this would have been unfortunate, but it would still have been an incident, an even better one to be exploited. Rhodes was always ready to sacrifice a sprat to catch a herring—always ready to give way in the small things if he could have his own way in the great.

Money meant power to Rhodes. He had no conception of money as money and was careless of it. Power he was not careless of. Credit? Has any man ever had more with a continent in his pocket? Rhodes had few personal wants. His beautiful home he loved, but it was a part of the power pattern—a casket. Women he was not interested in, and it is on women directly, and indirectly, that most money is spent. Yet his diamond fortune and his empire were built upon the fashion he created for diamond engagement rings, vanity and value the Achilles' heel of all women.

Rhodes sent his secretaries crazy with his carelessness. When his income was a quarter of a million sterling, he was overdrawn for nine months of the year and paying interest of five thousand pounds on his overdraft. He was even paying interest on his charities.

"You don't seem to care for money," someone said to him.

"I never tried to make it for its own sake. It's a power. I like power."

Rhodes did not care for the things that money could buy—fine houses, women, horses, yachts, servants—for the very good reason that he did not need to spend conspicuously to show his importance. He was important, one of the most important men in the world in his time, and these things, these possessions which he despised, were latent in his power. Because he could have them, and every one knew he could have them if he wanted, he could reject them.

"One is called a speculator," he once said. "I do not deny the charge. If one has ideas one cannot carry them out without having wealth at one's back."

Having got the wealth he had the power. And having the power he had its instruments—a devoted following, credit which he need never estimate, the backing of an Empire, and the friendship of a Queen.

Like one of his own diamonds Rhodes had many facets. He had, too, the brilliance and the hardness of a diamond. The apparent contradictions of his character are merely those of facets. He must be seen in his total brilliance; in the fire of his mind; in the hardness of his determination; in his integrity as much as in his lack of it; in his consistency as much as in his inconsistency; in his faults, which were great as his virtues were great. Of him it could never be said that anything was small. He was the enemy of the little; a believer in the great. To-day with the perspective of the years we can see him as he was—the prototype of the modern dictator, the modern financier, the jingo, and the final and completely modernised specimen of the old Elizabethan adventurer. Beyond evil and good in ordinary terms, Rhodes was great, a master of men in a world that even then demanded masters. There was nothing democratic about him. The fact that he did not worry about the origins of his friends means nothing since the moving force of his life was the security of England, and government by an élite which was merely a euphemism for an aristocracy of brains. Rhodes despised those who thought of money as an end. Money was a means to him—the only sure means of achieving anything.

But Rhodes, the diamond which could not be scratched, was about to meet another diamond. To meet Kruger who was without brilliance, who resembled a commercial diamond--a bort: the bort that would split Rhodes by his own instrument, his best friend—Doctor Leander Starr Jameson.

CHAPTER EIGHT

THE RAID

WHOLE BOOKS have been written about the Jameson Raid. It was a conspiracy, a filibustering expedition, a piece of land piracy, the rescue of an oppressed minority. It was this and that. Actually it ran the gamut from a Guy Fawkes plot to an Australian Bushranger's hold up, from treason to tragedy, from tragedy to comedy, from arrant cowardice to reckless courage. It was finally an expression of the times and the people of those times, and remains, historically, an action, in the military sense, which links the Battle of Majuba where the British were defeated in 1880 to the Peace of Vereeniging where the Boers laid down their arms in 1902.

Thought precedes action. And thought precedes conspiracy. A number of men having thought about their wrongs for long enough begin to conspire. That the wrongs in this case were largely imaginary does not alter the case. Most people are ready to feel aggrieved about something, most ready to sign a manifesto of complaints; while others are ready to organise the dissatisfaction they have promoted to achieve the ends that they desire. Though the majority cared not a fig for the vote and few wished to become burghers, the Uitlanders were all, by the fact of their presence in Johannesburg, adventurers, and as political material highly inflammable. They resented the Majuba defeat. They resented much more than this that the Golden Rand lay within the South African Republic, and if they could not change geology they were ready, or thought they were ready, to change geography. Gold was the primary cause of the raid, since if there had been no gold there would have been no Uitlanders, no grievances or problems, and certainly no desire on the part of any one to acquire the bleak Highland plateau of the Transvaal. Jameson—and Rhodes, though he was supposed to have had nothing to do with the raid—believed that the Uitlanders, the foreigners in Johannesburg, would rise and join the force that had been assembled at Pitsani on the Bechuanaland border. The truth was that the Uitlanders were doing very well and only liked to talk about rising. They liked to conspire and play cowboys and Indians. They did not want to fight. They wanted to play in their spare time, and make money in their working hours. As a result their conspiracy was the most open in the world—the most comic. Bryce, who was there at the time, wrote: "People have talked of conspiracy, but never except on the stage was there so open a conspiracy. Two-thirds of the action went on before the public. The visitor had hardly installed himself in an hotel in Pretoria before people began to tell him that an insurrection was imminent and that arms were being imported, that Maxims were hidden. Guns would be shown to him if he cared to see them."

Its later stages were equally comic. A messenger gave away the exact plans; and when all arrangements were made, the revolution was delayed because the day chosen—December 28—was in Christmas week, which was race week. These were only some of the errors made by the hard-headed, practical businessmen who organised the revolution.

The Reform Movement as it was called was headed by Charles Leonard of the National Union; Lionel Phillips, a partner in Wernher, Biet and Company; Colonel Frank Rhodes, Cecil Rhodes's brother; George Farrar, a mine owner; and John Hays Hammond, the American mining engineer, who was Rhodes's consultant. Hammond in his *Autobiography* says: "The Reform Movement as a whole was Fascist rather than Bolshevik in its nature. Direct action was finally undertaken by a group of hard-headed, successful, conservative men of affairs, not by hot-headed irresponsible radicals. It was the moneyed element in the revolt that finally assumed leadership."

This is strange justification for what appears to have been nothing but a *Putsch*, a march on Rome, an attempted *coup d'état*. Nothing could have been more democratic than the South African Republic, for though Kruger was called a dictator he was a patriarchal one and ready at any time to abandon power. He was indeed always threatening to do so, and this—blackmail by threat of abdication—was his main source of strength. So here was the beginning of a pattern that we now know so well: a grasping at riches and power, a misused minority the excuse, with the trimmings of incidents, agents provocateurs, irregular troops fanatically devoted to a single man, a furious imperialism, the use of threats, the massing of men, the marching, the demonstrations, the petitions, the threats, the broken promises and bribes—the first modern reflowering of the cult of a leader.

Had the raid succeeded instead of failing, Rhodes would have been the master of Africa and perhaps of England, for he had gripped the imagination of the British. Everything was in his favour as far as the national mood was concerned. England was at her strongest, her poets at their most lyrical crescendo. What country was there to compare with England then? France recently defeated was a republic trying to reach a stable form of government. Germany was still an infant power, America isolated by vast oceans and her own desire for isolation. Belgium, Portugal, and Spain were all negligible. Had Rhodes taken the Transvaal, he would have gone on and England would have been behind him.

Only Kruger stood in his way. Kruger, whom Hammond met and described in 1893 as "a shepherd peasant leader. . . . He was then sixty-eight years old. His massive frame still showed evidence of that brute physical strength which had become proverbial. A huge nose, a large firm mouth, keen eyes partially obscured by swollen lids were set in a heavy rugged face surrounded by a ragged fringe of beard. His forehead sloped back to where the long, grizzled hair swept up in a defiant mane. . . ." Kruger was a typical Boer, and "the Boer burgher was in no way interested in mining: he was a peasant with the conservative and suspicious nature of that class. But he was more than this: he was cunning, brave, and stubbornly intent on keeping what he regarded as his birthright."

The Uitlander problem was summed up by General Joubert when he said: "There are two riders but only one horse in the Transvaal. The question is which rider is going to sit in front, the Uitlander or the Boer."

Fundamentally it was the problem of two rival cultures which was coming to a head again. On the one hand was a simple patriarchal pastoral society, on the other an urban industrial civilisation. In the Transvaal in 1895 there were eighty-five thousand Uitlanders and sixty-five thousand Boers, of whom only twenty-five thousand were males over sixteen. The foreigners had bought more than half the land in the Transvaal and owned nine-tenths of the assessable property. Most of them, according to Phillips, who was in a position to know, "cared very little about the franchise," and did not mind whether the Vierkleur or the Union Jack waved over Johannesburg. What they said they wanted was the redress of their grievances—English to be taught in the schools; freedom from commando duty; and reduction of taxes. From these causes the Reformers believed an incident could be built up.

Loch, the High Commissioner, informed the Colonial Office that "in case of an uprising the Uitlanders were bound to win if they had rifles." This belief seems to have been based on the number of Uitlanders—eighty-five thousand to twenty-five thousand Boers. In conversation with Lionel Phillips at this time Loch hinted at the desirability of obtaining arms to defend Johannesburg pending British intervention. A main grievance, but one below the surface, was the fact that Kruger refused to allow the new Delagoa Bay Railway to be British-owned and gave the majority of votes to the Dutch in a corporation shared among the Dutch, Germans, and Boers.

This kind of self-protective measure was very annoying to the British, that is to say, to Rhodes.

To finance the revolution an account was opened in the books of the Chartered Company under the heading "New Concessions" on which Colonel Frank Rhodes was entitled to draw. Part of the balance stood in the names of Colonel Rhodes, Lionel Phillips, Percy Fitzpatrick, and John Hays Hammond at the Standard Bank of South Africa in Johannesburg. There was another account at the Standard Bank at Mafeking and the Pitsani Camp Account on the books of the Chartered Company which dealt with the immediate expenses of the force held at the border.

Cecil Rhodes could naturally take no leading part in all this. He was Prime Minister of the Cape Colony and would have alienated his Dutch followers if they had had the faintest idea that he was attacking the independence of the northern Republic. It was assumed that if the revolt could be spontaneously generated from within, Great Britain was certain to intervene on the behalf of her citizens.

The spontaneous revolt was being carefully worked up. Jameson's rôle was not to lead the revolt but to come in to stop bloodshed which would put his foray in a good light internationally. He was supposed to lie on the Bechuanaland border at Pitsani, a hundred and eighty miles west of Johannesburg, with fifteen hundred fully equipped men. Each man was to carry an extra rifle to arm the Reformers in the town, and the reason given out for his presence was "the necessity for a show of force to overawe the natives.". Jameson's orders were to stay in position for the six months that would be required to prepare everything in the Transvaal.

As Rhodes said at the time, "The only justification for revolution is success."

In the meantime, as a build-up, more petitions were sent to Kruger, more deputations visited him, more demonstrations were staged and more hardships of these outland Englishmen were reported in the British press at home. It was to some extent a repetition of the set-up used before the invasion of Matabeleland, an example of "manufactured evidence which is the homage that aggression offers to democracy."

At last Kruger was irritated into saying, "If you want your rights, why don't you fight for them?"

A German Uitlander hearing this remark said, "This is the last straw that broke the camel's back that killed the goose that laid the golden egg."

Arms continued to flow into Johannesburg, though only burghers had the right to possess them. They came from England to Kimberley, where they were received by Gardner Williams, the American mining engineer who was in charge of the de Beers diamond properties.

To get the arms and ammunition into Johannesburg was a harder matter. The gun-smugglers took the risk of being sentenced to seven years' imprisonment. However, a system was finally devised—guns and ammunition were loaded into Standard Oil drums which were provided with a false bottom so that "if the customs men turned a spigot a convincing trickle would run out." These drums were consigned to Mr. John Hays Hammond.

One train in which guns were loaded had a collision and Colonel Rhodes and Hammond prepared to bolt. "We have the fastest horses in the country," Colonel Rhodes said to Hammond. "If necessary we can make a bolt for Natal where we'll be out of danger of extradition. We could even go to Rhodesia where we'd be absolutely safe."

However, they did not have to bolt. Before their preparations were complete, they received a wire which said, "There has been a collision between two trains in one of which are some of our friends but they are entirely uninjured and will arrive at Johannesburg to-morrow. Be sure to secure proper hotel accommodation for them." The friends, of course, were the guns hidden like Ali Baba's thieves in the oil drums. The conspirators enjoyed using these codes. A consignment of guns was advised by a telegram, "Am sending you a diamond full of fire." The leaders all had code names: Doctor Harris was known as Cactus; Colonel Rhodes as Toad; Jameson as Zahlbar; Rhodes as Umbegangan; Johannesburg as Giovanno.

Hammond's idea was to secure the Boer Arsenal at Pretoria, where there were stored fifteen thousand Martini-Henry rifles, much ammunition, and three or four Maxims. To achieve this end he obtained the lease of a property—for mining purposes—just outside Pretoria and assembled there "fifty hard-boiled Americans of adventurous spirit." They knew there was no gold there, but were content as long as they were well paid. Most of them had been discharged from mining companies under Hammond's management for drunkenness and disorderly conduct. Another of Hammond's ideas, and one which seemed perfectly feasible once Pretoria was in his hands, was the capture of old Oom Paul himself. "I felt confident," he writes, "that when subject to this other environment, he would prove more receptive to our ideas." No wonder Mr. Hammond says this revolt was Fascist and that its organisers were hard-headed, calculating men of property!

Jameson's forces were in two divisions. The Bechuanaland Police under Major Raleigh Grey at Mafeking and the main body of Chartered Company Police who had been withdrawn from Rhodesia under Jameson himself at Pitsani. Sir John Willoughby was to command the combined forces. This was the same

Willoughby that Rhodes had sent to Portuguese East to be "shot in the leg."

One of the messengers Jameson used as couriers between himself and the Uitland Reformers was an old Etonian who, meeting with two other old Etonians, had a reunion party in which he told them all he knew. Word of this came to Hammond, who sent the young man back to Jameson with a letter that he told him to deliver in person: "My dear Jameson, for God's sake don't send any more damn fools like the bearer of this letter. He has divulged the entire plans to two Englishmen who are here with us. It will not make any difference, as they are loyal and will help us all they can: send the bearer into the interior of Africa where he will be lost for months."

Nor was Jameson's choice of officers much more felicitous than his choice of messengers. Infected by Rhodes's passion for that noblest work of God, the English gentleman, he apparently chose for his subordinates men who, though well bred, were all but mentally defective. Mounted upon that other noblest work of God, "the racehorse," these gallant men performed prodigies of inefficiency.

Lieutenant Colonel Sir John Willoughby, Bart., was an officer in the Royal Horse Guards, the Blues—a regiment whose main purpose was to ride their immense black horses beside the royal coaches, carriages, and victorias when they were drawn through the streets of London. Major the Honourable Robert White was an officer in the Royal Welsh Fusiliers; another colonel was a Grenadier Guardsman; Major Raleigh Grey came from the Sixth Dragoons. The Honourable C. J. Coventry added another title. There were in addition a number of young Guards officers attached to the staff; and one invalid officer, who happened to be staying in Mafeking for his health when Jameson set out, went along in his own cart in civilian clothes "to see the fun."

Sir John Willoughby was a well-known hunting man and had won a Derby. The others were all charming men of the highest social standing. It would have been as inconceivable for them to send the port round the wrong way as for them to send their scouts out the right. Taken as a whole, this collection of gentlemen presented the spectacle of the gentleman theory *reductio ad absurdum.* Against them they were to find men who, like their leader and President, had all begun life "as shepherd lads."

The Johannesburg preparations went very slowly. Jameson, getting impatient, wired, "Inform weak partners more delay more danger. Do all you can to hasten the completion of the works."

On December 18 Hammond wired to Rhodes, "Flotation would have to be postponed because of Biet's illness." Biet wired back, saying he did not want his illness "to interfere with the flotation" —the flotation being, of course, the revolt of the Uitlanders. December 28 was now decided on as the date, but this was again changed because it was race week and the Uitlanders did not want their Christmas week's racing disturbed.

Then there was a further complication. It appeared that Jameson intended to insinuate the British flag into the proceedings and carry it into Johannesburg and that Rhodes agreed with his suggestion.

Many of the Reformers were Americans and had no liking for the Union Jack. Even many of the British had no desire so see it fly in the Transvaal. What they wanted was reduced taxation and greater freedom, not the order and taxes which would come with a British administration.

But to Rhodes and Jameson everything had to be done for the flag and by it. By this time the lute which had never been too sound was thoroughly rifted. Jameson doubted the zeal of the Reformers, the Reformers doubted Jameson's intentions, and even the sluggish Boers were becoming aware that something was up. Probably they had been aware for some time. Harris wired to Jameson: "We suspect the Transvaal is getting slightly aware." Slightly aware! This shows how little any of them knew the Boers. Men who could see the sunlight glint on a buck's horn or the twitch of an ear three hundred yards away! How could they have failed to notice all this coming and going, or hear the talk that went on?

January the fourth was now set as the "date of flotation." In order to blind the Boers to the imminence of this event, an open forum for the discussion of Uitlander grievances was scheduled and announced for January 6—two days after the uprising. That is to say, the attack was to take place during negotiations.

Among the demands of the Reformers were: Representation in the councils "according to our numbers and vested interest"; proper control of public moneys; independence of courts; possession and control of railways and public works; abolition of monopolies and equal rights for the Dutch and English languages.

"This sweet and reasonable document," as the *Standard and Diggers News* called it, was read by Kruger. "Their rights," he said. "Yes, they'll get them over my dead body."

Nevertheless, the proposed mass meeting accomplished its purpose. It deceived the Boers, since it never occurred to them that any one would move before that date. They were a simple people.

The telegrams now increased in number, in the quality of their redskin and cowboy content, in the obscurity of their code. People were now sending telegrams to each other that no one understood, not even the Reformers. Rutherford Harris, for instance, on his return from England sent a message about "the veterinarian and his horses" and signed it "Godolphin." Who was Godolphin and why? Harris was "Ichabod." Was he trying to disguise himself from himself?

Doctor Wolff had become the "Rand Produce and Trading Company." Jameson was sometimes "the veterinarian" and his men "horses," or he was the "contractor" and his men "boys." One *alias* was not enough for any one; to be exciting the thing must be really mysterious.

The revolution was "the flotation" and alternatively, "the Polo tournament." Colonel Rhodes wired on this occasion: "Tell Doctor Jameson Polo tournament here postponed one week because it would clash with race week." Jameson wired back, "Surely in your estimation do you consider races of the utmost importance compared to the immense risks of discovery daily expected by which under the circumstances it will be necessary to act prematurely?"

Here we have one party wiring in code and the other not.

On December 29 the Reformers in Johannesburg received a wire from the Cape: "In view of changed conditions Jameson has been advised accordingly." That meant Jameson had been stopped. They also received one from Jameson saying, "I shall start without fail to-morrow night." Rhodes had cabled Harris, "My judgment is that it is a certainty." He meant a certain success.

From England Rhodes got other cables. "Chamberlain sound in case of interference by European powers, but have special reason to believe wishes you to do something about it immediately." Another telegram, again to Rhodes from England: "Delay dangerous. Sympathy now complete, but will depend very much upon action before European powers given time to enter protest which as European situation considered serious might paralyse government. General feeling on stock market very suspicious."

This seems to mean that England would have supported a successful "*coup d'état*" and been ready to accept a "*fait accompli*," but would have nothing to do with failure, which put the Reformers into the position of a secret agent caught spying in a foreign country.

On December 27 Rhodes wired to Jameson, who was afraid his concentration of troops was causing suspicion: "Not to be alarmed at our having six hundred men at Pitsani. We have a right to have them. If people are so foolish as to think we are threatening the Transvaal we can't help that."

He also cabled to his friend Flora Shaw in London: "Inform Chamberlain I shall get through all right if he supports me. To-day the crux is I shall win and South Africa will belong to England."

"Unless I hear definitely to the contrary shall leave to-morrow evening," Jameson wired to Rhodes.

"You must do nothing till all is clear," Rhodes wired back. Jameson answered, "Shall leave to-night for the Transvaal."

This telegram was delayed and before he received it Rhodes wired: "I yet hope to see things in Johannesburg amicably settled. On no account whatever must you move. I most strongly object to such a course."

This was not all. The Reformers were telegraphing to Jameson from Johannesburg too.

Harris in his *alias* of Ichabod wired: "All our foreign friends are dead against flotation and say public will not subscribe one penny towards it even with you as director. We cannot have fiasco." This was a reference to the Americans and others who objected to the British flag idea.

Jameson wired to his brother, Sam Jameson, "Let J. H. Hammond telegraph instantly all right."

Hammond answered: "Wire received. Experts report decidedly adverse. I absolutely condemn further developments at present."

Sam Jameson also wired: "It is absolutely necessary to postpone flotation through unforeseen circumstances until we have C. J. Rhodes's absolute pledge that authority of Imperial Government will not be insisted on."

Here was the crux of the situation—the Uitlanders did not want a stable government. Many of them were not British and they did not want a British government. What they wanted was what they had, only more of it. More freedom, more licence, and less control. In addition to this, the races were not yet over; the meeting lasted a week and the market was good. They were making money hand over fist. The time for revolution is when things are bad: nothing upsets a revolution quicker than full purses and full bellies. More, the Reformers mistrusted this flag business and the Chartered Company's aims. They felt they were going to be used to some purpose they did not fully understand. In this it turned out they were right. Rhodes had said to an envoy the Reformers had sent to tell him that they would not rise under the British flag: "All right. If they won't go into it they won't. I'll wire Jameson to keep quiet." But after leaving Rhodes, the envoy—he was *The Times* correspondent—met Doctor Harris, who told him Rhodes would not hear of a rising except under the British flag. Rhodes appears to have said it didn't matter about the flag merely to pacify the objectors. "Of course I would not risk everything as I am doing except for the British flag," Rhodes said to Harris.

None of this suited the Reformers, whose platform at least was direct—reform, not change. The Transvaal flag was good enough for all of them except a few ardent Britishers who wanted revenge for Majuba.

The Americans even went so far as to produce a Declaration of Independence of their own. A deputation of them went to see Kruger, who asked them, "On which side shall I find the

Americans if a crisis should occur?" They answered, "On the side of liberty and good government."

John Hays Hammond, addressing a meeting from which all but Americans had been asked to leave, said, "You all know what we are here for. I don't need to tell you how unjustly we've been treated by the Pretoria crowd. All I'm going to ask you is one single question. Don't you agree with me that we've reached the same point as the signers of the Declaration of Independence when they announced it was their right and their duty to throw off a despotic government and to provide new guards for their future security? That's all there is to it," he went on. "You won't find anything in the Declaration of Independence that limits this principle to latitude or longitude. It's a clean-cut issue to be faced by us Americans here and now. You know as well as I do that we won't stand for having a British flag hoisted over Johannesburg. All we want is justice from Kruger and his grafters." The assemblage applauded; a vote was taken and all but five of the five hundred present voted to take up arms against Kruger. A George Washington Corps was at once organised and pledged to support the revolutionary cause.

Another telegram now arrived: "The contractor has started on the earthworks with seven hundred boys. Hopes to reach terminus Wednesday."

It was followed by still another to Doctor Wolff, who was head of the Intelligence Department in Johannesburg: "Meet me as arranged before you left on Tuesday night which will enable us to decide which is best destination. Have great confidence and faith in J. H. Hammond, A. L. Lawley, and miners with Lee-Metford rifles."

Unfortunately Doctor Wolff had taken a holiday, and in Cape Town the other Intelligence chief, Doctor Harris, had also taken a holiday, so no one received Jameson's final message.

Nor did Jameson get Rhodes's final message because all the wires had been cut except the Pretoria wire which had been left open; so that while Kruger could get messages along the route, Jameson was cut off from the Reformers who should have ridden out to help him. The explanation of this mistake is both simple and interesting. Three days before setting out, Jameson gave his men three days in which to get drunk. They are supposed to have had several wagon loads of whisky and thirty-six cases of champagne. The trooper detailed to carry out the wire-cutting operation, in his alcoholic enthusiasm cut the wrong wire; and then, for good measure, cut and buried the wires of a farmer's fence.

F. E. Garrett, editor of the Cape *Times*, describes this incident:

An essential part of the plan was the cutting of the telegraph wire—"secure telegraph office silence," as one of the cipher telegrams put it. And one wire was cut, sure enough. The southward wire to the Colony was cut south of Pitsani and again south of Mafeking. But the really important wire running to Pretoria by way of Zeerust and Rustenburg was not cut by reason of the trooper who was sent to cut it being, in plain words, drunk. He started his errand carrying with him the most detailed and elaborate instructions. He was to cut the wire in two places so many yards apart, take it so far into the veld, and bury it so deep. He did cut certain wire and he did make an effort at least to bury it in the veld. But the wire cut was the peaceful fence by which a farmer kept his cows in. Then with good conscience he reeled back. In the whole tragi-comedy there is no grotesquer touch than this which the writer had from a resident on the spot.

Jameson now crossed the border with five hundred men, mounted on mediocre horses, and suffering from a hangover, instead of the fifteen hundred he was supposed to have. The Reformers were unready for him because the flag question was still unsolved and only a few of their rifles had arrived.

To the burghers, who for a long time had wanted to take action against the Uitlanders, Kruger always gave one answer: "You must give the tortoise time to put out its neck before you catch hold of it."

When Jameson crossed the border from Pitsani, the tortoise had stuck out its neck and Kruger struck. Except for the fact that the Boers had thought the attack would come later, after the demonstration which had been staged to deceive them, there was nothing unexpected about the attack. How could there have been, with all those telegrams, with all the unrest, with all the coming and going of Rhodes and his henchmen, and all the talk in the bars and hotels?

The Boers were a simple people, hunters and farmers, and because of this they were watchful, accustomed to sizing-up animals, both wild and tame, able to guess when a lion or a bull would charge, able to read the signs, not merely as well as the next man, but a little better, and as hunters able to wait their moment with a stolid and infuriating patience, refusing to be goaded into action till they were ready and had their opponent off balance. Then this sluggishness changed into dynamic action. Jameson had hardly crossed the frontier when the Boers were riding to meet him from a thousand farms—fathers, sons, grandfathers, all riding to join their commandos. The dirt roads of Africa were filled with mounted and armed farmers provisioned, as was the law, for a week. A single man would ride from his place and meet another, the two would meet more. The Boers' leaders, farmers too, mounted their horses and rode to the places of assembly where they would take command. Old Kruger himself sent for his old white horse that he had not ridden for eight years. When Mrs. John Hays Hammond went to see Mrs. Kruger on her husband's behalf when he had been arrested after the Raid, she said: "Yes, I will do all I can. I am very sorry for you all, although I know none of you thought of me that night when we heard that Jameson had crossed the border and we were afraid the President would have to go out and fight when they went and caught his old white horse that he had not ridden for eight years."

All Africa was up, from the President to the young boys on the farms, their minds clear, their purpose simple—the tortoise had stuck out its neck. The time had come to strike.

But no one was clear in Johannesburg. People were leaving the city. Women and children were being brought in and quartered in the clubs, men were drilling in the streets. Rhodes's newspapers—he controlled wholly or in part all the African press, that is, all means of propaganda—published manifestoes and tried to fan the flame of a populace that now, when rescue—that was the idea of the Raid—was near, became more and more apathetic. In fact, Johannesburg did not want to be rescued. What, after all, was the matter? Things were very nice as they were. They were making money. They were free to blackguard the President, the executive and the judiciary, they could write and say what they liked, they could do what they liked. Suppose the revolution succeeded, would a new government be so pleasant to live under? It had been a diversion to talk about it, but they preferred going to the races with the ladies of their fancy, to back the nags they fancied. And now the fat was in the fire: Jameson had crossed the border. The Contractor was coming—the Veterinarian was coming. There would be hell to pay.

And suddenly they realised that they were not soldiers, that they had not enough rifles, that they could not use the rifles they had. The cowboy and Indians game had been fun, but now the Indians were real. The more optimistic minority organised a reception committee for Jameson's victorious men—how could they fail?—The Majority sought solace according to their natures in dissipation or in prayer.

Jameson had not the faintest idea of what was in store for him in the Transvaal. He was an impatient man and he was dying of boredom from drilling his troops who, as bored as he, were continually deserting. He knew that the Boers suspected his purpose and that every day's delay would give them a better chance to prepare to meet him, but he despised the Boers. Above all, he mistrusted the Reformers in Johannesburg and said, "Rhodes had cold feet along with his Johannesburg friends." He thought every one had cold feet except himself and he was convinced that the job would be easy. Only a few weeks before the Raid he told a friend, "Any one could take the Transvaal with half a dozen revolvers."

So backing his judgment against that of Rhodes and of every one else, he started off. But not with the fifteen hundred men he had promised the Reformers, not with the eight hundred he had suggested later, not with six hundred, but in the end with less than five hundred, because many of his troopers refused to fight unless the Queen gave them orders. They, too, insisted on the flag and official sanction. The others who remained, heroes of the Matabele War, appear to have confused the plumed warriors of Lobengula with the Boer sharpshooters. For days before they set out, they had toasted each other. Jameson's address when he read them the letter of invitation from the Reformers had moved them to drunken tears: "Thousands of unarmed men and women and children of our own race will be at the mercy of the Boers. We cannot but believe that you and the men under you will not fail to come to the rescue of people who will be so situated."

Colonel Willoughby congratulated the troops "on their smart appearance and hoped they would give a good account of themselves," and the "army" marched. They had, besides their rifles and revolvers, eight Maxims, three machine-guns, and, for transport, six Scotch carts and a Cape cart. Their hearts were full of pride, their bellies full of whisky.

Yet almost at once things began to go wrong. The spare horses, forage, and rations they had expected never came. They did not come because Doctor Wolff, who should have seen to it, was having a holiday and no one knew that they were expected to come. Their horses, which never had been very good, were tired, but still they pressed on, expecting to meet reinforcements and rations; and to make matters worse, wherever they looked there were Boers. On every hill and kopje—scouts, small parties. They did not attack them, they merely rode on their flanks. It was terribly hot. The rains were late and had not broken. Jameson did not know that owing to the mistake in cutting of the telegraph wires the Boers knew about his attack eighteen hours before the Reformers heard he had started.

Then they did take some action. They withdrew the arms they had stored at Irene which they had been going to use in their attack on the arsenal at Pretoria. Why, instead of getting these arms back, were they not employed? According to Garrett: "The reason is simple: even to absurdity. The Johannesburg leaders had just discovered that the Boers keep Nagmaal—Christmas and New Year are great times to take communion. At the end of December and the beginning of January, Church Square at Pretoria was white with the tents of outspanned wagons. Bearded farmers and fat vrous, families by scores of wagons, drawn from the Pretoria district up to several days' distance, had come to town to partake of Nagmaal; and in each wagon along with the Bible came a rifle—in case of game on the way, or thieves, or other need . . . Pretoria was a ready-made garrison. So when

Jameson suddenly precipitated matters and the Johannesburgers went to spy out the land at Pretoria, lo! the Church Square was thick with Boers ... the geese of the Capitol were not more useful to Rome than the Boers in Church Square were to Pretoria. Once again the Boers say, 'We were saved by our religion.' "

It seems incredible that this cardinal factor of religion in Boer life should have been ignored by the organisers of the rebellion. First their own race week, then the Boers' religious week. ...

Jameson led his men along the road that led from Malmani to Krugersdorp. On Tuesday morning he reached the first stage station and after a short rest pushed on. By midday Wednesday the column reached the outskirts of Krugersdorp, only twenty-one miles from Johannesburg. And now the Boers, who had been riding round the Raiders, began to close in. They had let the Raiders get tired, had let them exhaust their horses, had all but herded them—as they herded a fat giraffe or eland bull near to camp before they killed it.

Jameson's scouts reported the Boers entrenched in a strong position on the ridges in front of them. The tactical situation had an historical precedent. Jameson's men were in the same position as the French knights had been in the Battle of Crécy when they faced the British long-bowmen, and like them they "fell slain or sore stricken, almost without seeing the men who slew them." But it seems doubtful if the officers in charge of this foray had studied much military history. There was indeed some question as to who was in charge.

Sir John Willoughby was theoretically in command, but a difference as to seniority had arisen between him and Colonel White. It seems that "sometimes Jameson gave an order, sometimes Sir John Willoughby, sometimes one or the other of the Whites, and sometimes Major Grey." At any rate, one of these men, acting as the French armoured knights had acted, and with equal dash, chivalry, and stupidity, ordered a charge across the marsh that separated them from the Boer sharpshooters. What these troopers could have done had they reached their objective, since they carried no sabres, seems not to have been considered. Their only course would have been to have used their rifle butts to club the Boers. They did not, however, reach their objective. The Boers, who had been shelled with shrapnel, simply lay low and not one was hit—"except one man who had the skin taken off his thumb and went on firing." A scout, allowed to come near them, returned, after surveying the prostrate and motionless Boers, saying that most of them were killed. These dead men watched the cavalry—some hundred strong—deploy and start off. One thousand yards, five hundred, three hundred, two hundred—at this point they splashed into the water and the Boers opened fire—cross-fire from all round. The charge slowed up, faltered, and failed. Only forty men got back to the British lines.

The column now moved southward, hoping to turn the Boer position, and then, unable to go on, camped for the night. Right through the hours of darkness the Boers harassed them, firing into the camp, killing and wounding a few men and stampeding the horses.

Jameson's position was bad, but he was not yet in despair, and he sent a message by runner through to Johannesburg: "Am all right, but should like a force sent out to us."

At dawn the column moved again, found itself under continual fire, and halted while Jameson and Willoughby revamped their plans. While they were talking, they saw two youths, apparently from a neighbouring farm, idly watching the troops. Thinking that they would know the country, Willoughby asked them the best road to Johannesburg. The Reformers' intelligence service evidently had not gone in for map-making. One of the Boer boys answered in good English, "If you follow this road for about ten miles you'll come to Doornkop and from there you can't miss the way."

The lucky coincidence of two boys who spoke English being on the spot to direct them after the Boers had checked them seems to have struck no one. After all, who would have expected the Boers to do a thing like that? The Matabele didn't do things like that.

Jameson's men now rode straight into a *cul de sac*. They had either to stop or throw themselves at rising ground in which there was ample cover for the Boers who were waiting, safely hidden, for them. Cronje, who three days before had been sitting peacefully on his farm, had got his commando into position before them. First the Raiders had been herded, by Boers riding on their flanks, into a marsh, and now they had been led by guides into this trap. Back? There was no way back, for the Staats artillery had appeared on their left, northern, flank and opened fire. After an hour of fighting, eighteen Raiders had been killed and forty wounded; and the white flag went up.

Ignorant of what was going on here, the flag question was still being discussed in Johannesburg. The Vierkleur, the Union Jack, and even the Stars and Stripes had been suggested. But while they were talking about these notable pieces of bunting, Jameson, their rescuer, hoisted the white flag over Farmer Brink's outhouse at Doornkop. The white flag used on this occasion was not, as a matter of fact, "a torn shirt plucked from a weary trooper," but was the white apron of an old Hottentot Tanta—Mammy—who was standing somewhere at hand on the farm, and it was borrowed from her to be waved as an emblem of peace. The Raid and the Battle of Doornkop were over.

Jameson sent Cronje a message: "We surrender provided that you give us safe conduct out of the country for every member of the force."

Cronje answered: "Officer, please take note that I shall immediately assemble our officers to decide upon your communication."

The Boer was a democratic force. The officers were the leaders elected by their men and entitled to speak for them.

Half an hour later Willoughby received the following letter: "The answer is that if you will undertake to pay the expense you have caused the South African Republic and if you will surrender with your arms, then I shall spare the lives of you and yours. Please send me a reply to this within thirty minutes."

Willoughby answered: "I accept the terms on the guarantee that the lives of all will be spared. I now await your instructions as to how and where we lay down our arms. At the same time I would ask you to remember that my men have been without food for the last twenty-four hours."

After the surrender the Boers maintained that their guarantee of safety did not apply to Jameson or the other leaders and arrested them. Much was made of this in the press later. Hammond writes, "I am convinced that the Boer intent at the time was to secure Jameson's surrender as simply as possible and that later deliberate suppression of the terms was Kruger's idea of diplomacy in dealing with us in Johannesburg."

The Boer alternative would have been very simple—to have lain where they were behind the rocks of the kopjes and slaughtered the helpless and exhausted Englishmen who struggled in the cup of the valley, to the last man.

By this time the Boers were tired of all this trouble with the Uitlanders. Slow to get angry, they were also slow to calm down. They wanted to make an end. They clamoured for Jameson's execution. Commandant Henning Pretorius even went down to the Cape, where he found the original beam that had been used by the English to hang the Boers condemned to death after the Slagtersnek Rebellion in 1816. He found it built into a farmhouse at Cookhouse Drift, bought it, and demanded that it be used to hang the leaders of the Raid. So strong was the feeling that when the President was informed by Chamberlain that he would be held responsible personally for the safety of the prisoners and had the beam placed in a museum, it had to be guarded in case it was taken out and used in a lynching.

A commando of four hundred men which was riding through Pretoria before the capture of Jameson called on the President. Their leader said: "President, we have come to greet you and at the same time to inform you that when we have captured Jameson, we intend to march straight on to Johannesburg and shoot down that den of rebels in it. They have provoked us long enough."

The President replied: "No, brother, you must not speak like that. Remember there are thousands of innocent and loyal people in Johannesburg and others have for the most part been misled. We must not be revengeful."

"You, President," the commandant answered, "you speak in vain. What is the use of clemency? It is only because we have shown the rebels clemency too long that they have gone so far. My burghers and I are determined to put an end to this sedition for good and all."

Kruger says: "Thereupon I lost my temper, or at least pretended to, and said: 'Very well, if you will not listen to me, you can depose me from the Presidency and govern the country after your own fashion.' The Commandant now calmed down and said, 'No, President, I did not mean that: we are quite willing to listen to you, but we have been terribly provoked.' I too answered more calmly: 'Well, if you will listen to me, do what I say and leave the rest to me.'"

This was the temper of the Boers. This was also the dictatorship of President Kruger. They did what he said or they could rule in their own fashion. They could not rule in their fashion, they were too used to Oom Paul. He alone had saved them from the British before and might have to save them again. For the Raid was war. It was a preliminary and unauthorised skirmish, but it could never have taken place had the feelings of the English been against it. Now that it had failed, the Raid was repudiated. Had it been successful, it would have been acclaimed. But one thing at least had been accomplished for Kruger. The Raid had smashed Rhodes, his enemy, politically. Jameson had upset his apple-cart.

CHAPTER NINE

THE FALLEN IDOL

THE PYRAMID of revolution had been based upon sand—upon the vacillations of the Uitlanders, many of whom were not only not British, but were violently anti-British. The cement that bound this fantastic structure together—desire for personal gain through obtaining greater political representation—was also the solvent that destroyed the cement when the revolutionaries saw their fortunes jeopardised or found their lives to be in danger. The plus was also, even before the Raid, a minus, where any advantage was almost immediately cancelled out by a corresponding disadvantage, and the algebraic formula, that Rhodes had so often equated, refused this time to come out.

Leaving much if not most detail to his subordinates, Rhodes had picked the wrong man in Jameson. His conquest of the Matabeleland had been a fluke, a gambler's throw which had won his master an empire and broken a black king, but one which might equally well have ended in disaster for every white man, woman, and child north of the Limpopo.

The Raid had been another gamble or had appeared to be a gamble to Jameson, and one which he thought he had every chance of pulling off. He had thought the Transvaal could be taken with "half a dozen revolvers." Even Rhodes had said he thought it "certainty," but his opinion was, to some extent at least, predicated on Jameson's reports of the situation. And he should have known Jameson's restless impatience. According to John Hays Hammond's *Autobiography*, early in their association he had been given an example of it. "A disease had broken out among the natives working on the mines at Kimberley. Was it smallpox, or was it a comparatively harmless malady which, on black skins, was known as counterfeit smallpox? Other doctors diagnosed the former, Jameson the latter. Most men would have hesitated and given the public safety the benefit of the doubt, but Jameson stuck to his own opinion in the teeth of everybody, declaring that when the thing was so perfectly clear, it was absurd to dislocate the whole mining industry by a panic quarantine. This element of the affair, the fact that scepticism as to the smallpox suited the books of the great capitalists, embittered the controversy, for it made Jameson's obstinacy take on the flavour of too little scruple as well as of too little caution. It need only be added that Jameson's opinion turned out to be absolutely wrong."

Jameson, despite his charm, was a hard and ambitious man. "The heroic death of Wilson's patrol on its daring quest was more due to Jameson's inspiration than to that of Major Forbes. . . . But then the daring was so nearly rewarded by success—and what success!—that the risk was considered justified. Intimates declare that Rhodes 'was really more cut up than Jameson.'" It was this Jameson, the reckless gambler, who led the Raid which had been the one thing it should not have been—a fiasco. Despite the casualties, it had not even succeeded in being tragic. Looking back at it now, the reasons for its failure are obvious, but first let us look at the forces employed. Behind the whole scheme as the general, though unseen, manager was Cecil Rhodes. who had the tacit backing of the British Prime Minister.

His instruments were the financiers in Johannesburg and the big industrialists. They were the organisers of the Uitlander fifth column, which was supposed to act when Doctor Jameson struck with his storm troopers from over the border and got into action against the Boers, who would then have been attacked from front and rear. John Hays Hammond's adventurous Americans in Pretoria were to act like paratroopers and capture the person of the President, who in their hands would have "changed his views."

That everything went wrong was due to the times. Rhodes was using the tactics of 1940 with the instruments of war current in 1896. Success, as we have since seen in such an operation, requires armoured cars, motor-cycle patrols, planes, tanks, radio communication, and sub-machine guns. Rhodes failed because the armaments he employed were the same as those of his enemies, who could use them to better effect. The Boers had greater mobility and greater fire power. Few of the Uitlanders could rid or even shoot well.

And though Rhodes controlled the newspapers, they failed as

instruments of propaganda, since you cannot force people to read. You can only force them to listen. Had he had the radio he could have built up general enthusiasm by repeating the wrongs, real and imagined, suffered by the mining population. In addition, before such a coup can be effective, the capitalistic economy, of which at that time Rhodes was one of the chief exponents, must be broken down. The financiers at the top of the Reform Movement were not the only financiers in it, they were merely the biggest, and the small fry were not ready to risk their fortunes in what was really a political adventure, but one which had no real political programme or clearly defined end. There was no fanaticism among the Reformers or among Jameson's troops. On the contrary, the only fanatics were the Boers, who believed in their Bibles and the sanctity of their soil.

While Kruger was sending a boy to catch his old white horse and his messengers were galloping over the Transvaal veld to raise the burghers, Rhodes was pacing up and down, wondering what Doctor Jim would do. Had he got his wire? Had he moved? What was happening? In God's name, what had happened at Pitsani? What had happened in Johannesburg?

Schreiner, his attorney general, Olive Schreiner's brother, was no comfort to him. "People will be saying you are mixed up in this," Schreiner said.

"People will say . . ." What were people not saying in these days! Every group was cut off from every other group and each had its own version. Even after Jameson's capture the Reform troops who had done nothing to rescue him were forming up to welcome him into the city, the bands under the auspices of the Reform Committee were ready to play Jameson and his heroes in. The ladies got ready bouquets to shower on them—"It should be roses, roses all the way." Johannesburg was a boom town. As the mouthpiece of the Committee put it: "What was initially a grave crime on the part of Doctor Jameson, his gallant officers and men, becomes by sheer stress of events a magnificent achievement. Its success will silence all criticism of his conduct. It will be justified by the event. He may claim fairly, if he gets through after repulsing every commando sent to stay him, to be the saviour of the situation because we ardently believe his junction with our own forces will end the campaign. It will compel unconditional surrender . . . we have to establish ourselves first; reflection will have to come afterwards; there is no backward path and returning."

Meanwhile, the commandos, that Jameson was to "brush aside and push on," had cornered and defeated him. But Kruger was still in doubt as to the issue and was ready to meet the British High Commissioner, "as I have received information that Doctor Jameson has not given effect to your orders and has fired on my burghers." When Rhodes heard of this message he said: "Kruger's in a tight place. He comes crying to the High Commissioner, ' Please come and help me, Jameson has been firing on my poor burghers.' "

But next morning the telegrams began to pour in. The line to Mafeking had been repaired and the news was bad. Schreiner looked for Rhodes to tell him. Rhodes was not to be found. He was wandering in the woods on the mountain behind his house. Wandering, communing with himself as Kruger had done long years before when he had been lost for days. Kruger had returned a changed man, but it did not take Rhodes days to change; a day was enough. When Schreiner met him in the evening he knew. Schreiner had nothing to tell him. He was a changed man, a broken one.

"Yes, it's true," he said. "Old Jameson has upset my apple-cart."

Schreiner said he had some telegrams.

Rhodes said: "Never mind, it's all true. Old Jameson has upset my apple-cart. I thought I had stopped him. I sent messages to stop him. Poor old Jameson. Twenty years we have been friends and now he goes and ruins me. I cannot hinder him. I cannot destroy him. Go and write out your resignation."

Rhodes himself had already resigned. He was a broken man. Schreiner says: "He was absolutely broken down in spirit, ruined," The golden bubble had burst, pricked by Jameson and his troopers. The golden bowl shattered, the silver cord cut. He had tried to stop Jameson and had failed. Then it looked as if his luck had held and that Jameson had got through after all. His depression was followed by exaltation. He would manage everything. He owned the press. He had the wonderful advantage that not one of his associates, including Hofmeyr, ever doubted his honour or his word.

Then the blow fell. One of his friends says: "His face was horribly changed from the exultant man of the night before. He paused to speak, checked himself and jumped into a cart that was waiting to drive him to Rondebosch, then as he started, turned that dreadful face over his shoulder and jerked out in that odd falsetto voice that he sometimes has: 'Well, there's a little history being made—that is all.'"

What remained to Rhodes were the pieces. But what can be made of the shards of greatness? What defence had he? What was left that could be saved?

To start with there was cover. There was the letter of invitation from the Reformers asking for help. It had been left undated for just such an emergency, though the emergency had been considered in terms of success rather than of failure and the cover designed to meet foreign, not English objections. Doctor Harris was back from his holiday—a week-end's shooting or fishing?—and became active. He cabled Flora Shaw in London a copy of the letter, so that it should be published immediately in the *Times*. He changed the date from December 20 to December 28, which made it impossible for Jameson to have received it, by post or messenger, when he had read it to his troops. So even here in the forging of a document which had been designed for forgery, Rhodes was unhappy in his choice of lieutenants. It appeared in the *Times* on New Year's Day, and England burst into a fury of anger against the Boers, sorrow for the victims, love for the brave rescuers who had fought against hopeless odds and admiration for Doctor Jim who had led the forlorn hope.

Alfred Austin, the new poet laureate, produced a doggerel that expressed the sentiment of the country:

> I suppose we were wrong, were madmen.
> Still I think at the Judgment Day,
> When God sifts the good from the bad,
> There'll be something more to say.
> We were wrong, but we aren't half sorry,
> And as one of the baffled band

I would rather have had that foray
Than the crushings of all the Rand.

Another of Austin's efforts showed Jameson as going to the rescue of the English women; many of them ladies of a very doubtful virtue whom he described as "the girls of the gold reef city."

Rudyard Kipling also gave tongue.

Majuba was recalled. Rhodes's press—it was the press of all Africa—began to whitewash, to apportion blame, to excuse, to explain and repudiate. Everybody repudiated everybody. The single exception was Rhodes, who, repudiated by all, refused to repudiate Doctor Jim.

The Kaiser telegraphed to Kruger congratulating him. The German Consul General at Pretoria presenting the Kaiser's compliments asked Kruger if he could bring up some German Marines from Delagoa Bay to protect his consulate—the German warships were more or less based there now. And German Marines in Pretoria might lead to bigger and better things for Germany. If one of them got shot, someone would have to come to protect the Marines. It would have provided another historic "incident." The German troops had had itching feet. Kruger laughingly assigned him fifty bearded burghers to protect his consulate. These lounging farmers, smoking, spitting, and leaning on their rifles, were not deemed necessary by the consul.

Hofmeyr insisted that Rhodes dismiss Jameson from the administration and take legal action against him. Rhodes said: "I couldn't do it. Jameson has been such an old friend. I cannot do it."

Rhodes spent the days following the Raid in a dream. He stared unseeingly through the people who came to see him, he looked unseeingly at the telegrams that were put on his desk. For forty-eight hours he did not undress. For five nights he hardly slept. He walked unceasingly, meaninglessly, a lion caged by the bars of failure, a man almost maddened by the thoughts of what success would have meant. When Hofmeyr assured Rhodes that he was still his friend, Rhodes said: "What am I to do? Live it down? How can I? Am I to get rid of myself?"

Hofmeyr's suggestion was that Rhodes resign from Parliament

and exile himself in Rhodesia. Then, after some years, he might regain the confidence of the Bond and re-enter public life at the Cape. But Rhodes had no years to waste. This error, the very fact that what had happened had happened, was due to this lack of time, to his efforts to force Time, to hurry Providence, to perform a Cæsarean operation upon the womb of Time and extract events from it. Oddly, the events were there within that womb; more than the germ, almost the infant, was there. Its features were those of the Union that Rhodes desired so much. It was the child he had wished to father, but in his haste to see it he had killed it. Only later was a new father found for a new child. The father was war, bloody and long; the godfathers Smuts and Botha. But owing to this first accident, the features of the newborn Union were marred by the political telegony of a consummation that had failed.

The Union of South Africa of to-day is not Rhodes's Union. The Rhodesias are out of it. The other colonies, states, and protectorates are out of it. It is the Bond's Union. Africa for the Afrikaaners and the South Africans—a Dominion of the British Commonwealth, but a foster child, as it were, uneasy about its adoption and uncertain of its ancestry: relatively satisfied with a good home, yet wanting to break away: a nation psychologically divided against itself, its mind cut with the schizophrenia of being and yet not belonging. The Raid, added to the other incidents—the hangings of Slagtersnek, the battle of Boomplaats, Majuba, the War of Independence, the Peace of Vereeniging, and the concentration camps—all play their parts in this national neurosis. This wilful remembering of wrongs and wilful forgetting of benefits can all be traced back to Jameson and through him to Rhodes.

Haste, which Rhodes was so against in his youth; compromise which had been the talisman of his success in his middle years, were forgotten. He had destroyed, in a single day, in a single hour—that hour which it took Jameson's men to ride over the frontier—the structure he had built so painfully and for so long. Time was against this man as it had been against Lobengula. But since there was so little of it, he must hurry more. *So little done, so much to do.*

Hofmeyr's advice galvanised Rhodes into action. It was all

he needed—the spur on the blood horse, the cut of the whalebone on his raw shoulders. He turned on his adviser. Hofmeyr had presumed to dictate to "a young king, the equal of the Almighty." They never met again. Hofmeyr said he felt as a man feels who suddenly finds that his wife has been deceiving him. Rhodes felt only anger, pride, and a renewed urgency.

Hofmeyr had said he was still his friend, but he felt himself betrayed. He declared it was hard not to use the word "perfidy." "I could explain better," he said to Rhodes, "if you had ever been a married man. You were never married. I have not yet forgotten the relation of perfect trust and intimacy which a man has with his wife. We have often disagreed, you and I, but I would no more have thought of distrusting you than a man and his wife think of distrusting each other in any joint undertaking.

"You will not pretend," he went on passionately, "that you have mixed yourself up with this outrage from an overwhelming democratic sympathy with the poor, down-trodden working men who are now drawing big wages on the Rand?"

"No," Rhodes answered, "I shall not pretend."

This was the end of the friendship that might have welded Africa into a unit without war or hatred; that might, to continue Hofmeyr's simile, have married the English and Dutch Africans and united them in the rich homeland of their birth.

Schreiner, however, gave Rhodes encouragement. "Whatever you suffer and whatever you seem to have lost, or to be losing, don't let them induce you to do anything small." The small was impossible to Rhodes, but the second-rate was forced upon him. Unable now, through the loss of his power to compromise with others, Rhodes had to compromise with himself; to surround himself with small men, sycophants, and Yes-men. He had neither the time nor the strength to argue. He must go on at all cost, and at any cost, with any kind of associates.

Political pimps, panders, and place-seekers he now tolerated—giving them, with a gesture of contempt, the financial crumbs that fell from his table; despising them, he used them; not in these last days, even bothering to name his horses after them. There was not even time for irony.

In this reversal of himself, Rhodes was complete: whatever can be said for or against him, he was a complete man, a whole-hogger, a diamond of the first water—each facet was perfect. He now really became a jingo and the head of the jingo party which he had refused to touch with a barge pole earlier in his life. He went out for the native vote. It did not exist, nor does it yet, but he hoped to bring it into use and to use it—the great Rhodes was ready to accept power on the Kaffir and Bastaard and Cape coloured vote. What did it matter, Time pressed so hard? He could use them, couldn't he, to get in? And once in the saddle what matter the stirrup he had used?

Africa was the horse he had ridden and it had thrown him. Now he tried to mount Africa from the off-side with a black blinder over its eyes and a jingo bit in its mouth. The last desperate race was on. The horse was good, the jockey—he knew himself—a master rider. The others, his opponents, he still despised as lame, sluggish, without staying power, without courage or stamina. How desperate the race was to be even Rhodes never guessed. He lived to see it almost run, but there were always new laps, new courses. It had never occurred to him that the Boers would really fight in the end, that the fight once it began could last three years, or that after nearly fifty years its repercussions would still be apparent.

But now after the Raid, his first fall, he was concerned with the tightening of his girths and seeing to his gear. He sat down to ride. He rode with bravado. A cable from the New York *World* asked him if he had declared South Africa independent.

He gave the New York *World* his own version of what had taken place and backed it with extracts from the African—his own—press. He informed America that the Uitlander population was largely composed of Americans. A lie—there were Americans, some hundreds or even a thousand of them—but he wanted to gain American sympathy. At Kimberley, on his way North to the Rhodesians, "who never bit me," he made a fighting speech. At Kimberley he was still the king diamond, and while he was here in his personal kingdom he was recalled to England by the board of the Chartered Company.

The golden girls and the boys of the golden city were in hysterics after the failure of the Raid. To start with, the bottom had dropped out of the market—and after all, the market was the important thing. Wasn't the idea of the Raid to send the market up in a booming spiral? All this political talk was nonsense, a blind for those patriotic fools who thought of England instead of money and had not the sense to cash in on England. The first man to get the news of Jameson's surrender held it up till he had disposed of his shares. What was going to happen now? What did happen?

Even the people who were there at the time know very little about what happened. So many things happened in little water-tight compartments. Before, during, and immediately after the Raid the committees were busy giving birth to new committees, and the committees to sub-committees. Each giving birth hurriedly, each forming boards and dissolving them, each passing resolutions and cancelling them—like protozoa the little affiliated groups broke from each other by this process of painless sub-division in the hope of evading responsibility or making money. Interests separated themselves from interests, individuals from individuals. Some men sent their wives away, others followed their wives; others sent for their wives now that the revolution was off. All watched the market, which was the golden pulse of Africa. But from beating fast in the fever of preparation for the Raid, it almost stopped after its failure.

One event of political importance did take place. The Uitlanders, to prove that they wanted only reform and not government by England, flew the Transvaal flag, the Vierkleur, but flew it upside down. This was a testament of their policy, and they said it in bunting. It was also a testament of their state of mind. The Reformers also "guaranteed with their persons that provided the government allowed Jameson to come in unmolested, he would leave again with as little delay as possible."

Unhappily, when they did this, Jameson was already on the point of surrender. When they heard this, some of the Reformers were furious, some were terrified—what would happen to them now?—others heaved a sigh of relief. They had not been rescued after all. They suddenly saw how embarrassing a rescue, and the orderly government it would imply, would be to them—the gamblers, the brothel-owners, and saloon-keepers. The Reformers repudiated Jameson. Jameson repudiated the Reformers. If it had not been for their cowardice, he said; if it had not been for his foolhardiness, the Reformers said. And where was Charles Leonard, the Reformers' leader?

He had disappeared after his last mission to Rhodes. He never reappeared. Hofmeyr, Rhodes's collaborator in his plan for Union, wired to Kruger repudiating "Jameson's filibusters." Chamberlain in England used the word "filibuster" too. A convenient word in which to cloak failure. The Kaiser had put his finger into the pie by congratulating Kruger. London repudiated the Kaiser. The Little Englanders came in howling against Rhodes, the Charter, the Rhodesians themselves, and raised the ghosts of the Matabele dead. Labouchere wrote: "If ever men died with blood on their heads, they are the men who died in the Raid, and if ever prisoners deserved scant mercy, Jameson and his comrades are those prisoners. They may thank their stars they have fallen into the hands of men who are not likely to treat them as they themselves treated the Matabele wounded and prisoners."

Hofmeyr said, "If Rhodes is behind it, he then is no more a friend of mine."

John X. Merriman said, "Mr. Rhodes is unworthy of the trust of the country."

Harcourt said, "Put money in thy purse and then call it expansion of empire, and the progress of civilisation."

Wilfrid Blunt wrote: "Those blackguards of the Chartered Company in South Africa under Doctor Jameson have made a filibustering raid on the Transvaal and have been annihilated by the Boers. Jameson is a prisoner. I hope devoutly he will be hanged."

Hofmeyr demanded an inquiry of Chamberlain and called for "a radical change in the government of the B.S.A. Company now that such a rule has proved to be a source of danger to the public peace of South Africa."

The directors of the Chartered Company, who would have profited most by success, requested Her Majesty "to institute a full inquiry into the circumstances attending the incursion of Doctor Jameson." Such a request looked well, Sarah Gertrude Millin says, and since it was out of their hands it could do no harm.

This was the price of failure: repudiation and disgrace; friend denying friend; brother, brother: a frantic and disgraceful rush of each man to protect his own skin, his own fortune, his own reputation. Towering over all the others stood Rhodes. Shaken to the depths of his soul, a ravaged man, a ruined man, but a man courageously, almost contemptuously, ready to face the music: ready to go down fighting, retorting bitingly, when, after speaking of the "unctuous rectitude of his countrymen," a reporter asked him if he did not mean "anxious rectitude." "No, unctuous," Rhodes said. Still insistent that England was made great, not by her politicians but her adventurers, still certain that the justice in wild places was not like justice in places that were tamed. Still contemptuous of British policy which he described as "philanthropy—plus five per cent." Rhodes was no philanthropist. And no man to be satisfied with a five per cent security. His mind was incapable of such minor calculations.

It was in this mood Rhodes returned to face his directors, his shareholders, and the Government of England, and thus that he met the Parliamentary Inquiry on February 16, 1897: a great man with the ghosts of England's great behind him: the ghosts of all the British adventurers, buccaneers and generals and admirals who had ever faced an inquiry or court-martial for the sin of failure.

In Africa others were being tried, too: the sixty-four leaders of the Reform Movement. In Johannesburg the panic grew. The worst had happened. Worse than being rescued was to have been nearly rescued and for the rescue to have failed. The crowds, which, if they had not been ready to fight for him, had been ready to go out and welcome Jameson when they heard he was near the city, dissolved. The American desperadoes who had been going to capture the Pretoria Arsenal drifted off. This operation of John Hays Hammond's could only have achieved success by surprise; the same applied to his idea of capturing the President. All possibility of surprise had gone with Jameson's timing his attack so that it fell on the Christmas Nagmaal.

Johannesburg was first menaced by bodies of Boers and then occupied by them. The principals were arrested in their houses and clubs. The market had gone to hell. Kruger's proclamation that he looked "upon only a small number of crafty men within and without Johannesburg as rebels," and his appeal to the inhabitants to behave in such a manner that he could appear before the Volksraad "with the motto, Forgive and Forget," would not put the market right again. Threats of closing the mines began to come in. The burghers were collecting the firearms the Reformers had issued. And even here things went wrong. In order to impress the Boers and back up their claims, the Reformers had pretended to have thirty thousand rifles and some guns. This boast boomeranged when the Boers found only eighteen hundred rifles and three damaged Maxims. They refused to believe that the rest were not hidden somewhere.

Kruger, writing of the rebellion, said that the only man among the so-called Reformers who understood his business was Colonel Rhodes. "All the others were theatrical revolutionaries." At any rate, sixty-four were soon in jail, and they were an odd mixture of nationalities. Seven were Americans, twenty-three English, sixteen South Africans, nine Scotsmen, one Welshman, one Turk, and seven of other nationalities. "They were thrown into prison which reeked indescribably of the Kaffir prisoners who had previously occupied it." Du Plessis, the head jailer, a cousin of Kruger's, admitted that "the prison was no place for gentlemen." The property of the prisoners was under interdict. Business in Johannesburg had come to a standstill and the town was patrolled by Piet Cronje's burghers.

The prisoners now began manœuvres for their freedom. The first measure was to cancel all orders for mining machinery and to inform the Boer Government that the mines would cease operation. This was a serious threat, for with the rinderpest killing the Boer cattle, the gold mines were the only thing that kept the country going and their shutting down would work untold misery on the people of the country.

It was a good card to play: a trump. But it did not halt the trials. And only at the trials did the full story of the Raid come out; most of the Reformers being ignorant of everything that had happened except for two facts: the first that Jameson, "the Contractor," had started; and the second, that he had been defeated and had surrendered at Doornkop. Their great surprise was the letter of invitation. As far as they were concerned, they imagined that they had withdrawn it. They may have verbally.

A.P. L

They may have repudiated it as they had repudiated so much else. But the letter was there. It had been captured with the rest of Major Robert White's other papers in a despatch box that contained his diaries, cipher keys, codes, and notebooks. The point was that this letter had been given to Jameson, and that Major White, as a magistrate in Bechuanaland, had certified it a true copy. More, while in jail in Pretoria he had confirmed his own affidavit.

Major White said later he did not remember signing the confirmation of the affidavit, but it was suggested that he had done it in order to regain possession of some of his own private papers which were given to him in exchange. The Boers still clamoured for the death sentence to be passed on the leading organisers of the Raid. Judge Gregorowski pronounced the sentence—"That you be taken to the place of execution and there to be hanged by the neck until you are dead. May Almighty God have mercy on your souls."

This was the sentence that had been passed on the Boers at Slagtersnek. And the prisoners were returned to their cells to await execution. Only one person could stay it. That was the President, and it was assumed that only outside pressure would succeed in influencing him. This seems entirely incorrect. Kruger was a consistent man. And there was his argument with the Free-Staters to be remembered: the time that he said it was lawful to threaten with death—but not to execute the threat.

There is also the ironic humour of the President to consider. By commuting the sentence he appeared magnanimous, but by allowing it first to be passed, he put himself in a position of authority where he could exercise his magnanimity. He certainly —to use a Boer word—gave them all a good "skrik"—a fright; and a sigh of relief went up in England when it was finally decided that the leaders should be fined twenty-five thousand pounds each and told not to meddle with politics again.

Jameson and his officers were sent back to England for trial, where, by a wavering jury which felt that they were heroes, they were sentenced to prison terms that varied from five to fifteen months without hard labour.

After one of the prisoners—Major Grey—had committed suicide, the others were ordered to make a statement offering any extenuating circumstances they could urge on their own behalf, with the result that ten prisoners were released, twenty-four had their sentences commuted to three months, eighteen to five months, and four to one year. Colonel Wools-Sampson and Karri-Davies refused to submit petitions and their cases were not reconsidered. The Boers, who were suffering from the loss of business due to suspension of work at the mines, were only too glad to close the matter officially and let England carry out what justice she would against Jameson and those of his officers who held commissions in the British Army.

There are, however, some interesting sidelights on the trial.

Barney Barnato, for instance, soon after it was over, went to the Pretoria Club in black, with mourning crêpe round his top hat, where he met Judge Gregorowski and attacked him for the way he had conducted the trial.

The judge replied in Dutch: "Mr. Barnato, you are not a gentleman. I was appointed to put down the rebellion and I have done so to the best of my ability."

Barney, who could not understand him, said, "Maybe you're right, but still you're a damn rotten judge."

Barnato then gave five thousand pounds to the Boer Government to alleviate some of the distress caused by the Raid and wanted Kruger to release his nephew, Solly Joel. But Kruger refused to discuss the prisoners, so Barney tried a new tack. He ordered two marble lions as a gift for the President on his birthday. "Oom Paul pretended not to know what lay hidden under the tarpaulins on his front porch and the pleasure evinced by these two grown-up children over the secret helped to bring a feeling of amity into the dealings between Boer and Uitlander. On Kruger's birthday a religious service was held in the parlour, and then the two lions were unveiled in all their gleaming majesty. In a halo of whiskers these three monarchs of the veld confronted the camera."

While in prison the wives of the prisoners used to smuggle in delicacies to their husbands. "Mrs. Solly Joel used to come with the crown of her hat filled with cigars, a bottle of cream in her skirt, and a brace of ducks in her bustle. Mrs. Hammond wore a large sausage round her waist. In the big sleeves of the period ladies were able to conceal tins of sardines, beef essence, condensed milk, and other delicacies."

One of the English prisoners, talking to Sullivan, an American, said, "The Boers can't get away with this."

"Like hell they can't," Sullivan said. "They are doing it, aren't they? Let me tell you," he went on, "these Boers can do anything they want to you except one thing."

"And what's that?"

"They can't put you in the family way."

Mark Twain happened to be in Africa at the time on a round-the-world lecture tour, and visited the prison. John Hays Hammond, who knew him, said, "Mr. Clemens, I am certainly glad to see you again. How did you ever find your way into this God-forsaken hole?"

"Getting into jail is easy," replied the humorist. "I thought the difficulties arose when it came to getting out."

To the reporter who interviewed him Mark Twain said he "was very pleased with the jail; he had found some very charming gentlemen there and he thought it was an ideal rest cure for these tired businessmen. He only regretted his stay was so short that he could not take advantage of the peaceful conditions in the jail to rest his own tired nerves. He said he could not imagine a place where one would be less troubled by the importunities of his creditors, and the only feature he did not like about the jail was that there were too many lawyers among the prisoners, and somehow or other he never could hit it off with lawyers."

It was about this time that some of the Reform Committee who had been freed swallowed their pride and went to Kruger to petition for the pardon of their friends. This interview is described by John Hays Hammond as "the famous dog interview. Kruger maundered on about dogs, and how the little dogs had been punished, but the big dog [Rhodes] had escaped, and how the little dogs crawled to lick their master's boots after being punished."

This description is particularly interesting because it shows a lack of understanding of the Boer characteristic of talking in bucolic similes and parables, and because in the same book—his *Autobiography*—Mr. Hammond uses this whipped-dog simile when discussing the flogging of natives which he appears to consider admirable. "Afterwards the natives would come to the managers, and thank them as a dog crawls to lick the hand of its master after a deserved whipping." But of course the hardheaded businessmen who mismanaged the rebellion could not be compared to naked savages working five and six thousand feet underground in temperatures "running as high as 120 degrees Fahrenheit with a relative humidity of from 90 to 100 per cent. This causes many cases of heat stroke." There is also some interest in discovering that the phrase "tired businessman" was originated by Mark Twain in the Pretoria jail.

The tragi-comedy of the *Putsch* that failed was over, its grandiose conception a fizzle, its end epitomised by the words of the great American humorist which are immortalised in almost every joke about a pretty stenographer and her employer. Thus do we span the years from Pitsani to Burlesque; and with the jokes are the dead, and the gold and the diamonds, the barefooted Kaffir running to fetch Kruger's old white horse, Rhodes saying, "Jameson has upset my apple-cart," smart women with roast ducks concealed under their bustles, and the awful continuity of history—of cause and effect.

CHAPTER TEN

INTERLUDE

IN RHODES'S TIME the market was Rhodes. "Kaffirs"—that is, African shares—excited universal and speculative interest. Whenever there was a chance of trouble, as there had been over the question of the drifts, the Kaffir stocks rose in value, on the assumption that the trouble would be for others—the Matabele or the Boers—and the benefits for the British stockholders.

The British public was much incensed at the Reformers in Johannesburg to whom was attributed the failure of the Raid. They were made the scapegoats, the subjects of journalistic cartoons, and music-hall skits. The Reformers were furious with Jameson for allowing charges of cowardice to be levelled against them. Had the Raid succeeded, Majuba would have been revenged, a great and rich territory added to the Empire, and everybody would have made money and been happy.

Instead, another disgrace had been added to Majuba and England had been made a laughing stock. There was plenty to laugh about and lampoon—race week in Johannesburg which had delayed the Raid; the flying of the South African flag upside down; the cutting of the wrong telegraph line—but the laughter was bitter. At the back of it was the thought, some one must fix "those damn treacherous Boers." How dared farmers pick up their guns from their chimney corners, ride out and fight Englishmen and defeat them? It was only a little over a hundred years ago that the American colonists had done the same thing. Oddly, Jameson, though condemned to prison, was never really blamed for his act. He lived to become Prime Minister of the Cape, a baronet, and a privy councillor.

In 1895, at the time of the drift trouble, Chartered shares had stood at nine pounds. By the time of the Raid, they had fallen to five pounds five shillings. It was thought that the Raid, if successful, would send the shares up again, but instead, as it failed, they fell in January to three and one-eighth pounds. The graph of the Chartered shares rose and fell on the ride of rumoured wars and the promise of the gold to be gained by such a war. An adventure in Mashonaland, and up they went—there was gold in Mashonaland. But there turned out to be no gold in Mashonaland, and down went the shares. There was gold in Matabeleland. Of course, that was where the gold was. War with Lobengula. Up go the shares again. No gold, or at least not much, in Matabeleland. Down they go again. The only really rich gold lay in the South African Republic. An argument over the drifts. Some troopships on their way back from India are halted. War—or near war. *We will take the Rand.* Up they go again. Kruger made concessions. No war. *Down they go.* The Uitlanders are going to revolt. Jameson is going to ride in. *We are going to take the reef this time.* Up. Jameson is captured. Down and down goes the fever chart of avarice.

The question now arises: What if there had been no Raid?— Or What if it had been successful?

Almost certainly in either case Rhodes would have succeeded in his plan of a South African Union. Had there been no Raid, it would have been achieved by peaceful penetration through the Bond; and had the Raid succeeded, the job would have been done under the guise of restoring order.

The real reason for the Raid was to foment disorder, in order to have an excuse for restoring it. The contrary political elements involved must be remembered. Rhodes was handling some very doubtful factors. The Bond was against an Africa under the British flag, but wanted a United South Africa. Here the Bond was against Rhodes and with Kruger, who wanted a South Africa for the Afrikaaners from the Zambesi to Simonstown, which was exactly what Rhodes wanted for the British—except that he wanted all Africa north of the Zambesi as well. Next, there were the Uitlanders in the Transvaal, who did not wish to come under British dominance and who only wanted their wrongs redressed. They, like the Bond members, felt they were being used by Rhodes, so that to achieve his ends he had to deceive both parties and draw the wool over Kruger's eyes as well; and for once Rhodes gambled with too many imponderables.

Politically his plan was sound, but he was without instruments for implementing his plan. The whole thing presented itself to him in its over-simplified form as a matter of power, of the fitness of things, of conformity to his working theory of the British Empire rather than as a matter of abstract-right sentiments—of Liberty, Equality, and Fraternity. Rhodes did not believe in these things. His sympathy for the British miners in Johannesburg was for Englishmen rather than for miners. "He accepted the idea of government by the people as he accepted any other part of the great British system that had spread over the world, but he believed that this was only the outer cloak for the inner reality of government by the few."

It was his dictum that in any part of the world there are only a few people who matter and that these can pull the rest almost any way they want, provided they pull together. That is to say, that in principle Rhodes was against the party system, and his acceptance of a pseudo-democracy was like his acceptance of the capitalistic system—a good arrangement by which the masses were shaken up and the few, the élite cream, were given the chance to rise to the governing surface. Hofmeyr says he never heard Rhodes express any sympathy for the Uitlanders. Nor could he have much, since he taxed the Rhodesian gold far more highly than Kruger taxed that found in the Transvaal. To Rhodes the Uitlanders were pawns to be moved, to be goaded into a revolution that would require his intervention.

Rhodes's genius worked on an established pattern. He was like a cowboy who stampedes a herd of cattle and then, when they have exhausted themselves, rides up with a few trained oxen and leads them to the slaughter-house. But the Uitlanders, if they did not know what Rhodes was doing, appear at least to have sensed it. What if a successful Rhodes introduced a new régime and, flushed with victory and the gold it now possessed, chose to inaugurate a really tough system of government? Might not Rhodes's finger then be thicker than Paul Kruger's thigh? Might they not be chastised—that is, taxed and kept in order—with British scorpions instead of Boer whips that could always be bought off? This uncertainty was certainly a factor which precluded a full and enthusiastic participation of the Uitlanders in a real rebellion. A little rebellion was good. It might even be amusing; but a real one was something else.

The plot was actually simple. What Rhodes proposed was this: The Johannesburghers—that is, the dissatisfied financiers and miners—were to formulate an ultimatum which naturally the Boers would treat with contempt. The revolutionaries were then to take possession of Johannesburg and declare a provisional government just as the Boers had done in the War of Independence. The same night they were to go to Pretoria, seize the arsenal and the seat of government, and then issue to South Africa and the outside world an appeal proposing to submit to a plebiscite of the entire white population of the country. It was thought that this coup could be executed without the Boers having time to fire a shot. Rhodes relied on speed and secrecy plus the force Jameson was to lead in from Pitsani over the border. The secrecy was, however, non-existent, and Jameson's force inadequate in numbers and inefficient in action.

The moment the trouble began and life and property were presumed to be in danger, the pretext for Jameson's entry would have been established. His force would hold off such Boer commandos as did rise and march, and to avert civil war and chaos the British Government would have to step in. Then Rhodes himself, using all his influence as Premier of the Cape and co-leader with Hofmeyr of the Bond, would come into the picture; and, as administrator, would mediate between the Dutch and the British whom he had got involved and must now, to save his position with the Bond, turn against—at least nominally —by declaring South Africa independent and separate from England, but a part of the British Empire called the United States of South Africa. In this way Rhodes would have appeared to the Boers to have saved them from the British and to the British to have saved them from the Boers. Then, as master of the richest part of the continent, he could have proceeded by negotiation, purchase, and war to have absorbed all Africa. From the Cape of Good Hope to the Mediterranean it would have been British red. Already master of the world's diamonds, Rhodes would have become the master of most of its gold—and copper.

But it was not to be. Even Rhodes had bitten off more than he could chew. Jameson could not wait for the Uitlanders. Instead of rescuing them he made a desperate raid. And the Uitlanders, because they could not decide on a flag and because it was race week, because they had insufficient arms and training, and because they were really very content with things as they were, refused to rise. The plan to capture the Pretoria Arsenal and the more daring one of seizing Kruger fell through because they had forgotten that the Boers were religious and had assembled in great strength to worship in their capital. So that Pretoria, far from being a pushover, was an armed camp. As to the secrecy, there had been very little of it. What was the good of a secret if it could not be enjoyed?—and to be enjoyed it must be told. Even the code used was the Bedford McNeil Mining Code, a copy of which was to be found in every telegraph office in South Africa. Duplicates of every message were kept, and, as a contemporary writer said, "Never was a plot plotted in the manner of this plot. It was a system of conspiracy by double entry."

The plan to capture the copper market, which was part of Rhodes's greater Africa scheme, Mr. Hammond says, "was formulated round our camp-fire. The Sécrétan Copper Syndicate, which had aimed at buying up the bulk of the world's stock of copper, cornering the market and boosting the price, had collapsed ignominiously a few years before. But the brilliant and erratic Frenchman, Sécrétan, had given me much useful information which I passed on to Rhodes and his associates. . . . The Rothschilds, who controlled the Rio Tinto copper mines in Spain and an important copper mine in Mexico, would have entered the new syndicate. My plan was to leave for the United States . . . in the hope of acquiring control of several of the great copper properties there. Unfortunately the Jameson Raid diverted my attention. After that, Rhodes went to Rhodesia to quell the native uprising and the whole gigantic plan fell through."

In terms of finance, cartels; in terms of names like Rothschild or in terms of properties like the Rio Tinto, 1895 is very near us to-day. The super-colossal syndicate that Rhodes envisaged controlling the world's gold, diamonds, and copper would have been the foundation for his great society of wealth that would have controlled the world, the octopus that would have swallowed every utility, every natural resource, and have held all governments vassal to these new financial barons.

The discovery of copper in South Africa was due to the sharp eyes of Burnham, the American scout. He found a Matabele warrior whose girl wife wore a bracelet of pure copper round her leg. Trade copper was common enough, but pure native copper was extremely rare. That the girl was a Matoka was indicated by the fact that her two upper incisors had been removed. On being questioned, the girl said her husband had captured her in a raid and that there was plenty of copper in her country.

It is typical of Africa, where the unexpected is so often the rule, that an American plainsman and Indian fighter should be the one to lay a trail that led from a captured slave girl's bangle to the Roan Antelope and Northern Copper Mines and link them to the London Stock Exchange, the Paris Bourse, and Wall Street. Burnham also discovered coal—the Wankie coal fields—through another native story, when some Kaffirs told him where there were "black rocks that burn."

Not only Africa, but all the world at this time—the last ten years of the last century—was in turmoil. The end of the Victorian era, which died, not with the old Queen, but with the outbreak of war in 1914, was in sight. Though few had the eyes to see it or the ears to hear the approaching storm, the tempest was mounting. Men and nations rode on the ground swell of future cataclysm smugly content that they were in control of events and unaware of an historic process which ignored both men and nations.

Here are some of the straws in that wind: The Dreyfus case in 1894 and Emile Zola's *J'Accuse* in '98, which led to the separation of the Church and State in France. The Cuban Revolution against Spain in '95, and revolts in Portugal against Carlos I. The defeat of the Italians at Adua in Abyssinia in '96. Federal insurance in Switzerland in 1890. Pope Leo XIII., the workingman's Pope, pointing out that the possessing classes had important moral duties in an encyclical in '91. In '97 the German occupation of Kiao-chow on the Chinese coast. Universal manhood suffrage in Norway in '98. The gold standard introduced in Russia in '97. Armenian massacres in '96, the insurrection in Crete and the Turco-Greek War in '97. The Spanish-American War in '98. The conquest of Madagascar by the French in '94. The Sino-Japanese War in '94.

Selected arbitrarily from the history of this period these events indicate a change of tempo. The terrible American Civil War was over, as was the Franco-Prussian War. Garibaldi and Bolívar were established as heroes in the minds of the common man. The Suez Canal had contracted the world by joining the Far East to the West. An invisible psychological canal had also been cut between the masses of men below and the kings and hereditary rulers—a hole breached into the dam autocracy, and the political movement was from aristocratic rule towards democracy and pseudo-democratic plutocracy.

This change was implemented by the inventions of the last half-century. In 1855 Whitworth applied the principle of rifling to small arms. The Bessemer process followed, then came the first iron-clad frigate. Winchester introduced the repeating rifle, Gatling invented the machine-gun; trans-Atlantic cables were laid, velocipedes and typewriters invented. Telephones and rotary presses, phonographs, incandescent electricity came into use, Nordenfeldt built the first submarine, smokeless powder and high explosive were introduced. The gasoline motor car and Diesel engine were followed by Marconi's wireless and the cinematograph. The non-rigid airship and the French seventy-five quick firer that revolutionised field artillery were all invented and many in use before 1900.

These were the instruments of power, speed, and destruction. For good or ill they were there, and their coming presaged change. They were the products and the servants of a new kind of men. Now at last the mathematics of propaganda and destruction could be seriously applied and operations of all kinds be scaled up enough to satisfy even the most ambitious—total war at last was becoming possible.

With the rising of the socialist tide the instruments of counter-revolution rose to combat it. It was the old tactical equation of the weapons of offence catching up with and surpassing those of defence. It was, in other terms, the political marriage of those two incompatibles—the secret ballot and the machine-gun—in the hope of producing an offspring that would be named the *Status quo*, or, if that failed, *A près nous le déluge*. It marked the diversion of mankind into two camps. In the one the believers in the ballot; in the other the believers in force should the ballot method go against their interests.

Rhodes could by no stretch of the imagination be described as a democrat. He could, without any stretching of the truth, be accused of not believing in the secret ballot, of using force when persuasion failed, and of buying men whom he could not intimidate or lead by the nose by his instruments of propaganda.

Modern Fascism could, indeed, be said to have begun with Cecil Rhodes. A book could be written, "From Rhodes to Hitler." He was the first man to organise business politically, his diamond industry was the first great cartel. His was the dream of an élite, a secret society, that ruled whole continents by money controlled by a single source. His hope was for a greater British Reich. He assumed and believed that his name would live, not one thousand but four thousand years.

Never until recent times has a single man been worshipped as Rhodes was, and he had no radio to use in putting his ideas before the public. A celibate, a demagogue, endued with powers which transcended those of ordinary men, Rhodes was, as Spengler has suggested, a new type. In him could be seen the shape of things to come—the individual of such massive proportions that he could upset the equipoise of nations, an actual superman, a phenomenon. Rhodes had the dream of Nordic superiority, a penchant for big blond men, a dislike of and perhaps a contempt for women. Rhodes saw people as masters and servants.

Condemn or condone, fight or follow, love or despise as we may, such men cannot be examined as other men. They are not men in the full sense of the word. They are acts. They live by their acts and die of them. They are at once effects and causes: causal and effectual men of a curious and sterile completeness which defies the imagination. Their mechanisms are different, though their outward appearance is the same as that of others. They are as different as a watch would be if, instead of having works within its case, it was activated by a speck of radium. Having energy, they develop it in a way foreign to our understanding. Napoleon, Bismarck, Julius Cæsar are relatively simple, but the great Fascist is not. He is great because he is big as a mountain is big. A mountain is neither good nor bad: it exists. A great Fascist is like a volcano, his dangerous energy the result of the upheaval of a molten mind. A possible explanation of such men could be that they are the results of an upheaval in the human psychological pattern and a part of a new and unpredictable political pattern.

Rhodes, with the acquisition of Rhodesia, with the Boer War of which he was a contributory cause, ended, in a final brilliant upsurge, the British Empire principle and the British jingo cause.

The war, once it was over, was seen for what it was—something to be ashamed of. Yet this war caused the Union of South Africa and gave birth to a new Dominion, a new partner in the British Commonwealth.

If there is ever a United States of Europe, it will be due to Hitler's producing a bond of misery that is stronger than dislikes and suspicions that separated nationalities and which could never have been overcome by other means. If there is a revival of Christianity, it will be due to the appearance of this anti-Christ and his admirable presentation of what happens to people who abandon the Christian ethic.

Mussolini's dream was the pale echo of Rhodes's; his conquest of Ethiopia an inglorious aping of the conquest of Rhodesia.

The interests which placated Japan and Italy are the same in principle as those which backed Rhodes in his march up Africa.

And if Manchukuo, Abyssinia, Czechoslovakia, and Spain were modern acts of aggressions, they only followed the pattern set by Rhodes. These are unpalatable truths, but such truths must be faced and considered, for only by them can our present troubles be understood. We tend to look at politics as if they had been born out of nothing and were not part of the historical process. The politics of to-day are to-morrow's history, and if we know nothing of yesterday's history, how can we understand the politics to-day?

To see the pictures of South Africa in the eighties and nineties, we should imagine it as a struggle of personalities, interests, and cultures. Imagine a Brigham Young in possession of most of the oil land in the United States. Imagine a single man at the head of Standard Oil first making war on an Indian chief, on the assumption that his land also had oil, when it proved to be barren of it, attacking Brigham Young.

The Mormons in America resembled the Boers in many ways, though the Boers were not polygamous. Kruger's state stood somewhere between that of Lobengula's and Haile Selassie's.

It was in addition a white state and Christian. Its error was that it resisted aggression; its glory that of Greece; its Thermopylæ the battles its farmers fought on the vast plains of Africa.

And all this is near to us in time. Only a relatively few years ago Rhodes's name was news. Now it is history. Still fewer years ago Hitler's name was news. Now it is history. To-day's news is to-morrow's history. For its makers look in the daily press: less at the men than at the shadows they cast.

And—till Hitler came—no single man in recent times cast a greater shadow over the face of the world than Cecil Rhodes.

Though Cecil Rhodes associated himself with the Elizabethans, he was a modern. They were lusty fighters and brigands; lovers, equally apt with the sword and the lute; great trenchermen, boastful and ready to carry out their boasts. They were the adventurers, the pirates of the Spanish Main. It is questionable how much they fought for England and how much for the wealth they seized to lay at the feet of their Virgin Queen. Both they and Rhodes served queens. There is something romantic about a queen—even the motherly old widow at Windsor that Kruger described as a "kwai vrou," a bad one to cross. But here the similarity between the Elizabethans and Rhodes ends. Rhodes to achieve his ends used every method and every device. He used money to buy and bribe men, to obtain control of interests and of land. He used the tactic of infiltration. He bought and used the press, the then only known method of propaganda. "There was no reason," he said, "that a man should not be properly reported," and obviously a man is best reported by his employees.

He more or less invented the minority problem as a political lever, and when this minority became a majority, he then used the majority problem. For the first he claimed sympathy, the few oppressed by the many; for the second he claimed power, pointing out how absurd it was that a majority, which owned half the land and paid all or at least nearly all the taxes, should be without representation. He did not believe in war—"Give me breakfast and then we will talk about blood." But he was ready to make war inevitable, to create those incidents which cause war and then to step in as mediator to stop it. Mediation, compromise, the steel enclosed in the velvet glove, was his forte. Rhodes the Colossus was a manipulator of men and events. Inevitably one day his luck was bound to desert him, one day both men and events to betray him; the time when his part would be played and his usefulness as a creator in the pattern of history ended.

Someone had to destroy the Matabele, who had destroyed hundreds of thousands. Rhodes did this. A régime of barbarous cruelty was destroyed. But there was no reason to destroy the Boer Republics, no reason to incorporate those who hated England, and had fled her over a thousand miles of wilderness, into the Empire. The dream of a world at peace was a fine one, but its accomplishment by enslavement savours of sophistry. Understanding the employment of money, understanding the extraordinary attraction of man to riches, Rhodes was incapable of understanding that the Boers would rather be free than prosperous. The Boers were a nation of farmers, a people without historical precedent, and, as such, a nut that even Rhodes had no instrument to crack.

Rhodes, who was in his person the embodiment of empire, indirectly ended empires. Rhodes, one of the greatest of Englishmen, indirectly brought discredit upon England. And still he towers, a man above others: a man blessed and cursed by the gods.

He had destroyed Lobengula. Now he was himself destroyed by his own instrument, by his best friend. He was repudiated by Hofmeyr, and with Hofmeyr went the Bond and the hopes of a South African Union. Gone, too, was his premiership. All that was left was his fortune and his North, for his health had gone, too, what was left of it, and his confidence in his star. The run of luck had turned against the gambler. The complexity of his prestidigitation had been too much for him. Dropping one of the balls he was juggling, and fumbling for it, the others fell, breaking like eggs about him.

Perhaps Rhodes had used too many people, perhaps he had hurried too much, building upon the sand of his luck with the mortar of his urgency. He had played the Cape Dutch of the Bond, hoping to use them to form his Union. He had played the Reformers also, hoping to use them. He had played his gold and his diamonds against old Kruger. For England he had risked and lost his reputation and now still worse was to happen. The rinderpest was sweeping down from the North killing the cattle of his settlers and the natives with tremendous impartiality. And the Matabele who had been conquered refused to stay conquered: they rose, and with them the Mashonas who had once been their slaves. Rhodes's cup was full as he stood in London facing his accusers. He stayed in London a week and returned to his beloved Rhodesia—and the rinderpest.

This was the cattle plague that Egypt had known in the time of Moses. It had been present in Abyssinia in 1893 and now in 1896 it had reached Rhodesia and was spreading on. It was the cause of the second Matabele War—the rising that took place and which, as if Providence regretted what had happened to Rhodes, permitted him to regain his own self-esteem and the confidence of England.

The rinderpest is a disease caused by an undetermined virus. It is the French *peste bovine*, the Italian *peste bovilla*. It is an Oriental disease and is supposed to have been brought to Europe by the Huns from China: it raged in Europe intermittently until about 1880. It broke out in England in 1865, being brought there by cattle imported from Finland. In Africa it had been confined to Egypt till about the year 1890 when it spread south.

The nature of the disease is described as an acute, febrile, contagious, and infectious disease of cattle and ruminants caused by an invisible virus which during the course of the attack is present in the tissue fluids and secretions. Its symptoms are a high temperature of 104 degrees, or 105 degrees, accompanied by a diphtheritic discharge of mucus from the nasal membranes and mouth which is followed by ulceration and encrustation. Diarrhœa soon sets in; the evacuations are mixed with blood and mucus. In the last stages of the disease, the animal becomes very weak and greatly emaciated. It lies with its head turned towards a flank and is unable to rise.

The Boers, who for a long time had known the disease in its less virulent form, had discovered a method of immunisation by inoculation, using the bile of an animal which had died of the disease. This method was investigated and elaborated by Robert Koch in 1897. But in 1897 it was too late to save the cattle in Matabeleland. The method pursued there was to slaughter the infected herds and even those which had been exposed to infection. This was the straw that broke the back of that doubtful camel of peace in Matabeleland. For the Bantu culture is a cattle culture; his cattle are his joy, his life, and his tradition.

Bantu marriages are in essence a cattle-trading operation. Ten cows being paid—lobola—by the suitor to the father of the girl he wishes to marry. Five wives would then cost fifty cows. Divorce arguments are always about the return of these cattle which have been paid by the husband and about the calves born during the marriage. A Bantu rarely kills cattle. He counts his riches in cattle by quantity and not by quality. A hundred bad cattle bring more credit and prestige to the owner than fifty good cattle. This cattle culture is the reason that the native reserves are eroded by overstocking, and is a major African problem. The Herero Rebellion against the Germans in West Africa was as much due to thefts of their cattle by their German masters as the misuse of their girls and women.

It was obviously impossible to explain to the Matabele that their cattle were dying because of an invisible virus, and that the only way to save even a few of them was to slaughter the infected herds. What is invisible is not there and this was just another white man's trick to break them. Within a year only five hundred head of cattle were left of a hundred thousand in Matabeleland. And with the cattle died the game—the buffalo and the buck—in millions. To an agricultural and hunting people this was the calamity of calamities. The rinderpest was one of the godparents of the South African poor white. After it had passed, thousands of people, black and white, had nothing left of their beasts but their skins.

CHAPTER ELEVEN

M'LIMO

IN 1895, two years after the conquest of Matabeleland, Bryce found "Everybody was cheerful because everybody was hopeful." Prices had reached a height "which nothing but a swift and brilliant prosperity could justify."

Rhodes had called for "Homes and more homes," and they were springing up. The quick-growing trees he had planted in Bulawayo were already fifteen feet high, and the streets, according to his order, were laid out so wide that an ox wagon with a full span of sixteen oxen could turn in them. There was a cricket ground, a polo ground, and talk of an opera house.

The white men in Rhodesia were Rhodesians, British conquistadors, a master race towering above the conquered peoples. They were not businessmen like the people in Jo'burg whom they despised. In their glory they thought of the natives as instruments and not as men. They conscripted labour, often brutally, at ten shillings a month. They beat the Kaffirs and then forgot them. This was their error, this forgetfulness, or their ignorance of the native mind which can accept anything but injustice. The native understands a loose form of slavery for a conquered people much better than conscripted labour where he is worked hard and given payment in money which he does not know how to use. Above all, the natives did not understand why their cattle should be slaughtered. And then, to add to the disaster of cattle sickness to which they had been exposed—the rinderpest infection—the locusts appeared in Matabeleland for the first time in the memory of man. Everything that happens, from the death of an ox, the sickness of a child, or the coming of the grasshoppers, is believed by the Kaffirs to be due to witchcraft. Before the white man came, there had been none of these things. Now, there was cattle sickness, and the young mealies were being eaten by locusts. The white men had bewitched the land and M'limo must counter it. Maddened by famine, furious at injustice, the Matabele went to the prophet's cave. And he told them to rise.

The mouthpiece of M'limo said the white man's medicine had gone weak. He would give them mouti—medicine—that would turn the white man's bullets.

The settlers living on the isolated farms they had built, or on the little mines they had started, were contemptuous of the Matabele. The war was over: the Matabele finished. They forgot who the Matabele were: that they were Zulus: a proud warrior race. And as for the Mashonas, why, even the Matabele had despised them, calling them dogs. But if the Mashonas had hated the Matabele, they hated the British still more.

True, the Matabele had raided. They had stolen cattle and women. But that in a sense was orthodox. Things had always been that way. The herds bred up again and the Matabele made good husbands to the girls they stole. But when the English came they settled:' they stayed: they made them work; and so the Mashonas joined with the Matabele under auspices of the oracle of M'limo. From their point of view there were many favourable signs. Jameson had been defeated in war by the Boers. All but forty-eight police had gone with him on his expedition—and the settlers were unsuspicious.

And on March 20, the day Rhodes landed at Beira after a week's stay in England, they attacked. The arch-wizard of M'limo, the oracle of the Matopos, had planned well.

The Matabele had not been completely subdued in 1893, and had been waiting for a favourable moment to drive the white men out of their country; and the witch-doctors, the servants of the oracle, had inflamed and organised the people, while Providence had played into their hands by bringing drought, locusts, and finally the rinderpest, to prove to them that their cause was just and the gods of the Matopos angry that they tolerated their subjection. Jameson was not only away and in prison, but with him were the police officers who knew the country and the only armed white force. If the young warriors on the Insesi River, forty miles from Bulawayo, had not grown impatient and started out to kill the settlers three days before the set time of the full moon, probably not a white person in the entire country would have escaped slaughter. The house servants were to be armed and to kill their masters and through this the rebellion was discovered, not in time, but in time to save complete disaser. A Mashonat woman carrying wood on her back was seen to be staggering under her load. It was examined and assegais were found to be concealed inside the wood. This discovery removed the chance of complete and overwhelming surprise.

Still it was bad enough, and many settlers—men, women, and children—were murdered before resistance of any kind could be organised, or rescue parties could go out to bring in the isolated ranchers and prospectors. The witch-doctors had given the Kaffirs medicine to protect them—a magic drink which would make them invulnerable to the white man's bullets; and convinced of its efficacy, blood-drunk with a lust to kill and revenge themselves, the Matabele and Mashonas attacked everywhere under the old captains who had led them in Lobengula's day. The settlers, traders, prospectors, and miners who were not killed were driven into laager in the towns where the men formed themselves into irregular regiments, and having made arrangements for the defence of the women and children, rode out to attack the larger bodies of Matabele. Rhodes joined one of these columns and behaved with almost reckless courage. He was desperate: this was a blow at his North—at all that was left to him.

But this was not a simple neat little war like the first one against the Matabele. They had learnt cunning and did not charge in their thousands against the white men's guns. They hid and skulked in small parties. They hit and ran. They attacked and withdrew to the mountains they knew so well. True, after the first days of surprise they killed fewer people, but few of the Matabele were killed and the Europeans were penned up in the towns and villages in a state of siege. By July nothing had been achieved and a thousand imperial troops were sent to help the irregulars. In a fortnight they had lost twenty per cent of their strength. Regular troops were of no use for this kind of operation. Boers could have finished it: five hundred Boers, such as Kruger had offered to lead against the Zulus, but not the country lads who composed the British army.

If the war went on, the Company would be ruined. The new issue of shares had just paid off the Matabele War of 1893; this rebellion was costing four thousand pounds a day and was expected to cost anything up to five million pounds before it was over. In Rhodes's words, they had to "hunt the Matabele in the bush and in the stones and in the kopjes in a country nearly half the size of Europe."

But this was not the only difficulty. The rinderpest which had caused the rebellion came in to help the Matabele. The nearest railhead was six hundred miles away. It always had been, but goods had come up by ox wagon. Now they had to come by mule wagon, since the oxen were all dead. The added expense was enormous. In terms of to-day, the difference between a mule and ox transport would be that of trucks and passenger cars. Mules had to be fed; oxen did not. Mules were used to drawing coaches and light vehicles fast; oxen were perfect for drawing heavy wagons slowly. I have driven four mules forty miles in ten hours in four-wheeled spider over rough roads. This is the ideal use of mules. Oxen would take a load of two tons fifteen miles a day. In addition, both the mules and mule drivers were hard to find.

So here we have Rhodes the financier, the visionary empire-builder, coming straight from facing his shareholders in London into a rebellion of savages complicated by a cattle disease of Oriental origin. All over Rhodesia farmhouses were blazing or in ruins. All over the country were the scattered dead.

Here is Melina Rorke's description of a devastated farm: "It was lighter now, and through the gaunt, leafless branches of the trees I saw the house partially burnt away, its blackened timbers falling apart to disclose a still blacker interior. I saw swaying from the limb of a tree on my right the body of a man. I knew from the limp white hands that it must be Doctor White, but there was nothing else to identify him. His stomach had been slit open—to permit his spirit to escape so that it shouldn't haunt his murderers. His face had been hacked away and ants were swimming greedily all over him. Beyond, across a tangle of berry bushes, sprawled the nude body of a white woman;. she had been repeatedly stabbed with spears and a knobkerrie had been thrust up into her body. Above her, dangling by one leg from a bit of wire that had been twisted round a limb of the tree, was the blood-coated body of a little white girl whose brains had been dashed out against the tree trunk."

This was the situation Rhodes had to remedy if he was to save his North. Round Salisbury alone a hundred and twenty white people had been killed. The positions the Matabele had taken up were the traditional ones of Kaffirs who were hard pressed. They hid in caves and sallied out to raid, but the caves in which they hid were not isolated. They could not be bottled up in them or smoked out. There were a great number of caves, many of which communicated. Nor were there only a few hundred Matabele and Mashonas: there were thousands of them. Pressed in one direction they moved forward in another. Unless Rhodes did something, this was the end of Rhodesia. His settlers would abandon the country, the Chartered Company go into liquidation, and while the British Government was inquiring into this new disaster, the Boer commandos would cross the Limpopo and take possession.

What Rhodes felt is best expressed by the letter he wrote to Harcourt: "We start to try and make junction with Bulawayo. We are two hundred and fifty men and the Bulawayo column is five hundred. There are about six thousand natives between us and Bulawayo and we may make a mess of it. . . . I would be sorry to think that you thought I was capable but not honest. I have tried to unite South Africa and no sordid motive has influenced me. You might say why do I write; certainly not to mitigate your censure, but in case we come to grief, I wish you to know that I feel that whatever you have said of me you have said from a sense of public duty. . . . I am still pleased to think that you had an affection for me. But remove from your mind the idea of a sordid motive. This letter is written because I do not know what will happen during the week. . . . You will be pleased to think I understood your reasons, but I could not go from here to an uncertainty without saying, ' Blame me as much as you like, but do not do the cruel thing of attributing my conduct to sordid motives.' Good-bye." It would have been terrible to Rhodes to be considered small or sordid.

At this juncture hope came in the person of a young district commissioner named Armstrong. He said he had a Matabele boy who had come to him with a plan for killing the chief priest of M'limo, who had planned the rebellion. He had killed all his family and he thirsted for revenge. He said the witch-doctor could be caught in his cave by surprise. It might be a trap, but the chance seemed worth taking and Major Frederick Burnham agreed to go with Armstrong and test the Matabele boy's plan.

The cave was not the priest's home, but his church. It was sacred and no one dared enter it. When he spoke in a loud voice at the cave's mouth, an echo was heard, and this was supposed to be the utterance of the Great Spirit. Near the cave was a village, and here, when Burnham and Armstrong arrived, a whole Matabele regiment was waiting to be rendered immune to the white man's bullets, "a feature of the ceremonial being the skinning of a live ox and eating it raw."

Leaving their horses hidden in a thicket, Burnham and Armstrong succeeded in reaching the cave by creeping on their bellies and screening their movements with branches of mimosa thorn held in front of them. Once in the cave, they waited for the prophet. They described him as "a man about sixty years of age, very black, sharp-featured, with a cruel, crafty cast of countenance."

Burnham shouted, "You claim to be immune to the white man's bullets, stop this one," and shot him through the body just below the heart. The mouthpiece of God was dead. Immediately the village was in an uproar. To create the diversion necessary for their escape, Burnham had decided to fire the village. His first match went out, but with the second the thatch of a hut took. As the fire spread, the Matabele abandoned the pursuit to put it out and the white men reached their horses and escaped.

This destroyed the M'limo myth and induced the timorous to surrender, but the more bitter and dangerous fighters united under Babyaan, an old induna, and continued to carry on a savage guerrilla war from the mountains.

This could have gone on indefinitely. England was not ready to help Rhodes any further and his own fortune could not support a prolonged war.

Now Rhodes the gambler, the man who understood timing and calculated risk, rose to his full and gigantic stature. This country was Rhodesia—named after him. He identified himself with his creation. Having made it he must save it. "I am here," he said later, "and you have done me the favour of giving this country my name. My return will be to make this country as great as I can."

Could anything be more suitable, more dramatic, or indeed more necessary than that Rhodes should save Rhodesia?

He decided to go to the Matabele alone. He would deal with them. Good luck or Providence had given him another chance. By an act he would show them—the curs and jackals that yapped at his heels—the kind of man he was.

The link between Rhodes and the Matabele was Tembu, a young and devoted native. It was part of the pattern of Rhodes's life that when he needed a man to serve him that man was at his side. Tembu had fought the Matabele and knew their ways. Rhodes was convinced that the Matabele were ready to make peace, that they only fought because having begun they did not know how to stop. On this conviction he was about to stake his life.

Tembu's instructions were to get into touch with the Matabele; and armed with field-glasses, some food and a blanket, and accompanied by two other Kaffirs, he set out.

Hiding by a stream, Tembu heard two Matabele girls who had come to fetch water talking of the hunger and troubles of their people. Tembu called to the girls, told them that he had come to see if a parley could be affected with the chiefs, and gave them a piece of his shirt-tail for a flag, which, if the chiefs agreed, they were to raise in a conspicuous place. Tembu said he would wait four days during which no fighting would take place. After that, if the flag was not raised, the armistice would end and the fighting would go on.

On the fourth day an emissary appeared from the Matabele. But it was not a warrior or a captain. It was an old woman, a wizened crone with sagging breasts, who had been one of Moselikatze's wives.

Then under the burning noon sky of Africa, amid the piled rocks, the kopjes, the drought-smitten trees standing with their shadows a black pool beneath them, the half-civilised Tembu and his companions faced the indunas—thin with war, wounded, dressed in kilts of wildcat tails and leopard, plumed with black ostrich feathers, and armed with assegais and kerries. And with the chiefs was the wizened wife of their old king who had led them to Rhodes's emissary.

Yes, they would meet Ulodzi. Yes, they would talk.

With this news Tembu returned to his master. The chiefs would meet him if he came with only three men.

Many of the old-timers in Rhodesia were against Rhodes's going. It was a trap. Look what had happened to Retief when he went to talk to Dingaan, they said. Dingaan's words, "Kill the wizards," still rang in the ears of Africa.

This was one of the grandest moments in Rhodes's life, a dramatic moment, and one that he appreciated for what it was. He might make a mess of it—but if he didn't Rhodesia was saved; his North—and with it his reputation. Here was a chance to retrieve a political mistake by an act of personal bravery.

Accompanied by Johann Colenbrander to interpret for him and Vere Stent the journalist he set off. Tembu guided the party. The track they took led through a wilderness of forest and kopjes. About them on the hills they saw Matabele watching. When they reached the appointed place, there was some argument about whether they should remain on their horses or dismount. Rhodes gave the order to dismount.

"Dismount, of course," he said. "It will give them confidence. They are nervous, too. How do they know we have not an ambush for them ready behind the hill?"

Then the chiefs appeared bearing the shirt-tail flag.

"This is one of the moments that make life worth living," Rhodes said.

Twenty chiefs squatted round the flag.

"Mehle M'hlope," Colenbrander said—"The eyes are white."

"The eyes are white, Chief Great Hunter," the indunas answered.

"Is it peace?"

"It is peace, my father."

Then, to quote from Sarah Gertrude Millin's biography of Rhodes:

"Somabulane spoke up. He spoke at length, dramatically in the most dramatic of languages—his native liquid Zulu. With gesture and pantomime he told the story of the Zulu nation. The tale of Moselikatze's flight from T'Chaka, of his conquests, of his being driven north by the Boers, of other wars, of the fights at Bulawayo. He told of how the white men had come to Lobengula entreating protection, asking for permission to hunt and dig, asking for meat, asking that young girls be sent to them—asking,

asking. And when asking failed, taking; and still this was not enough.

"Not the half of Lobengula's kingdom did they want, but the whole of it. They had come between the Matabele and their vassals the Mashona. The eyes of the other chiefs reddened with anger as they sat and listened to their wrongs, to the story of their wars and the fury of their fight. Somabulane went on, 'The white men had conquered the land that they of the long shields had taken from the Mashona.' He told how his king had been driven into exile and had died. He told how peace had been refused to Lobengula, though his gifts of peace had been taken. Then he went on with the present wrongs of his people, speaking of the tyranny of the commissioners, of the abuse of a warrior people by the native police, of the slaughter of their cattle and the abuse of their young women. 'You came,' he said, 'you conquered. The strongest takes the land, we understood that. We lived under you. And then you treated us as dogs. Is it not better,' he asked, ' to die than to live as dogs?' By now the Matabele chiefs were trembling, eager as hounds. Their eyes, red with anger, turned from the white flag of peace to the spears that they had planted in the ground beside them.

" 'Who treated you as dogs ?'

" 'The native police and commissioners,' Somabulane answered.

" 'Once I myself came to Bulawayo to pay my respects. I brought my indunas with me and my servants. I am a chief. I sat till the shadows were long having come before the dew was dry. I sent to the chief magistrate asking for food—that an ox should be killed. And the answer came that the town was full of stray dogs—dogs to dog. We might kill them and eat them if we could catch them.'

" 'These things will cease,' Rhodes said. 'There will be no more native police. Tell him that such things will not happen again. Now I want to know, is it peace? Are the eyes white?'

"Somabulane threw down the reed he had in his hand as a token. The sun was going down when the chiefs stood up. 'It is peace.'

" 'How do we know it?' Colenbrander asked again.

" 'You have the word of Somabulane, of Babiaan, of Dhisilo, chiefs of the house of Kumalo.' "

A week later there was another meeting. This time Rhodes had four white men with him and two of them brought their women. But instead of the chiefs being there, a mass of warriors appeared with their arms in their hands. Rhodes told them to put down their weapons and dismounted from his horse. The older men prevailed upon the younger and the arms were flung down. Rhodes gave gifts of salt and tobacco and food. The Matabele praised him and gave him a new name—"Lamula M'kunzi"—the separator of the fighting bulls.

For weeks, for months the indabas—the talks—went on, chief after chief coming in to see Rhodes, each with a special story, each demanding a special justice—to none was time of importance. To each this was a God-sent chance to tell the history of his personal life, his exploits and the saga of his race. Rhodes heard a thousand versions of the history of the Zulus and the Matabele. Never more pressed for time than now, Rhodes had never wasted time like this. He listened to all and answered all in the same way. "Tell them they are fools. If they do not want peace, why do they not come down here in the night and murder me and all of us? The thing would be very simple. They need only send a few of their young bloods one night—twenty-five would be enough—and the business would be over. If they were not fools, they would do this—they would have him, and him, and him, and him"—he pointed to his companions. "Tell them if they want peace, then why do they not all come and shake hands with me and then they could go back to their wives and children and be happy."

More chiefs came. They brought their wives. They brought their babies to see Ulodzi. Meanwhile, Rhodes was wanted in England. The English wanted him to appear before a select committee of Parliament "appointed to inquire into the origin and circumstances of the incursion into the South African Republic by an armed force."

When Rhodes received the summons, he answered: "The investigation can wait. I am busy fighting the Matabele."

He had fought them, he had made peace with them. He had kept his promise to them, giving the chiefs back their authority and supplying the starving people with a million bags of mealies which he ordered on his own authority and was ready to pay for out of his own pocket.

But one incident nearly wrecked the peace indabas. Some of Rhodes's men had discovered and opened up Moselikatze's tomb. They had thought to find treasure with his bones. The chiefs came to Rhodes in a fury at this new desecration. He went back with them to see what had been done. Round the tomb were thousands of shouting Matabele. Their dead king had been affronted, his spirit was hurt. His ghost, more terrible than the living man, was loosed upon them by this act.

In the tomb the skeleton had been disturbed. The ground had been dug up. The objects buried with him—his wagon and furniture, bottles, and weapons, cook pots and utensils—were scattered. The head of the skeleton rested on its high bones, but the empty sockets still looked north.

Rhodes was as indignant as the Matabele. The robbers were punished. The Matabele were allowed to repair the damage and were paid while they worked, and to appease the dead king's spirit ten black oxen were bought by Rhodes and sacrificed.

On this day Rhodes found his burial place among the Matopos, the mountains that had been the toy things of the gods. "I shall be buried here," he said. Death was near him and it was time to think of his burial, to make certain that his tomb should match the grandeur of his life, that in death he should lie with kings and heroes.

Having settled Rhodesia, settled his settlers and his Matabele, settled on his mausoleum, it was time for him to go back to England and settle with those who decried him. To face the full blare of the music and "the unctuous rectitude" of those who would have cheered him had he come to them as a victor with all Africa in his hand.

CHAPTER TWELVE

A FOURTH TERM

THIS was the calm before the storm of Africa—the almost calm—the pseudo—for the hot air was breathless with coming storm and, though the leaf on the tree was still, it was vibrant with the coming event, foreshadowed by Majuba and the Raid. These had given the British a craving for vengeance and had put anger into the slow Boer heart. And the golden apple still lay beneath the rough veld of the South African Republic. The gold, that had been the cause, was still the cause.

In London, Rhodes faced his shareholders and the parliamentary select committee. Endless witnesses were called, endless speeches made by all, directly and indirectly, concerned with the Raid, and what at the end merged quite clearly was the fact "that Jameson had indeed ridden into the Transvaal." That is to say, the matter was all but hushed up by giving it such a detailed examination that it died from over-exposure. So well was everything ventilated and for so long that public interest was exhausted and the matter blew over. Anyway, it had been staged more for foreign consumption than domestic. It was said that documents were withheld because they compromised the great—the Prince of Wales, the Kaiser, the Queen herself, and Chamberlain. There was a nice little shifting about of officers in the Colonial Office. Many were removed and then given other jobs; officers in the army were censured and transferred. A great stir was made, and under the cover of the smoke screen, everything was allowed to settle down again so that at the end the differences were imperceptible; but nevertheless there was a general feeling that justice had been done and honour satisfied.

One thing, however, did happen. Lord Milner was sent out to Africa.

But in the relations of the South African Republic with Europe there were certain changes. The Kaiser, who had congratulated

Kruger on his repulsing the Jameson Raid, reversed himself when he understood how nearly he brought Germany to war and had been reprimanded by Queen Victoria, who was his grandmother. Kruger was reported to have described himself as disgusted, and saying, " I have a contempt for a man who is afraid of his grandmother."

When at a later stage war between the South African Republic and England appeared certain, the Kaiser—perhaps Kruger's remark had been reported to him—told his general staff to prepare a complete plan of campaign, to be used by the British army against the Boers, which he submitted to Arthur Balfour. It would seem likely that this plan was one which he had himself considered using if the opportunity had occurred for the conquest of Africa, and that he now proposed to ingratiate himself with his grandmother by sending it to her. One thing is certain—that to prepare any such plan his intelligence agents must have been active for a considerable time. This plan of operations was so good that, with minor changes, it was used by Lord Roberts.

In the years which had elapsed since Germany first established herself in German South-West Africa, she had built strategic roads which were a threat to British interests from the Cape to the headwaters of the Nile. She planned to build up an enormous legion of black soldiers and, waiting for the trouble which must inevitably take place, would have been ready to help the Boers. But the hostilities broke out too soon, and so, making the best of a bad job, the plans were put at the disposal of the English. New troubles were bound to occur and the chance would come back.

This happened fifteen years later in the First World War when certain Boer leaders made a compact with the Governor of German South-West Africa to announce the independence of the South African Republic and declare war against England. Fortunately this rebellion was put down by General Botha, who, having fought the British in 1899, was now far-sighted enough to see with many other Boers that South Africa's future was best secured as a member of the British Commonwealth rather than as a German colony, for once the English had been beaten their dream of independence would have vanished.

The Germans tried the same plan again in the Second World

War even before it began. It was squashed by three hundred South African police armed with machine guns occupying all the key points at Windhoek on the eighteenth of April, 1939.

There can be no direct severance with the past, no actual division between one war and other wars, and it is more than certain that this fear of Germany was a contributory factor in causing the Anglo-Boer War. It was the cause of the statesmen. Rhodes was definitely bent on thwarting German aims. In consequence there was a good general pattern: the one of high politics, of the statesman, which appealed to the governing class; the one of economic gain which moved the middle-class financiers and investors; and the one of revenge for Majuba and the Jameson defeat, which appealed to the jingos—and finally the sentimental appeal of an oppressed minority of Uitlanders for the mass of the public.

On the twelfth of May, 1898, Paul Kruger took oath for the fourth time as State President of the South African Republic. He obtained 12,858 votes. Schalk Burger got 3750 and Joubert 2001. Kruger appointed Jan Christian Smuts as Attorney General. "Smuts," Kruger wrote in his *Memoirs*, "will yet play a great part in the future history of South Africa." And Smuts, a world figure to-day, is a link between to-day and yesterday, between two world wars and the Boer War.

Kruger saw not only into the distant future when Smuts would be great, but into the near future, which is only a projection of the immediate present. The Raid, the second attempt on the independence of the Republic, had failed, and now, he said: "Mr. Chamberlain was to be set to work to try whether he could be more successful. With his assistance Jameson's Raid was to be replaced by a gigantic British raid."

A proposal now came from London that President Kruger should come to England, and suggested that a kind of Home Rule be established in Johannesburg: that is, that a country be established within a country. Naturally this fell through, and by its falling, by the very fact of its ever having been proposed, the inevitable conflict came still nearer. To meet this new threat the Republic bought more arms. Still more were ordered when the Raid investigations, which showed that Mr. Chamberlain was not so innocent as he had been represented, were over. Further straws in the wind were the fact that in the House of Commons Mr. Chamberlain declared that Rhodes "was a man of honour and that there existed nothing which could effect Rhodes's personal position as such." And the further fact that Jameson having been condemned to prison was soon released on account of illness, but recovered his health immediately afterwards.

The League at Johannesburg drew up a petition to the Queen enumerating their grievances. A second petition was also drawn up and signed by twenty-one thousand British subjects and sent to London. To offset the first two, still another petition was drawn up, signed by twenty-three thousand Uitlanders of all nationalities, who declared they were satisfied with the administration of the country.

Rhodes was out of South Africa now. The war, as yet unblooded, was between Kruger and Chamberlain, with Milner as Chamberlain's instrument. But if Rhodes was out, his interests were not, nor his followers. It was merely that he stood aside; enough had been pinned on to him. He wanted, if he could, to salvage his dream, to mend the golden cup and splice the silver cord. Acknowledged leader of the jingos, he was of it but not in it, and actually the enemy of Milner who he saw would force bloodshed by his tactlessness.

Yet, even though he knew this in his mind, Rhodes refused to believe it in his heart. He could not believe in war, or at least not in war with white men fighting against white men. A raid was one thing and a war quite another. But Milner was no compromiser; and when the Boers were ready to compromise, not Rhodes, the man who had said he could make a deal with the Mahdi, but Milner, the cold, precise, aristocratic stand-patter, sat at the conference table.

At this meeting, according to John Hays Hammond, "Kruger employed his histrionic talent so effectively as to bring tears to his own eyes; the only reaction in the mind of the Englishman was disgust."

The facts according to Manfred Nathan, were these: "Milner said: 'Why not have an advisory council, made up of those who are not burghers of the state, but who represent the Uitlander interests of the community?' The President asked, 'How can strangers rule my state? How is it possible?' He then broke down and cried, ' It is our country you want! It is our country you want!' He bent his head between his hands while the tears coursed down his weather-beaten cheeks."

It is interesting to note here how the same act, this act of a man weeping, is treated by the prejudiced observer. Kruger weeps at the thought of war and it is theatrical. Rhodes weeps over Pickering's watch and chain and it is an admirable expression of sentiment. Rhodes wept on several occasions—and why not?— On his return from Rhodesia after the Matabele Rebellion when he was met by crowds at every station; in Cape Town when people ran after him shouting, touching his clothes, the hem of his garment. Tears poured down his face as he said, "Such appreciation as this generally comes after a man is dead." There was something prophetic about his "after a man is dead," for Rhodes, though he did not know it, was dead.

There is no record anywhere of Paul Kruger's dramatic gifts. He had none. What he had were the emotions of a simple man who raged and stormed when he was angry and wept when he was sad. A man who had seen much of war, who had killed many men with his own hand in war, was here faced in argument by the blank mind of a diplomat, an ex-financial secretary of Egypt, an English aristocrat trained from childhood in the school of absolute stoicism, a man who could not understand that any one should show sorrow: trained so highly that his ability to feel had probably been destroyed. How then could the minds of such men meet? On what grounds or basis? If only it had been Rhodes, who was emotional, dramatic, who had an appreciation of the great moments of personal life and the high moments of history! Rhodes was great enough to be awed by circumstance, at the wonderful concatenation of strange events when they occurred. But Sir Alfred Milner knew nothing of this. He was Chamberlain's servant, the representative of the Conservative Party in Africa.

In this issue each side—the British and the Dutch South Africans—saw themselves as white and their opponents as black. Each accused the other of treachery, of falsifying documents, of lying. Probably each was, to some extent at least, right. But the fact remains that had the Transvaal held no gold, there would have been no war. Had it been what the Boers wished it to be, a vast farming plain and a great lowland hunting ground, instead of one of the richest territories in the world, there could have been no quarrel. Even the secondary motive of getting there before the Germans would not have existed, since it was the gold the Germans wanted too. And this is the paradox, that the Boers, in the end, had to fight for something they did not want. Had they been able to keep their veld and give to England the riches that lay beneath it, they would have done so, and been glad to get rid of what they, in their simplicity, thought the source of all evil. But the British, to get at the mineral wealth, had to hold the surface rights that the Boers had fought and bled for, and here, on this basis, the facts are clear and every conference and every despatch merely points them.

Diametrically opposed as they were, probably Rhodes and Kruger could have settled things had they been able to meet and had Rhodes been given the authority to act. He said this himself. "Perhaps the best thing would be if Kruger and I could meet." They had met at Fourteen Streams and again later, but their first meeting had set Kruger against Rhodes because they had not been alone. Warren the soldier, with his dragoons, had been there and Boers had unpleasant memories of dragoons; and Mackenzie had been there and the Boers hated missionaries. Yet the ends of the two—of Rhodes and Kruger—were similar: the good of Africa; Africa for the Afrikaaners; Africa for the South Africans.

Perhaps Rhodes could have arranged for Africa to belong to the Afrikaaners, as it does to-day to the South Africans, and for it also to have remained within the framework of the British Empire. When it comes to saying what Rhodes could or could not achieve by compromise, especially if the other side was ready to compromise, it is hard to see failure. This would have been particularly true if the meeting could have taken place before the Raid when Rhodes had the South African Bond behind him and could have offered a share in his North to the Boers. But all this is an *If.* Instead, Kruger went to meet Milner at Bloemfontein, in the neutral ground in the Free State.

From the time that the investigating committee closed its proceedings in London, there was an unending stream of despatches from England which continued till war broke out.

Each was intended to prove England's case and to excite anger against the Boers. Sir Alfred Milner was the last man to have been sent to Africa as High Commissioner. He tried to treat the Boers as he had the Egyptian fellahin, and actually said on one occasion that "the power of Afrikanderdom must be broken." He was another Lanyon, another man used to governing coloured men, and unable to adapt himself to a people like the Boers. The British had no tradition and no precedent for such a state of affairs except in America, where their methods had lost them those Colonies.

To meet the threat of almost certain war, the South African Republic entered into a still closer association with the Orange Free State and it was resolved "that the rights granted to a Transvaaler in the Free State should be those granted to a Free-Stater in the Transvaal, only the franchise being left untouched."

Incident now followed incident. The Bunu incident was the first of the new series. In 1898, Bunu, the king of Swaziland, murdered one of his indunas and was summoned to appear before the court at Bremersdorp. He arrived with an armed suite and refused to face the justice. An armed force was sent to fetch him. Sir Alfred Milner now intervened and Banu fled to Zululand, where he was under British protection.

The next trouble came through a branch of the South African League, which at the instigation of Rhodes protested when some coloured persons who were British subjects were arrested for being without passes in the Transvaal.

Another incident occurred when a policeman following a murderer broke, without a warrant, into the house where he had taken refuge. This received much space in the British press.

But the question of franchise was the real issue: a franchise which would have given the Uitlanders possession of the Republic.

President Steijn of the Free State accompanied Kruger to the conference. According to Kruger, Sir Alfred Milner showed not the least desire to come to an agreement. He would not meet Kruger's compromises and Kruger found his suggestions impossible to agree to. The conference came to nothing and ended in the two principals questioning the authenticity of the signatures of the petitions which were under discussion. Kruger pointed out to Milner that a number of signatures appearing on the petition to the Queen appeared spurious.

Milner said, "Very well, we will investigate the matter." He then asked if the counter-petition did not also contain false signatures. Kruger denied this. Milner then said, "Let us drop the subject." And to Kruger's suggestion for further deliberation he said he "considered it unnecessary and that the conference was ended."

On his return to Pretoria, Kruger suggested to the British agent there that all future differences between the two governments should be settled by an arbitration tribunal. This letter was dated June 9, 1899. In July a bill was passed in the Volksraad which reduced the length of residence in the country necessary to obtain the franchise, gave full franchise to all sons of foreigners born in the Republic immediately they attained their majority, and increased the representation of the gold fields in each Raad by four members.

While this bill was being passed, the Intelligence Department of the War Office in England had already issued military notes on how war should be waged against the Republic, and Lord Wolseley had laid his plans before the Government for the conquest and seizure of the two republics.

The British agent in South Africa meanwhile refused the Republic's proposal of arbitration. On August 19 the State Secretary of the Republic made an alternative offer to the British agent, offering further concessions in the hope that the controversies between the two governments could be settled. On August 26, Mr. Chamberlain, during a garden party in his house at Highbury, said: "Mr. Kruger dribbles out reforms like water from a squeezed sponge and he either accompanies his offers with conditions which he knows to be impossible or he refuses to allow us to make satisfactory investigation of the nature of these reforms. The sands are running down in the glass . . . the knot must be loosened or else we shall have to find other ways of untying it."

These reforms Mr. Chamberlain spoke of were the full franchise of Uitlanders in Johannesburg which even the Reform leader, Lionel Phillips, had acknowledged most of the people cared "not a fig about." The Uitlanders as a whole outnumbered the Boers, but the English Uitlanders did not. They were a minority which was represented as repressed and down-trodden. The propaganda tune varied between this minority story and its exact opposite—the fact that the Uitlanders outnumbered the Boers and therefore should have control of a country in which they had only a temporary interest. The term "Uitlander" in the English press included the total foreign population, who were represented to be English. Nothing was ever said about the land ownership qualification which was part of Kruger's platform. If a man owned land, he had a real stake in the country; if he owned shares in stock or mineral rights, he had only a financial stake which he could administer from home or liquidate at any time it suited him to do so.

On August 31, Sir Alfred Milner telegraphed to Mr. Chamberlain: "The purport of all representations made to me is to urge prompt and decided action; not to deprecate further interferences on the part of Her Majesty's Government. British South Africa is prepared for extreme measures. I fear seriously that there will be strong reaction of feeling against the policy of Her Majesty's Government if matters drag."

Further notes were exchanged, further propositions proposed by both sides which were acceptable to neither. The matter of suzerainty came up again. And while all this was going on, Rudyard Kipling met Rhodes and became his guest at Groot Schuur. It is impossible to ignore Mr. Kipling as a political factor. His verse was the song of Rhodes's England. He was more than a poet, and less than one; he was the lyrical expression of England, of imperialism, of an upper-class old-school-tie kind of Spartanism. His "if you can keep your head when all about you are losing theirs" amounted to a creed.

And now the penultimate instrument of actual war was pulled out of the political bag. The link between the politics of peace and those of war was put into effect. British troops began to march North. On the seventeenth of September, the State Secretary asked the British High Commissioner for explanations regarding the concentration of troops on the frontier of the South African Republic. This time it was not a few filibusters and police. It was a force of regular troops.

The High Commissioner replied that they were there "to

defend British interests and in order to prepare for possibilities."

On September 22 the mobilisation of an army corps for South Africa was announced in England. On September 28 it was stated that the greater part of that army corps had sailed.

The burghers now rode out from their farms again and mobilised on the frontiers waiting for an attack by England. There were further exchanges of letters, despatches, and notes. It was clear, Kruger says, that Chamberlain was playing for time so that he could assemble more troops in Africa. Oddly enough, this fitted in with Kruger's own plan. He was waiting for the rains to come. It was early spring in the Transvaal and the rains fall there through the spring and summer. His force of mounted burghers were dependent on grass to feed their horses and the driven cattle which they used for food when on commando.

The president of the Free State tried to arbitrate and its Volksraad adopted a resolution in which it declared "that no cause for war existed." Nor would it have existed if there had been no Witwatersrand, no speculators in gold shares, no people demanding revenge for Majuba or who felt disgraced because Jameson's foray had failed. The English now objected to the concentration of Boers on the borders of Natal. The President answered that it was "the natural result of the constant increase of British troops and their movement towards the Transvaal border." Concentration had produced, as it must, a counter-concentration.

The High Commissioner replied that the British troops were there "because of the natural alarm of the inhabitants of exposed districts and were not comparable in magnitude with the massing of armed forces on the borders of Natal by the Government of the South African Republic."

The President replied on October 3 that he "did not consider the movement of British troops had been necessitated 'by the natural alarm of the people in exposed districts' nor in fact had he ever thought that there were any fair grounds justifying such movements."

Meanwhile every one moved and counter-moved. The more men the British moved, the more the Dutch concentrated. The more the Boers concentrated, the more the British moved, and the more troopships sailed from England with reinforcements.

Both sides were now in a position where neither could withdraw and yet neither was ready to attack. It had not rained yet, so the Boers were not ready to move. Enough troops had not yet arrived, so the British were not ready either. Both sides were hoping that some face-saving miracle would occur by which they would attain their object without war. The English were convinced that the Boers would not fight, or if they did would not fight for long against regular forces. Their belief in regular troops remained pathetic. The lesson learnt in America had never really gone home.

On October 4, the British High Commissioner said that "no good purpose would be served by recrimination, but that the present position was that burgher forces were assembled in very large numbers in the immediate proximity of Natal while the British troops only occupied certain defensive positions well within these borders."

This was the trick of pretending that the aggressor was acting in self-defence and trying to force the threatened country to act first and thus justify punitive action. He continued, that "he would not despair of peace, and felt that any reasonable proposal from any quarter would be favourably considered by Her Majesty's Government."

On October 5, the President replied that he was "prepared to make a proposal, but that the British troops should be withdrawn from the frontier and that those now on the water should not be landed." On October 6, the High Commissioner regretted that he "could not accede to conditions which hampered the freedom of action and disposition of Her Majesty's troops."

The President answered that he had no doubt that Her Majesty's troops were intended for the defence of Her Majesty's possessions, but that the same purpose could be accomplished in another way and he would be willing to assist in its being effected. But the point was that it was virtually an act of hostility on the part of Her Majesty's Government to be continually increasing their forces during negotiations.

On October 7, both Republics, the South African and the Orange Free State, placed themselves on a war footing and the Parliament in London called out all reservists.

Of this period Paul Kruger writes: "Any one who views these

matters impartially must admit that the British Government . . . did their utmost to cause the negotiations to fail and to bring on war. The Government of South Africa saw what the British Government wanted, that a collision was inevitable, and the British were only waiting to send their ultimatum until sufficient troops had arrived in South Africa to overwhelm the Republic from all sides. When it was realised that a war was inevitable and that concessions availed nothing, extreme measures had to be resorted to." And on October 9 a letter, the so-called ultimatum, was sent to the British agent.

This ultimatum was a remarkable one, since it suggested that England had no right to interfere in the internal affairs of the Republic. It emphasised the fact that Her Majesty's Government had assumed a threatening attitude in all discussions and had finally broken off discussion on the subject. It demanded again that all points of difference should be settled by arbitration, that British troops be withdrawn from the frontier, and that reinforcements be checked. It demanded an answer by Wednesday, October 11, not later than 5 p.m., and ended by saying that if no answer was received by that time the Government of the Republic would be forced to regard it as a declaration of war.

On October 11, Mr. Green brought the reply of the British Government to the effect that the conditions demanded by the Government of the South African Republic were such that "Her Majesty's Government deemed it impossible to discuss." At the same time he asked for his passports. The Volksraad of both the Transvaal and Free State declared themselves "ready to risk their lives and property for their rights and their liberty."

The Boers' efforts at appeasement had failed. It was war. War for the Vierkleur, for the Union Jack. It was the parting of Boer men from their wives and their homes and work to face an unknown destiny. For the British it was to have been a picnic. It was. It was a picnic that lasted three years, in which a hundred thousand died and that cost a hundred million sterling.

The Boer War is a definite part of modern contemporary history. Ending a century, it ended also an empire. Beginning a century, it started a Commonwealth and a Commonweal.

To this, then unknown, end did the Boers ride out—twenty thousand of them against two hundred thousand; a small free people against an empire; mounted farmers against the best that Europe could provide. To this end the graves both Boer and British scattered over the veld of Africa. "The blood" that Kruger had prophesied when gold was discovered in the Transvaal was about to flow. "The breakfast" that Rhodes preferred to blood had been set upon the table by the Boers, but the British refused their hospitality.

Part Three

Blood

Blood must flow. . . . —*Adriaan de la Rey.*

CHAPTER ONE

THE STORM

BOTH SIDES in this war considered themselves to be in the right. Behind each were imponderable psychological factors—hatred, on the part of the Boers, who, remembering the past, felt the independence they had given up so much to gain was once more, and finally, threatened. The demand for franchise by the Uitlanders had been, to the Boers, no more than a means of gaining by peaceful methods that which was, now that this device had failed, to be obtained by the armed forces of the British Crown.

On the British side there was contempt for this absurd little Republic of farmers which stood in their way, and a desire to revenge themselves for the defeat at Majuba. Blood, as Adriaan de la Rey had said, was equally and to both the only answer. To each, their own blood and that of their enemies. By blood are nations made and broken, by blood bound together or separated; by its flowing in war are new combinations set up, new amalgamations formed, new peoples born and old destroyed. Only to-day, when we have seen too much of it, can we begin to understand the possibility of other settlements, but even to-day, before those settlements are made, much fresh blood must flow in battle, in revolution, and in murder. Like the men full-fleshed and choleric from whom the barbers once drew blood, so nations, full-fed and choleric, demanded that blood be drawn. This choler,.this anger, was and is the basic fact of war. Granted that it is an effect and not a cause, and that the cause of this inflammation in the body of the people is the government which produces it, war still remains impossible without anger and a belief in its justice, no matter how perverted it may be.

The point in this case is that both the English public and the Boer burghers were behind the war. Though each would have preferred to gain its point without war, fear of war was insufficient to produce the compromise that could have stayed it.

"Obstinate old Kruger"—"Acquisitive Empire-minded British"— are words easily bandied. But the Boers were with Kruger. They considered their homes and liberties at stake, and the British were behind Chamberlain and Milner in believing themselves put upon and insulted. The Boer War has been described as the last *gentleman's war*. There is even a book of that title, but men who are killed, whether in gentlemanly fashion or not, are dead, and their women—the colonel's lady or Judy O'Grady—are widows and their children fatherless. The Boer War was, however, remarkable, with a few outstanding exceptions, for its lack of atrocities. Neither the Boer farmer nor the Empire private soldier had a talent for sadism. It was a simple war fought by simple men.

But the tree of the past could not be prevented from bearing its fruit among the Boers—that of the scaffold at Slagtersnek where the British had by their executions turned rebel leaders into political martyrs—the last insanity of statesmanship; while the British were still smarting under the sting of their defeats. The English bulldog spirit was up, and against it was set that of the Dutch—that of Van Tromp who had sailed with a broom at his masthead, that of the Lowlanders who had cut their dykes and resisted the might of Spain.

The Republican Administration was accused of taking bribes. It has been proved that many Boers did accept bribes. But who tempted them and why? And is the tempter free of blame? The Boer Administration was accused of ignorance. They published reports in the Volksraad, saying that using dynamite was firing at God; that it was impious to destroy locusts, since they were a plague sent by the Lord; that the word "participate" should not be used, since it was not found in the Bible; and many considered postal pillar boxes both extravagant and effeminate. Naturally, some of the British in South Africa resented being ruled by men like this, but with equal naturalness the Boers resented the idea of being out-voted and consequently ruled by Uitlanders whom they considered to be without respect for God's law. To some extent this was a religio-political war. For to the Boers, religion and politics were inseparable. President Burgers fell because he was a godless man.

"You see that flag," Kruger said to a friend, pointing to the

Vierkleur flying over state buildings. "If I grant franchise I may as well pull it down." And though Rhodes was out of power now, his words represented the opinion of the British in South Africa when he had said, "Of course I would not risk everything as I am doing except for the British flag."

The Raid which ruined Rhodes's prestige had only settled Kruger more firmly in the saddle, the one man's political poison being the other's political meat. As Kruger said of himself, "If one gets a good ox to lead the team, it is a pity to change him." The Raid had in addition given the Boers the sympathy of the world. The President's magnanimity to the prisoners taken in the Raid made people forget his faults. His feeling about the Raiders was expressed in one of his canine similes—"It is not the dog which should be beaten, but the man who set him on to me." This man, of course, was Rhodes, and all who thought like him. There is a certain irony in the fact that the President had armed his country for the coming struggle by using the money obtained by taxing the mines. If there had been no mines to tax, there would have been no money in the treasury for weapons. But also if there had been no mines, there would have been no need of weapons. So the cause of war supplied the Boers with the means of waging it, as the diamond mines of Kimberley had, by the wages they paid to the Kaffirs who worked in them, enabled the Matabele to buy guns to fight Rhodes.

Into South Africa now began to drift, on the wings of the storm, the *condottieri* of all Europe—the soldiers of fortune who were ready to hire out their battle skills to the highest bidder.

There is some uncertainty as to the numbers the Boers could put in the field, but twenty-five to thirty thousand would seem to be about the number. The voters' roll is not accurate because of possible abstentions from voting. In addition, the fighting age of the Boer is probably five years younger than the voting age, and if there were men of seventy riding out on the commandos, there were also boys, thirteen and younger. "These men, all of them, young and old, were brave, hardy, and fired with a strange religious enthusiasm. They were seventeenth-century except for their rifles. Mounted on their hardy little ponies, they possessed a mobility which practically doubled their numbers."·

An observer who watched the commandos ride to war on October 12 said: "Their faces were a study. For the most part the expression worn was one of determination and bulldog pertinacity. No sign of wavering there, nor of fear. Whatever else may be laid to the charge of the Boer, it may never be truthfully said that he is a coward or a man unworthy of the Briton's steel."

Sir Arthur Conan Doyle wrote of the Boers, "Could we have such men as willing fellow citizens, they are worth more than all the gold mines of their country."

Among the Boers there was a German corps, a Hollander corps of about two hundred and fifty men, and an Irish-American corps of about the same number who rode under the green flag and the harp. There were also men from almost every other country.

On October 20, 1899, the first shot was fired at the British by the Doormberg Commando. Rhodes had not believed that war would come until that shot was fired. As far as he was concerned, "A Samoan chief might as well make war on the Empire. . . . It is only temporary trouble in South Africa. Kruger will, at a push, give anything. . . . Nothing will make him fire a shot. . . . There is not the slightest chance of war. . . ."

Why wasn't there? What had Rhodes learned about the Boers if he could think this? What had he learned of history, which he studied so much, if he could not see that they would fight? They had fought before and won before. Kruger felt himself and his nation surrounded; to use his own words—"kraaled like an ox." And what did the Black Veld Boer know of England or the outer world? His ignorance on such subjects was only equalled by the English ignorance of the Boers. Truly, "what do they know of England who only England know," or of Africa who only know Africa? Rhodes knowing both should have known better.

One can only believe that his wish was the father to his thought, and that having sired this opinion, he stuck to it till the first shot was fired. Perhaps he thought the Boer mobilisation was simply an armed protest. Perhaps he did not think, but only hoped.

Even among the Transvaal Boers there were men who were against the war. De la Rey spoke out against Kruger and the war party in the Volksraad. It was a bitter scene. The President taunted those who were against him, accusing them of cowardice.

De la Rey, the son of Groot Adriaan, rose for a second time to face Kruger. "I shall do my duty as the Raad decides," he said. Then he turned on the President, "And you will see me in the field fighting for our independence long after you and your party who make war with their mouths have fled the country."

These were the words of a prophet. He was in the field at the end of war, as one of the best Boer generals and an undefeated one, long after Kruger, as he had prophesied, had fled. But in the beginning things went well for the Boers—so well that had they pushed their initial advantage home, they could have overrun the country. They had at this time an excellent chance to win. The British forces at Dundee and Ladysmith fled in disorder after some skirmishes and a pitched battle. Joubert, the Commandant-General, however, had never believed in the war and did not pursue them and force the issue. Instead he used his mounted guerrillas for the one purpose to which they were the least suited. He besieged for months towns in which the British had garrisons, and for months the British held out, knowing that each day reinforcements were landing and irregular troops of Colonials were being formed and trained. Had the Boers pushed on in a mounted Blitzkrieg, a form of warfare to which the British were quite unused, and reached the sea—with the Cape Colony pledged to neutrality—it would have been hard to dislodge them. With all Africa behind them, with ample supplies of provisions, and world opinion on their side, it would have been difficult for the British to land enough troops to recapture the country. But this opportunity was lost.

At the outbreak of war Kruger was seventy-four—too old to fight himself, but he had prepared well. He had his trained artillerymen. He had his guns from Schneider and Creusot. He had hired trained officers, Germans, Russians, and Frenchmen. He had volunteeers from all parts of the world. A clean sweep over Africa and a negotiated peace was what he hoped for. He did not expect to hold conquered territory, but to use it as a lever in the final negotiations. It was for this reason, at a later stage, that the war, which was already lost, was continued. The Boers hoped for a change of government in England. If Chamberlain went out and a Liberal Government came in, they felt they would get what they wanted.

At first the news was encouraging for the Boers. Natal and the Cape were invaded. Kimberley, with Rhodes in it, was besieged. This was a new war for independence, a war for permanent freedom, and into it Kruger threw himself, body, soul, and fortune. He lent the treasury half his savings—forty thousand pounds, interest free, and did not expect to see it repaid. He worked as he had never worked before. He was in his office from nine till twelve and from two till five every day. At two every morning he was awakened and worked till four. At six he got up. His doctor, Albert Heymans, was always with him, for his eyes were worse than ever, more puffy, more bloodshot, and more painful; and his kidneys were giving him much pain. He not only worked in his office, but went out into the field.

At Glencoe, where there had been a slight setback, he refused to shake hands with the commandants. "Were I but five years younger," he cried, "I would have shown you myself what facing the enemy means—even if they were in a tenfold majority." The commandants were ashamed, for the President was no armchair strategist. He meant what he said and they knew he could have proved it.

With Johannesburg in the palm of his hand, Kruger did nothing to destroy the city, though it was the cause of all his troubles. There was nothing vindictive about him—a characteristic that he shared with Rhodes. What went on in Kruger's mind and in that of the other older Boers can best be gathered from his wife. She was described in 1900 as sitting in her back stoep knitting her husband's socks for the coming winter with her youngest great-grandson playing at her feet. She was dressed in her usual black silk and wore her white cap. She would not leave her house. If she accompanied her husband, she felt she would only be an encumbrance to him. "You don't know how this war weighs on me in my old age," she said. "Long years ago I came to the Transvaal with my parents on the Great Northern Trek. We were always retreating—as our people have always done from British power and British lands. If I were to tell you the troubles, hardships, we went through! If I remember how we women and children had to hide many a night in the reeds at the river side, half in the water, hiding from bloodthirsty Kaffirs who would not hold back from the most atrocious deeds to white women, and I think of how these worries and other troubles have continued ever since, my heart feels sore that the evening of our lives should be darkened by this awful, this unnecessary bloodshed between people of our kind and race." She told how her husband had been shelled at Abrahams Kraal; of how he had been covered with dust and, roaring with laughter, had said, "How well the Queen's pills burst!"

The President had at the fighting fronts five sons, six sons-in-law, and thirty-five grandchildren, apart from innumerable other more distant relatives.

The Boer War was a rebellion, a civil war, in which brother fought brother, for there had been much inter-marriage between the English and the Dutch. Two of General Botha's sisters had married Natal Carbineers and many burghers had English wives. Some Boers from the Cape fought with the British while others came North to join the Republican commandos. Those who fought against the British were considered traitors by the Cape authorities, while those who fought for them were called renegades and fratricides by the Boers. As in the American Revolution there were colonists on both sides; and the leaders in both wars, having been born under the Union Jack, were considered mutineers.

When Deneys Reitz, the son of the President of the Free State, joined a commando at seventeen, Joubert, the Commandant-General, said to him, "I started fighting younger than that." Reitz saw a good deal of the President at that time and says he "had an uncouth surly manner and he was the ugliest man I have ever seen, but he had a rugged personality which impressed all with whom he came in contact. He was religious to a degree, and on Sundays, he preached in the queer little Dopper Church he had built across the street." Of Joubert Reitz says: "He was a kindly, well-meaning old man who had done useful service in the smaller campaigns of the past, but he gave me the impression of being bewildered at the heavy responsibility placed upon him and I felt that he was unequal to the burden. One afternoon he showed me a cable from a Russian society offering to equip an ambulance in case of war and, when I expressed my pleasure, I was astonished to hear him say that he had refused the gift. He said: ' You see, my boy, we Boers don't hold with new-fangled ideas. Our Bossie-middels—herb remedies—are good enough.'"

That young Reitz was right in his estimate of the Commandant-General was proved by the course of the war. After the action at Nicholson's Nek the British army retreated, and again I quote from Reitz: "Shortly after the surrender I heard one of the captured officers exclaim, ' My God, look there!' and turning round we saw the entire British force that had come out against us on the plain that morning in full retreat to Ladysmith. Great clouds of dust billowed over the veld as the troops withdrew and the manner of their going had every appearance of a rout. There were about ten thousand soldiers, but General Joubert had far more than that number of horseman ready to his hand and we fully expected to see him unleash them on the enemy, but to our surprise, there was no pursuit. I heard Christian de Wet mutter, ' Los jou ruiters! Los jou ruiters!'—Loose your horsemen!— but the General allowed this wonderful opportunity to go by, a failure that would cost us dear in days to come. . . . I was told that when officers came back to implore Piet Joubert to follow, he quoted the Dutch saying: ' When God holds out a finger don't take the whole hand '—meaning that the Almighty had helped us sufficiently for one day and that it did not behoove us to presume upon His bounty. . . ."

Here is exposed another facet of the Boer character—their belief in the principle of "Gut genog'—good enough; of "Alles sal regt kom"—All will come right; of leaving things to God and time instead of riding one's luck when luck is smiling. It is the defect that balances the virtue of Boer patience. Through this attitude of mind the Boers lost their chance of driving the English out of Africa in the first months of the war. The English spirit, rising in anger, fanned by reverses, is described by Sir Arthur Conan Doyle, who said: "If there were any who doubted that this ancient nation still glowed with the spirit of its youth, his fears must soon have passed away. For this far-distant war, a war of the unseen foe and the murderous ambuscade, there were so many volunteers that the authorities were embarrassed by their numbers and pertinacity. . . . Many young men-about-town justified their existence for the first time. In a single club, which was particularly consecrated to the *jeunesse doré*, three hundred members rode to the wars." Perhaps this is why it was such a "gentleman's war."

But while the Boers were besieging the towns, British reinforcements continued to arrive and Lord Methuen was able to drive the burghers back to Magersfontein, where they made a stand under Cronje and de la Rey. But he advanced against the new position in close order and suffered two thousand casualties, of which a thousand were in dead. This checked the attempted relief of Kimberley. General Gatacre then attacked in the direction of the Stormberg in another drill-book formation and found himself in a position commanded on three sides by the Boers. Hundreds more British troops were killed and captured.

General Buller fell back on Chieveley and began organising a new army which he led against General Botha, who had succeeded to the post of Commandant-General of the Boer forces after the death of Joubert. Attacking in four sections on a front of eight miles, Buller was decisively defeated and was prepared to surrender. He heliographed to General White in Ladysmith to use up his ammunition and surrender with his twelve thousand men. White, however, determined to hang on. Here again victory almost came to the Boers. If White had obeyed his orders, the war would have been over.

The position was now very much what it had been after Majuba in 1881, but the Boers waited for the British to make peace instead of attacking vigorously. Since the first part of the pattern of the War of Independence had been duplicated, surely the second part must follow the same course. It was obviously the Lord's will.

However, these new defeats infuriated the British. The prestige of the Empire was at stake. "Bobs"—Lord Roberts of Kandahar—with Kitchener as his chief of staff, took command. More reserves were called up, one hundred thousand of them, and were employed against the Boers, who never had more than twenty thousand men in the field at one time. Six hundred British were killed in a savage battle at Spion Kop, but then the tide began to turn. The reinforcements by sheer weight of numbers began to push the Boers back. Roberts, using the plan which the Kaiser's staff had given to Queen Victoria, began his great round-up.

Cronje was surrounded, and, refusing to abandon his wagons and escape with his men, which he could have done, stood, fought until resistance was no longer possible, and then surrendered with four thousand burghers. He had engaged Robert's fifty thousand men and one hundred guns with four thousand men and five guns. The prisoners, Conan Doyle says, "were the most singular lot of people to be seen at that moment upon earth—ragged, patched, grotesque, some with goloshes, some with coffee pots, umbrellas, and Bibles their favourite baggage. So they passed out of their ten days' glorious history. A visit to the laager showed that the horrible smells that had been carried to the British lines and the swollen carcasses that had swirled down the muddy river were true portents of its condition. Strong-nerved men came back white and sick from a contemplation of the place in which for ten days women and children had been living. From end to end it was a festering mass of corruption, overshadowed by incredible swarms of flies. . . ." Some Boer women, such as Joubert's wife, had always accompanied their husbands on commando, but at this stage of the war unattached Boer women and children of all kinds drifted in—rendered homeless by the destruction of their farms; they were what we should call refugees to-day.

Many Boers, despondent and exhausted, now gave up the struggle. Their horses were starving and hardly able to carry them, their clothes were in rags, and they were having difficulty in getting enough rations to live on, yet the people's faith in the President remained firm. He came among them to encourage, to exhort, to pray, to censure, to praise. Three times he went to different fronts in his light wagon. Once he was nearly taken prisoner. Knowing he was near, General French launched a cavalry attack to capture him, but the Johannesburg mounted police checked the charge of French's troopers. According to Captain Van Asselberg, the military attaché from Holland, one hundred Boers stopped the advance of five thousand cavalry by continuous and effective rifle fire.

Roberts now began burning the farmhouses, because, he said, with some justice, that it was impossible to tell if the Boers hanging round them were actually out of the war and working their properties or merely resting between battles. The Boers had no uniforms and tended to drift to the war and back as they needed rest, having had it, felt inspired to fight again. Cattle, sheep, and horses were lifted by the British and irregular Colonial troops, crops were destroyed, the women and children rounded up into camps, and the men and boys sent overseas to the West Indies and Ceylon as prisoners of war. This ruthlessness, though in the end it wore the Boers down, was something they never forgave. And worst of all, many thousands of women and children died in the camps to which they had been sent. Everything seemed to go wrong there. Supplies were short; women from the warm parts of the country died through a shortage of blankets when transferred to the High Veld. Without understanding sanitation or the use of the latrines, and with a kind of passive resistance to all orders, the prisoners suffered from enteric and other epidemics, and died. For a farming people, accustomed to wide spaces, confinement alone, coupled with anxiety about their men and fear for the future, was enough to produce a state in which they were susceptible to any illness that struck at them. In Bloemfontein there is a monument to the twenty thousand Boer women and children who died. The excuse the British gave was that these women could not be allowed to starve, or be left at the mercy of the Kaffirs, who, at that time, if they were subdued, were far from completely broken, and longed for revenge against their now helpless masters. This is an unpleasant picture, but it is impossible to leave it out or to gloss it over. As Sherman's Ride is remembered in the Southern States, Robert's scorched-earth tactics are remembered in Africa. But Kruger remained undaunted. "Even if it goes so far that I am sent to Saint Helena, let us persevere," he said, "for then the Lord will bring back the people and set it free."

Then came the stroke that ended the first phase of the war. Roberts relieved Mafeking, which, under General Baden Powell, had held out against the Boers.

Mafeking cancelled out Majuba. It cancelled out the Raid. It cancelled out the thousands of British dead, or at least caused them to be forgotten in the wave of hysteria that struck London when the news came in. Flags waved in every hand, they hung on every building. There was dancing in the streets, hansom cabs were festooned with bunting and decorated with flowers.

England went mad, for the relief of this relatively unimportant town meant the surrounding of the Transvaal and the end of the war. Mafeking, overnight, ceased to be a town and became a verb. "To Mafeking" came into the English language.

For a brief instant the *furor Teutonicus*—the mad German mixture of hate and lust and pride—overcame the British phlegm.

CHAPTER TWO

LONG CECIL

THE STORY of Kimberley from the beginning of the war to its relief is a story by itself. To begin with, the Cape Administration never thought Kimberley to be in any danger and a secretary wrote: "I am directed to assure you that there is no reason for apprehending that Kimberley or any part of the Colony either is, or, in any contemplated event, will be, in danger of attack. Mr. Schreiner is of the opinion that your fears are groundless and your anticipations in the matter entirely without foundation."

On October 12, a few hours after Kruger's ultimatum had expired, Cecil Rhodes had arrived in Kimberley, *just in case*, for Kimberley was the diamond-linch-pin that held the wheels of his chariot in place and de Beers still the centre of the financial web that he had spun. Kimberley was Mr. Rhodes. Mr. Rhodes was the King of Kimberley till the Boer horsemen appeared on October 15, and then Colonel Kekewich and his chief of staff, Major O'Meara, took command. That any one but he should give orders in Kimberley staggered Rhodes; that soldiers, of whom he had a profound contempt, should do so, did more than stagger him. It infuriated him.

The situation had not been improved by the Mayor's message. Hearing that Rhodes was coming, he had telegraphed to his prospective visitor: "Under all circumstances would ask you to postpone coming."

But Rhodes was not going to be stopped by a telegram. He arrived on the last train that came into the town before it was invested. Why should he not come? Who was the Mayor to try to stop him when he had practically made Kimberley in the first place, and practically owned it in the second? He came and immediately fell out with the military commander. Rhodes took orders from no one, particularly from a soldier. He had a poor opinion of military men. His conquests had been without them and his defeats were largely due to them. Soldiers, he thought, spoiled everything. Soldiers and missionaries had the common denominator of obstinacy and dogma. They could not see big.

So here was Rhodes besieged in Kimberley. Jameson was also besieged—in Ladysmith. Neither was a welcome visitor, for there were no two men whom the Boers would sooner have captured. The officer in command in Kimberley and Rhodes were scarcely on speaking terms the day after his arrival there. Indeed, when General French did relieve the town, he demanded Rhodes's arrest; while Lord Methuen before his defeat sent a message saying: "On my entry into Kimberley, Mr. Rhodes must take his immediate departure."

There were some curious factors in the siege of Kimberley, one of which was the use of an observation balloon by the British forces attempting to relieve the town. This sign of hope from the outer world was first seen on December 10. Far on the southern horizon, a little golden speck shimmered against the blue African sky. It was Methuen's balloon gleaming in the sunshine. It remained, however, merely an interesting phenomenon and helped Kimberley no more than a soap-bubble. And Rhodes, unused to being cooped up, got busy.

Among the de Beers' mining engineers at Kimberley was an American—a Mr. Labran of Detroit—who not merely installed searchlights, constructed an armoured train, a telephone system, a cold-storage plant for the cattle, which, owing to the Boers, could no longer be grazed outside the town and had to be killed; but in addition he constructed in the mine workshops a heavy gun from a billet of hammered mild steel, complete with ammunition in twenty-four days. This gun was called "Long Cecil" and did excellent service. All this was typical of Rhodes and his men—indefatigable, undefeatable, enterprising—without him Kimberley would have fallen. He organised, he constructed, and all they—those damn soldiers—did was to fly balloons. But the unorthodoxy of it all did not go down with the regular officers of the British army. Rhodes went about offering advice, much of it good, to every one. He acted as if it were his war and that he had a right to direct it. He even wrote to Lord Roberts, demanding that he relieve the town and telling how it should be done. "Your troops," he said, "have been more than two months within a distance of a little over twenty miles from Kimberley and if the

Spyfontein hills are too strong for them, there is an easy approach over a level flat."

Nothing happened, and two months later he wrote again and demanded "full power and no one to interfere with me . . . reply sharp as otherwise I am going to the Cape."

This was a fine way to talk to the Commander-in-Chief! It is perhaps a pity that the running of the war was not put into Rhodes's hands because he saw the stupidity of it which no professional soldier could. If war were recognised as stupid, there would be no wars and no more professional soldiers—something that Rhodes would not have regretted. It is sometimes forgotten that the keenest advocates of armaments and of wars are soldiers, since world peace would destroy their profession.

Conan Doyle, however, writing on the siege of Kimberley, takes another point of view about "the notorious but painful fact that there existed, during the siege, considerable friction between the military authorities and a section of the civilians of whom Mr. Rhodes was chief." He says: "Among other characteristics, Rhodes bears any form of restraint very badly. . . . He may be a Napoleon of peace, but his warmest friends could never call him a Napoleon of war, for his military forecasts have been erroneous and the management of the Jameson fiasco inspires no confidence."

The Napoleonic simile is a common one. Conan Doyle uses it again: "This remarkable man stands for the future of South Africa as clearly as the Dopper Boer stands for its past, has both in features and in character some traits which may, without extravagance, be called Napoleonic. The restless energy, the wide fertility of resource, the attention to detail—all these recall the great emperor. So does the simplicity of private life in the midst of great wealth. And so does, finally, a want of scruple where an ambition is to be furthered, want of scruple, for example, in that enormous donation to the Irish Party by which he made a bid for their parliamentary support, and in the story of the Jameson Raid. A certain cynicism of mind and a grim humour complete the parallel. But Rhodes is a Napoleon of peace. . . ."

The interest of this extract from Conan Doyle's history of the Boer War is that it was written by him in 1900 before the end of the war and before Rhodes's death; and in the fact that Conan

Doyle, an admirer of Rhodes, definitely calls him the organiser of the Raid and openly writes of Rhodes's bribing the Irish members of Parliament.

To return to Kimberley. Rhodes was fed up with the whole business, with the war which he considered unnecessary, with its conduct, assuming it to be necessary now that it had begun, and above all, with the army and its commanders who wished to arrest him as soon as the town was relieved. Once safely out, he washed his hands of the war and decided to return to his North where he was appreciated.

En route for Rhodesia, when Lord Roberts had declared the war was won, Rhodes addressed an anti-Boer meeting in Cape Town and told his audience that the Boers were not beaten. Only Krugerism was beaten. "The Dutch to-day," he said, "are just as virile, just as unconquered, as they ever were, the country theirs as much as it is yours. When the war is over, you will have to live together and work together exactly as in the past." Both Rhodes's premises were right. The war was not over. It did not end as it should have done with the fall of Pretoria and the flight of the President. And when it did end, as Rhodes had said, the Dutch and English lived side by side as they had before. Fortunately, South Africa had men, Boer generals, who saw this too. Men like Botha, Smuts, and de la Rey. Had Rhodes lived, things might have gone even better, but agony was piled on to agony as more and more things went wrong for him. Even Jameson now turned against him. "Rhodes," he wrote to his brother, "has done absolutely nothing but go backwards."

There are fires in the grounds of Rhodes's home at Groot Schuur, his trees are felled, animals in his zoo poisoned, and still he is not beaten. With all that he says, "We shall not relax our efforts, by our civilisation and the efforts of our people, we reach the Mediterranean."

"Talking of the North," he goes on, "give me your confidence because your hinterland is at stake and I am the only man who can work the North with the South. . . . Whatever your personal feelings may be regarding me, you will get the country and I shall only get six feet by four."

His ideas of race began to change. "Race feeling," he said, "I cannot have in me, because my feelings is that the best man must come to the front, whatever his race may be. You cannot live on race feeling. It will not give you new lands for your children."

H. J. Whigham, who was a war correspondent and travelled North with Rhodes, describes his disillusion with the war and throws some new light on his character. He says:

When French relieved Kimberley in 1900, I went as correspondent of the *Morning Post* round to the relief of Mafeking via Cape Town, Durban, Lourenço Marques, Beira, Salisbury, Bulawayo. On arriving at Beira, through which port the British were shipping troops up to Rhodesia for the relief of Mafeking, I found that Rhodes, who had been released from Kimberley by General French, had also come round to Beira on his way up to Rhodesia.

He was bored with the war which hadn't gone so well as he expected, and so he chartered a steamer, loaded it with prize cattle pigs, sheep, and poultry, which he was taking up to distribute among the farms in Rhodesia. So far as he was concerned the war was over.

I ran into Harry White, one of the Jameson Raiders and now a war correspondent, and a friend, of course, of Rhodes. He told me that Rhodes had chartered a special train to take his prize animals up to Rhodesia and he offered me a seat and berth in his compartment on the train.

The train started off in the afternoon after a lot of ceremonies and champagne-drinking on the part of the Portuguese officials who were entertained on his train by Rhodes. The first few miles of the journey were on a two-foot gauge line across the Punjive flats to the point where we met the railroad up to Salisbury which was built on the regular South Africa gauge.

There we had to tranship to the broader-gauge train which awaited us; and that was a job. Half the prize animals broke loose and made for the jungle, pursued by Kaffir porters with flaming torches. Finally, however, they were rounded up and we settled down for the night journey. I happened to have a delectable pâté in my scoff box which I wrapped in a wet handkerchief and attached to the door of our compartment.

I woke up in the morning to find the train at a standstill, our engine having broken down. Tony, Rhodes's faithful man, was much disturbed because he had left Beira in a hurry and forgotten to bring sugar with him for the Great Man's coffee. Rhodes settled that matter by going off into the jungle and discovering a Kaffir kraal where the natives gave him some sugar, greatly to Tony's relief.

I noticed, however, that Tony in the confusion had stolen my pâté which he kept as a peace offering for Rhodes.

Finally we got our engine working and our train proceeded to climb the big rise through Portuguese Africa, winding its way through the most magnificent primeval forest full of game and orchids and all sorts of surprises.

A few hours later we came upon a trainload of New Zealand troops in a siding, suffering also from engine trouble. It was obvious that we couldn't attach the troop train to our rear with any hope of getting anywhere. Rhodes might, of course, have lent the New Zealanders our engine, as they were combatants and we were not; but that never occurred to him. He did, however, hitch on their dead engine to our tail, saying that he would take it up to the railroad shops in Rhodesia and get it fixed up for the soldiers. The engine was hitched on, but very soon, as the grade got steeper, our locomotive got tired. So we unhitched the dead engine, left it right there on the track, and proceeded on our way with a clear conscience that we had done our best. At sundown we emerged on the top of the plateau across the border of Rhodesia on the vast expanse of the veld. "Now," said Rhodes, "we're in a real country, thank God." He was determined not to admire the magnificent forests through which we had been passing. They were not in Rhodesia and therefore not worth bothering about.

I found the great man extremely simple, pleasant, and frank as we sat and talked with him in his compartment all that afternoon. His big bulk, ruddy complexion and greying hair went curiously with his high, almost falsetto voice. He was not by this time interested in the war which had been dreadfully muddled, he thought, until his friend, Lord Roberts, took over charge. But he was full of interest in Rhodesia. He loved the veld which no doubt agreed with his lung weakness, but he particularly loved the veld of Rhodesia.

Doctor Jim told me afterwards that when the British Government was holding its inquiry about the Jameson Raid, the one thing Rhodes feared was that they might take his name off the map. He was fond and proud of Rhodesia, and when I came to drive over that wide landscape, with its lush grass and picturesque clumps of trees and the long vistas leading away to distant blue ranges, I could see that it was something to be proud of.

Rhodes loved the veld, he loved all of South Africa, but he had no understanding of Afrikaaners, certainly not of the Boers. In the summer of 1899 I happened to be playing tennis with a British Member of Parliament, a Conservative, and a business man, and not by any means enamoured of Joe Chamberlain. He objected very strongly to the rather high-handed manner in which Joe was leading the country into a war which would be costly and long-drawn-out. He told me that he had met Rhodes at dinner the night before, and when he told Rhodes how much he objected to the Chamberlain policy as leading the country into disaster, Rhodes said he couldn't see how any one could fear a war with the Boers. In all probability Kruger wouldn't fight, but if he did the British could march from the Cape to Pretoria with twenty thousand men and the whole business would be over before Christmas. Unquestionably Chamberlain believed this, even though the way might have been doubtful, and so Rhodes was very largely responsible for the war. And being a man of most decided character, he still thought he was right when I went up with him to Rhodesia. He thought the campaigns in Natal and up on the Modder River had both been messed up by incompetent leadership, and he was quite annoyed when he was besieged in Kimberley. He had confidence in Bobs, but anyhow he knew the war would end in the right way sooner or later, and he wasn't going to bother about it; and so to him it was far more important that his cattle should get to Salisbury than that the New Zealanders should get to Mafeking, which in fact they never did until long after Mafeking was relieved. There was something typically Rhodesian, or perhaps British, in the picture of this big Englishman chartering a private steamer and two special trains and passing them right through the battle lines, and brushing the war aside as a silly nuisance which men of less calibre had to attend to. . . .

This was Rhodes—the Napoleon of peace—who could ignore the war which he had helped to cause, and in the midst of it decorate the country he loved, which had taken his name like a wife, with a chaplet of prize bulls, a waist-belt of stallions, and ear-rings of prize-winning pigs. Only an Englishman could be mad enough for this, or great enough. The humour of the situation must have escaped Rhodes. It never occurred to him that he could be funny—great, tragic, yes—but not funny. It is probably impossible for a man to be great and have a sense of humour.

CHAPTER THREE

MR. RHODES OF RHODESIA

It was a long time since Rhodes had first said: "The North is my thought.' "Co-operation is my thought. ... Federalism and the Union of South Africa." Since then he had made his thought come true; had welded Mashonaland, Barotseland, Manicaland, and Matabeleland into Rhodesia, the land where he was king. He was inspired by the North, and the North was inspired by him, its sire. Even the Matabele, whom he had twice defeated, called him father.

"They can't take it away from me, can they?" he said after the Raid. "You never heard of a country's name being changed ...?"

Rhodesia was his child: like a father he saw it grandly, romantically. It was beautiful to him as it had been to others before him: To Moselikatze, when he came out of the maze of the Matopos, and to others, before the Zulu renegades.

These lands lie in the lower central part of Africa. They touch its very womb. To the north is the Congo Basin and the East African Rift. To the west is Angola; to the east Nyasaland and Portuguese East Africa.

The history of Rhodesia is unknown, but has been reconstructed on the basis of its mysteries, its ruins, the thousands of excavations in gold-bearing quartz veins, that are scattered through the country. These diggings, hundreds of yards in length, are more or less continuous on the surface and rarely exceed a hundred feet in depth. The ore was extracted by building fires against the veins and then, when it was well heated, dashing water against the rock, which caused it to crack and disintegrate. The fragments were then crushed in pans of hard rock and the powdered quartz was washed in a stream. Sometimes a sheep-skin was placed below a small waterfall to catch the heavier particles of gold which were washed into the wool, turning it into a golden fleece, while the lighter quartz was carried away.

The gold was then melted, poured into soapstone moulds, and

converted into ingots. At the time of the British occupation, many furnaces sunk in the solid rock still contained cakes of gold, which would suggest that the miners were driven off in a great hurry, or died of some sickness, rather than an orderly abandonment of the country. There is the possibility that the warlike northern tribes, the mother tribes of the Bantu nations, attacked the gold workers at a time when their own country was unable, through other troubles, to protect them. This would be analogous to the attacks on the Britons by the Picts and Scots when the Roman Empire was disintegrating. What has not been discovered in which nation it was that, in these early times, developed these gold mines. What early prospectors dared this tropic wilderness? What expeditions of bearded, long-robed men, armed with bronze spears and swords, came here? How did they prepare their reports? To whom did they submit them? There is plenty of evidence that the mines were worked in a desultory fashion by the Arabs and Portuguese and even the Mashona after these people had gone. But who were the original people? The key to the mystery lies hidden in the Zimbabwe ruins. These forts and temples are built of shaped granite blocks laid in even courses without mortar. Doctor David Randall-MacIver and Miss Caton Thompson both consider Zimbabwe to have been built by Bantus in the fourteenth or fifteenth century. But against this theory is the fact that there are no native legends or traditions about them. Sir Harry Johnston says that no Bantus could have created such complex structures without Semitic teachers. Theodore Bent, another expert archeologist, ascribes the Zimbabwe civilisation to Sabæan or Phœnician origins. Kane agrees with him that the ruins are Semitic. Professor Raymond Dart says the earliest workings were begun between 4000 and 3000 B.C. Professor J. W. Gregory thinks the gold recently excavated at Ur came from these mines. Among other curious things found among these ruins are: a Roman coin, found in a shaft seventy feet deep, near Umtali; beads which are referred to Ptolemaic Egypt and pre-medieval India; ingot moulds of soapstone in form of an X, such as were used by the Phœnicians in Cornwall, and soapstone birds similar to those of Assyria where they were used in the worship of the Assyrian Astarte, or Venus. Many emblems symbolic of the female element in creation and phalli were also found. Nowhere could the phallic cult have been more suitable or seemed more natural than in Central Africa, which epitomises fecundity in the richness of its flora and fauna, in the lushness of its forests, in the numbers of its people.

It has been suggested that the gold for King Solomon's Temple came from Zimbabwe, since the mines are only about two hundred miles inland from Sofala which was famous for its gold export in King Solomon's time. There is evidence of a road leading into the interior from this port and it seems probable that the ships built at Ezion-geber—I Kings IX: 26 ... "And King Solomon made a navy of ships in Ezion-geber"—were to be used for trade with India or down the African coast. Again, I Kings X: 22, "once in three years came the navy of Tharshish, bringing gold, and silver, ivory, and apes, and peacocks." The voyages along the east coast of Africa would have been facilitated by the monsoons—the trade winds of the Indian Ocean. That King Hiram brought back Negro slaves from the land of Ophir to work on King Solomon's Temple is certain, since the sculptures of the period show men with unmistakably Negroid features at work. It is estimated that these unknown miners took one hundred and fifty million pounds' worth of gold from the Southern Rhodesian fields. John Hays Hammond, after examining the ancient workings, wrote to Rider Haggard and asked him why, in his book, he had located King Solomon's mines "within a few miles of where I believe I had seen them." Haggard replied that he had placed them there because he felt its almost inaccessible character would prevent any Yankee mining engineer from penetrating there and reporting that Rider Haggard's King Solomon's mines did not exist. "And thus," he went on, "imagination precedes reality." But romantic speculation does not end here. There are Bushman drawings which suggest that even Chinese bowmen, in peaked hats, reached the east coast of Africa. Nor did these ancient miners work only in Rhodesia. They penetrated the Transvaal and took some two thousand tons of tin from the Rooiberg Mountains. This, expressed in terms of bronze, amounts to thirty thousand tons, and which, again expressed in terms of weapons, amounts to a great number of spears, swords, knives, and battle-axes.

This, then, is the history of Rhodes's Hinterland. We see

the ancient Bantu people enslaved by a race of engineers and miners from the North; we see them, the exploiters, destroyed, perhaps by the Arabs; we see a later penetration by slavers and gold-seekers; we see the Bushmen driven out and killed by the bigger black men; we see the bigger black men eaten up by still bigger black men—Moselikatze's Zulus who became the Matabele —and the Matabele themselves destroyed by Rhodes's white men under the leaderships of Doctor Jim. We learn that it was at Mombasa, not so far up the coast, that Vasco da Gama dropped his anchor in 1498. That at Melinde, sixty-odd miles still farther north, he picked a pilot, "a Moor of the Guzerat nation," who used charts divided into small squares by meridians and parallels to take him across the Indian Ocean to Calicut. This Indian and Far-Eastern trade must have existed for centuries—gold, ivory, gums, slaves, baboons, ostrich feathers, rhinoceros horn for poison cups and aphrodisiacs being the African exports, while silks, spices, peacocks, and objects of Oriental art were imported.

It was from Sofala that Francisco Barreto led his ill-fated expedition of a thousand white men into Monomopata's country. This land, this coast, was all fabulous; infamous with cruelty, soaked with blood, dusted with gold, rich with ivory, gems, and slaves. It was a challenge. It had always been a challenge. It was a warm, dark-green slate upon which many men of many races had made their marks. It is not surprising that Rhodes should love this land and find it exciting, that he should wish to add the final and most glorious page—written in English—to a book begun in hieroglyphics.

Immensely old, Africa remains still new. Theoretically conquered, Africa remains unmoved by conquest. For who will conquer the fevers, the ants, the tsetse fly, the floods and droughts? Who will survive in Africa—the Negroes who originated there or the white races that have superimposed themselves upon it?

Africa has penetrated the world. It is a breeding place, fecund, dark, and warm, whose tendrils have reached out into the Indies, into the United States, where one man in ten is a Negro. It has crossed the Caribbean into South America. It has mingled with Indians, with Chinese, with Portuguese and Spaniards. Its culture is prevalent in every night club from London to San Francisco, from Nassau to Singapore. The drum was born in Africa, which is the mother of the drum—the big war drum, the talking drum, and the tom-tom. Still to-day with giant bombers overhead there are witch-doctors and leopard men in the Bush; there are pygmies and giants. Still to-day there are mysteries in this land that is inviolate, that sleeps like a giantess forever spawning black men who run with pink-soled feet upon its little paths. To him, the Negro, Africa is no mystery—it is his home.

The history of Asia we know, of Europe, but not of Africa. The Boer and Matabele wars are episodes, important perhaps because they are near to us in both time and history, but no more than two episodes, among thousands. What knowledge have we of Africa? Some descriptions of the voyages made by the early Portuguese, the obscene documentations of the slave trade, the journals of du Chaillu, the memoirs of Stanley, of Livingstone, the writings of hunters like Harris, and later of Frédéric Selous, the paintings of Daniels, Cape Archives dating from the seventeenth century . . . no more than this except the mysterious rock paintings of the Bushmen, the stone ruins and the old mine workings.

We know that the hundreds of tribes that inhabit Africa spring from three main stocks: the Negro, the Hamite, and the Bushmen. The Negroes inhabit Central and West Africa. Generally speaking, they have been prevented from spreading north by the Sahara. The Hamites, who are so called because they are supposed to be descended from Ham, the second son of Noah, include the Bergers, Tuaregs, and Copts of Egypt, the Ethiopans and Somalis. The Bantu, who are the "Kaffirs" of the Boers, are Negroes with a mixture of other blood. As Sarah Gertrude Millin puts it: "Trailing down Africa they mingled with those Hamites who include not only the Egyptians, Nubians, Abyssinians, and such others, but also the Hottentots; and they met in what is now Portuguese East Africa, but was long years ago a great Eastern Arab state, the Eastern men who landed at the port of Sofala to trade in slaves, gold, and ivory. These Hamites and Semites chiselled away the Negro thickness of the Kaffirs' faces. They gave the Kaffirs their name—*Kaffir*, an unbeliever."

This is about the limit of our knowledge. Rhodesia was the cockpit of Africa, a melting pot, a mausoleum, a mint, a zoological garden, and an archeological museum. In addition—and here is the dual key to Rhodes's adventures—it was not only supposed to contain gold formations rivalling those of the Rand, but its highlands were healthy and suitable for colonisation by white men; that is to say, that white men and women could live and breed there, and raise their young Rhodesians.

Rhodes's interest in animal husbandry was secondary to his interest in human husbandry. He bought the best beasts so that fine men should be built from their meat. It was to these Rhodesians that Rhodes came after the relief of Kimberley, bearing gifts, and with promises—to the people of his North, "who have never bitten me." This was the country, these were the people, of his dream that had come true. The creation that had been formed in a black, despotic vacuum, they were, as it were, the sperm of an empire, the tiny nucleus that must grow into a world state.

Me, my, mine—our country, our future, our hopes, our thoughts. The North is my thought. The North was the dream, Rhodesia the corner-stone of the great pyramid that was to be raised on the gold, diamond, and copper industries. They supplied the blood, Rhodes the brain, his settlers the brawn.

What is this fascination that Africa exercises over men? Not merely Cecil Rhodes, but over all those who have known her, who leave her but almost inevitably return, drawn back by some inexplicable force.

Is the Wegener theory correct? Is Africa really the mother continent of the Southern Hemisphere from which the others have split in a kind of gigantic geological calving?—South America on one side; Madagascar, India, and Australasia on the other? Looking at a world map, the pieces seem to fit nicely. The bulge of Brazil into the Gulf of Guinea, Madagascar into Mozambique. Is Africa, in fact, the great divide of the southern continents, and the cradle of the human race? Is then a man, any man, who goes to Africa in a sense going home? Does he, without knowing it, thus satisfy some primeval urge? Does the country strike some hidden, psychological chord of memory?

As America is a melting pot of modern man, the country where many races are being blended into a new type, Africa is the country where in the distant past the residue of many ancient races were driven. As the ancient Britons were driven into the mountains of Wales, as later the American Indians were driven farther and farther west, so were earlier types of men driven from Europe into Africa. *Homo Rhodesiensis*, although apparently a more primitive and simian type than *Homo Neanderthalensis*, was found, unfossilised, among the remains of animals still living in Rhodesia, which leads one to suppose that *Homo Rhodesiensis* was living quite out of his geological period in Africa, thousands of years after his kind had become extinct in Europe. The Bushmen are contemporary, living fossils, the last examples of a type of man that once inhabited Europe. So are the tiny pygmies that build their nests of leaves in the dark forests of the Congo. The matings of all these breeds with both white and black men, their merging into the Griqua Bastaards and Cape coloured people, like those of the Australian aborigines, the American Indian, and New Zealand Maori, tend to prove that extinct races of men were never really exterminated, but were absorbed by the more advanced type, killing the men and taking the women. There is probably no reason but one of æsthetic taste which would prevent a modern white man from producing offspring with a Neanderthal woman should he come across one. Africa is the home of the giant anthropoids which are nearest to us—the gorilla and chimpanzee—while, to get back to Wegener, the only other anthropoid apes—the orang-outang and the gibbon—are found in the East Indies and India. All monkeys are found in South America, Africa, India, and the East Indies. Leopards are found only in these countries, and there are geological resemblances—most precious stones, diamonds, rubies, and emeralds come from South America, Africa, India, and Australia; opals from Australia, Honduras, and Mexico. There are ornithological resemblances in the rhea of South America, the ostrich of Africa, and the cassowary of Australia. There are botanical resemblances and etymological resemblances, which, if they do not prove Wegener's theory, at least make it an interesting hypothesis.

Many of these things were unknown to Rhodes. The Broken Hill skull and the Taungs skull had not been discovered in his time, but he had been much influenced by Darwin, who said: "It is probable that Africa was formerly inhabited by extinct apes closely allied to the gorilla and the chimpanzee; and as these two species are now man's nearest allies, it is somewhat more probable that our early progenitors lived on the African continent than elsewhere."

It was things like this that excited Rhodes, that drew him on towards the dark interior. Ambition, politics, empire, power, were the obvious drives that racked him; but behind these were the urge of curiosity, of romance, and a sublimated virility that wished to tear the veil, not from the body of a woman, but a continent.

Rhodes, as we have seen, was not interested in money; for him it was only a tool. Paul Kruger was not interested in romance, or beauty, or history, or progress, and here, too, they clashed. Kruger was a domestic man. Rhodes, unmarried, a man to whom home, except the abstract idea of "England, home, and beauty," made no appeal. Kruger was without curiosity. The world, he believed, had been created in six days as was stated in the Book of Genesis: to him nothing was controversial. Not only did he have an archaic sense of time, but of timing. His timing was that of the hunter and farmer, excellent for those purposes; whereas Rhodes's sense was of the future, always the future; the present meant little to him. To-day was no more to Rhodes than the rung which he must climb to attain to-morrow.

An example of Rhodes's sense of timing is given by Fitzpatrick when he describes his negotiations for the sale of a parcel of diamonds worth half a million sterling. What he wanted was a cash offer for the whole lot made on behalf of all the buyers present. They could agree among themselves afterwards as to the proportions they would take, and how the payments should be made, but he alone, acting for the de Beers shareholders, would decide whether the offer they made was adequate or not. The diamonds were laid out on sheets of paper exactly fitting a teak trough twelve inches wide. The sheets overlapped each other like the tiles of a roof and the diamonds on each sheet were carefully sorted and graded by the de Beers experts—the work, perhaps, in a parcel of this size, of several months. The diamonds in each little heap were identical.

The first offer made was not enough and Rhodes said so. He said. "I know the value as well as you do," and, turning to Brink, said, "That's not good enough."

A few minutes later, the buyers agreed to a much higher price which Rhodes accepted.

At this time the diamond market "was in a very nervous condition and it was realised that the sale, releasing of a mass of stones, would have a very serious effect upon prices." Every one knew this, but the buyers each thought that he would be first in the field and re-sell quickly. All knew the enormous advantage of buying well-classified stones. Rhodes, when he signed the contract, had said, "I can make no contract with you binding you to hold these stones off the market . . ." "The buyers were all rivals and none believed that everybody would exercise this restraint or comply with Rhodes's wishes . . . After all, business is business," Harris says. However, all agreed with Rhodes and there was a little chaff about his idealistic touch. Everything was now signed. The lawyers were finished and Rhodes said, casually: "All right, you will get the stones to-morrow when payment is made. They will be here in the de Beers office. Brink will take care of them for you. . . . Come along, Brink, put them away . . . and you understand, delivery to-morrow morning against payment.

"For a moment every one was happy. Then Rhodes strolled across the room to speak to Brink from the head of the long trough where the diamonds lay grouped on their white paper. A wooden bucket was at the other end of the trough, and as Rhodes told Brink to put them away, he raised the head of the teak trough and shot the whole in a cataract into the bucket. He did it with the most natural movement, just as indifferently as one would toss an old newspaper on to the table. He did not say a word to those round him; was seemingly quite unconscious of what he had done and strolled out of the room without showing any sign of what had happened.

"Believe me, the faces of our people were a treat . . . the whole work of sorting was wiped out in one second and for six or eight months the entire output was kept off the market as surely as if it had been locked in the de Beers' safe. Someone said, 'My God, we have not a word in the contract about the grading or classifying. We just bought the output. . . .' Then someone else said, 'How the Christian beat the Jews!' and there was a roar of laughter such as you would only get from a gathering of Jews, who can, after all, enjoy a story at their own expense. And mind you, Rhodes was perfectly right. Our stones were locked up, but when we could sell them we realised a much better price than we could possibly have done at the time. His judgment was completely justified."

Rhodes was the master of diamonds and the diamond men. He understood time in relation to both, for here it was computable in pounds sterling, in dollars and cents—in carats.

But when he had gone to see Kruger in Pretoria soon after he had his concession from Lobengula, he showed no understanding of time—so eager was he to turn to-day into to-morrow that he lost to-morrow. He appeared to see the President on a Saturday morning. The President said his burghers were in town for Nagmaal. He always reserved the Saturday of Nagmaal week for his burghers. And Sunday?—he did no business on Sunday. Rhodes could wait till Monday or he could go.

"The old devil," Rhodes said to his companion. "I meant to work with him, but I'm not going on my knees to him. I've got my concession and he can do nothing." No one had asked Rhodes to go on his knees. Kruger had asked him to wait while he, Kruger, listened to the grievances of his burghers and prayed to God.

What is appropriate has much to do with the time element, and what is good at one time and in one place is bad in another place at another time. An example of this is the story of Kruger once opening a new synagogue "in the name of Jesus Christ." It was things like this that infuriated Rhodes—the fact that he had been hindered throughout his career, not by a great nation, but by an uneducated farmer. He felt to the end that "Kruger wasn't a fit opponent for him." That he was a fool, not worth powder and shot. Kruger, "the old devil," could go to hell because he chose to keep the Sabbath. The war—years later—could go to hell. Because they would not run it his way, Rhodes proceeded to ignore the war, by-passing it as he commuted between Rhodesia and London in this period of conspicuous eclipse, as he had commuted between Kimberley and Oxford in the days when his star was rising.

Someone at this time said that the best thing to do about Rhodes is to ignore him. "Ignore him!" Edmund Garrett said. "As well ignore Table Mountain ... you just try and ignore him."

The war dragged on. Rhodes continued to ignore it. But he was getting sicker and sicker. In February, 1902, he was on his way back to Africa for the last time, and though he may not have known that, he knew his end was near. He sat for hours by himself thinking. Jameson and Fitzpatrick were on the boat with him. "You'll see it, and I won't," was Rhodes's refrain. His one relaxation was bridge. He asked for a book only once. Fitzpatrick gave him Lincoln's *Plan of Reconstruction.* After a while, he put it down and said, "I've enough to do thinking of our plan of reconstruction without bothering about his." The heat worried him. In the tropics he could not sleep and breathed only with difficulty. A bed was made up for him on the chart-room table and all the portholes were left open. Then he caught a bad cold. . While this was still on him, he was thrown from the table in a storm and so badly bruised that he could not move for days. But he kept giving directions to his friends. He kept saying what he had done and not done. He said, "I ought to have told Schreiner." He said, "You must get along with the Dutch. . . . They are fine people . . . we are all South Africans." These were instructions for after the war. He said, "You've got to remember this: it's no good giving the public an idea. You've got to hit them over the head with it, and keep on hitting." Hitting. . . . What ideas were hitting Rhodes now in his illness and despair?

Bigelow had described Kruger as unique, but he was not that; he was merely great. Rhodes was great and unique. There was no one to take his place and he knew it. He had lived less than six hundred months. His work was not done; scarcely, in his own mind, begun. God was a doubtful factor, and though he too had dead friends, he had no certainty of meeting them. He was worried about his work, about his name. "Do you think they'll change its name?" Rhodesia must stay on the map. His name must live for four thousand years. He must be buried with a savage king, with the heroes who had died with Wilson. His wills, the half-dozen he made, must be political documents.

What memories came back? Did he think of Lawley, his friend, turning on him once when he lost his temper and saying, "Look here, Mr. Rhodes, it's no use squeaking at me like a bloody rabbit, because I'm not frightened of you." Did he think of how he, suddenly losing his temper with the portrait of himself that hung in the board-room of de Beers', slashed it with the knife he was playing with? Did he think of the Matabele, his children who called him "the separator of the fighting bulls," or of Lobengula? Did he think of his ventures, his friends, his servants, his successes and failures? Did he think of Barney Barnato's suicide, of the way he himself had been black-balled at the Travellers Club in London? Did he remember that Simon Bolïvar, who also had had a country named after him, had died when he was only forty-seven?

Did he think of women? For it was a woman who, against his doctor's advice, had brought him back to Africa—a princess. This was a fine thing for the great Rhodes, the misogynist, to find himself caught up in a scandal with a part-worn Polish adventuress! It was the kind of joke that the gods reserve for men like Rhodes. First they arm them with lightning, then they garnish them with a tubercle, and finally finish them with a Radziwill. It would seem that only a woman can save a man from women, but Rhodes, the master of paradox and irony, who had laid so many trap lines for others, had forgotten that he too could be trapped. Rhodes, who so well knew the weaknesses of others, had ignored his own. Despising women, he had underestimated them; not perhaps their achievements, but the trouble they could cause if scorned—or even if they are not scorned.

Rhodes, once he had got out of Kimberley, had spent his time in Cape Town, Bulawayo, London. There was money to be raised for his Cape-to-Cairo railway. Two million pounds—three million pounds. There were troubles, arguments with shareholders; letters and telegrams by the hundred the minute he went away. When he came back and faced them, he could do what he liked with his shareholders. He was a sick man, very sick. In London they told him he would live longer if he stayed there quietly. There was no time to stay quiet. His heart was pumping purple blood into his inflated cheeks. Sometimes it faltered, all but stopped, and then pumped again madly. His lungs were failing. A big man mentally and physically, he had overdriven himself all his life. He knew no other way of living, even if to live this way was to hasten death. Even death, for him, must come fast if it must come. Then, as if the Fates wished to hurry on the final act, he found himself involved in a forgery case and decided to return to the Cape to give evidence against the Princess Radziwill, whom he had befriended and who in return had forged bills in his name. It fitted into the ironic pattern of Africa, that it should be a woman who should betray Rhodes, who had had so little to do with women. He did not care for women. "I don't want them always fussing about," he said. Once, when he dined at the Palace, Queen Victoria asked him if he were a woman-hater. "How can I hate a sex to which Your Majesty belongs?" was his tactful answer. She then said, "What are you engaged on at present, Mr. Rhodes?"

"I am doing my best to enlarge Your Majesty's dominions."

Large, enlarge, big, bigger, biggest—always the same theme song.

Rhodes was the most eligible bachelor in the world, and women knew it. They wrote from all over the world offering themselves and saying how much better off he would be married. They even wrote when they were married themselves. They all wanted to mother him, to be his mistress, his friend, and perhaps to share the pinnacle that he climbed.

One of his secretaries said: "As regards Rhodes's relations with women, he led an absolutely innocent, open, and simple life. I knew exactly what he did and where he was. He seldom went to private parties, probably not more than twice in twelve months. There were few nights in which he had not guests for dinner. After dinner, he invariably played bridge until he felt sleepy and usually left us abruptly for his room."

But despite his dislike of women, one of them, this middle-aged Polish princess with remnants of a haggard beauty, was to plague him. She had met him by arranging to travel to South Africa on the same ship and interesting him in her conversation. She often came to Groot Schuur to see him and occasionally acted as his hostess there. After stating alternatively that she was his mistress, or his fiancée and was going to marry him, she forged his name on a cheque for twenty-nine thousand pounds.

Avoiding women all his life, he could not avoid the Princess. Knowing nothing of women, his end was accelerated by this adventuress.

CHAPTER FOUR

THE SCHOLARS

TIME, that Rhodes had raced so long, was catching up with him, but he would go down fighting. Again in his mind, he went over the things he had done . . . his diamond mines, the northern empire that had his name, which he had built upon the rings that circled the virgin fingers of the world's betrothed . . . the thing of cool beauty that he had made of his house . . . his scholarships which, drawing the right kind of men together, would eventually form the élite which he believed so strongly should rule the world.

Rhodes had chosen his scholars rather oddly. "Thirty per cent for literary and scholastic attainments; twenty per cent for fondness of and success in manly outdoor sports, such as cricket, football, and the like; thirty per cent for qualities of manhood, truth, courage, devotion to duty, sympathy for and protection of the weak, unselfishness and fellowship; twenty per cent for the exhibition during school days of moral force of character and of instincts to lead and to take an interest in his schoolmates."

"It is ridiculous," he said, "to lose one's ideas by death." These Rhodes scholarships were another means of carrying on his ideas after death, or he thought they were.

Rhodes assigned these scholarships to each state and colony and added five to Germany after meeting the Kaiser. The Kaiser was to choose them personally. Oddly though he had thought much about the United States, neither Rhodes nor his attorneys knew that there were more than the original thirteen states in the Union, with the result that the United States of America has more Rhodes scholars than all the British Dominions put together. This ignorance has led to the charge that Rhodes was attempting to regain the United States through his scholars.

It was brought up again recently. Here is the story as reported by the New York *Herald Tribune:*

Dr. Frank Aydelotte, director of the Institute for Advanced Study at Princeton, New Jersey, and American Secretary for Rhodes trustees since 1918, defended yesterday the record made by American Rhodes scholars and charged that George Sylvester Viereck, convicted Nazi propagandist and agent, published an attack in 1916 against them similar to the recent "exposure" by the *Chicago Tribune*, which scented a plot against the United States by Rhodes scholars.

In a stinging denunciation of the *Tribune* and Representative Clare Hoffman, Republican, of Michigan, Dr. Aydelotte also decorticated the *Tribune* and Mr. Hoffman for opposing "the deepest intellectual and spiritual interests of our civilisation."

Dr. Aydelotte, moreover, denied the *Tribune* charge that Rhodes scholars organised into a secret society to tear up the Declaration of Independence and make America a British colony.

Concerning Viereck, under sentence of one to five years in prison on conviction of having violated the foreign agents' registration act, Dr. Aydelotte said the precursor of the *Tribune* attack on Rhodes scholars appeared in a publication known as *The Fatherland* which the German agent put out during the World War.

The purpose of the journal, according to Dr. Aydelotte, was avowedly to fan pro-German sentiment in the United States and was bitterly anti-British and anti-French. *The Fatherland* attack on Americans who studied at Oxford University as Rhodes scholars appeared in the edition of March 22, 1916.

Dr. Aydelotte said the article was entitled "The Great Conspiracy" and was described by Viereck as the most important piece it had been his privilege to publish.

"It exposed 'The Cecil Rhodes conspiracy against the United States,' using the same misstatements which have lately been repeated by the *Chicago Tribune*," Dr. Aydelotte continued.

He contended that just as the *Tribune* dragged in Wendell L. Wilkie, Viereck's publication charged that many prominent persons in public life, including the late Dr. Charles Eliot, former president of Harvard University, "had likewise been bought with Rhodes's money."

The *Tribune* accused former Rhodes scholars of acting in

concert with "Eastern admirers of royalty," "international bankers," and Mr. Wilkie for cooking up a grandiose plot to destroy American independence.

Dr. Aydelotte observed that "the *Chicago Tribune*, however, goes a little further than *The Fatherland*. The *Tribune* assailed all old Oxonians, whether Rhodes scholars or not," said Dr. Aydelotte, and it made the statement that any man who had himself educated in a foreign country, "no matter what country it was, must fall under suspicion with the Rhodes scholars."

By such an assertion, Dr. Aydelotte said, "the *Tribune* thus placed under suspicion several signers of the Declaration of Independence and a long line of distinguished American scholars and divines" who in the last hundred and fifty years have studied in European countries, Canada and in Latin-America.

Dr. Aydelotte characterised as "most outrageous" the fact that Mr. Hoffman and the *Tribune* in discussing the war record of the Rhodes scholars "have completely ignored" about two hundred and fifty who are in the armed forces. He pointed out that since there are fewer than three hundred and fifty former Rhodes scholars of military age, "this record is one which could hardly be matched by any similar group."

Summing up, Dr. Aydelotte said the Rhodes scholarships have stimulated establishment of similar plans by American philanthropists to bring Englishmen here to study. The Rhodes scholarships, he continued, also resulted in the establishment of other similar foundations for international study, "which have made an immense contribution to American life."

The *Chicago Tribune* and Mr. Hoffman, by assailing the Rhodes Scholarships and similar foundations, Dr. Aydelotte concludes, "treat with cynical contempt the effort for international understanding which through the elimination of war" will enable Americans to preserve the American way of life and ideals.

This accusation and defence are interesting in that they show the influence of the past on the present and illustrate two trends of thought: those of the internationalist who wants free exchange of ideas and of the nationalist who believes in isolation and fears the contamination of the outer world.

The characteristics Rhodes demanded from his scholars were

ones that he did not possess himself, and perhaps in consequence admired. Sports bored him, he was no good at them. He had not been a leader at school and took little interest in other people's affairs. That the Rhodes scholars have done so little except become admirable husbands and fathers of families shows how little Rhodes really understood the qualities required for greatness in others. Abnormal himself, he admired the normal. Almost, the requirements of a Rhodes scholar epitomize that which is most normal, admirable, and dull. Or did Rhodes really believe in these bourgeois virtues, which he once described as "smugness, brutality, unctuous rectitude, and tact?" There remains only the doubtful possibility that the scheme might have been more deeply laid. Granted Rhodes's hypothesis of a world led by a secret society controlling all the wealth, these scholars might have fitted into it as administrators—as buffers between the masses and the controlling secret body. They would have been the managers of a "Managerial Revolutionary Era" and the screen behind which the great international industrialists and financiers operated.

One thing remains certain, it is constantly reiterated and once more proved by his scholarships that apart from Africa, Rhodes's idea was the restoration of the Anglo-Saxon unity destroyed by the schism of the eighteenth century, and the foundation of "so great a power as hereafter to render wars impossible."

In these days of his, vision after vision must have come to him.

Speaking of the railway bridge that was to span the Zambesi on his Cape-to-Cairo line, a line that is not yet completed, he asked his engineers if the spray from the falls would splash the train. He said, "I want it to splash the train."

Speaking of the trees that lined the three-mile avenue to Government House in Bulawayo, he said, "You say I shall not live to see the trees grow. I tell you that, in imagination, I already see people passing and repassing under their shade."

"Get that avenue through," he said when he was dying, "we have got to fulfil our promise to give shade to the nursemaids in the afternoon."

Probably Rhodes did not give a damn about the nursemaids. But he cared about the trees, and about the children playing under them, about the thoughts they would think beneath the canopy of leaves—thoughts of the greatness of Rhodesia and of Rhodes himself. Those were special babies—the first batch of blue-eyed, tow-haired little pioneers and pioneeresses to be born north of the Limpopo—children of other men's bodies, they were the children of his mind.

Rhodes thought of himself, of his acts, and of himself again. These hours were a summing-up, the casting of his final balance sheet, a last effort to prove to himself and to others that he was not in the psychological red. "They ask you to believe that I am the most dreadful man in the whole country—what have they done for you? . . . Sit down and think that the man whom they denounce so vehemently has done more for you, in a practical way, than any one else in South Africa." The "they" in this case were the Bond leaders with whom he had broken, but it was also the psychological "they" of all men—the outside forces, the people who do not understand.

Compare this questioning of the spirit with Kruger's certainty that he had done right. Kruger had done right according to his lights, but Rhodes was not sure he had. He craved authority. He must be told he had done right. He must have testaments to prove himself right, must have countries named after him, scholarships in his name, avenues of trees, a great house, a great tomb, streets in his towns where a full span of oxen could wheel, where the drivers, as they clapped their whips and shouted at the oxen, would think of Rhodes and the convenience he had given them. He must if he could become God. First rich, then powerful then all-powerful. That had been his pattern. "I am Rhodes"—not even Cecil John Rhodes. There was no "Tell the gentleman I was a shepherd" here, and no understanding of the man who, like Kruger, could speak that way. Nor was there in his heart any understanding of why he had failed, or why all must fail, who, in the pageant of man's progress, tamper even benevolently with destiny, playing both ends against the middle.

When Rhodes got off the boat at Cape Town, he was so changed as to be almost unrecognisable to his friends. His face was bloated, his hair grey and wild, his eyes protuberant and strained, his skin a livid purple.

At this time his gait is clumsier, his voice breaks more often into a falsetto. He is passionate, furious. He stands like a lion turning at bay and then suddenly is humble and ashamed; and each day he is more sick. The jackals of his own race, who had once followed him so slavishly to profit from his kills, now scoff at him.

Kruger was also and aptly compared to a lion. But though he was in exile, he still had the whole-hearted support of his people. The Boers, who were now in 1902 going down, were united against a common foe and united in their belief in God and the justice of their cause, whereas Rhodes, having regained at least some of his prestige, was doubted by all but his most fanatical followers.

Rhodes seemed like an octopus to Kruger. Wherever he turned, Rhodes had thrown out a tentacle. Rhodes always forestalled him, Rhodes always outsmarted him.

Rhodes saw himself as the wedge which would crack open the world, exposing it to Anglo-Saxon domination. There can be no question about Rhodes's gifts or his greatness. He believed that he would be remembered for four thousand years, so great was his confidence in himself and his mission.

Sir Percy Fitzpatrick saw Rhodes at a bazaar in the Town Hall at Wynberg when he had first been elected to Parliament. He says: "He was extremely good-looking in an unconscious way. He was tall, looking easily over the heads of those about him. Within a few minutes—seconds, it seemed to me—the whole room appeared to have gone crazy. It was disgusting . . . elderly ladies who should have known better, grown-up girls who should have had more dignity, little flipper-flappers and kids who were without shame, swarmed round him. They mobbed him. It made one's gorge rise. . . ."

A few years later Sir Percy was working with Rhodes. It was the same with every one. He exerted a most extraordinary charm over most people. Barney Barnato said, "He tied me up as he ties up everybody. You can't resist him. You have to go with him." He could charm the very birds down from the trees, charm his enemies into his own personal circle, charm his friends into a devotion that went beyond devotion into love and hero worship. Brains, wealth, looks, power—he had them all. Men were ready to die for him. Women in multitudes were ready to be loved by him, importuning him. Olive Schreiner, the author of *The Story of an African Farm*, was among those said to have pursued him, and then, failing to attract him, wrote a book called *Trooper Peter Halket of Mashonaland*, a venomous attack on the actions of Rhodes in Matabeleland. She told how this monster Rhodes had crushed the noble savage; how the poor natives had been staked to anthills and otherwise tortured; and how this land-grabber had defeated the Will of God.

So the end of Rhodes's life was pestered by two women: one writing a novel in which he appeared as the villain, the other forging the name he had refused to give her.

Rhodes was angry at dying—"So much to do, so little done." His anger at the woman who had brought him back, at the scandal that linked their names, was now switched to anger against Time itself and the woman became the lesser evil, the instrument of Time that was hastening his end. Twenty-nine thousand pounds was nothing to him—nothing was anything if only he could get more time. The woman was prosecuted, convicted, sentenced, and finally, after her release, wrote a book about Rhodes and her life with him. By that time Rhodes was dead. But now, at this instant, he was living—a dying man, at Muizenberg in a little tin-roofed cottage. Sitting up in bed here he gave his evidence about the forgeries.

Worshipped by his followers, they could do nothing for him now. One of them, Marshall Hole, says, "I revelled in the idea that I was engaged in his work and felt that for him I would go through fire and water." These men, who thought of him as the Master, waited anxiously all over Africa for news of his health, and other men, those who hated him, waited too.

Aware of what his end would be—and how could he be unaware of it?—Rhodes wrote to his friend, "At any rate, Jameson, death from the heart is clean and quick. There's nothing repulsive about it. It's a clean death, isn't it?"

Like all men, he wanted a quick and easy death, almost demanded it as a right. Surely a man who had laboured so hard should be entitled to a peaceful end; surely a rich man should be able to buy it.

Death is a subject about which we are all supremely ignorant. We only know that we all must die; that dying is the final experience of life, but one of which there can be no record. Some men die hard and some easily. Some die at peace, feeling their work is ended; others fight death off, wrestling with it; and Rhodes was one of these. He was not like Kruger, who waited for his end patiently, more than ready to welcome it. Was not his wife waiting for him? His old Tant' Sann whom he called Ouma? Were not his old friends? Was not God Himself? In his mind Kruger did not fear meeting God. He felt that he had done his best. He had lived nine hundred and forty-eight-odd months —nearly the thousand that is man's span. He had left a vast progeny. He had done enough, and he was tired. Others would take up the plough that he laid down.

Now that Rhodes was really dying and he knew it, did he think of Lobengula's death?—the Lobengula he had robbed and broken? Did he think of anything when he walked from room to room in his great white house? It was hot at the Cape that summer—the hottest summer they had had for years. The hydrangeas he had planted on the mountain behind his home hung their great greenish heads, the leaves on the tall oaks wilted under the burning sun. There was no breeze from the Atlantic on the west—none from the Indian Ocean on the east. The shimmering glare of the mirage was all that met his tortured eyes. He unbuttoned his clothes, he kept drying the sweat from his forehead, he kept running his hands through his hair as he fought for breath. Lying down he could not breathe, so he sat up. Then he could not breathe sitting up. Standing by the window, it was a little better. But how long could a man stand at a window and stare at Africa, at the gardens he had made, at the trees he had planted, at the wild beasts he had roaming in his enclosures?

Through the trees that he had had trimmed, he could see the mountains. How hard and stark they were! How little they had changed in a hundred thousand years! How little they would change! Then he was taken to his cottage on the shore. If there were a breeze at all, there would be one here. If only there would be a breeze that would blow air into him, into lungs that could not draw it in for themselves! But there was no air and it was hot, hotter than ever. Ice was packed above the ceiling of his room. A boy pulled at a punkah all day. Its creak sent him nearly crazy, and all it did was to move the stagnant air from one place to another. Each day his driver got the horses ready to drive him to his farm in the Drakenstein Mountains. It might be better there.

But Rhodes wanted the cold. Summer at the Cape was winter in England. He would go to England—get out of the sunshine. He was a Nordic, he needed snow and rain and cold. If only he could be cold! If only he could be under the leaden sky of his native land again! Perhaps, too, he wanted to die at home. A man, like a beast, tends to drift back to his native place when his end is near. Sentiment, a sense of race, or a desire to see and smell the things he smelled and saw as a child.

A cabin was got ready for him. It was equipped with electric fans, oxygen, and special refrigerating pipes. Nothing was too good for Rhodes.

But on the day he was to have left, he died.

His last words were, "Turn me over, Jack." They had the simplicity of Nelson's "Kiss me, Hardy." It was April 22, 1902, and the Boer War had only a month to go. Eight men and no women were with him when he died.

In his last will, Rhodes said, "I admire the grandeur and loneliness of the Matopos and therefore I desire to be buried in the Matopos on the hill I used to visit and called ' the View of the World,' in a square to be cut in the rock on the top of the hill, covered with a plain brass plate with these words thereon, ' Here lie the remains of Cecil John Rhodes.' " No date, no place of birth or death, the names of no parents. He was to lie apart, separate from mankind; a god, begotten of no one, begetting no one, cognisant of nothing but empire, at once the master and the slave of his idea.

Escorted by mounted police, his body, covered with an old battle-scarred Union Jack, was taken to the Houses of Parliament in Cape Town, where it lay for a day and a night. The Archbishop of Cape Town preached a funeral service and took as his text: "Know ye not that there is a prince and a great man fallen this day in Israel."

A prince and a great man, but now no greater than other dead men, a man equalised by death in which all men are equal.

His body went North on the maiden trip of the new train he

had ordered. It was draped in black and purple. The coffin was placed in the old de Beers special carriage that he always used. At stations and sidings, two Cape police troopers stood on guard with arms reversed, while a bugler sounded the "Last Post" and crowds brought wreaths to lay upon the catafalque.

A pilot train preceded the Rhodes Special, an armoured train accompanied it, flooding the night with searchlights, for it was still war.

In Rhodesia, the coffin was put on a gun carriage drawn by twelve black oxen. The Matabele swarmed like bees over the wild hills where M'limo's oracle had lived—the Matopos where their great chief Moselikatze lay buried, looking with eyeless sockets to the north.

This new chief was to lie near him, the white chief whom they had named the "separator of the fighting bulls," their conqueror and their saviour. "Our father is dead . . . the king is dead . . . Ulodzi is dead." And then for the first time, they gave a white man the royal salute . . . "Bayete!—Bayete!"—the salute of the Zulu kings, of Dingaan and T'Chaka, of Cetywayo, of Moselikatze—and now of Rhodes. Rhodes had joined the kings. He had been buried like a king. His acts alone remained, and the war that he had said would never come went on.

There is a certain interest in this necrophilic symbolism—in the idea of a dead man carried in his own triumphal car—in Rhodes's body being drawn to its last mountain resting-place by a span of black oxen like the bodies of the native kings who had preceded him. It seems to show man's desire for continuity, and is psychologically related to Hitler's dictating his terms to a beaten France in the historic railway carriage at Compiègne in which the Armistice of 1918 had been signed. Another parallel is the general's charger led, at a military funeral, saddled, with his master's boots reversed in the stirrups. Unknowing, modernity turns back to the unknown past for its symbols and taboos when facing the unalterable facts of life—birth, marriage, and death. Even Rhodes had to be buried like a savage chieftain in a chieftain's burial place. What chord was struck in his heart when he recognised this spot as his last resting place? What made him wish to lie in a cave hewn from virgin rock, sealed with brass, in this wild, tumbled playground of the Gods? It was an odd choice for a mining magnate, a super-businessman, or would have been if he had ever seen himself as that. Flags, soldiers, gun carriages, and sacrificial oxen—sacrificial, even if they were not sacrificed. His avenues of trees that, in principle, were sacred groves. His belief in luck and lucky men. It is "good to have a minister with luck," he told the people of the Cape when speaking of himself.

Lucky Rhodes, unlucky Rhodes. *Happy? Good God, no!* . . . His words come back, they still echo in Africa and over the world. The stone of his personality which he flung so whole-heartedly into the pool of world politics, still sends out its rippling circles. Never was there a more practical man, never one with more understanding of the implacable gods who lived in the peaks of Africa. "My church," he told a bishop once, "is up the mountain" —and then his "fifty per cent chance that God exists." He meant a fifty per cent chance that Paul Kruger's personal God existed. Rhodes's gods were mountain gods. Who denies that they exist? But they are dangerous. They are the devils that tempt men from high places.

It has been said that modern history begins with the American and French Revolutions. Seen in terms of fallen kings, of mass citizen armies, of industrial progress and the slow liberation of the masses, this is true, and the lives of Paul Kruger, Cecil Rhodes, and Lobengula were lived out in the later stages of this period of change and expansion.

Kruger was born in 1825. In 1836, the first overland contacts with the Pacific Coast were made in America. In 1835, England abolished slavery. In 1861 the American Civil War took place. In 1870, the Suez Canal was opened and Germany, defeating France, became a great power. In 1897, Queen Victoria had her Diamond Jubilee. In 1900, there was the great exhibition in Paris.

The seventies were the period of expansion, of discovery, of ruthless enterprise. The humanitarians of the eighteenth century had given way to the common-sense materialists. Charles Darwin had cracked the nut of religious orthodoxy. The peasants, attracted from their farms, were breeding workers like flies, and dying like flies in the new centres of industry. Railroads were creeping over continents—arteries that fed the rich blood of raw materials into the hungry hearts of factories, and all over the world new thoughts were entering men's heads. The principle of aristocracy had begun to break down and was merging into plutocracy on the one hand, and greater literacy and an increased franchise were giving the working masses political power on the other. These two ideas of privilege without aristocratic responsibility, and government of the people, by the people, are the roots of the troubles which rend the world to-day. From them stem fascism, communism, democracy, and socialism.

As the Spanish War, in our time, was a microcosm of the present war, Rhodes's aggressions were a microcosm of the modern wars for empire—that is, for raw products and markets of the previous but recent era.

De Tocqueville said, "It is not the mechanism of laws that produces great events but the inner spirit of government." And the inner spirit which animated Rhodes, and the England of his time, was that of fascist imperialism. He believed, as some believe to-day, that the world should be rebuilt by "enterprising men who have freedom of action, not by politicians; by the establishment of governments with the integrity to deserve the respect of the intelligent minority and strength to command the obedience of the multitude."

Rhodes made money to enter politics and used politics to increase his power. That Rhodes was relatively benevolent changes nothing in principle. His aim was to build up a machine, and such a machine, once built up, could easily fall into evil hands. On no basis could Rhodes be called democratic. Nor could he, on any basis, be considered aristocratic. He despised the idle, was, in essence, a man who believed in living dangerously and by direct action. His beliefs made it impossible for him to understand Paul Kruger, who was essentially democratic, for though many of his actions were arbitrary and autocratic, he was always ready to resign his position. His treatment of the natives was harsh, but the British were little better in this respect, and the Boers had at least the justification of their religious beliefs—to them, the Kaffirs were the children of Ham and service was their destiny. A backward, religious, democratic people, the Boers were defeated by the British industrial reactionaries, and progress was forced on the unwilling free republics.

The main interest of the past is its bearing on the present, and the future. Historically, the Anglo-Boer War, the Matabele War, and the Kaffir wars of the last century are only yesterday. Historically, Rhodes and Kruger are our own contemporaries. Many men are still living who remember them. Highlighted by the letters, reminiscences, and despatches of those who knew them, but with the rancours of immediacy toned by time, the perspective and the pattern, not only of their acts, but of the consequences of their acts, is now apparent.

Contemporary history can legitimately be considered to have begun with the rise of Germany, with the new development of finance, and the final rush to achieve empire before it was too late, as the earlier phase can be said to stem from the American Revolution.

Rhodes, in his time, was not a fascist, because the term is relatively new, but his own contemporary and friend, John Hays Hammond, writing later, calls him one. Spengler considered him "fascist," and his methods were, to some extent at least, those of Mussolini and Hitler. Rhodes's pioneers were, to all intents and purposes, black shirts; his leaders operated outside the law. He intimidated with threats of force, he bought men and parties, he spoke of Nordic superiority. He believed in a Saxon élite and tried to found one with his Rhodes scholars. Strange accidents happened to those who opposed him, and if documents were not falsified at his instigation, they were at least distorted to suit his convenience. He understood the modern use of money as power, and the cartel as a means of industrial control. He thought of the masses as labour, and promoted class legislation based on colour. He created, not a Reich that would last a thousand years, but a name which he said would be remembered for forty centuries. He was a man inspired, one whom others delight to follow. He was in fact a leader, a man on a white horse, a dictator —and still a dictator, though his aims were good. He was without belief in the democratic process of secret ballot. A man outstanding in his time and breed and representative of both his time and breed. At once the first and last perfect specimen of a type of Englishman, who, reaching his ultimate development in him, died, because at heart the English are not capable of fascism, and instead of going on from there, shied away from it.

It seems likely that the present fascist and communistic phase of human development was essential to progress; that finally, in a hundred years' time, the period which began in 1776 and still continues will be seen as the world revolution and world civil war, which occupied the time between two great phases of civilisation —the division between the immense period of scarcity when we were dependent on slave labour and the coming period of plenty when the machine tool and science will replace much of the labour and set men free.

Rhodes is understood better to-day because of Hitler, who has exaggerated his every act. And Hitler is more easily understood because Rhodes preceded him. Despite the misery Hitler has caused, in five hundred years even Hitler may be seen as the cathartic, which, though it has all but destroyed civilisation, yet succeeded in saving it. Only by the black can the white be highlighted. Only by the anti-Christ is Christ proven. Only by the anti-social act is the social act appreciated. Rhodes believed in a fifty per cent chance of God. Hitler destroyed God by removing the balance of hope that Rhodes had left the world. Rhodes wanted to know who voted against him so that he could bribe them. Hitler wished to know so that he could destroy them. Certain men are the instruments of history, but to achieve anything they must fit into that history. There have been a thousand Rhodeses, a thousand Hitlers, but for success there must be a niche into which they can fit. They are, as it were, super-contemporaries, perfect pegs for the perfect holes which circumstances prepares for them.

Paul Kruger, too, was a perfect example of his time and people. And if Rhodes is described as an early fascist, Kruger could be described as an early democrat. Neither fits into our present definition except as approximations, but their struggle was in effect a war between two ideals, two ways of life—the material and the spiritual. Both Rhodes and Kruger failed. Yet, oddly to-day, long after their deaths, both have succeeded. Rhodes's dream of a United South Africa may soon come true. The Rhodesias and West Africa seem likely to enter the Union, and his hope for closer relations between the United States and the British Empire is an accomplished fact. But that the Empire, since his time, would change into a Commonwealth was something Rhodes did not foresee.

Kruger's dream of an Africa for the Afrikaaners has come true. The Union is a free Dominion and the Uitlander element which caused him so much trouble has been absorbed, at least politically.

The ends of these two men are achieved, though not in the manner that they envisaged. They both died sadly, Kruger alone in Switzerland, Rhodes in Africa with "so much to do, so little done"—and yet their dreams went on.

Purged of Rhodes's imperialism, purged of Kruger's isolation, the dreams themselves, as ideas, were *greater* than those who conceived them. Time was against these three—Kruger, Lobengula, and Cecil Rhodes—only Lobengula lived and died in vain.

But when Rhodes, the prince and great man, fell in Israel, Paul Kruger, the last of them, was still alive.

CHAPTER FIVE

COMMANDO

THE BOERS knew that the relief of Mafeking meant that the end had come—though they still had forces in the field, all regular, co-ordinated resistance was at an end except in the Far North. They had only one hope—a change in the British Government—if they could only hold on till there was an election. While Rhodes was dealing with his pure-bred livestock, his interests; while he was forcing himself, trying to outrun Time, the Boers were hanging on to Time's coat-tails, fighting desperately for inconclusion, since conclusion, in their favour, had become impossible.

Sarel Eloff, the President's favourite grandson, was captured at Mafeking. Other members of the family were wounded. One at least was killed. It became obvious that the President must leave Pretoria. For a time he had the idea of leading his burghers himself in the Zoutpansberg, but he was too old to take the field again. On May 1, 1900, Lord Roberts began his march from Bloemfontein to Pretoria. On May 29, Kruger left his home and the wife to whom he had been married for fifty-four years. Accompanied by his doctor and his secretaries, the President went east towards the Portuguese border. A provisional government was established in a saloon carriage at Machadadorp, where he continued to direct operations and receive the commanders who came to see him. On June 5, he learned that Roberts had entered Pretoria. The enemy had now finally parted him from his wife. She was behind the lines. Undaunted, the old man telegraphed to his commanders: "We have resolved to fight to the end. Be faithful and fight in the name of the Lord, for those who flee and leave their positions or run away from commando are only fleeing straight to Saint Helena."

The cold of the Machadadorp High Veld drove the President on into the Low Country. His next stop was Waterval Onder, where he lived in a cottage. "Here," he said, "I spent the happiest two months since my departure from Pretoria."

With the news of Botha's reverse at Dalmanutha, another move was made, this time to Nelspruit. Lord Roberts now issued a proclamation stating the Transvaal to be annexed, and on September 3, Kruger countered it by a proclamation of his own, in which "he did hereby proclaim, in the name of the independent Republic, that the aforesaid proclamation is not recognised, but is by these presents declared null and void. The people of the South African Republic are, and remain free and independent people, and refuse to submit to British rule. . . ."

Meanwhile, the British troops were advancing on Nelspruit and to avoid capture, the President had to get out of the Transvaal. A council of delegates was called. It was resolved that the President should go to Europe to seek help for the Republics, and that in his absence, Schalk Burger, the Vice-President, was to take his place. On December 10, the following proclamation was published:

"Whereas the great age of his honour, the State President, renders it impossible for his honour to continue to accept the commandos; and whereas the Executive Raad is persuaded that his honour's invaluable services can still be profitably employed in the interests of the land and the people, the Executive Raad does hereby resolve to grant his honour a six months' furlough, in order to proceed to Europe and there promote our cause. . . ."

Kruger says: "I had to bid good-bye to the men who had stood beside me for so many years, and to leave my country and my people, my grey-haired wife, my children, my friends, and the little band of lion-hearted fighters who, surrounded as they were on every side, had now to make their way through an uninhabited district to the north of the Republic, there to recognise and recommence the struggle. But I had no choice. . . ."

On September 10, Kruger left Nelspruit. The first night he slept at Crocodile Poort, the next at Hector Spruit, then he went on to Komatipoort, where he got his last look at the Transvaal before he crossed the Lebombo Mountains, the range which, as boy and deputy field cornet with his father, he had declared to be the boundary between the South African Republic and Portuguese East Africa. His final weeks in his country had been spent in the great game reserve that he had created among the palm scrub, bush, reed beds, and great green-barked fever trees of the

Low Veld; spent in the last stronghold of the game, which as a young man he had seen spread in its thousands over the whole face of the land. An old lion himself, Paul Kruger was retreating through the lion country with hunters on his spoor. There had been opposition to the establishment of this game reserve or Wildtuin—wild town, as the Boers called it. The rinderpest had killed off not only domestic cattle but thousands of buck—wildebeest, kudu, and buffalo—and Kruger marked off this great game reserve, seeing that if nothing was done to prevent it, the game which had swarmed in the old days in Africa would be exterminated. Or, as he put it, "If I do not close this small portion of the Low Veld, our grandchildren will not know what a kudu, an eland, or a lion looks like...."

The establishment of this sanctuary in the troubled time between the Jameson Raid and the Boer War throws a further light on Paul Kruger's love of his land and all that lived in it. The objectors were those who had winter grazing farms in this area or who hoped to get them. The motion to set aside this land for a reserve was passed in the Raad, but the following day, Stoffel Tosen, member for Piet Retief, and some others, came to see the President about the matter.

Kruger's answer to them was that he would give any one who wanted a farm freehold if they would live there for just four months of the year—"from October to January." These are the fever months and his offer was not accepted. To have done so would have been suicidal.

Theoretically Lord Roberts was right when he said the war was over—with Kruger gone and the Free State and Transvaal annexed, it was over. But the Boers still fought on. The English who had laughed gaily at Kipling's poetic licence when he had written, "Fifty thousand horse and foot going to Table Bay," now found that Kipling, far from exaggerating, had been overconservative. Many times fifty thousand were going to be required before the end.

The war was over. But it did not stop. It was being continued "in the mountains" as Smuts had said it would be. The loss of the capital, which might have shocked an industrialised nation into submission, had small effect upon the Boers. Pretoria was not Africa.

Johanna Brandt, describing the occupation of Pretoria by the British, says: "In perfect order but weary unto death, the British troops marched in. Thousands and thousands of soldiers in khaki, travel-stained, footsore and famished, sank to the ground at a given command in the open square facing Government Buildings. Some of them tried to eat the rations they had with them; others, too exhausted to eat, fell into a deep sleep. One old warrior, looking up into the face of the girl who stood above him, said, in a broken voice, ' Thank God the war is over.' She bent towards him and answered in a voice vibrant with passionate feeling, ' Tommy Atkins, the war has just begun.' "

And so it had. The guerrilla war of armed bands and commandos that was to astonish and infuriate the English for nearly two years more with its unorthodoxy, and that was, in the end, to make them change the composition of some of their own forces from "horse, guns, and foot" into irregular mounted infantry that operated with the same methods as the Boers. Infantry were useless against the Boers, who could always get away from them. Cavalry were equally useless because they were not much more mobile than the foot soldiers, and were trained to the use of steel—the sabre and the lance—on an enemy that was supposed to wait and allow itself to be charged. Their only firearms were single-shot carbines, and they had to use one man out of every four as a horse-holder when they dismounted to fire. They were, in addition, mounted on "chargers"—big horses that stood sixteen hands and over and needed twelve pounds of oats a day to keep them going. These magnificent animals were absolutely unable to forage for themselves even when there was grass in abundance. Conan Doyle, in his history of the war, says: "A battery which turned out its horses to graze found that the puzzled creatures simply galloped about the plain and could only be reassembled by blowing the call that they associated with feeding, when they rushed back and waited in the lines for their nosebags to be put on . . . It was no uncommon sight to see a trooper, not only walking to ease his horse, but carrying part of his monstrous weight of saddle gear." In discussing the lessons of the war he says: "There is one change that must be effected. That is to relieve the cavalry horse of the seven stone (98 pounds) extra weight which is carried and which brings the creature on the field of battle too weary for his work. . . . It is not an exaggeration to say that the Boer War was prolonged for months by this one circumstance, for we should certainly have cut off the Boer retreat and captured their guns, had our horses not been handicapped so severely."

The Boers now, by the pattern of the logistics they had evolved, were enabled to trade space for time in a terrible game of tag, while they waited for the British Government to fall. If there were a change of government, the British, they felt, would give up the war. It was unpopular with many people. So the Boers fought on, living on food they captured, fighting with captured rifles and ammunition, and riding captured horses.

There were three phases in the Boer War. The first was a series of Boer victories that ended with what the British called "Black Week" and the battle of Colenso on December 15, 1899.

The second phase was a series of British moves under Lord Roberts and Kitchener which defeated the Boers and ended with the capture of Pretoria on June 5, 1900.

The third phase was one of guerrilla warfare which lasted till May 31, 1902.

At the outbreak of war on October 12, 1899, the British had only about twenty-five thousand men in South Africa, and the Boers had some sixty thousand—had they been able to place every man in the field at once. They were, in addition, highly specialised soldiers for this kind of warfare and had some excellent heavy artillery. Under a general more vigorous than Joubert, they should have driven the English out of the country.

Joubert's plan—good enough, if he had not stopped to invest Ladysmith—was to drive through Natal and capture Durban. He succeeded in brushing Sir George White aside at Laingsnek; suffered a setback at Elandslaagte and then won another battle at Nicholson's Nek. It was at this juncture that he failed, for he used his highly mobile troops to invest towns which should have been by-passed—Ladysmith, Mafeking, Kimberley.

Methuen now succeeded in driving the Boers back at Modder River, but Cronje won a victory at Magersfontein, frustrating Methuen's efforts to relieve Kimberley, and Buller, commanding in Natal, failed at Colenso to cross the Tugela and advance on Ladysmith.

A.P.　　　　　　　　　　　　　　　　　　　　　　　　　　　O

Phase two began when Buller was relieved of his command and Roberts took his place. Cronje, defeated at Paardeberg, was obliged to surrender. Bloemfontein was captured and the Free State annexed as the Orange River Colony. On May 17, Mafeking was relieved and the invasion of the Transvaal begun. On June 5, Pretoria was occupied, and on September 3, 1900, the Transvaal was once more annexed as a British colony.

This briefly recapitulates the actions which took place and the ebb and flow of the tide of war.

Kruger left the country at the beginning of the third and final phase of the struggle. He was now on his last errand, an errand of despair; he was seeking help in Europe. It was his third visit. He might come back; but as he left, he knew he would never see his Sanni again. Too weak to travel with him, she was also too weak to live without him. His wife, seventy-five years of his life, and his country, were all behind him—to the west behind the Lebombos. In front of him was Europe, his mission, and— there is little doubt that he knew this too—his end.

When Kruger got to Lourenço Marques he went to the house of Pott, the Consul General, without the public being aware that he was in the town. But almost on the first day of his arrival he ran into new trouble. The British Consul put every obstacle in his way. Pressure was exerted to prevent his receiving visits from the burghers who had come with him or from those who lived in the city. The Portuguese Governor immediately invited the President to stay in his house. When Kruger hesitated, the Governor threatened to use force. This was one of those "or else" invitations and it was in the Governor's house that he passed his seventy-fifth birthday with the burghers shouting their greetings to him from the street. It had been arranged that the President should sail for Europe on the *Hertzog*, the first ship that was leaving, but the Governor's invitation prevented this. The Governor could not—simply could not—let his guest leave so quickly and Kruger was forced to stay—almost a political prisoner in Government House, till the Queen of Holland offered him a passage on a Dutch warship. He still hoped faintly that in some way his wife would be able to go with him, but when the doctors said such a trip would be fatal, he gave in and sailed alone.

On October 21, he embarked on the *Gelderland*. She coaled at

Dares-Salaam, where the Germans offered him a banquet, which he declined. He did not want dinners in his honour, he said. He wanted military assistance—or, if that was impossible, moral support. After some rough weather, during which he was seasick for the first time, he landed at Marseilles on the twenty-second of November. In the Mediterranean, the *Gelderland* passed five British warships and the captain manned the ship, ready to fight if attacked. But after some manœuvres, the British men-of-war passed by. The docks at Marseilles were lined with cheering crowds. Doctor Leyds and Piet Grobler, members of the South African deputation who had preceded the President to Europe, came out in a longboat to meet him. There was the hope that if Germany, France, and Russia protested strongly enough and demanded the cessation of hostilities, England would agree to arbitration. No one expected any of these powers really to go to war on the Boers' behalf, but the delegation felt that diplomatic pressure from all three might help them.

The President was received everywhere with great enthusiasm, with speeches, with banquets, with shouts of "Vive les Boers! ... à bas les Anglais!" President Loubet sent an escort of steel breast-plated cuirassiers to meet him in Paris. One wonders what the old farmer soldier thought of the French dragoons with horsetails hanging from their helmets. War to him was a stern business, not a parade. Money poured in from all sources, but the French Government would not commit itself. It must be certain of Germany first.

Kruger then went to Belgium—more cheers, more ovations, more speeches. In replying to one of them, the President said, "he had not come to be festively received because of the sorrow in which his country was wrapped. They have burnt our farms," he said, "and driven our women and children into destitution. I hope God will not abandon the Boer nation. But if the Transvaal and the Free State are to lose their independence, it shall only happen when both nations have been annihilated with their women and children."

His next stop was at Cologne, in Germany, where he waited an invitation to an audience with the Kaiser. At last news came. The Kaiser "regretted that he was unable to see the Boer ambassador, as he was away on a hunting trip." Kruger's little jest about a man who was afraid of his grandmother had bitten deep.

While the President had been on his way to Europe, things had moved fast, just as they had when Lobengula had sent his emissaries to Queen Victoria and Rhodes had got in first. The treaties of friendship between the South African Republics and Germany had been broken by a new treaty, superimposed upon them, with England. Count Hatzfeld signed documents which he admitted constituted the abandonment of the Boers in return for certain rights in Africa and a free hand for the Germans in Samoa. The last treaty, like the last will, is the one that counts. Naturally, neither the Boers nor Samoans were consulted or even informed of these decisions.

By this act, Kruger was no longer an ambassador. He was an ex-president and an exile. He became seriously ill. He had counted on help through some Divine Providence, and the disappointment was too much for him. He had asked for bread and had been given a stone. He nearly died of pneumonia and would have, had he been a less strong man. For a while, he lived in Holland, but the news from Africa did not help his recovery. After the fall of Pretoria, the Boer generals—Botha, de la Rey, and de Wet—had reorganised their forces into guerrilla bands and were raiding the long British lines of communication, and inflicting much damage, but early in 1901, the British, seeing no end to this campaign, which had turned from a colonial campaign into a first-class war, organised a great drive across the Eastern Transvaal. On a front of seventy miles they cut a swath of devastation. This policy, calculated to shorten the war, lengthened it by a year—and its memory for fifty years. The bitterness of this African "Sherman" drive is still in the mouths of those who suffered it, and in those of their descendants. Even the *Times* history of the war, which certainly was not pro-Boer, said: "The policy of intimidation totally failed, as any one acquainted with the Dutch race and Dutch history could have foreseen. Applying the system against a white race defending their homes with bravery and resource, which has rightly won the admiration of the world, was the least happy of Roberts's inspirations. . . ."

The whole civilised world was upset about the struggle. Everyone offered suggestions. The Prime Minister of Canada, Sir Wilfrid Laurier, wrote Lord de Villiers urging him to influence the Boer leaders and end the war. Lord de Villiers answered, "I quite agree with you that President Kruger ought to have displayed more liberality towards the newcomers, but I fear that the exaggerated and distorted accounts which have been sent over of Boer oppression have affected your judgment in the same way as they have affected the judgment of the great majority of the British public people. The policy you say ' of admitting settlers simply to make Helots of them is intolerable.' I have travelled a good deal over the world and have nowhere seen a more flourishing people than these so-called Helots were before the war. They looked with utter contempt upon the President and his people and I quite agree with Lionel Phillips that the great majority of them did not care a fig for the franchise. . . . Chamberlain, of course, did not wish for war if he could attain his objects without war, but those objects were utterly inconsistent with the continued independence of the state. The negotiations should be read by the light of the historical events which preceded them, and if so read, I cannot understand how any impartial person, with any sense of justness or fairness, can support Chamberlain's action. A supreme tragedy is being enacted in Africa. The British people are accusing and punishing a whole people. Their minds have been poisoned by a venal press and by the lies which have been sown broadcast over the land at the bidding of a capitalistic clique, which owes all its wealth to the liberal gold-mining laws of the Republic. . . . But with these people—the Boers—the preservation of their independence is a sacred mission. It may be a foolish sentiment, but I cannot help respecting it. To us, it may seem foolish and indeed wicked to prolong a war which can have only one issue, but to them, submission, especially after the declarations of the British Government, probably appears to be nothing short of a crime."

Here in an historic document is one of the earliest mentions of a "capitalistic clique" which since then, and in so many forms, has appeared so often in the press.

Leaving Cologne, Kruger returned to Holland, where he dined with the Queen and thanked her for all that she had done for him. He then visited Amsterdam, where a solemn service was held in the principal church for the Boers. At The Hague, he caught cold and developed inflammation of the lungs, of which again had he been less rugged, he would have died. The man seemed unkillable, but only perhaps because his time had not yet come.

At Utrecht, where he stayed two months, he underwent an operation on both eyes; they had troubled and harried him for many years. From there he moved on to Hilversum, where for eight months he lived at the villa Casa Cara with his suite. While he was here, he visited many Dutch towns, paying particular attention to the churches in each—among them "the old church at Dordrecht where the Synod of 1618 to 1619 was held which exercised so great an influence upon the church to which I belonged. I also visited Kampen, the Mecca of the Protestant church. Shortly after my return to Hilversum, I received the heaviest blow of my life. A cablegram informed me that my wife was dead. My profound sorrow was consoled by the thought that the separation was only temporary and could not last long; and my faith gave me strength to write a letter of encouraging consolation to my daughter, Mrs. Malan. . . ."

The President then went to stay for a fortnight at Scheveningen with Mr. Wolmanans "to distract my thoughts a little. I then went back to Hilversum, where I lived in absolute retirement, interrupted only by the necessary conferences, and devoted myself entirely to the perusal of my Bible."

For the rest he says, "I had throughout the war replied to every inquiry . . . that my confidence was unshaken still . . . and to the generals I applied the text from the Corinthians: 'For to their power, I bear record, yea, and beyond their power they were willing of themselves.'"

Sometimes there was good news, such as that of a meeting held at the Queen's Hall in London by English Boer sympathizers, in which it was suggested that some man of good counsel should be sent to South Africa instead of "that wretched penny-a-liner Lord Milner."

The Liberal Party at the time was at its lowest ebb and such protests did nothing to help the Boer cause except to prove that all England was not behind the war, only the major and most official part of it. Another and more practical piece of good news was the capture of Lord Methuen by de la Rey in February, 1902. The President rejoiced greatly over this victory, but when it was suggested that Methuen be kept a prisoner, he said, "I cannot approve of that and I hope de la Rey will release him without delay, for we Boers must behave as Christians to the end, however uncivilised the way in which the English treat us may be."

But most of the news was bad. But Kruger saw that nothing was to be gained by submission. Whatever happened, they would lose everything; but fighting on, they would save their honour and might even be able to get better terms as the British got tired of spending so much in capital and in blood. There was still a faint hope of French and German support, or at least of protests, which would shame the English into agreeing to arbitration. In March, 1902, there were some negotiations between Botha and Kitchener, of which nothing came except the President's message to the Boer leaders "that the generals in the field must decide." He had led too many men himself not to know that it was for the man on the spot to decide what must be done. But in his mind were words he had spoken earlier, "If I were young and strong enough, I would die at the head of the last commando."

And now in May, 1902, came the tragic end of this farmers' war. It began with the argument between those who wished to fight on, all but naked, nearly starving, on starving horses, outlaws in their own land, and those leaders who wished to save what was left of the nation. At last the bitter-enders gave up, still protesting that it was better to be dead than unfree, but prepared, since the majority had agreed to it, to surrender and live on.

CHAPTER SIX

THE END OF A WAR AND A PRESIDENT

THE END is best described by the men who were there. Deneys Reitz, who was serving under General Smuts, wrote: "A meeting was to be held at Vereeniging, on the banks of the Vaal River, with a view to discussing peace terms. A safe-conduct was enclosed under which he [General Smuts] was to proceed through the British lines. . . . The men were the real tragedy. They had endured against great odds, facing years of peril and hardship without pay or reward, and they still had so much faith in the cause for which they were fighting that when the news trickled through next day that General Smuts was to go on a peace conference, they were convinced that the British were suing for terms and were ready to restore our country. . . . It was pitiful to listen to their talk and see their faces light up when they spoke of having won through at last, and I, for one, had not the heart to disillusion them . . . so steadfast was their trust. Next day we set off. We were met by Colonel Collins. Our escort took over our horses and after singing our commando hymn and firing a volley into the air, they wheeled round and galloped away cheering towards their own side, to the manifest interest of the English officers and troopers lined up beside the road."

Then follows a description of the journey to the British Headquarters. "Here I underwent record promotion. When an officer of hussars asked General Smuts who I was, the General explained that on commando there were no social distinctions, but he had brought me along because he thought my father might be at the conference. After telephoning to the authorities to tell them that the son of the Transvaal State Secretary was with the party, as an orderly, he said, ' Young man, you are Chief of Staff to General Smuts.' "

They then proceeded by sea to Cape Town, where they transferred to H.M.S. *Monarch* till they were able to go North by rail. Reitz goes on:

"I do not know what was in the minds of my companions, but perhaps they, too, were thinking of the long road we had travelled, of camp-fires on mountains and plains, and of the good men and splendid horses that were dead.

"It took us the better part of a week to reach Kroonstadt in the Northern Free State, where Lord Kitchener was to meet us. Soon after our arrival, he rode up to the station on a magnificent black charger, followed by a numerous suite including turbaned Pathans in Eastern costume, with gold-mounted scimitars. His retinue waited outside while he came to our compartment to talk. He was anxious to bring the war to a close, for he referred again and again to the hopelessness of our struggle, telling us that he had four hundred thousand troops in South Africa against our eighteen thousand. . . . He said he was prepared to let the burghers retain their horses and saddles in recognition of the fight they had made and that the British Government would help to rebuild the farmhouses destroyed, the burning of which he defended, on military grounds. General Smuts accused him of having unfairly executed our men in the Cape, and this, too, he justified, on the plea that we had used khaki uniforms.

"The journey continued for another day and a half, until we reached a point where a party of horsemen sent by General Botha was awaiting us. They had brought spare horses . . . and striking across country, we travelled two days over bare and deserted plains to the place where the Commandant-General was expecting us. Here about three hundred men were assembled. They were delegates from every commando in the Eastern Transvaal, come to elect representatives to the peace conference to be held at Vereeniging and nothing could have proved how nearly the Boer cause was spent than these starving, ragged men, clad in skins and sacking, their bodies covered with sores from lack of salt and food. Their spirit was undaunted, but they had reached the limit of physical endurance, and we realised if these haggard, emaciated men were the pick of the Transvaal commandos, then the war must be irretrievably lost. Food was so scarce that General Botha himself had only a few strips of leathery biltong to offer us, and he said that but for the lucky chance of having raided a small herd of cattle from the British a fortnight before, he would have been unable to hold the meeting at all. . . . Next day the elections were held. Even in adversity, the Boer instinct for speeches and wordy wrangling asserted itself, and the time was passed in oratory and with the nomination and re-nomination of candidates. ... Next morning the gathering dispersed, the men riding off on their hungry horses to rejoin their distant units, while General Botha and the successful deputies started back for the English blockhouse line ... at Standerton, we entrained for Vereeniging.

"I knew little of the actual conference, as I was not a delegate, but the outcome was a foregone conclusion. Every representative had the same disastrous tale to tell of starvation, lack of ammunition, horses, and clothing, and of how the blockhouse system was strangling their efforts to carry on the war. Added to this was the heavy death toll among the women and children, of whom twenty-five thousand had already died in the concentration camps, and the universal ruin that had overtaken the country. Every homestead was burned, all crops and livestock destroyed, and there was nothing left but to bow to the inevitable. ..."

The difficulty was to tell the men that peace had been signed and that they who were still in the field and undefeated, must surrender their arms and come in. Reitz continues the story:

"Most of them took it calmly, but some cursed and vowed that they would never surrender. ... The depressing ceremony of handing over the rifles now took place. It was presided over by an English officer who sat at a table beneath the trees, with a regiment in reserve close by. Despite his protests, our men fired away their ammunition into the air, smashed their rifle butts, and sullenly flung their broken weapons down before putting their names to the undertaking that each man was called upon to sign, that he would abide by the peace terms.

"When my father's turn came, he handed over his rifle to the officer in charge, but refused to sign. He said that though he was one of the signatories of the Peace Treaty, he had told Lord Milner at the time that he was setting his hand to the document in his official capacity as State Secretary to the Transvaal and not as a private individual, and Lord Milner had accepted his signature on that basis. The officer pointed out that he would not be allowed to remain in the country, and my father agreed. ..."

Most men signed and rode off on their different ways to search for what remained of their families and to set about rebuilding

THE END OF A WAR AND A PRESIDENT 427

their ruined homes; but many, like the Reitz family, preferred exile—and only a South African can understand what this means, for there is no country to which the Boer can go which is like his own, no sun like his, no space like his veld, no people like those he was brought up among.

General de Wet expressed what he felt about the defeat in his book, *Three Years War*: "To every man there, as to myself, this surrender was no more and no less than the sacrifice of our independence. I have often been present at the death-bed and at the funeral of those who have been dearest to my heart—father, mother, brother, and friend—but the grief which I felt on these occasions was nothing to be compared with what I now underwent at the burial of my Nation."

The peace was a great blow to the old President. His wife was dead, his children scattered, his nation lost, and he himself in exile. Kruger's cup was full, and the great river of his life, the many days that were its waters, was nearing the final sea. He now spent his time in prayer and thought. He wrote his *Memoirs*. He saw the friends who came from Africa to visit him.

Lobengula was gone. Rhodes was gone. Of the three great figures that had dominated the African scene, only Kruger remained: Old Kruger, in exile with his pipe and his Bible. The Bible was big and heavy; the pipe was big and heavy, too, with a long, thick, curved stem. In his waking hours it never left his mouth, except when he made a speech or did his devotions.

When the news that peace had been made came to Kruger, he said, "My grief is beyond expression. I cannot say more." But his faith was untouched. The "old bull" could not be tamed. He could only wait for the end with the strange dignity that is given to men who have lived much and long and are aware that death itself is a part of life—the final experience, and one which will bring them at long last into the presence of the God they have spent their lives serving. Kruger's heart was emptied of words. His work was undone, his people broken, and his own life shattered utterly. His wife had died alone. His son Tjaart had died in Pretoria. Another son had been killed in the war. Each mail brought more news of grandsons wounded and killed, of cousins, nephews, friends.

Kruger could no longer sustain his granite front. He was used up. He passed into a state of torpor from which he only roused himself to lash out at his enemies. He was like an old wounded buffalo standing with lowered head and making its last abortive charges. This was the end of his life, the late evening of it, almost the night. He thought about the past, about the future, of Africa—and as Rhodes had done he exhorted his friends and consoled them. And to them—the friends who came to visit him, the old soldiers, the generals—story after story about their old President must have occurred. Still living, Kruger was already a legend.

There was the story about a burgher who once went to a meeting primed with drink, and complained about the liquor concession. "What good is it?" he asked the President. "Can't you feel it in your body?" was the answer. Another man complained about the high duty on imported flour which came from Australia; and the President said, "Je julle wil Ouma se brood eet, dan moet julle darvoor betaal"—Yes, if you want to eat grandma's bread—meaning Queen Victoria—then you must pay for it.

Then there was the story of his pyjamas. They had been given to him in England. When he showed them to his wife, she said, "Throw away that rubbish and put on your nightshirt."

On another occasion, in his last Presidency when talking to Commandant Schutte, he said, "There is strength in the old bull yet," and forced the Commandant into a chair despite resistance and pinched him playfully but unmercifully, between the thighs.

Meeting a boy on one of his trips about the country, the President asked, "And how are things in your part of the world?"

"With us, President, things go well except for the rinderpest."

"And have you lost many cattle?"

"No, President, not one."

"And how is that?"

"Because, President, we haven't any cattle." This boy also got a pinch.

The President was in fact a pincher. He pinched the ears of his state artillerymen as he pinched the ears of children, only harder. To him, his people were his children, and a hundred years ago pinching, both as a caress or a punishment, was more common than it is to-day.

Then there was the story of the young Hollander who came to the President looking for a job. It appeared that he was well educated, knowing, among other things, Dutch, English, French, German, Greek, Latin, history, geography, mathematics, and astronomy. Having listened to the list, the President blew out a great cloud of smoke, and said, "Do you need clever people in Holland?"

"Yes," said the young man.

"How is it, then, that you did not stay there?" the President asked.

Once, when he had argued very rudely with Doctor Leyds, he woke him in the middle of the night to say that he had been wrong to speak so sharply. This shows Kruger in an interesting light. It was more than an apology, which could certainly have been delayed till next day. It would appear to show that he was unable to sleep until a wrong he had done had been righted.

In the troubled times that preceded the war, a considerable amount of money was spent by the South African Republic on the secret service. An old friend of Kruger's made a special trip to Pretoria to ask him what all these secrets were that cost such a lot of money. The President said they were state secrets, but his friend persisted. At last the President leaned towards him and said, in a subdued voice, "Can you keep a secret?"

His friend said eagerly, "Of course I can."

"So can I," said the President.

When the question of a good road between Pretoria and Johannesburg was brought up, Kruger said that building roads was a waste of time and money, "as roads were good when the sun shone and bad when it rained." This in brief was the nature of roads.

As a young man returning very hungry from commando, Kruger came upon some Boers camped and eating. When they refused to share their meat with him, Kruger left them, went to the river near by, emptied the powder out of his horn, filled it with water. Then he came back to the fire and addressed the feasters, telling them the miseries he had suffered on commando made life not worth living. Their treatment of him had completed his misery and he was now about to put an end to his troubles. He raised his powder-horn and threw it into the fire. When the men leaped to their feet and bolted, Kruger sat down and finished the meat they had abandoned.

There is a second suicide story told of the President. On another commando there was a melancholy man nicknamed "Mal Jan"—unlucky John—who talked continually of cutting his throat. The Commandant believed him and each day detailed a burgher to watch over him. When Kruger's turn came, Mal Jan moaned and said to-day he was really going to kill himself.

"Do you really want to cut your throat? Kruger asked.

"Certainly, Paulkie. The world is too full of trouble."

"Then wait a minute," Kruger said. He left him and came back with an open razor. "There you are," he said, "now you can cut your throat."

"But Paulkie . . ."

"Cut, cut, man," Kruger shouted, "this is your opportunity. Cut your throat properly."

"But Paulkie . . . I'm afraid it will hurt me, it is so sharp."

"Well, then, you are cured, you loafer," Kruger shouted, and took up his sjambok to finish the cure.

When in 1892 electric light was installed in the President's house in Pretoria, burghers who had heard of this marvel used to come and ask to see how it worked. Kruger, holding his hand on the switch, faced the light and blew hard. The light went out and his visitors went away much impressed. "Magtig! the President blows hard," they said. "Did you notice the light was inside a glass?"

Kruger loved jokes. At the opening of the Pietersburg Railway, he challenged Sammy Marks, the Jewish magnate, to run a race with him, saying, "If you win, you become President. If I win, you become a Christian." In 1884 in Holland, he was asked by the theological professors of the College of Ministers to preach a sermon. He refused because "I cannot enter the pulpit if learned men like you are present." They said, "President, go into the pulpit, we won't be there." He then agreed, but the following Sunday he noticed them creeping into the church. They had forgotten that the President had been hunter before he had become an elder. When the time came for the sermon, he chose the text from II Corinthians XII: 16, "But be it so, I did not burden you: nevertheless, being crafty, I caught you with guile."

Once he said to Sir James Sivewright, "If I had your education, I should be leading the whole of South Africa by the nose," Sivewright replied, "That might be so, President, but you might have got into a groove and never been heard of again."

Yet Kruger's education was sufficient for him to understand what lay under the stock-market fluctuations. He did not think the mining industry was unduly burdened and wrote: "The principal reason why some mines give no profit and others less profit than the shareholders would have liked to see was to be found in over-capitalisation, in the floating of companies on worthless properties. . . . The great financial houses had everything in their hands and caused prices to rise or fall as they pleased, and the public was the victim of their manœuvres."

To the stories of his operating on his thumb when he blew it off, and his setting his cart back on its axle with a broken leg and driving it home, must be added an incident related by Doctor Leyds, who was in Lisbon with him when it took place. The President had a violent toothache. "For a while he paced up and down the room seeking relief. Then he pulled out his knife and cut the tooth out of his jaw by patience and persistence."

The Reverend Doctor J. H. Hertz gives this comparison between Rhodes and Kruger: "Of the five strong characters of all countries who have of late decades been most in the eyes of the world, two men have been products of purely South African conditions—Cecil Rhodes, who was an archangel's sweep over human affairs, whether to create or to ruin; and the other one that huge antediluvian monster who has strayed into the world some four thousand years too late, who combines the titanic will of a Cromwell, the mother wit of a Lincoln, with the shrewdness of a Richard Croker, and the education of a Red Indian— Stephanus Paulus Kruger. To understand Kruger it must be realised that he moved all his life in a circle to which the average South African is accustomed. He played the same games, saw the same scenes and natural wonders, loved the chase, devoted his talents to the solution of the same political, social, religious, and moral problems as those with which we are concerned to-day. He was a man of the people; he grew up with the people; he lived for the people." He was Oom Paul, the uncle, not merely of his many nephews and nieces, but of his race.

Kruger knew no niceties. In his early days he was a prodigious eater. After saying grace, he fell to without uttering a word and finished his meal. Then he said grace again and left the table. General Smit said, "Yes, if Old Paul comes to a table which has food on it, he eats it clean as far as he can and leaves as quickly as possible."

Now that the war was over, many Boer leaders came to Europe to see Kruger—General Lucas Meyer, President Steyn, Reitz, Botha, de la Rey, Christiaan de Wet. They came to collect funds to help re-establish the Boer women and children who had lost their men. They had a good reception in England and elsewhere. Towards the end of 1902, the President attended a service in the Cathedral at Utrecht with his generals and preached a short sermon.

A strange old man, this pioneer hunter, soldier, and president —a farmer—a preacher attended by his unsoldierly farmer generals, who with them had held an empire at bay for three years, and had cost England 22,000 soldiers dead, and 223,000,000 pounds sterling in money. The generals must have contrasted this scene in the Cathedral with the one at Vereeniging where they had all been gathered to sign the peace; where, bearded, in farm clothes ragged from war, they had been met by Kitchener, resplendent in uniform, surrounded by turbaned soldiers with drawn scimitars. But this panoply, so useful to daunt and impress the native tribes, had no effect on the Boers, who dislike vanity.

There is a story about de la Rey, who in later years received many presentation watches, which illustrates this Boer characteristic. He had been presented a gold watch by "another old chap. It was very funny, it was as big as half an orange. You've never seen a watch like that. I asked him what it was, and he told me it had belonged to his family for a hundred, two hundred years ... more, perhaps. I asked him if it kept good time, but he said it was not for that. I showed him my watch." De la Rey had a large-sized nickel watch and used a leather voorslag—whiplash —as a chain and told him he "should get one like mine. It never gave any trouble. I had it years before the war. Of course you don't want a watch round the farm, you know when to eat and go to bed and get up; and that's all you want."

De la Rey was then asked if he had other presentation watches and he said there had been more than he could remember, "twenty or thirty, perhaps. Out on the farm there was a box full of them." He took out his own watch again. "This is the kind you want if you need a watch at all."

There was never a more typical old-time Boer than Paul Kruger. He epitomised all that was good in them and all that was bad: the bad, for the most part, being his refusal to accept modern standards and his effort to substitute the laws of the Bible for those current in the late nineteenth century. For Kruger there was no higher authority than God.

Kruger was a man who could not give in, who could never bend, and who, even now, in exile and waiting for death, was in no way broken. He believed that Africa belonged to his people. He said. "Ons voortrekker het die land schoongemaak; ons is geregtig tot die vet van die land"—We voortrekkers made the land clean; we are entitled to the fat of the land.

But the fat was now gone: the blood spilled to take the land and that spilled to protect it was wasted.

The winter of 1902, Kruger spent at Mentone on the French Riviera, where he was well cared for in a luxurious villa home in the midst of palms and orange trees; and consoled by the thought that he had always done what was right, and that if his countrymen were suffering it was not his fault. His health did not improve and his stay was prolonged. His friends, Louis Botha, Schalk Burger, de Wet, and de la Rey, visited him again there to clasp his hand.

He had had several slight strokes, but even these were not enough to smash his iron frame, and he performed his last public act telegraphing to the Het Volk Congress at Pretoria, "Seek out of the past all that is noble and elevated and build on that." The news of the surrender of his people he had accepted as "God's will. . . . I am satisfied my generals could fight no further or we could have had no women, children, or nation left. . . ."

In 1904, it was thought he should go to Switzerland for the summer. The shores of the Lake of Geneva in Switzerland was a strange place for the President of the South African Republic, the veteran of Kaffir wars and hunts, the Voortrekker boy of three-quarters of a century ago, to find himself waiting for death to take him. All his life he had seen death by war, by misadventure, by age and sickness. Thoughts of his own end must have entered his mind in those years, but never this one—never the thought that he would die like a woman in bed, an alien and an exile, at the edge of a little inland sea.

Rhodes had died a month before the end of the war, but Kruger was not a man to take satisfaction in death, even that of his enemies. He had seen too much of it. He was near his own end, waiting for it to come, thinking about it, confident of meeting his dear wife again, his young burghers who had died in the war, and his old hunting companions and associates. To those who had come to him weeping, to tell of his wife's death, he had said: "The Bible says we must be strong in misfortune." Then he took up his pipe again and continued reading the Bible.

After the war, he could have gone back to Africa, but he was too proud for that. His daughter and some grandchildren were with him. His valet, Happe, his doctor, Heymans, and his minister, Doctor Los, attended him.

His last message, dated Clarens, June 29, 1904, was to Botha. There was neither anger nor bitterness in Kruger's heart nor need for haste. He had lived a long time, and time to a Boer is a different dimension—an incalculable, related to his belief in God. He wrote:

"Dear General,—With all the sorrow and sadness which are my lot, and with all my heart, I thank you who having come together to deliberate about the future thought about your old States President, and by that have proved that you have not forgotten the past. For those who wish to create the future must not lose sight of the past ... much that had been built up is now destroyed and annihilated; yet with unity of purpose, that which now lies in ashes can be re-established. Never forget the serious warning which lies in the saying, 'Divide and rule.' May these words never be applied to the Afrikaaner people. Then our nationality and our language will live and flourish. What I myself may be allowed to see of that future lies in God's Hands.

"Born under the British flag, I shall not die under it. I have learned to accept the inevitable—the thought that I shall close my eyes in foreign lands an exile, almost alone, far from relatives and friends whom I shall never see again; far from the African soil which I shall never tread again; far from the land to which I dedicated my life in opening it up for civilisation and where I saw my own nation weeping. But the bitterness thereof will be softened as long as I may cherish the conviction that the work once begun will be continued, for that hope and expectation will sustain me in the knowledge that the end of that work will be good. So be it.

"Out of my heart, the depth of my heart, I greet you and the whole nation.

"(Signed) S. J. P. KRUGER."

How like Rhodes, with his "Does it matter what people say about it as long as our work goes on and work survives the worker?..."

Both Kruger and Rhodes were dedicated. Both approached the same problem, though from utterly different angles. The one was dead and the other dying, yet both knew the work would go on; that once begun, the process of ferment that would make Africa must continue. A fortnight after Kruger had written to Botha, he caught another chill. Pneumonia set in again and on the fourteenth of July, Bastille Day, he died.

Holland which had brought him from Africa took back his body. *Die Battavia VI.* was specially equipped for the purpose. At the Synodical Hall of the Huguenot Memorial in Cape Town, the coffin lay in state for five days while the nation came to pay tribute to the dead President. There were wreaths from all countries and General Botha conducted the funeral service. On December 16, Dingaan's Day, the funeral took place in Pretoria. Botha had accompanied the body and at every station Boers came to honour the dead State President as others had come when Rhodes's body had been taken North.

Thus for a second time the body of a great man had gone North over the same track in two years, with the same panoply of mourners, flags, crepe, and flowers, each watered with the tears of his followers. Only the followers themselves were different, for the Boers had not regretted the death of Rhodes and the British were not sorry that Oom Paul was dead. But the form was the same, and the centre of each procession was the same—

its core a dead man who had been great, who had been loved and hated, who had served, according to his own lights, his people well.

So the third great man died, anti-climactically for a hero, as had the others. Not leading a last charge, but fading away stifled by the weight of his years and disappointments; and Time, which was against these three, had given Kruger, who never tried to hurry Time, the longest life.

EPILOGUE

THE BIRTH OF A NATION

THE STORY of Africa does not end with the Boer War or with Paul Kruger's death, any more than it began with the Great Trek or the discovery of gold and diamonds. And even if some aspects of the lives of Kruger, Rhodes, and Lobengula have been dealt with—there remain loose ends to be tied; there remain hypotheses to be suggested; there remain links in the chain of circumstance to be re-examined.

With German atrocities once again a matter of discussion, their treatment of the Hereros at the turn of the century should be thought of, and the fact remembered that Reichsmarshal Herman Goering's father was the Governor of German West Africa at the time they took place. Before the Germans took German West Africa in 1892, there were a hundred and fifty thousand native-owned cattle. In 1902, they had there forty-six thousand. By 1905, they had none. And in 1907, to force their labour, the Hereros were forbidden to own cattle. In 1892, there were eighty-five thousand Hereros. In 1911, after the rebellion, only fifteen thousand survived. These figures are self-explanatory. As to the other German African colonies—the story is the same. I quote German and American authorities.

In March, 1906, Herr Babel, leader in the Reichstag of the Social-Democrat Party, said, "The German Government has simply abolished the existing civil laws of the natives in the German colonies. . . . We have lost the sympathy of the Black Race." In 1907, Herr Dernburg, the German Colonial Secretary, visited the German colonies in Africa and reported to the Reichstag: "It makes a very unfavourable impression on one to see so many white men go about with Negro whips. . . . Labourers are obtained under circumstances which are not to be distinguished from slave hunts. . . . It has happened that settlers have seated themselves at the wells with revolvers and have prevented the natives from watering their cattle, to compel them to leave the latter behind."

An American Consul, Mr. Alexander Powell, in 1913 reported that "there is not a town in German East Africa where you cannot see boys of from eight to fourteen years, shackled by chains running from collar to collar, guarded by soldiers armed with rifles, doing the work of men under the deadly sun. Natives with bleeding backs are constantly making their way into Belgian and British territory with tales of maltreatment by German planters. . . ."

When the Maji Maji rebelled in East Africa, a hundred and twenty thousand of them were killed.

Sarah Gertrude Millin says: "The whip-chain-forced labour system prevailed in all German colonies. And should the Nazis ever return to Africa it will (as they themselves declare) do so again."

Thus does the web of German brutality bind us to the past of Africa. The past is history. The speculative future is based upon that past and upon to-day, which to-morrow will also be history.

Mommsen, the great German historian, said, "The war in South Africa was at bottom a fight between the sixteenth and the twentieth centuries." Actually, the Anglo-Boer War, like the present World War, was two wars. It was a war for territorial expansion and, as such, fitted into what can be described as the general pattern of the wars of the past; but, in addition to this, it was a war of two ideologies, and thus it fits into the World War design of to-day. It was a civil war, and as such related to the American Revolution, the American Civil War, and the recent Spanish Civil War.

Kruger's work in welding South Africa together has been compared to that of Simon Bolívar in South America. This is an exaggeration which has only a certain foundation of truth. Kruger was able to unite the Boer factions into a single people, but the South Africa of to-day—the Union—has been welded into a further unity with a flux of gold and blood; has been bound by lead and steel; has been watered with the tears of its women and created by the marriage of the gun and the Bible. Kruger and Rhodes and Lobengula were instruments of history, who like other instruments—like Hitler, or Churchill, or Stalin, or Roosevelt—were dependent upon the times in which they lived for their stature, or their infamy.

The Boer War is not the true past. It is not even distant in either time or space. Many who fought in it are still alive; the others our fathers and grandfathers may have met. There is no lag in historical memory, each man remembering old men who remembered other older men. The veterans of the Civil War must have met in their childhood men who fought in the War of 1812, some of whom may themselves have fought in the Revolutionary War of 1776. So it goes on, actual memory overlapping actual memory into the endless past, till it touches the fringe where there was no written word, and still history is remembered, passed on by word of mouth in fable, folklore, and myth.

And Africa, once so distant, is now next door. Science and the inventions that the Boers hated have contracted the space they loved. Kruger's hope of a united South Africa has come true, though not in the way he hoped. Rhodes's dream of a British Commonwealth is consummated, through the genius of the man who was his enemy—Jan Christiaan Smuts—and once again the dream is proved greater than the apparently accomplished fact.

Good or bad, the past is past. It has been embodied into life; into our lives, and these three—Paul Kruger, Lobengula, and Rhodes—are among the heroes, the great men of whom songs are sung. Their virtues and vices enhanced by the glamour of time—overlauded, overdecried—they were once but men living as others, but cast in a greater mould, born to a destiny, almost against their will. Lobengula had no wish to be king: the witch-doctors of the Matopos made him king. Kruger, had there been no Trek, would have been a farmer, like his father. The British made Kruger as previously they had made Washington. And Rhodes, but for his weak lungs, might have been a village parson. Cause and effect, percussion and repercussion, made these men what they were, but having been, they remain monuments in Africa. Strange men to be judged; great men who died exiled, alone, or failures; who, having drunk the cup more fully than most, set it down more empty. They drained it to its last most bitter dregs.

After death and burial of great men, as much as little, comes the reading of the will—the publication of the material assets left by the deceased. Spiritual legacies are subject to controversy and vary according to individual points of view, but money and property have clearly defined values—they represent the crystallisation of residual energy, and as such throw a light upon the life of a dead man. Lobengula left no will. His real estate, the whole of Matabeleland and Mashonaland, had been taken from him. But he did leave his accumulation of gold extracted from his people and the diamonds they had stolen for him when they worked in the mines. What he left behind him in material assets was the legacy of a tyrant, the result of extortion, robbery, and theft. The exact amount is unknown, but it was considerable, and has never been found, though even recently expeditions have gone in search of it. His body is said to have been discovered on the banks of the Manyana River and inspected by Arthur Huxtable, the district commissioner for native affairs. But among the relics, old guns, bullet-moulds, saddles and gear, there was no money, no diamonds, no gold or ivory.

There is a legend, too, about Kruger's millions. Though people still seek them, they are non-existent. What he left, he left mainly in farms and cattle. The money he had given to his country to prosecute the war was not repaid to him and he left the Transvaal its creditor.

Of these three men, only Rhodes left a fortune.

Had the idea of a British Commonwealth been suggested in 1877, Kruger might have consented to join it, and the War of Independence and the Anglo-Boer War have been avoided. Had he had to negotiate with a man like Sir George Grey, there would probably have been no conflict. Had he and Rhodes been able to meet on friendly terms, there might never have been war, for Rhodes had taken over Grey's original idea of the federation of all the countries which made up the British Commonwealth, with the United States as an outside partner.

But these *Ifs* remain *Ifs*. What happened, happened, and the bitterness of these wars still lives to-day and will for another thirty years or so, until all who were alive at the time in Africa are dead. Human misery, unhappiness, and hate can only live as long as the man or woman or child who suffered lives. With their deaths, direct memory dies too, and the residual historic memory is weakened, generation by generation, becoming more objective as it fades.

Ons Land—Our Land of South Africa—as the Boers call it, was thus born. Out of the Cape Colony by the Trekkers, with whom Paul Kruger marched as boy, it reached upward into the north across the Vaal and east into the land of the Zulus that became Natal. The Free State was born, Bechuanaland taken, and Rhodes, leaping the Limpopo, came to the Zambesi and the borders of Portuguese East Africa.

Rhodes's dream of a British Africa and a British dominated world has not come true. But his hope for a rapprochement between England and America an agent for world peace has come, at least provisionally, to pass. His desire for a great South African Union seems more possible than it was even in his own time, and his desire for a world governed by business, or, in our terms, of cartels and monopolies, is too near the truth to suit many people. Rhodes and his dreams are still a factor in this changing world. The government by an élite, though not necessarily the one he had chosen, is likely to come, since the world is now too complex to be ruled by the accidents of trial and error. And world peace is likely to come his way—through alliances of power, rather than the balance of power, which has proved too precarious for safety. Thus, right or wrong, and right and wrong, Cecil John Rhodes made his mark and left his imprint upon the face of a continent, an empire, and a world in which many are able to criticise him, but none are great enough to judge. Had Rhodes been greater, he might have been worse—a British Hitler. Had he been less great, he might have been nothing. As it was he fitted—a great round peg into the great round hole of his period, pinning his time flamboyantly to Africa, centring attention upon Africa—upon his love; holding time, for the brief instant of his passing, still with the weight of his personality, and then dying, as he had lived, loved and hated—a separator of fighting bulls.

Rhodes was able to reduce the mountain of his desire to the molehill of the immediately possible, and by moving a thousand molehills, create the mountain of his desire. Proclaiming the truth from the housetops of after-dinner oratory, his true meanings were rarely understood by the man in the street. "Too much too soon" he realised was as bad as "too little and too late." and his was the principle "that the idea of gold" was as good as gold itself. His politics were a form of banking in which the assets were kingdoms, mortgaged by pigmentation. Understanding that effects were the results of causes, Rhodes was able to create such causes as would promote the effects he desired.

Rhodes, for all his affection for men—in his case certainly surpassing the love of women, since he did not like women—has never been accused of homosexuality. In all the dirt that was flung at him by his enemies, this charge at least was avoided. They certainly called him everything else, and it seems possible that, as he was a new type of man in other ways, he was new in this also—an asexual. One of those who, passing beyond the ordinary hetero-sexuality of the common man, that the French call *l'homme moyen sensuel*, was beyond bisexuality, beyond homosexuality and was literally asexual—beyond sex. It appears to have had no meaning to him except as a human weakness that he understood and could exploit in others. Had his life been different from what it was, he might, owing to his tubercular tendency, have become obsessed with sex as was D. H. Lawrence, for instance, because, although unattracted by women, he was fantastically attractive to them long before he reached the pinnacle of his fame. Or, on the other hand, he might, because of his dislike of what in his day they called "the fair sex," and his love of men, have become truly homosexual. Instead, his instinct was sublimated and his passion was for a continent and an empire.

It seems possible that he could not feel the beauty of women as he could not feel the quality of a gold mine. What he felt emotionally was diamondiferous ground—"I could not feel this," he said, when shown the gold reef of the Rand.

Essentially, beauty is something that is felt and is not seen. We do not say this is beautiful when we look at it. Indeed, if we are told something is beautiful, we are set against it. What actually happens is that when we look at an object, something happens to us. What this something is, no one has yet decided, but it is felt in the heart, and then we say, "This is beautiful!" It can be a woman, a horse, a picture, or a great hole dug into the earth—the central core of a diamond pipe. What to Rhodes was beauty was to Kruger its antithesis: mines, wire fences, railroads, big towns, factories. What the one loved, the other hated. What the one admired, the other despised. The virtues of both men, could they have been combined in a single individual, would have made a man who was nearly a god: the vices of both, in combination, a super-criminal. I have suggested that Rhodes was the prototype of the modern fascist dictator and that Kruger was a democrat; but this is an oversimplification, for Rhodes was a democrat in the sense that he had no use for idle aristocrats, or indeed idle men of any kind. Capacity was what interested him. While Kruger, who believed fanatically in democracy and freedom, also believed in complete white superiority, in a *Herrenvolk* that was set by God to hold the black children of Ham in subjection and servitude. So that even here in South Africa, where issues were relatively simple, we get the intermingling of currents of opinion and belief. Yet to some extent Rhodes was the prototype of the modern fascist as he was also an expression of an earlier kind of adventurer. He can be seen as a connecting link between Warren Hastings, the House of Rothschild, and Hitler. As Hitler was influenced by Wagner and the old German gods, so was Rhodes influenced by the spirit of the British empire-builders, the pirates who gained an empire by accident, and the philosophy of Ruskin. He was perhaps the final flowering of the British Imperialist whose feelings were expressed in the poetry of Kipling. Rhodes was a student of Greek and had absorbed much of the Greek sophistry. He was a reader of history and Machiavelli did not escape his attention. Nor did the organisation of the Society of Jesus, from which he drew his inspiration of the world ruled by an élite. This was the basis of his Rhodes scholarships, which could be called the forerunners of Hitler's "leader schools." However great the difference between a Rhodes scholar and a *gauleiter*, the idea in both cases was to produce leaders. There are other parallels. Rhodes's belief in the Nordic race, his theory of the survival of the fittest, the simplicity of his dress, and his power of dominating crowds by his oratory.

Nothing is quite new in history. The repetitions are there continually and only slightly changed. The assassin appears in a lounge suit instead of a toga: the headsman in evening dress and top hat instead of in black tights and mask. Incidents have always been found: minorities always used: messengers often killed, or delayed till their messages were valueless. There is nothing new in seeing expediency disguised as justice or might masquerading as right. Thus, with many reservations, the Anglo-Boer War can be considered as a fascist war upon a democratic Christian state. For this reason, it excited the world in a manner that was unusual and not approached till the Spanish Revolution in 1936-39. The Russo-Japanese War of 1904-05 and the Balkan War of 1912 were ordinary wars which followed the ordinary pattern. In England there were many pro-Boers as there were all over the world. The terminology of modern ideology had not yet come into use, but the rapacious Jingo of 1900 was, to all intents and purposes, the Fascist of 1939. They would have found more matters they agreed upon than disagreements.

It has been said that we have little true democracy to-day; that "it is unable to persist because it has never existed, self-government having, for technical and mechanical reasons, been long impossible. The masses may depose their leaders, but only to exchange them for others..." Democracy, in its truest sense, could and did exist among the Boers, because they were a small people and devoid of those "technical and mechanical reasons" which prevent the functioning of self-government by the people. The South African burgher had rights, was in fact the freest man in the world; one who lived for little else but his freedom, and was prepared to sacrifice everything, even life, to retain it.

Rhodes was not a "Hitler," but they had certain qualities in common. Lord Roberts was not a "Rommel," but he and Rommel would have understood each other. Abyssinia was much more civilised than Matabeleland, but somewhat the same thoughts must have passed through Haile Selassie's mind when he was attacked as went through Lobengula's. The Boer leaders and generals were not soldiers, but commanders of partisans: "guerrillas" Lord Roberts called them. Kruger, Joubert, Cronje, Botha, and Smuts were all farmers. Yokels, if you will, men who owned and worked their land themselves, who were as adept at cattle-breeding as at war and much preferred it. A group of Boer leaders looked like a group of farmers in their best clothes assembled in the market place of a country town; with their heavy, often home-made shoes, their top hats and old frock coats; with their shoulders bowed with the muscles of hard labour and hours in the saddle, their faces burnt by the suns of their many summers; their hands horny from whip stock and plough handle. They were not city men. They hated cities. Their eyes were used to distances—the vast distances of their native veld. Most were without what we call education, but they were wise as only the simple can be with a belief in God and a knowledge of Nature, and love of right and freedom. The Boers were obstinate, stupid men, uncouth, rough, without delicacy or diplomacy, but astonishingly uncompromising. Hot-blooded beneath a heavy exterior, swift-moving despite their apparent clumsiness, this little army of sixty thousand burghers challenged the might of England and fought England off for three long years. Despite the deaths they suffered and the wounds, despite the burning of their farms and the ravishment of their herds, despite everything, against hopeless odds, they fought and were finally conquered, but not beaten.

Lobengula fell before Rhodes; Rhodes fell before Kruger; Kruger fell before the whole power of an empire intent upon crushing him; and with him fell the Boer Republics. But a process cannot be arrested. A greater South Africa has been reborn out of her blood and tears, out of her dead Kaffir fighters and hunters, out of the farmers and soldiers who died in war and of disease. Though dead, both Rhodes and Kruger live on. Time took the impress of their moulds and the Union of to-day is cast from the matrix that they carved from the red granite of Africa's kopjes. Cleavage there is still, and bitter memory and recrimination; but it is a small thing compared to the other forces that are at work—the love of country and the thought of the two world wars in which South African Dutch and South African British have fought side by side.

This period of early strife between black and white, and white and white; between men who were, in their time, among the greatest, belongs to a past that is over, but which being historically pregnant gave birth to a new people—the South African of to-day who is neither Dutch nor British—who is a South African, the custodian of a tradition, the master of a sub-continent.

The world of the last century was not republican. It was, by and large, royalist, imperial, with the accent fading, it is true, but still the accent, on the divine right of kings. The United States of America was still considered a rebellious colony. France, which was in its third republican stage, was not considered quite respectable. Switzerland was scarcely known. Republics were associated with revolution and rebellion. They were not regarded seriously or considered to be permanent political structures. So it is not surprising that the two little South African farmer republics were held in some contempt. After all, in Africa alone, there had been a number of small republics which had failed— Stellaland, Goshenland, Lydenburg, and Zoutpansberg. This republican business was just a phase, and the idea of democracy; unpractical and unrealistic. President Masaryk's definition of a democratic state would have been considered lunacy in 1900: a state "wherein human beings do not use one another as a means to personal gratification; where each man, woman, or child is recognised as something intrinsically valuable." That is democracy. It is the ultimate ideal of political organisation, of society, the aim of humanity. Except for their treatment of natives, the Boers were one of the first democratic states to fulfil every one of President Masaryk's conditions, and politically ahead, rather than behind, their time. The mistake made by the English was their failure to understand the way the Boer Republics were organised. They were military: each man by law having to bear arms and to be in possession of arms, which is something most of the more industrialised and highly developed pseudo-democracies of to-day dare not permit. Still speaking in terms of masses and proletariat, the difference between Africa to-day and Rhodes's Africa is that a black, working, and partially educated mass has arisen which presents completely new problems.

When Kruger wept at the thought of war, he thought of his people who would fight; they were his own relations, his descendants, his friends, and their sons and grandsons. Milner did not think in those terms, he could think objectively of men as pawns. To him it was the soldiers that fought, the men of whom a Boer said, "Yes, I know the Queen buys them for a shilling." Kipling was the poet of the day, and in Kipling's words:

It's Tommy this, an' Tommy that, an' Tommy go away,
But it's thank you, Mister Atkins, when the band begins to
 play . . .
For it's Tommy this, an' Tommy that, an' Tommy wait outside,
But it's special train for Atkins, when the trooper's on the tide . . .

Then, in those days there was no people's army, no talk of a people's war. The masses of all countries were cannon fodder. Theirs to obey, and not to reason why.

But the Boers, under their field cornets and commandants, were following in war the men they had elected to rule over them as magistrates in peace. Their peacetime duty was to control grass-burning and pasturage, to prevent the ill-usage of servants and settle legal arguments. Throughout Boer history, these leaders were regarded as the pillars of the state, the bulwarks of these infant commonwealths and indispensable to their political system.

Again, there has been an odd repetition of events. To-day, free men are fighting men who are not free. The private soldier of the British army in 1900 was no more free than the German in 1914 to 1939. This, with the fact that the Boers were fighting for their own country and in country they knew, is the only explanation of the fight they put up. That they were damned as guerrillas by Lord Roberts because of their unorthodox methods of fighting is a repetition of Gentleman Johnny Burgoyne's curses at the Americans a century before and another of the military echoes that go down the gallery of battles. The Boers had an International Brigade of Irish, German, American, and many other nationalities and they set the stage for another International Brigade—that of the Spanish Civil War. It can be said that there is danger in parallel and analogy, but there is even graver danger in ignoring them, and refusing to face the pattern of human change in terms of trends. The present British outlook can only be understood by looking back on that old Imperial England, which is dead; by looking from a war of aggression for the conquest of a gold field to the present war; by thinking of the Boers fighting for their plains and mountains and the British for their skies; by looking from Empire to Commonwealth, from Boers fighting Englishmen to Boers fighting with Englishmen in North Africa; by turning from Kipling to Sir William Beveridge; from Kruger to Masaryk; from Smuts, the attorney general and commando leader, to Smuts, the Prime Minister of South Africa, British field marshal, and a power in the councils of the world.

There are many definitions of fascism, none conclusive because, being without an ethic or philosophy, fascism is an elastic and fluid term. But it is born of feudalism and industry. It is a counter-revolution against the revolution of men who, tired of leading "lives of quiet desperation," are determined to be free. It is total, and the seeds of its destruction lie in its totality, for there is no absolute. Essentially it is the politic of bringing all forces—economic, financial, geographic, and military—to bear upon an opponent and an endeavour to secure gains by threats alone. It is the art of making psychological war by means of demonstrations of force, the use of traitors, fifth-columnists, and finally, if war becomes necessary, of applying total national resources to make total war. It is a belief that the means—any means—are justified by the desired ends, with the implication that certain races are supermen; and thus fascism is anti-Christian, denying at once God and the equality of man in His eyes. The Fascist believes in armed force and the social pyramid with a mass of slaves at the bottom and a single leader at the top. It is the antithesis of democracy with its government by debate and committee. It is, in its final application, the *reductio ad absurdum* of centralisation, and anti-social in its refusal to employ the talents of an opposition. Almost any man who is a financier or an industrialist employing a great number of workers, and who thinks there is a fifty per cent chance in the existence of God, is susceptible to fascism if it is presented to him in a palatable form. Cecil Rhodes was such a man—an example of Spengler's new man of power. To offset this type, a second new type has arisen—the complementary *plus*, the man of political good will— Smuts is such a man. That he was born in 1870, the year which was taken in the beginning of this book as a key year in modern history, appears to be no coincidence.

Another key year was 1902, when the Boer War ended. Queen Victoria had died in January, 1901. Edward VII had replaced her on the British throne, and the great men of our era had arrived in the wings of the stage. In those years that separate 1870 from 1902, much history had been made and many historical figures been born or matured. In 1902, Franklin Delano Roosevelt was a young man of twenty. Winston Churchill was already a member of Parliament. Stalin was a young man of twenty-three and Hitler a boy of thirteen. New movements were gaining strength—world movements with world affiliations, labour groups, capital groups, religious groups, youth groups.

Kruger was the human bridge that spanned the river of time which flowed between the muzzle-loading pioneer days and the days when it went down, pinned by the rattle of the machine-gun to the barbed-wire entanglement. Lobengula exemplified the last stand of the barbaric spear against the mounted man with firearms. Rhodes foreshadowed the mastery of the industrial, political giant, epitomising the assets and defects of a system, which in his time was just reaching its crescendo. But in terms of South Africa, and perhaps of the world, we are left with another bridge—General Smuts—who almost proves, by his own life, his thesis that human nature is changing and that a great mutation is taking place which will produce a new type of disinterested, non-attached man.

Jan Christiaan Smuts, the field marshal of to-day, the State Attorney to Kruger, was the son of a farmer member of the Cape Parliament. He could not read till he was twelve. At twenty he headed both parts of the law tripos at once at Cambridge, an unprecedented event. He feared going to college because he was afraid it might corrupt him, but while at college replied, as president of the debating society, to Cecil Rhodes when he addressed the students. After listening to him, Rhodes said, "This fair-haired young man will go far." Little did the great Rhodes think that he would go as far or farther than he had himself, or that later Kruger would use almost the same words when speaking of him. Smuts, with General Louis Botha, was responsible for the Union of South Africa. Smuts helped to draft the plan for the League of Nations that was advocated by President Wilson, and it was Smuts who, by his famous "Commonwealth of Nations" speech, changed the name, and in consequence the substance, of what had been the British Empire. As Rhodes had been influenced at Oxford by Ruskin, Smuts was influenced at Cambridge by Walt Whitman. In the Boer War, Smuts had his first contact with Winston Churchill, who was then a war correspondent. Smuts was State Attorney when Gandhi, attacking the status of Indians in South Africa, was in continual trouble by breaking the laws relative to coloured persons. Here again is the overlap of history, the string of time that ties Smuts, Churchill, and Gandhi to Kruger and Rhodes; that ties Hitler into the pattern of Africa through Smuts; that makes Kruger and Lobengula and Rhodes, who are dead, only once removed from us who are living.

Smuts, Kruger's commando leader, was at Versailles in 1919 and a power there, while Hitler, the corporal, was with the beaten German army. Hitler, duplicating history, signed in 1940 the French armistice in the railway carriage at Compiégne and then took the car to Berlin, where the British Air Force, which he had despised, are said to have destroyed it. Poetic justice, romance, paradox, though left out of history books, are true history—are psychological factors which impress the souls of men by their impact.

Three years after the Boer War, Smuts went to England to ask the new Liberal Government for responsible government for South Africa. "I saw," he says, "Churchill, Morley, Elgin, Lloyd George, Campbell-Bannerman. The only one I had met before was Churchill. I came across him when he was taken at Ladysmith. He asked me if I had ever known of a conquered people being allowed to govern themselves. I said no, but we did not want to govern ourselves without England's assistance, and that was the truth, we could not." Smuts went on: "The Boer has fought for independence, the Englishman has fought for empire. All have fought for what they considered highest. Now *the highest is Union* . . . and there is only one thing the people of South Africa can do—become a united people . . ." Here Smuts wore both the mantle of Kruger, who had united the northern Boers, and of Rhodes, who had hoped to unite all Boers with all British people. Only a few years later, during the First World War, when Smuts went to England again, Churchill wrote: "There arrives in England from the outer marches of the Empire a new and altogether extraordinary man. The stormy and hazardous roads he has travelled by would fill the acts and scenes of drama.

He has warred against us; well we know it. He has quelled rebellion against our own flag with unswerving loyalty and unfailing shrewdness. He has led raids at desperate odds and conquered provinces by scientific strategy. His astonishing career and his versatile achievements are only the index of a profound sagacity and a cool, far-reaching comprehension."

The first Prime Minister of the Union of South Africa was General Botha. Smuts followed him. Then came Hertzog. Then Smuts came back to power. Groot Schuur, the house that Rhodes bought and left to the nation to be occupied by its prime ministers, has never had an Englishman living in it since its donor died. This is due to the Boers, apart from being more numerous in Africa than the British South Africans, having greater political genius.

Noel Busch, in his article in *Life* on Smuts, gives an excellent picture of the General and the Boers, who in forty years have changed very little. He says: "Among other peculiarities of Afrikaan South Africans is the fact that money, *per se*, does not greatly interest them. Addicted to competitive talking rather than earning, they often live like *Tobacco Road*, but usually think like philosophers. What infuriates Afrikaan South Africans about the British South Africans, is not so much that the British are richer, as that being richer, they think that they are therefore better off. Boers in general are far too sure of themselves to feel the need of small pretensions. Doornkloof (General Smuts's home), though more luxurious than most Boer farms, is otherwise representative. Tea is served by Mrs. Smuts from an oilcloth-covered table on the screened-in portion of the porch next to the kitchen. Outside his grass, Smuts's chief interest at Doornkloof is his celebrated library, reached by a passage, also book-lined, opposite the front door. Smuts spends most of his evenings there and would doubtless often sleep in it as well if, among the massive polished stinkwood desks, poisonous arrows, aluminium chairs, *Punch* cartoons, animals' skins, flags, assegais, and air-cooling apparatus, there were room to pitch a cot. Since there is not, he has two small bedrooms near the library, one indoors next his bathroom, and the other outside on the porch. Next to his iron outdoor bed, there has stood for thirty years a certain kitchen chair which Smuts finds handy as a lampstand.

Back of the lampstand and the bed there rests on its side for no special reason an empty wooden box. Bits of railroad track are placed inside the box in order to prevent its tipping over."

Speaking of himself, Smuts says: "I have sampled the world and human nature at many points and I have learnt that it takes all sorts to make a world. But through it all my conviction has only deepened that there is nothing in the nature of things which is alien to what is best in us. There is no malign fatalism which makes fools of us in our dark striving towards the good. On the contrary, what is highest in us is deepest in the nature of things, and as virtue is its own reward, so life carries its own sanctions and the guarantee of its own fulfilments and perfections. That is my ultimate Credo; and it is not founded on hearsay, but on my first-hand experience in that cross-section of the world which I have lived through. This is no doubt a slender basis of fact for so large a conclusion. But the final convictions are not inductions from experience, but insights into it. I remain at heart an optimist." Of his own people he says: "The temper of South Africans is curious and full of individuality. They are only a handful of whites ... each private thinks he is a general. ... Look at the other dominions, no quarrels, no problems. Everything smooth and easy, how empty! how dull! Now—there isn't a single problem under the sun we haven't in this Union of ours. Black, yellow, brown, and white, we have them all. ... Can it be said we are a peaceful nation? Of course it can't. But it cannot be said we are not an interesting nation. How exciting life is here! How there is a passion here that creates a kind of genius!"

And speaking of money, again he says, "What would I do with money? Money would only be a nuisance to me." It is this almost dislike of money which still differentiates the Boer from most other races. It is less prevalent to-day than it was, but it is still there, and is due to a great extent to a dislike of ostentation, of what Veblen calls conspicuous spending. A rich Boer lives very much like a poor one, and, on analysis, most money is spent, not on necessities but on impressive luxuries. This is the basic psychological reason that South Africa, with its great riches, has a population of only two million white people. The South African prefers to be a small frog in a big puddle and wants neither the competition nor the crowding of a modern society.

The history of the Boer is the history "of escaping from the next man. Of demanding privacy, which to him is happiness."

White South Africa still sleeps, while the Black, which has slept so long, begins to stir. This is both the past and the future of Africa—the relationship between the black and white, and the difference between the sleep of an impossible isolation and a consciousness of the world and South Africa's place within it. It is the interplay of these forces which have made her history. Rhodes, Kruger, and Lobengula in the past were political catalysts. Come what may, Africa remains, and history, which is lodged in the story of her great men, must continue to bear fruit, for an historical event—a war, a massacre, an insult, or an act of courage—is not a tree which can be rooted out branch and stem from the hearts of a people. All that can happen is that the tree can die slowly or alternatively can be rejuvenated by additional grafts. It is as political horticulturists that these great men must be considered—as master gardeners, who, if they desired different blooms and different fruits, at·least, desired blooms and fruits, and wished, each in his own fashion, for what he thought to be best for his country and his people. There can be little comparison between them, for each in his way served his turn and his time, each was the flower of his race and period and as such representative of it.

Oil and water cannot be compared. They have no common denominator except that both are liquids. They cannot mix without the addition of an emulsifying element. This element was the freedom that Smuts obtained for conquered republics by gaining Dominion status for the Union.

The future of Africa is almost impossible to predict. Certain facts, however, are apparent. Its riches, except for gold and copper, are still almost untouched. Industrial expansion has been forced upon it by the war. The so-called native question will have to be dealt with and the gradual education of natives will create a local market for consumer goods. It seems possible that the affiliation of all African colonies, dominions, and dependencies into a single block is at least becoming theoretically possible. In addition, there is the probability that South African agriculture will be vastly stimulated by the discovery that organic matter in the form of carbohydrates—sugar, starch, cellulose—can replace oil. In Africa there is a practically inexhaustible supply of such carbohydrates reproduced under natural conditions at least once each year.

General Smuts, speaking of the native question, says: "With us there are certain axioms now in regard to the relations of white and black; and the principal one is 'no intermixture of blood between the two colours.' It is probably true that earlier civilisations have largely failed because that principle was never recognised, civilising races being rapidly submerged in the quicksands of the African blood. It has now become an accepted axiom. In these great matters of race, colour, and culture, residential separation and parallel institutions alone can do justice to the ideals of both sections of the population. The system is accepted and welcomed by the vast majority of natives; but it is resented by a small educated minority who claim 'equal rights' with the whites. It is, however, evident that the proper place of the educated minority of the natives is with the rest of their people, of whom they are the natural leaders, and from whom they should not in any way be dissociated. Far more difficult questions arise on the industrial plane. It is not practicable to separate black and white in industry, and their working together in the same industry and in the same works leads to a certain amount of competition and friction and antagonism, for which no solution has yet been found. Unhappy attempts have been made in South Africa to introduce a colour ban, and an Act of that nature is actually on the Statute Book, but happily no attempt has yet been made to apply it in practice. It empowers the Government to set aside separate spheres of work for the native and the non-native, the object being to confine the native to the more or less unskilled occupations or grades of work. The inherent economic difficulties of such a distribution of industrial functions, the universal objection of the native workers, and the sense of fair play among the whites will make its practical application virtually impossible. No statutory barrier of that kind should be placed on the native who wishes to raise himself in the scale of civilisation, nor could it be maintained for long against the weight of modern public opinion. As a worker the white man should be able to hold his own in competition with the native. Industrial, as distinguished from territorial, segregation would be both impracticable and an offence against the modern conscience."

This theory would appear to be tenable at present, but is probably doomed to failure in the future when educated natives will wish to move socially among their white economic equals. It would appear impossible, on a basis of colour alone, to create permanent barriers between people who are civilised. The desirable does not enter into the argument—only the possible. It would have been desirable that no slaves should ever have been exported from Africa. It would have been desirable that the native culture of the Bantu tribes should merely have been modified and not destroyed. But these are the problems of the future, and will be dealt with by the future leaders of South Africa. Whoever they are, they will not be able to love their land more greatly than the great men of the past. To the South African his country is his life. It is incomparable. Smuts cannot be said to love Africa more than Kruger did. Kruger cannot be said to have loved Africa more than Rhodes. They merely loved two different and incompatible Africas.

There can be little comparison between Rhodes and Kruger, little comparison between the bull and the eagle. The eagle Rhodes saw the world a pattern beneath him and stooped with folded wings upon his prey. The bull Kruger knew and loved his land and would bear no encroachment upon it. Seeing less than Rhodes, he felt more, or, if not more, more personally, of men and soil and less of space and power. The one was objective and the other subjective. Rhodes loved England, the Empire, and a few men, such as Pickering, Jameson, and Beit. Kruger loved Africa, all of it, its veld, its rugged mountains, its dry sandy river beds, and all his people. The width of vision of the one was only paralleled by the narrow integrity of the other. Both Kruger and Rhodes shared one physical characteristic—they were big heavy men, but the resemblance ended there; for Kruger in his youth was a great athlete and hunter, while Rhodes was always a poor shot and despised games. Rhodes's voice was high-pitched, Kruger's a bass that roared when aroused. Kruger was an elder, practically a minister, of the church when he was not a farmer, soldier, or political leader. Rhodes was a financier when he was not a politician. Kruger was a family man, the father of a multitude, while Rhodes was never in his life known to express anything but a dislike of women. Kruger loved animals and made a reserve for them; Rhodes had a private zoo. Rhodes drank champagne and brandy; Kruger smoked almost continuously, but never touched alcohol. Rhodes went to Oxford; Kruger had only three months' schooling in his life. Rhodes believed in imperial expansion; Kruger believed in isolation. To Rhodes, money was power; to Kruger, it was the source of all evil. Rhodes's dream was a world free from war through a gigantic Anglo-Saxon racial block; Kruger's dream was of a world governed by the Word of God, which, oddly, if every one believed in and acted on the words of our Lord, would produce the same result. Thus, approaching the same problem from opposite ends, Rhodes and Kruger met on common ground, though it is doubtful if either of them ever saw the question in this light. Lobengula, caught between the upper and nether millstone of these two men, was ground to pulp. Then, inevitably, the stones having nothing more to grind, were forced to grind upon each other.

Thus, simply, ends the story of these three men and those who accompanied them on their journey through life. Much has been left out, much oversimplified. If some of the deductions are right, others, because of human fallibility and prejudice, are bound to be wrong. But a picture, well drawn or ill, of our land remains.

It is easy to pull down the great: easy, because it is easier to destroy them than to emulate; easier to take sides than to try to understand. Yet these men were great—Rhodes, Kruger, and Lobengula towered over the other men of their time and race. Their story is a part of our story, part of the history of our race and of our time. At once an example and a warning to heroes, despots, and bigots—an example of great men who died unheroically in bed.

They are dead, but Africa lives on, its last battle perhaps fought, and a Nation at last and truly born.

THE END

APPENDIX I

SOURCES

THE MAIN SOURCES used were:

Manfred Nathan's *Paul Kruger.*
Paul Kruger's *Memoirs.*
Sarah Gertrude Millin's *Cecil Rhodes.*
Hugh Marshall Hole's *The Passing of the Black Kings.*

The books listed, and many others unlisted, were also used in a lesser degree and their inclusion is due to a wish to show range of this African source material and to suggest titles to those who wish to pursue the subject. Lobengula is not well documented and much that has been written about him is obviously biased and no more than a justification of the Matabele wars. There is less about Kruger than Rhodes, for the Boers of fifty years ago were not a literary people—one book, the Bible, was enough for them.

Barnard, Lady Anne. *South Africa a Century Ago.*
Birkby, Carel. *Zulu Journey.*
Black, W. T. *The Fish River Bush.*
Brandt, Johanna. *Petticoat Commando.*
Burlingame, Roger. *Engines of Democracy.*
Cambridge History of the British Empire, vol. VIII, *South Africa.*
Chilvers, Hedley A. *Out of the Crucible: The Yellow Man Looks on: The Seven Lost Trails of Africa.*
Cloete, The Hon. H. *The History of the Great Boer Trek.*
Columbia Encyclopedia, The.
Cory, Sir George E. *Owens Diary: The Rise of South Africa.*
Creswell, W. *Our South African Empire.*
Cumming, Gordon. *A Hunter's Life in Africa.*
De Wet, C. R. *Three Years War.*
Doyle, A. Conan. *The Great Boer War.*

Du Val, Charles. *With a Show Through Southern Africa.*
Encyclopedia Britannica.
Engelenburg, Dr. F. V. *General Louis Botha.*
Farson, Negley. *Behind God's Back.*
Fitzpatrick, Percy. *The Transvaal from Within: South African Memories.*
Fitzsimons, F. W. *Snakes.*
Fleming, Rev. Francis. *Kaffraria and Its Inhabitants.*
Fort, Seymour. *Life of Beit.*
Fuller, Claude. *Louis Trigardt's Trek.*
Gardiner, Captain Allen, F. *Narrative of a Journey to the Zoolu Country in South Africa.*
Garret, F. E. *The Story of an African Crisis.*
Green, Goodwin E. *Raiders and Rebels in South Africa.*
Haggard, Rider H. *The Last Boer War.*
Hammond, John Hays. *Autobiography.*
Handbook for Farmers in South Africa.
Harris, William Cornwallis. *Wild Sports of Southern Africa.*
Hole, Hugh Marshall. *The Making of Rhodesia: The Jameson Raid: The Passing of the Black Kings: Lobengula.*
Hone, Percy F. *Southern Rhodesia.*
Juta, Marjorie. *The Pace of the Ox.*
Juta, Rene. *The Cape Peninsula.*
Kerr, Montague. *The Far Interior.*
Kruger, Paul. *Memoirs.*
Laidler, P. *A Tavern of the Ocean.*
Langer, William L. (ed.). *Encyclopedia of World History.*
Leigh, William. *Frontiers of Enchantment.*
Le Vaillant, François. *Travels in Africa.*
Lichtenstein, Henry. *Travels in Southern Africa.*
Liebbrandt, H. C. V. *Cape of Good Hope Archives.*
Livingstone, David. *Travels and Researches in South Africa.*
Lucas, Thos. T. *The Zulus and the British Frontier.*
Millin, Sarah Gertrude. *Cecil Rhodes: The South Africans: South Africa.*
Montague, Captain W. E. *Campaigning in South Africa.*
Mossop, Dr. E. *Old Cape Highways.*
Nathan, Manfred. *Paul Kruger: The Voortrekkers of South Africa.*
Newman, N. *With the Boers in the Transvaal.*

Nixon, John. *The Complete Story of the Transvaal.*
Oates, F. *Matabeleland and the Victoria Falls.*
Parr, Captain H. H. *A Sketch of Kaffir and Zulu Wars.*
Pettman, Charles. *Africkanderisms.*
Rainier, Peter W. *My Vanished Africa.*
Regan, W. F. *Boer and Uitlander.*
Reitz, Deneys. *Commando.*
Rorke, Melina. *By Herself.*
Schapero, I. *The Khoisan People of South Africa.*
Schreiner, S. C. Cronwright. *The Migratory Springboks of South Africa.*
Scully, W. C. *History of South Africa.*
Selous, Frederic Courteney. *Sunshine and Storm in Rhodesia: A Hunter's Wanderings in Africa.*
Selwyn, James. *South of the Congo.*
Simpson, T. S. M. *South Africa Fights.*
Smuts, Jan Christiaan. *Towards a Better World.*
South and East African Year Book.
Sowden, Lewis. *The Union of South Africa.*
Spengler, Oswald. *Man and Technics: The Decline of the West.*
Stathan, Reginald F. *Paul Kruger and His Times.*
Stevenson-Hamilton, Col. H. *The Low Veld.*
Stow, George. *The Native Races of South Africa.*
Trollope, Anthony. *South Africa.*
Tuller, Thomas. *Cecil John Rhodes.*
Walker, E. A. *The Great Trek.*
Wells, A. W. *South Africa.*
Wells, Carveth. *Introducing Africa.*
Wilmot, The Hon. A. *The History of Our Own Lives in South Africa.*

SOUTH AFRICAN NOVELS
  Dehan, Richard. *The Dop Doctor.*
  Schreiner, Olive. *The Story of an African Farm.*
  Young, Francis Brett. *They Seek a Country: The City of Gold.*

APPENDIX II

HISTORICAL SURVEY OF SOUTH AFRICA[1]

AT THE END of the eighteenth century, the Dutch were still in possession of Cape Colony, where they had established themselves in 1652. Cattle farmers continued to push the frontier of settlement eastward along the coast and northward into the veld. The Orange River was reached in 1760 and the Great Fish River in 1776.

1814, May 30. By the Treaty of Paris the British secured definite possession of the Cape.

1820. About four thousand British colonists (Albany Settlers) settled in the eastern coastal region by the British Government, giving the colony for the first time a noticeable English tinge.

1822. A proclamation provided for the gradual establishment of English in place of Dutch as the official language.

1826. The Cape Colony was extended northward to the Orange River.

1834. Abolition of slavery throughout the British Empire, with compensation to the owners.

Great invasion of the eastern regions by the Kaffirs, irritated by the constant encroachment of the Dutch cattlemen and farmers.

1835-1837. THE GREAT TREK of the Dutch (Boer) cattlemen and farmers to the north and the east of the Orange River. Irritated by the restrictions on slavery and by the sympathetic native policy of the Government, the Boers sought new lands and freedom from interference. About ten thousand moved northward. Under A. H. Potgieter they passed beyond the Vaal River and settled in what became the Transvaal. Those under Piet Retief crossed the Drakensberg and began to occupy Zululand and Natal, regions largely depopulated by the ravages of Chaka, the great military leader of the Zulus.

[1] Cape of Good Hope, Orange Free State, Natal, South African Republic, Rhodesia, German Southwest Africa. Condensed and reprinted from *An Encyclopædia of World History*, edited by William L. Langer, Boston : Houghton Mifflin Company, 1940.

1838, Feb. Retief and sixty followers were treacherously slain by Dingaan, the powerful king of the Zulus, who massacred the immigrants and thereupon destroyed Durban.

Dec. 16. Dingaan was defeated by the Boers, now led by Pretorius. The Boers thereupon settled in Natal (Republic of Natal).

1840. Dingaan was defeated by his rival, Umpanda, who became king of the Zulus and accepted the rule of the Boers. Immigration of the Zulus from Zululand into Natal continued unchecked.

1842. War between the Boers and the British in Natal. The Boers were repulsed and British authority established.

1843, Aug. 8. Natal was made a British colony. Thereupon many of the Boers departed, moving northward over the Vaal River.

Dec. 13. By treaty with Moshesh, powerful leader of the Basutos, Basutoland became a native state under British protection. A similar treaty was made with the Griqua chief. Thus many Voortrekkers were put under native jurisdiction.

1844. May 31. Natal was combined with Cape Colony for administrative purposes.

1848, Feb. 3. The British governor of the Cape proclaimed as British territory all the region between the Orange and Vaal Rivers and the Drakensberg. The Boers were disunited, but some, under Pretorius, opposed the British. They were defeated.

1850-1853. Great Kaffir War on the eastern frontier of Cape Colony.

1852, Jan. 17. By the Sand River Convention the British Government recognised the independence of the Transvaal.

1854, Feb. 17. By the Convention of Bloemfontein the British Government withdrew from the territory north of the Orange River. The settlers thereupon organised the Orange Free State, with a president and a volksraad.

1856, Dec. 16. Organisation of the South African Republic (Transvaal), after years of confusion. Pretorius became president, and Pretoria (founded 1855) the capital.

Self-destruction of the Kaffirs, who slaughtered their cattle in the hope, encouraged by their prophets, that the heroes of old would return and drive out the white man. The population, deprived of food, died of starvation, and in the end was reduced to about one-third of the original number.

1857, June 1. The South African Republic and the Orange Free State recognised each other's independence.

1860-1864. Pretorius was at the same time president of the South African Republic and of the Orange Free State, thus establishing a close bond between the two Boer states.

1865-1866. War of the Boers of the Orange Free State against Moshesh, the chieftain of the Basutos.

1866. Kaffraria was joined to Cape Colony.

1867. Discovery of diamonds near Hopetown, on the Orange River.

1867-1868. The Orange Free State defeated the Basutos, who had risen in protest against the cession of territory in 1866.

1868. Mar. 12. The British annexed Basutoland, following a petition by Moshesh. His lands were returned to him, despite the protests of the Orange Free State.

Forces from the Transvaal attempted to occupy Delagoa Bay.

1871. The town of Kimberley was founded and soon became the centre of the great diamond industry. The opening-up of this great wealth completely changed the economic setup in South Africa.

Oct. 27 The British Government annexed the diamond region (Griqualand West), which had been under the rule of the half-breed chief, Waterboer, under the authority of the Orange Free State since 1854. The Orange Free State vigorously protested against this action, which had much to do with stimulating Boer distrust of the British.

1871-1872. The efforts of the British to bring about federation of the South African colonies were frustrated by the opposition of the Cape Government.

1871. The government of Basutoland was taken over by the Cape Colony.

1872. Thomas Burgers, a learned Dutch minister from Cape Colony, became president of the South African Republic.

1875. Lord Carnarvon, continuing his efforts toward federation, arranged for an informal conference at London. As a result the claims of the Orange Free State to the diamond country was settled by a money payment.

1876. The Cape Government extended its influence up the west coast of Africa, concluding treaties with native chiefs as far as the frontier of Angola, but this policy was disavowed by the Home Government.

1877-1880. Sir Bartle Frere, governor of Cape Colony. His purpose was to push forward the work towards federation.

1877, Apr. 12. Annexation of the South African Republic by the British. This was intended as a step toward federation, but was a flagrant violation of the Sand River Convention. The Boers, under the leadership of Paul Kruger, protested vigorously, but without avail.

1877-1878. Kaffir War. As a result the British annexed all of Kaffraria, and in the following years (1879-1886) extended their authority to the north-east.

1877, Mar. 12. The British annexed Walfish Bay on the coast of South-West Africa. German missionaries had been active on that coast since 1842, and had, in 1868, appealed to the British Government for annexation.

1879. The Zulu War, against Cetywayo (king since 1872). Cetywayo had built up again the military power of the Zulus. Jan. 22 he defeated the British in a battle at Isandhlwana. Reinforcements were rushed to the front, and July 4 Sir Garnet Wolseley won a decisive victory at Ulundi. Cetywayo was captured Aug. 28 and peace was made with the Zulu chiefs Sept. 1.

1879. Foundation of the Afrikander Bond, a Dutch group designed to work for recognition of the Dutch language. Under the influence of Jan Hofmeyr it soon rallied most of the Dutch elements in the Cape Colony, but with a much larger programme of South Africa for the South Africans, with gradual elimination of interference from the British Government.

1880-1881. Revolt of the Transvaal Boers against the British. Dec. 30 a Boer republic was proclaimed by Kruger, Joubert, and Pretorius. The Boers repulsed a British force under Sir George Colley at Laing's Nek, and again defeated and killed Colley at Majuba Hill. The British Government, under Gladstone, was unwilling to contest the desire of the Boers for freedom, and Apr. 5 concluded the Treaty of Pretoria, by which the South African Republic was given independence, but under the suzerainty of Great Britain.

1880. Organisation of the diamond industry. Two great corporations were founded: the Barnato Diamond Mining Company and the De Beers Mining Corporation.

1880-1881. The "Gun War" in Basutoland Colony.

1882. Establishment of Stellaland and Goshen, two Boer states in Bechuanaland. This was part of the Boer expansion to the westward.

1883, Apr. 16. Kruger became president of the South African Republic.

1883, Aug. Lüderitz, a German merchant, purchased from the natives a large tract of territory north of the Orange River. When Lüderitz hoisted the German flag at Angra Pequena there was much excitement in London as well as at Capetown.

1884, Feb. 27. The Convention of London further defined the relations of the South African Republic to Great Britain.

1884, May. Fearful of German expansion eastward as far as the Transvaal and the cutting of the route to the north, the British, under the influence of Cecil Rhodes, concluded treaties of protection with the native chiefs of Bechuanaland.

1884, Aug. The Boers, under Joubert, attempted to establish a republic in Zululand and thus secure themselves access to the sea on the east.

1884, Dec. 18. In order to frustrate this move, the British Government annexed St. Lucia Bay to Natal.

1885, Sept. 30. The Bechuana territory was organised as British Bechuanaland (the region between the Orange and Molopo Rivers) and as the Bechuanaland protectorate (north of the Malopo).

1886. Discovery of gold on the Witwatersrand in the southern Transvaal. Gold had been found in various parts of the Transvaal before this, but the rich reefs were opened up only at this time. There was a wild rush to the Rand. Johannesburg was laid out. Rhodes and his associates took an active part in the financing and organisation of the industry, and his company soon controlled a large share of the business.

1887. The British annexed Zululand.

1888. Amalgamation of the De Beers and Barnato diamond interests, giving the De Beers corporation, under Rhodes, practically a monopoly of the industry.

1888, Feb. 11. J. S. Moffat, a missionary and agent of Rhodes, concluded a treaty with Lobengula, king of the Matabele, by which the latter accepted British protection.

1888, Oct. 30. In a further treaty Lobengula gave the Rhodes interest exclusive mining rights in Matabeleland and Mashonaland.

1889. The Cape Colony and Orange Free State concluded a customs union. At the same time the Free State and the Transvaal (South African Republic) concluded a defensive alliance.

1889, Oct. 29. The British Government granted a charter to the British South Africa Company, headed by Rhodes.

1890, July 17. Cecil Rhodes became prime minister of the Cape Colony. He enjoyed the support of the Afrikander Bond.

1891, June 10. Dr. Jameson was made administrator of the South Africa Company's territories.

1892, Sept. The first trains from the Cape arrived at Johannesburg. An immense traffic developed and the income from the railways came to be a vital factor in the finance of Cape Colony.

In Johannesburg Charles Leonard organised the foreign (Uitlander) element in the National Union, to agitate for better educational advantages, better police, easier franchise requirements, etc.

1893, Apr. 12. Kruger was elected president of the South African Republic for another term of five years.

1893, May 12. Responsible government was introduced in Natal.

1893. July. War of Lobengula against the Mashonas. The South Africa Company interfered, defeated the Matabeles and took Bulawayo. The chiefs submitted and the danger passed with the death of Lobengula.

1893, Nov. 13. By the Pretoria Convention Great Britain agreed that the Transvaal should have Swaziland, which, however, did not give the Boers access to the sea.

1894, Sept. 25. The British annexed Pondoland, thus connecting the Cape Colony with Natal.

1894, Nov. Rhodes paid a visit to Kruger and renewed his efforts to induce the Transvaal Government to join the other states in a customs union.

1895, May 3. The territory of the South Africa Company south of the Zambesi was named Rhodesia, in honour of Rhodes.

1895, June 11. The British annexed Tongoland in order to block the last possible access of the Transvaal to the sea.

1895, July 8. Opening of the Delagoa Bay Railway from Johannesburg and Pretoria to the sea. This gave the Transvaal at least an economic outlet free of all British influence.

1895, Nov. 11. British Bechuanaland was attached to the Cape Colony.

1895, Dec. 29—1896, Jan. 2. The Jameson Raid.

1896, Jan. 6. Because of his part in the Jameson Raid episode, Rhodes was obliged to resign as prime minister of the Cape Colony.

1896, Mar. In Rhodesia there was another rising of the Matabele.

1896, Mar. 17. The Transvaal and the Orange Free State concluded an offensive and defensive treaty, a direct reaction to the Jameson Raid.

1896, Sept. 26. Aliens Expulsion Act passed in the Transvaal. This, and the Aliens Immigration Restriction Act (Nov. 26, 1896), and various restrictions on the press and on public meeting, resulted in continuous friction between Great Britain and the Transvaal.

1897, Nov. 4. The railroad from the Cape reached Bulawayo, in southern Rhodesia. This line was intended by Rhodes ultimately to connect the Cape with Cairo.

1897, Dec. 1. Zululand was annexed to Natal.

1898, Feb. 10. Kruger was re-elected president of the South African Republic for five years.

1899, Mar. 24. The Uitlanders sent a petition with twenty thousand names, to Queen Victoria, recounting their numerous grievances.

1899, May 31—June 5. The Bloemfontein conference between Milner and Kruger, arranged through the efforts of President Steyn of the Orange Free State.

1899, Oct. 12—1902, May 31. The South African (Boer) War.

By the Treaty of Vereeniging (May 31, 1902) the Boers accepted British sovereignty, but were promised representative institutions as soon as circumstances should permit; the British Government promised a grant of £3,000,000 to enable them to rebuild their farms.

1902, Apr. 25. The Transvaal was granted a constitution, with an elected assembly. This arrangement was condemned by Botha as inadequate.

1906, Dec. 6. By a new constitutional instrument, the Transvaal was granted responsible government.

1907, July 1. A new constitution, with responsible government, was established in the Orange River Colony.

1908, Oct. 12—1909, Feb. 3. Meeting of a Constitutional Convention, first at Durban, then at Capetown. The older ideas of federation were now brushed aside and the sentiment spread rapidly in favour of union. The convention agreed on a scheme for a Union of South Africa.

1909, Sept. 20. The draft constitution was approved by the British Parliament as the South Africa Act. It went into effect on May 31, 1910.

APPENDIX III

NOTES ON NATIVE NAMES

HUGH MARSHALL HOLE, one of the best authorities on the spelling of native names, says:

"The study of South African history had been made unnecessarily difficult by the queer variations adopted by different writers in the spelling of native names of persons and places. These vagaries arise mainly from the fact that, as the natives in their aboriginal state had no knowledge of writing, Europeans have been obliged to fall back upon their own alphabets to express sounds which they do not always provide for, and in this respect everybody has been a law unto himself.... It is sheer pedantry to write the name of the Matabele King Ulopengule, as the missionary Thomas persists in doing, when the rest of the world calls him, and spells him, Lobengula, and the same applies to many other well-known Bantu names.... A Scottish journalist, possibly with a laudable desire to make things easier for his fellow-countrymen, calls the river in the north of Bechuanaland McLoutsie, on the analogy of McKenzie!..."

Ordinary Spelling	*Variants*
Bechuana	Boochooana; Bechwana (Lloyd)
Bulawayo	Gubuluwayo; Bulowaigo (Baines)
Dingaan (Zulu king)	Umtigana (Lloyd)
Khama	Kgama; Khame; Khâme (Lloyd) Khami
Kalahari (desert)	Khalahari (Lloyd)
Lobengula	Ulopengule (Thomas) Lumpengula (Mohr); Lopguela; Lopingula; Lopenula (Blue Books)
Matabele	Amandebele; ma-Tebele (Bryant)
Mantabele (Blue Book) Matabili	
Matopo (hills)	Amadobo (Thomas)

Mjaan (Matabele general)	Mtyana
Mziligazi	Mzilikazi (Posselt); Moselekatse (Moffat); Morelekatse (Blue Book) Masulakatse (Cloete) Moselikatze
Ningi (Lobengula's sister)	Mncencengni; Ningengnee (Selous); Nini (Cumming) Nina
Palapye (Mangwato town)	Palapswe; Phalapi; Palachwe; Palapshe, etc.
Zulu	Zoolu, Amazulu
Chaka (Zulu king)	T'chaka, Tshaka
Cetewayo (Zulu king)	Ketchwhyo
Panda (Zulu king)	Umpande

Index

Aborigines Protection Society, 222.
Abyssinian War of 1935-36, 249.
Adams, Major Gould, 229, 246, 252.
Africa, changes in, 186-87, colonisations of, 17, 18, 21, 178, 195; cultural conflicts in, 17; descriptions of, 32, 33, 189, 190; discovery of, 19; explorations in, 19; future of, 453-55; history and influence of, 19, 22, 389-92; inhabitants of, 15, 389-90; land disputes in, 234; products of, 19; rise of nationalism in, 220.
Afrikaaner Bond, 274.
Amatetwa, nation of, rise to power under Diniswayo, 75.
Anglo-Boer War (1880). *See* War of Independence.
Anglo-Portuguese-Congo-Zambesi Agreement Conference, 176.
Anstruther, Colonel, 142.
Atherstone, Doctor, 110.
Austin, Alfred, 313-14.
Aydelotte, Doctor Frank, 399-400.
Ayleward, A., 146.

Baker, Sir Herbert, 205.
Balfour, Arthur, 351.
Bantus, and Dutch, conflicts with, 20; history of, 17.
Bapedi, native tribe, 119; Burgers' forces defeated by, 113; national rise of, 112; Sekukuni leader of, 113.
Barnato, Barney, 137-39, 198-99, 231, 323, 396, 403.
Barotseland, 16, 385.
Barrett, Francisco, 388.
Bastaards, Griqualand settled by, 103-4; origins of, 104.
Basuto nation, 57.
Basuto War (First), 58; (Second), 72, 73, 275.

Bechuana, native tribe, 92; defeated by Matabele, 93.
Bechuanaland, 162-63, 218.
Bezuidenhout, Frederick, 30, 140.
Bezuidenhout, Johannes, 140.
Bezuidenhout, Piet, 140.
Belgium, 17, 195.
Bent, Theodore, 289.
Bethell, Commander, 162.
Biet, Alfred, 137, 190, 199-200, 214, 267, 271, 295.
Bigelow, Poultney, 53, 59, 168.
Bishop Stortford. *See* Rhodes, birth of.
Bismarck, Chancellor Otto von, 17, 162, 170, 172, 175-77, 196, 277.
Blunt, Sir Wilfred, 205, 319.
Boer Rebellion (1914), 18.
Boer Revolt. *See* War of Independence.
Boer War (1900), beginning of, 362, 368; Boers, allied in, 361; Boers, delaying tactics of in, 413-17, 419, 423; Boers, partial surrender of in, 374; campaigns in, 369-70, 373-74, 416-18; causes of, 291, 365-66; characteristics of, 371; comparison with recent wars, 446-47; conditions immediately prior to, 360-62; destruction of property in, 375; end of, 423-27; England's part in starting of, 351, 353, 356-61; Kimberley besieged during, 377-78; mobilisation of troops for, 359-60; phases of, 375-76, 417-18; Pretoria occupied during, 416.
Boers, appearance of, 34; characteristics and attitudes of, 28-29, 49, 68, 108, 109, 111, 131, 132, 153, 186, 275, 277, 283, 444-45, 451-52; civil wars among, 57, 70; and English, basis for conflict with, 29, 49, 187-88, 195; farms, houses, and provisions of, 15, 27, 39-40; fighting methods of, 72; take

471

Great Trek. (*See* Great Trek) ; life and customs of 42, 43, 68, 69 ; natives, conflicts with, 40, 92, 93 ; origins of, 15 ; slave raids of, 18, 55, 105 ; territorial expansion of, 163 ; war camp of, described, 146.
Bok, Edouard, 117, 119, 124.
Bolivar, Simón, 194, 396, 438.
Boshoff, 56, 69.
Botha, General, 351, 373, 380, 425, 432, 433-35, 449, 451.
Boukenhoutfontein. *See* Kruger, houses of.
Boyes, Lorenzo, 110.
Brand, President, 142, 165.
Brandt, Johanna, 416.
Britain. *See* England.
British Empire, additions to, 16-17.
Bulawayo. *See* Lobengula, palace of.
Bunu Incident, 356.
Burgher, Schalk, 352, 414, 433.
Burgers, Thomas François, 366 ; Bapedi fought by, 112-14 ; Kruger's opposition to, 112-14 ; South African Republic, President of, 111, 114.
Burnham, Frederick, 235, 253, 330, 343.
Burnham, Mrs. Frederick, 235.
Busch, Noel, 451.
Bushmen, Bantus' destruction of, 17 ; Kaffirs ancestors of, 15 ; slave raids on, 55.
Buys, Coenraad, 31.
Buys, Suzanna Lasya, 25.
Buys-Folk of Transvaal, 31.

Cameroons, 172, 177.
Cape coloured, origins of, 15.
Cape of Good Hope, colonisation by Dutch, 17, 20; products of, 68 ; rounding of, 20.
Cape-to-Cairo Railroad. *See* Rhodes, desire for.
Carnarvon, Lord, 114, 117-19.
Carter, author of *A Narrative of the Boer War*, 116.
Celliers, Sarel, 36.
Cetywayo, 120-21, 174.
Chadwick, Cooper, 225.

Chamberlain, Joseph, 116, 222-318, 350, 352-53, 357-58, 383, 421.
Chartered Company, 211, 231, 234-35, 238, 255, 261, 269, 298, 317, 319, 341.
Chartered Company Police, 293.
Chelmsford, Lord, 121.
Christelijk-Gereformeerde Church. *See* Dopper.
Churchill, Lord Randolph, 14, 210.
Churchill, Winston, 449-50.
Civil War (Boer), 56, 69-70.
Cloete, Francina, 25.
Colenbrander, Johann, 202, 222, 234-36, 242-44, 346-47.
Colenbrander, Maria (Mrs. Johann), 235, 242-44.
Colley, General George Pomeroy, 120, 142-45.
Columbus, Christopher, 19.
Congo, 19, 21, 134, 195.
Convention of London, 160, 162, 270.
Convention of Pretoria, 159.
Copper, discovery of, 331 ; Rhodes's cartel plans for 329-30.
Coventry, Honourable C. J., 294.
Cronje, Petrus Andries, 140.
Cronje, Piet, 305-6, 321.
Cruger, Frans. *See* Kruger.

Damaraland, 63.
Dart, Professor Raymond, 386.
Darwin, Charles, 15, 96, 186, 196, 197, 280, 391.
Dawson, James, 245.
de Beers, 131, 132.
de Beers Mining Company, 134.
de Branza, 195.
Declé, Lionel, 224.
de Gama, Vasco, 388.
de la Rey, General Adriaan, 164, 365, 368, 380, 422-23, 432-33.
Derby, Lord, 159-61, 163, 175.
de Villiers, Lord, 420.
De Wet, Christiaan, 372, 427, 432, 433.
Diamonds, discovery of, 14, 84, 103, 109-10, 131 ; fields, description of, 128 ; geologic origins of, 129 ; mining, method for, 129, 136-37 ;

INDEX

mining camps, description of, 129-30; stones, types of, 130; workers and miners of, 129-30; workers, treatment of, 136.
Dingaan, 36, 346; Boers attacked by, 79-80; cruelty of, 78; defeat of, 80; T'Chaka's death plotted by, 77; T'Chaka succeeded by, 39; Zulus led by, 39.
Diniswayo, Chief of Amatetwa, 75-76.
Dinzulu, 175.
Disraeli, Benjamin, 15, 106, 164, 172, 196.
Dominick, Major, 172.
Doornkloof. *See* Smuts, home of.
Dopper Church, 44, 65, 70; founded by Doctor Postma, 70.
Doyle, Sir Arthur Conan, 368, 372-73, 379, 416.
Dun, John, 17.
du Plessis, Gezina, Suzanna, Frederika, Wilhelmina. *See* Suzanna Kruger (Mrs. Paul).
du Plessis, Maria. *See* Maria Kruger (Mrs. Paul).
du Toit, Reverend, 159, 160, 274.
Du Toit's Pan, description of, 98-100.
Dutch, conflict with Bantus, 20; colonisations by, 17.
Dutch East India Company, 27, 68.

Edward VII, 14, 448.
Eliot, Doctor Charles, 399.
Eloff, Sarel, 413.
Emerson, Ralph Waldo, 195.
England, annexations by: of Griqualand, 103; of Santa Lucia Bay, 174; of South African Republic, 114-27, 141, 149-50; colonisations, attitude toward, 173; colonisations of, 184; Germany, relations with, 171, 260-61, 350-52; Jameson Raid, supported by, 297; social scene during 1880-1900 in, 213; South African Republic opposed by, in Boer War. *See* Boer War.
English, against Boers, 17, 186-87.

Exploration Company, 222.
Exploring Company, 218.
Exportation Company, 218.

Farmers' Defence Association, 274.
Farrar, George, 289.
Farson, Negley, 171.
Federation of South Africa, 126.
Ferry, Jules, 176.
Filibusters, 162.
Fitzpatrick, Sir Percy, 395, 403.
Forbes, Colonel Patrick, 253.
Fowler, Sir Robert, 160.
France, colonisations of, 17, 176, 195.
Frazer, Major, 67.
Free State, arbitration by, before Boer War, 359; Boshoff, President of, 57; Griqualand, claimed by, 103-04; joins South African Republic in Boer War, 356, 361; Pretorius as President of, 69; Pretorius makes claims to, 56.
Frere, Sir Bartle, 83, 110, 120, 122-23, 126, 129.
Freud, Sigmund, 14, 96.
Froude, James Anthony, 120, 129-30, 186.
Fulata, death of, 87; mother of Lobengula, 87.

Gandhi, Mohandas, 450.
Gardiner, Charles, 183.
Garrett, F. E., 300.
Gasibone, 60, 61.
Gazaland, 16.
Germany, colonisations by, 18, 134, 164, 170-73, 175-76, 195; desire for colonies, 17, 175-76; disappearance as colonial power in Africa, 22; England, relations with, 171, 260-61, 351-52; South African Republic, relations with, 260-61, 351, 420, treatment of natives by, 437-38.
Gladstone, William E., 17, 104, 105, 126, 127.
Glen Grey Act, 281-82.
Gold, description of Rand, 184-85; discovery of, 14, 84, 93, 181-83; financing of fields, 184; formation

of fields, 183-84 ; geologic origins of, 183 ; labour in fields, 184 ; mining, methods of, 385-86.
Goldfields Company, 261.
Gordon, General " Chinese," 176, 191, 198.
Goshen, Land or Republic of, 163, 166.
Granville, Lord, 170, 172.
Great Trek of 1836, 13 ; attacked by Matabele, 35-36 ; causes of, 26-28, 104 ; course of, 28 ; dangers on, 33 ; description of, 26-27, 32-34 ; food on, 34 ; merger of, 35 ; pace of, 31-32 ; women on, 35.
Gregorowski, Judge, 323-4.
Gregory, Professor J. W., 386.
Grey, Sir George, 440.
Grey, Major Raleigh, 293, 304, 322.
Griqualand, 102, 104.
Griquas. See Bastaards.
Grobler, Piet, 68, 157, 158, 169, 227, 419.
Groot Schuur. See Rhodes, houses of.

Haggard, Rider, 115, 186, 387.
Hammond, John Hays, 184, 186, 188, 201, 207, 242, 272, 289-90, 309, 330, 353, 387, 410 ; part in Jameson Raid, 292-94, 298-99, 306, 324.
Hammond, Mrs. John Hays, 101, 301, 323.
Harris, Sir David, 200.
Harris, Rutherford, 296, 299, 313.
Hartley, discovers gold, 93, 109, 182.
Hartwigs, Elizabeth, 25.
Hastings, Warren, 102, 214.
Hatzfeldt, Count, 171, 420.
Helm, 219, 221, 229, 232.
Herero, Rebellion of 1903, 18, 338.
Herreros, native tribe, 437 ; origins of, 171.
Hertz, Reverend Doctor J. H., 431.
Hervormde Reformed Church, opposition of, to Kruger, 70.
Heymans, Albert, 370, 434.
Hicks-Beach, Sir Michael, 119.
Hitler, Adolf, 333-35, 407, 410, 411, 443, 444, 449-50.

Hofmeyr, Jan Hendrik, 191, 198, 257, 274, 313, 314-16, 319, 328.
Hogg, British Commissioner, 56.
Hole, Marshall, 211-12, 404.
Hottentots, Bantus' destruction of, 17 ; descended from Kaffirs, 15.
Huxtable, Arthur, 440.

" Incident of the Drifts," 269-70.
Indian Mutiny of 1857, 68.
Indies, search for, 19.
Ingubobubo, 246.
Inyanga. See Rhodes, houses of.
Isaacs, Nathaniel, 76.
Italian-Abyssinian War, 18.

Jacobs, John, 249-50.
Jameson, Sir Leander Starr, arrest of, 306 ; arrival in Africa, 213-14 ; attitude of : on Africa, 210 ; on Boers, 208, 271, on England, 210, on natives, 208, on Reformers, 303 ; besieged in Ladysmith, 378 ; birth of, 207 ; characteristics of, 207-10, 214, 309-10 ; Chartered Company, administrator of, 235 ; condemned to death, 209 ; death of, 209, 210 ; description of, 207 ; health of, 207 ; imprisonment and trial of, 209-10, 322, 340, 353 ; Jameson Raid, part in, 209, 292, 300-02, 304, 312 ; Lobengula, treats with, 230-311, 251-2 ; Mashonaland, rôle in taking, 232 ; Matabeleland, rôle in taking, 239-41, 244-46, 251-52 ; Premier of Rhodesia, 207 ; Prime Minister of Cape Colony, 209-10, 326 ; Reformers' repudiation of, 307 ; Rhodes, friendship with, 102, 207, 209, 212, 272, 314, 380, 395 ; Rhodesia Horse, raised by, 269 ; Uitlanders of South Africa studied by, 261.
Jameson, Sam, 210, 294.
Jameson Raid, arms and supplies for, 292-93, 303 ; attack of, 300, 302, 304-06 ; causes of, 288-89 ; cut off from Reformers, 299-300 ; financing of, 291 ; military organisation of,

INDEX

293-94 ; nationality of Raiders, 320 ; officers of, 294-95 ; plans for, 292-93, 295-99, 329-30 ; reasons for failure of, 319 ; Reformers, part in, 295 ; Rhodes's part in, 292 ; sentence of leaders, 321 ; trial of leaders, 320-22 ; world reactions to failure of, 319.
Jeppe, 69.
Joel, Woolf, 198.
Johannesburg, 18, 156, 186.
John Company of India, 214.
Johnson, Frank, 231.
Johnston, Sir Harry, 174, 387.
Joubert, Frans, 142.
Joubert, Piet, 119, 124, 126, 141, 143, 155-56, 165, 167, 181, 290, 352, 371-72, 417-18.
Jorrisen, Doctor, 117, 187.

Kaffir War, 54.
Kaffirs, cattle, reliance on by, 338-40 ; descendants of, 15 ; origins of, 15 ; Rhodesians' treatment of, 339 ; slave raids on, by Dutch, 55 ; stock thefts by, 18, 29, subdued by, 20 ; as workers in gold fields, 184-85.
Kaiser William I, 162, 173, 183, 314, 319, 350.
Karri-Davies, Colonel, 323.
Kemp, Johanna, 25.
Khama, King of the Bechuanas, 215, 217-20.
Kimberley, besieged, 377-79, description of, 128-29 ; Rhodes at, 100-101.
Kipling, Rudyard, 14, 186, 202, 221, 314, 358, 414, 443, 446-47.
Kitchener, Lord, 373, 425.
Knutford, Lord, 218, 219.
Koch, Robert, 337.
Kruger family, settled in the Transvaal, 37.
Kruger, Frans, 25.
Kruger, Gerrit, 25.
Kruger, Hendrik, 25.
Kruger, Jacob, 25.
Kruger, Kaspar Jan Hendrik, 25.
Kruger, Maria (Mrs. Paul), 44, 45, 46.
Kruger, Stephanus Johannes, 25.
Kruger, Stephanus Johannes Paulus,

ancestry and parentage of, 25 ; anecdotes told about, 421-31 ; annexation of South African Republic by British opposed by, 114-17, 121-26, 141 ; Basuto wars, part in, 58, 72-73 ; Boer Civil War, part in, 71-72 ; Boer War, direct part in, 367, 369-70, 374-75, 413 ; birth of, 25, Burgers opposed by, 112-114, 116-17 ; Chamberlain, relations with, 343 ; characteristics, personal and physical, of, 20, 51, 53-54, 63-67, 168, 263-67, 290, 354, 371 ; childhood of, 25, 26, 31, 37, 43 ; children of, 45 ; Commandant in Rustenburg, 58 ; Commandant-General of the South African Republic, 72 ; commando, first one of, 36, 37 ; death and burial of, 20, 435-36; Deputy field-cornet to Delagoa Bay, 44, 48 ; Doppers, member of, 65 ; early military campaigns of, 48-50, 55-56, 60-61 ; education of, 37, 67, 431 ; England, attitude on and relations with, 31, 62, 174, 263, 353, 361 ; evaluation of, 16, 411, 431-32, 438-39, 449 ; exile of, 427-28, 433-34 ; farming in Rustenburg, 15, 63 ; Federation of South Africa, opposed by, 126 ; flees South African Republic, 413-15, 417-22 ; Free State and South African Republic dispute settled by, 69-70 ; To Free State government, services offered by, 57 ; full field cornet and service under Pretorius, 48-49, 56 ; Germany, relations with, 173-74, 260-61 ; Great Trek, part in, 16, 21, 26, 32 ; hatred of gold minings, 14, 181-82, 186 ; Hervormde Reformed Church, opposition to, 70 ; houses of, 44 ; hunting exploits of, 37-38, 43-44 ; " Incident of the Drifts " caused by, 269-70 ; Jameson Raid, attitude on and attempted opposition to, 301, 307, 320 ; Kaffirs, fought by, 73 ; last message of, 434-35 ; Lobengula, relations with, 157-58, 215-16 ; marriage to Maria de Plessis, 44 ; marriage to Suzanna du Plessis, 45 ; meets with Lord Milner, 356-57 ; President of South African Republic, 56, 155-57, 257, 266, 352 ; racial theories of, 21 ; Rhodes, comparison with, 63, 186-88, 190, 195, 392, 395, 402-03, 431, 435, 443, 455-56 ; Rhodes relations and conflict with, 63, 158, 165, 186, 240, 257-60, 355-56, 394 ; spiritual life of, 44-47, 58-60, 65, 97, trips to Europe, 117-19, 159 ; Uitlanders, described by, 267, Vice-President of the South African Republic, 124 ; Volksraad, first speech in, 153 ; War of Independence, part in, 147-50 ; world he lived in, 408-09 ; wounded, 51-53.

Kruger, Suzanna (Mrs. Paul), 45, 271, 301, 370-71, 405, 418, 422.

Labouchere, Henry, 222, 240, 319.
Labran, 378.
Lanyon, Sir Owen, 121, 123.
Laurier, Sir Wilfrid, 420.
Lawley, A. L, 299, 395.
Leonard, Charles, 268, 319.
Leopold II. of Belgium, 134, 170, 175.
Lewanika, chief of the Barotse, 217.
Leyds, Doctor, 53, 419, 429, 431.
Liberal Party, 422.
Lippert, 218.
Livingstone, Doctor, 48, 265.
Lobengula, King of the Matabele, Africa, influence on, 16 ; Allies against, 245 ; ambitions of, 20 ; attitude on gold minings, 14-15 ; death and burial of, 20, 255-56 ; descriptions of, 215, 224-25 ; early life of, 91 ; father, Moselikatze, 16, 85-86 ; father, reunited with, 91-92 ; father, succeeded by, 15-16, 21, 95 ; first battle of, 92 ; flight north of, 250-51, 255 ; Fulata, mother of, 87 ; hunt for, 253 ; Jacobs, advisor of, 249 ; Jameson, treats with, 251-52 ; Kruger, relations with, 57, 159, 216 ; Mashonaland, ceded by, 232-33 ; Matabeleland, protectorate given to Rhodes by, 218-20, 232-33 ; Matabele War, led by, 247 ; missions to England sent by, 222, 230 ; Nyumbakazi, foster-mother of, 87 ; palace of, 226-27 ; pride of, 215 ; Rhodes, relations with, 216-18, 230, 241, 244-46 ; Sara, foster-mother of, 87, 90, 91 ; Shippard, treats with, 227-29 ; sorcerers, control of, 223 ; Wilson Patrol, defeated by, 254 ; wives of, 224 ; Victoria, letters to, 221, 245.

Loch, Sir Henry, 258, 279, 291.
London Chamber of Commerce, 222.
London Missionary Society, 219.
Losikeyi, 223, 249.
Luderitz, Franz Adolph, 170-71, 175, 177.
Lys, Robert, 182-83.

Machabi, 162.
Magato, Kaffir chief, 58.
Maguire, Rochfort, 218.
Mahura, 61.
Majuba Hill, 117, 143-45.
Makapaan, Kaffir chief, 48, 50, 54, 55.
Mackenzie, Reverend John, 160, 163, 164, 166, 222, 277, 355.
Mampoer, 155.
Manicaland, 16, 385.
Mankoroane, 162.
Mapela, Kaffir chief, 49, 50, 55, 58.
Mapoch, 155.
Maritz, Gert, 78-80.
Marks, Sammy, 430.
Marx, Karl, 14.
Mashona, native tribe, 93, 236 ; annexation of Matabeleland, instigated by, 239 ; habits of, 233 ; join Matabele in Second Matabele War, 340.
Matabele, nation of, Boers attacked by, 39, 92-93 ; Bechuana defeated by, 93 ; cattle slaughtered by, 18 ; destroyed, 254 ; founded by Moselikatze, 78, 86-88 ; Great Trek attacked by, 35-36 ; Lobengula, King of, 15-16, 20, 95, 223 ; name, origin of, 36 ; natives attacked by,

INDEX

38 ; rise against Rhodesians by, 340 ; Zulus, break with, 38.
Matabele War of 1893 (First Matabele War), 246-48 ; capital taken in, 250 ; losses in, 248 ; method of fighting, 249.
Matabele War (Second Matabele War), 336 ; beginning of, 340 ; cause of, 336 ; English losses in, 343 ; fighting methods in, 341 ; first attack in, 340-41 ; Rhodes makes peace with natives in, 345-49.
Matabeleland, 16, 215 ; absorption by Rhodes, 239-40, 242-46, 385 ; ceded by Lobengula to Rhodes, 218-19.
Matapos. *See* Rhodes, tomb of.
Mauch, Karl, 93-94, 133, 171, 182-3.
Maude, Captain, 145.
Maund, 218, 221, 224, 233.
Memoirs of Paul Kruger, 26, 38-39, 61, 85.
Methuen, Lord, 373, 378, 422.
Meyer, General Lukas, 174, 432.
Millin, Sarah Gertrude, 101, 139, 166, 194, 196, 215, 233, 249, 268, 318, 346, 389, 438.
Milner, Lord Alfred, 203, 350, 353-58, 446.
M'limo, chief priest of, 334.
Moffat, 215-17, 229, 240.
Montague, Captain, 213, 226.
Montsioa, 56, 162.
Mormons, 334.
Moselele, 48.
Moselikatze, 93-94, Boers fought by, 85 ; death and burial of, 94-95, 215 ; Lobengula, son of, 16, Matabele nation, chief of, 16 ; Matabele nation founded by, 78, 86-88 ; T'Chaka, fled from 16, 40 ; tomb of, desecrated, 349.
Moshesh, chief of Basuto nation, 58, 59, 72.
Moshette, 162.
Munster, Count, 173.
Mussolini, 410.

Nagmaal, 41, 68, 96, 124, 303.
Namaqualand, 163.

Napoleon III., 13, 121.
Nathan, Manfred, 59, 154, 353.
National Union of Reformers, 258, 289.
Newman, N., author, *With the Boers in the Transvaal*, 146-47.
Ngwali, 88, 90, 92.
Nietzsche, Frederick, 186, 197, 280.
Ningi, 86, 134, 223-24.
Nkulumana, 86, 95.

Oates, Frank, 224-25.
Oosthuizen, widow, 183.
Orange Free State. *See* Free State.
O'Reilly, John, 109-10.
Origin of Species (Charles Darwin), 15, 96, 196.
Osborn, Melmoth, 115.
Owen, 78-80.
Owen, British Commissioner, 56.

Panda, 80, 175.
Parliamentary Inquiry of 1897, 320.
Parnell, Charles, 198.
Parr, Henry Hallam, 83.
Peters, Karl, 170, 175.
Phillips, Sir Lionel, 257, 289, 291, 357, 421.
Pickering, Neville, 102, 190, 200-201.
" Place of Slaughter," 76.
Pondoland, 279.
Portuguese East Africa, 16, 158.
Postma, Doctor, 70.
Potgieter, Andries, 47.
Potgieter, Hendrik, leader of Great Trek, 35, 36, 92-93.
Potgieter, Herman, 49.
Potgieter, General Piet, 50-51.
Potter, Mrs. Brown, 284.
Powell, Alexander, 438.
Pretorious, Commandant-General, 48, 54, 56.
Pretorius, Commandant Henning, 307.
Pretorius, President, 112, 141, Commandant-General, 56 ; Free State, President of, 70 ; South African Republic, President of, 56, 69, 104 : War of Independence, part in, 124-25.

Pretorius, Theunis, 48.
Prince Imperial (France), 121.

Radziwill, Princess, 397, 404.
Rand, 183-86.
Randall-MacIver, Doctor David, 386.
Rawstone, Fleetwood, 131.
Reform Committee, 237, 267, 269, 324.
Reform Movement, leaders of, 289; nature of, 289.
Reformers, demands of, 296, 298; Jameson repudiated by, 318; Jameson Raid, part in, 295; leaders of, tried and sentenced, 321-23.
Reitz, Deneys, 371-72, 424-27.
Retief, Piet, 27, 36, 78-80.
Rhodes, Barnard, 98.
Rhodes, Cecil, Afrikaaner Bond, alliance with, 274; arrival in Africa, 15, 16, 21, 98; attitudes of, 13, 15, 17, 20, 97, 102, 133, 192, 200, 284-85; attitude on natives, 196-97, 274-77, 281-84; attitude on Uitlanders, 327; Bechuanaland, relations of Rhodes to, 163-64, 216-19; Biet and Barnato, amalgamation with, 138-39; birth of, 97; Boers relations with, and attitude toward, 128, 166, 380; Boer War, part in, 82, 83, 96, 368, 377, 381, 383; Cape Parliament, elected to, 140; Cape-to-Cairo Railroad, desire for, 174, 238-39, 278, 396, 401; characteristics, personal and physical, of, 99, 102, 135-36, 192, 194, 196, 198-202, 214, 285-88, 335, 354, 379-80, 382, 403-04, 442; Chartered Company, officer of, 273; childhood of, 98; copper syndicate, plans for, 330-31, death and burial of, 205-06, 406-08; de Beers Mining Company floated by, 134, dying, 401-02, 404-06; early prospecting of, in Griqualand and Kimberley, 98-101, 103; education at Oxford, 100-101, 106-07; England, attitude toward and its expansion, 132-33, 173-74, 193, 195, 197-98, 219-21, 257, 279-81, 283; evaluation of, 333-36, 409-11, 449; family of, 97; financial dealings of, 103, 134, 138-39, 392-94; Freemason, 134; friends of, 272, 316; Germany, relations with 277, 352; Goshen, negotiations with, 163-64, 166; health of, 99, 100, 205, 277-78, 395-97; Hofmeyer, relations with, 192, 274, 314-16, 319; houses and library of, 202, 204, 380-81; influences acting upon, 197, 473; influence of, on Africa and world, 16, 441-42; Jameson, relations with, 102, 209, 212, 312, 314, 380, 395; Jameson Raid, part in, 292, 297, 310, 311; Kruger, comparison with, 186-90; 195, 392, 395, 403-04; 431, 435, 443, 455-56, Kruger, relations with, 194, 187, 216, 257-60, 355-56, 394; lands taken by, 290, 385; Lobengula, representatives treat with, 229-30; love for Rhodesia and Africa, 382-85, 390-91; Mashonaland, obtained by, 232-33, 385; Matabele, treats with, 50, 345-49; Matabeleland, taken by, 238-40, 245-46, 252; Matabele War (Second), part in, 341, 343-45; natives, attitudes about, 202; Parliamentary Inquiry into activities of, 320, 350; Pickering, friendship for, 102, 191; Pondoland taken by, 278; positions of, 261; Premier of Cape Colony, 16, 233, 261, 273; resignation and ruin of, 311, 314-15, 317-19, 336; Rhodesia, conquest of, 212; rivals of, 137, 222; South African Republic, desire for, 277-78; Stellaland, negotiations with, 164, 166; tomb chosen by, 273, 349, 406; wills of, 192, 396; and women, 105-06, 396-97, 404.
Rhodes, Herbert, 98, 100.
Rhodes Scholarships, 16, 21; assignments to, 398-400; basis for choice, 398; charges against, 399; characteristics demanded by, 400-01; origin of idea, 442; purpose to establish Anglo-Saxon unity, 401.

INDEX

479

Rhodesia, 107, 190, 254 ; colonisers of, 340 ; history of, 385-88, 390 ; natives, treatment in, 340.
Rhodesia Horse, 268.
Rinderpest, 337-38, 342.
Roberts, Field Marshal Lord Frederick, 142, 351, 373-75, 378-79, 413, 414, 444.
Robinson, Sir Hercules, 161, 163, 165, 216, 219.
Robinson, I. B., 183.
Roos, Tielman, 34.
Rorke, Melina, 137, 207, 235, 342.
Rosebery, Lord, 154, 260.
Rudd, 100, 134, 218, 229-30, 272.
Ruskin, John, 132, 133, 186, 196, 280, 443.
Rustenburg, 15, 64.

Sand River Convention, 48, 49, 116, 159.
Sara, foster-mother of Lobengula, 85, 87, 89-92.
Saulspoort. See Kruger, houses of.
Scheepers, Gerrit, 122.
Schiel, Colonel, 175.
Schoeman, Commandant - General, 56, 69-70.
Schreiner, 311-12.
Schreiner, Olive, 311, 404.
Sebitoane, 89.
Secheli, Bechuana chief, 36.
Sécrétan Copper Syndicate, 330.
Sekukuni, leader of Bapedi, 112, 120, 155, 175.
Selous, Frédéric Courtney, 222, 225, 231, 380.
Shaw, Bernard, 14.
Shaw, Flora, 297, 313.
Shepstone, Sir Theophilis, 105, 114, 119, 121.
Shippard, Sir Sidney Godolphin Alexander, 216, 219, 224, 227, 228, 229, 232.
Sigau, 279-80.
Sigidi. See T'Chaka.
Sivewright, Sir James, 431.
Slagtersnek, 18, 27, 29, 30, 117, 307, 322.
Slaves and slave trade, 17, 29.

Slocum, Captain, 265.
Smart, Sir Thomas, 210.
Smit, General, 66, 113, 148, 159.
Smith, Doctor Andrew, 83.
Smith, Scotty, 162.
Smuts, Jan Christaan, and Africa 439, 449-50 ; Attorney-General, election of, 352 ; birth of, 15 ; and Boer War, 424 ; and British Empire, 449 ; Dominion status for Union of South Africa obtained by, 453 ; history of, 449 ; home of, 451 ; and League of Nations, 449 ; on native question, 454-55 ; philosophy of, 452 ; as Prime Minister of the Union of South Africa, 451.
Smuts, Mrs. Jan, 451-52.
Snijman, Theunis, 70.
Somabulane, 346-48.
South African Bond, 258.
South African Republic, 56 ; army raised by, 154 ; Bapedi, war with, 112-13 ; and Boer War (see Boer War) ; Burgers elected President of, 111 ; democracy of, 289 ; England, relations with, 149-50, 355-61 ; finances of, 153-54, 159, 181 ; Germany, relations with, 175, 260-61, 351, 420 ; Griqualand claimed by, 103-04 ; Grobler, Acting President of, 68 ; Jameson Raiders fought by, 304-06 ; Kruger, President of (see Kruger) ; Orange Free State, relations with, 356 ; Pretorius as President, 56, 69 ; Shepstone takes over, 114 ; Swaziland taken by, 277 ; troops mobilised by, 359 ; and Uitlanders, 267-69, 357-58 ; war footing set up, 361.
Spengler, Oswald, 192, 198, 280, 410, 448.
Stanley, 133, 170, 195, 265.
Stead, W. I., 191-92, 195.
Steenkamp, Sophia Margaretha, 25.
Steijn, President, 356, 432.
Stellaland, Republic of, 163, 166.
Steyn, Elsie Francina, 25.
Struben, Fred, 183.
Swaziland, 278.

Tanganyika, 172, 177.
T'Chaka, chief of the Zulus, 16, 76, 185 ; ancestry of, 75 ; assassination of, 77 ; birth of, 75 ; brutality of, 77 ; children of, 77.
Tembu, 345-46.
Tennyson, Lord Alfred, 14, 221.
The New Republic, 174.
The Story of an African Farm, 404.
Thomas, Morgan, 94.
Thompson, 218, 230.
Thompson, Miss Caton, 386.
Three Years War, 427.
Tongaland, 154.
Tosen, Stoffel, 415.
Transvaal. *See* South African Republic.
Transvaal National Union, 267.
Trek. *See* Great Trek.
Trigart, Louis, 31.
Trollope, Anthony, 130, 186, 276, 284.
Trooper Peter Halket of Mashonaland, 404.
Twain, Mark, 265, 324-25.

Umbandine, King of the Swazi, 153.
Umnandi, 75.
Umnombata, 88, 91-92, 223.
Union of South Africa, 315 ; Dominion status for, 453 ; first prime minister of, 451 ; native question in, 283 ; origins of, 344.
Uitlanders, 15, 68-69, 110, 156, 267, 290-91, 294.

van der Walt, Piet, 149.
Van Niekerk, Schalk, 109-10, 164, 166.
Van Rensburg, 70.
Van Zweten, 271.
Vegkop, 36.
Venter, 56.
Vere, Stent, 346.
Victoria, Queen, 104, 160, 222, 350-51, 397, 448.
Victoria Agreement, 245.
Victorian era, 330-32.
Viereck, George Sylvester, 133, 399.
Voortrek. *See* Great Trek.
von Schlieckmann, Captain, 113.

von Weber, Ernst, 174.

Wahehe, tribe of, 172.
Walker, George, 183.
Wallace, Sir Mackenzie, 281.
War of Independence of 1880, 177, 173, 174 ; campaigns of, 142-43, 145 ; cause of, 352 ; first shot of, 131 ; Majuba Hill attack in, 144-45 ; native activity in, 162 ; peace terms in, 147-50.
Warren, Sir Charles, 164-66, 174, 355.
Waterboer, Nicholas, King of the Bastaards, 104.
Waterkloof. *See* Kruger, houses of.
Watervaal. *See* Kruger, houses of.
Weenen, scene of massacre of Boers, 80.
Wernher, Biet and Company, 261, 267, 289.
Whigham, H. J. 381.
White, Harry, 381.
White, Major, the Honourable Robert, 262, 294, 304, 322.
Wilde, Oscar, 14.
Williams, Gardiner, 292.
Willoughby, Sir John, 285, 294, 303-04, 306.
Wilson, Major Allan, head of Wilson Patrol, 253-54.
With the Boers in the Transvaal, 146-47.
Witwatersrand, 18, 106, 181.
Wolff, Doctor Henry, 213, 299, 303.
Wolseley, Sir Garnet, 124, 126, 174.
Wonderfontein, resolution of, 122.
Wood, Sir Evelyn, 67, 147-48.
Wools-Sampson, Colonel, 323.

Zaharoff, Sir Basil, 219.
Zimbabwe, 21, 386-87.
Zu Hohenlohe-Langenburg, Prince, 177.
Zulu War of 1879, 18, 84, 121, 175.
Zulus, native tribes of, attacks by, on Boers, 40 ; characteristics of, 75 ; composition of, 82 ; customs of, 82-83 ; origin and history of, 74-5 ; pride of, 225-26 ; T'Chaka becomes chief of, 76 ; warriors of, 80-84.